LANGUAG
EVALUATI
OF COGNI
DEVELOPI

LANGUAGE-FREE EVALUATION OF COGNITIVE DEVELOPMENT

NAT

Helga A.H. Rowe

Published by
The Australian Council for Educational Research Limited
Radford House, Frederick Street, Hawthorn, Victoria 3122

Typeset direct from Wang diskette to Itek typesetter at the ACER

Printed and bound by
Brown Prior Anderson Pty Ltd
Burwood, Victoria 3125

Cover design by Louise Coutts

National Library of Australia Cataloguing-in-Publication data

Rowe, Helga A.H. (Helga Anneliese Hildegard).
   Language-free evaluation of cognitive development.

   Bibliography.
   Includes index.
   ISBN 0 85563 419 7.

   1. Non-verbal intelligence tests. I. Australian Council for Educational Research. II. Title.

153.9'324

Copyright © ACER 1986

No part of this publication may be reproduced in any form without permission of the publisher

CONTENTS

List of Tables		vi
List of Figures		vii
Introduction		1

PART I	THEORETICAL CONSIDERATIONS	3
Chapter 1	The Concept of Intelligence	5
Chapter 2	The Model of Intelligence Underlying the NAT	27
Chapter 3	The Role of the NAT in the Assessment of General Ability	41

PART II	THE SELECTION AND DESCRIPTION OF THE NAT SUBTESTS	53
Chapter 4	The Selection of Items for Intelligence Tests	55
Chapter 5	Perceptual Tasks	65
Chapter 6	Conceptual Tasks	83
Chapter 7	Tests of Attention and Concentration	105
Chapter 8	Memory	115

PART III	THE INTERPRETATION OF PERFORMANCE ON THE NAT	133
Chapter 9	The Construct Validity of 14 NAT Subtests	135
Chapter 10	What the NAT Factors Measure	167
Chapter 11	The Interpretation of the NAT Score and the Ability Profile	181

PART IV	PRACTICAL APPLICATIONS	199
Chapter 12	School Achievement and NAT Performance: Validation of Theoretical Model	201
Chapter 13	Using the NAT as Part of a Larger Test Battery	217

References	239
Index of Authors	268
Index of Subjects	275

List of Tables

Table	Title	Page
5.1	The Correlation of NAT Subtests with Age	75
9.1	Summary of the Results of Principal Component Analyses on Different Samples	145
9.2	Results of Principal Components Analysis (Total Sample)	148
9.3.1	Results of Principal Components Analysis (Age 8 and 9 years)	149
9.3.2	Results of Principal Components Analysis (Age 10 years)	150
9.3.3	Results of Principal Components Analysis (Age 11 years)	150
9.3.4	Results of Principal Components Analysis (Age 12 years)	151
9.3.5	Results of Principal Components Analysis (Age 13 years)	151
9.3.6	Results of Principal Components Analysis (Age 14 years)	152
9.3.7	Results of Principal Components Analysis (Age 15 years)	152
9.3.8	Results of Principal Components Analysis (Age 16 years)	153
9.3.9	Results of Principal Components Analysis (Age 17+ years)	153
9.4	Results of Principal Components Analysis (Retarded Adults)	154
9.5	Results of Principal Components Analysis (Aboriginals)	155
9.6	Correlations of NAT Subtests with Age	159
10.1	Percentage Contributed to the 'g' Factor by Individual Subtests	170
10.2	Percentage of Subtest Variance Explainable by the 'g' Factor	172
11.1	Differences between Mean Scaled Score and Scaled Scores of Individual Subtests at the 15% and 5% Levels of Confidence, and Estimated Standard Errors of Difference between an Average Subtest Scaled Score and Each Individual Subtest Scaled Score	191
11.2	Differences between Mean Scaled Scores on the Perceptual, Conceptual, Speed and Accuracy and Memory Tests and Scaled Scores of Individual Subtests at the 15% and 5% Levels of Confidence: and Standard Errors of the Difference between an Average Subtest Scaled Score and Scaled Scores on Individual Subtests	192
11.3	Amounts of Reliable Specific Variance Contained in each Subtest of the NAT for the Total Sample and for each Age Goup	196
12.1	Summary of an Analysis of Variance of High, Average and Low Academic Achievers Based on 14 Subtests of the NAT	203
12.2	Probability Levels Resulting from Comparisons of Differences in Mean Values for the High, Average and Low Achievement Groups	205
12.3	Mean Scores and Standard Deviations for each of the 14 NAT Subtests, and for the Total NAT Score for the Three Groups of Varying School Achievement	211
12.4	Correlations Among 14 NAT Subtests for 90 High, Average and Low School Achievers	213
12.5	Correlations Among 14 NAT Subtests for the Group of High Achievers	213

12.6	Correlations Among 14 NAT Subtests for the Group of Average Achievers	214
12.7	Correlations Among 14 NAT Subtests for the Group of Low Achievers	214
12.8	Range of Significance of Intercorrelations for High, Average and Low School Achievers	214
13.1	Comparison Between NAT Scores and Standard Scores Yielded by other Tests	236

List of Figures

Figure	Title	Page
1.1	A Hierarchical Model of Mental Abilities (after Snow, 1978)	20
2.1	Simplified Model of a System	33
8.1	Memory as a Multi-store Model of Information Processing	116
8.2	Schema of some Major Categories of Memory Recognized in Current Theories (after Estes, 1982)	119
8.3	Information Plan through Postulated Short-term and Long-term Memory Systems	120
8.4	The Levels of Processing Model of Memory	121
12.1	Graphic Representation of Mean Scaled Scores Obtained by Groups of High, Average and Low School Achievers	204

INTRODUCTION

In the pluralistic society of the 1980s, culture-fair techniques for the assessment of cognitive development and functioning have become a necessary tool for competent professionals in education and in various branches of psychology.

The author shares the frequently aired view that much more theoretical and empirical research is needed before substantial gains can be expected in the validity of suitable procedures. At the same time, she recognizes the plight of those professionals who are required to report on the psychological functioning and educational achievements, including disadvantage, of minority groups, and to make valid recommendations for improving their opportunities. The latter concern and the hope that even a modest test battery might provide a basis for some of this much needed research led to the author's acceptance of the ACER's request to develop a non-verbal test of general ability, which can be administered to groups.

This book is concerned with the theory, interpretations and applications of the Non-Verbal Ability Tests, abbreviated as NAT. It is designed to help psychologists and teachers to clarify and define for themselves the role of the NAT in intervention-oriented psycho-educational and (where applicable) clinical assessment of individual children and adults.

The book is not intended as an introduction to psychological testing and test interpretation in general. It is assumed that the reader is familiar with the aims and procedures of, at least, traditional educational and psychological testing. A grounding in basic areas of measurement and statistics, cognition and developmental psychology is also assumed. Some sources of information for readers with insufficient background in these and other essential areas have been included where relevant.

The present volume will serve to provide the reader with an understanding of the major psychological skills and abilities that underlie performance on the NAT, its subtests and similar tasks. This understanding is essential for those who wish to interpret the scores obtained on the NAT battery, particularly if more advanced techniques of ability assessment such as profile analysis or 'syndrome analysis', as advocated by Luria (1966a, 1966b, 1973) and others, are also utilized.

Central to the rationale for both the production and the use of the NAT is the goal of contributing to an understanding of individual differences in intellectual performance and achievement. An aim of this book is to show how advances in experimental and differential psychology combined with psychometrics can yield progress towards that goal.

Essential aspects of the theoretical rationale and the interpretation of scores of the NAT battery are covered in this book. The technical aspects of test development are discussed in the *Manual for the Non-Verbal Ability Tests* (Rowe, 1985c), which accompanies the battery. In the present volume, every attempt has been made to explain the underlying logic of theories and analyses in simple terms, avoiding—even in the chapters reporting on statistical analyses—equations and mathematical complexities, which might frighten readers not schooled in their use. To the mathematician, some of the chapters may thus seem somewhat clumsy. The author would argue, however, that the elegance and effectiveness of mathematical statements are of no use to those who do not understand what they represent.

In the development of the NAT battery the first task was to identify major dimensions of the concept 'intelligence' that could be measured by means of a group-administered paper-and-pencil instrument. The emphasis was thus on establishing defensible dimensions of individual differences in cognitive functioning, possibly—at this stage—at some cost to the establishment of solid psychometric parameters for the instrument. The only justification that can be offered for this is that the author shares the view of Carroll (1980b, 1983), Sternberg (1977, 1980a), Whitely (1980a, 1980b) and others who believe that questions of scaling, and *statistical* reliability and validity are subservient to the basic questions concerning the scientific usefulness in assuming that separate, though interconnected, dimensions of ability exist, and if they are shown to exist, what they are, and what they mean in the context of psychological theory and the measurement of individual differences.

The information contained in this book is presented in four parts. In turn, each part is divided into a number of chapters. Part I, Chapters 1 to 3, is concerned with theoretical issues pertaining to the elusiveness of the concept of intelligence more generally, or to the understanding of intelligence as defined for the purposes of the NAT. Part II presents the theoretical and empirical framework surrounding the selection of the NAT subtests. Each chapter in this section relates to a particular dimension of intelligence as measured in the NAT. Part III is concerned with the interpretation of the NAT. The major focus in these chapters is on the results of various factor analyses, and on profile interpretation. Part IV focuses on applications of the battery and includes a detailed discussion of its use as part of a larger assessment procedure. Questions of test validity are addressed in both Parts III and IV.

In selecting the material to be included in the book an attempt was made to go beyond the subject matter usually present in the introductory chapters of test manuals. The aim was rather to capture a sense of the depth and the breadth of the assessment of individual differences in relation to the cognitive tasks included in the NAT battery.

The author hopes that the reader will find this book a useful guide to the application and understanding of the NAT battery as a whole, and to the role the individual tests can play in advanced assessment of general ability and in intervention-oriented psychological and educational diagnosis.

PART I

THEORETICAL CONSIDERATIONS

The main purpose of this book is to enable those concerned with the assessment of general and specific cognitive abilities to make use of the Non-Verbal Ability Tests (NAT). However, it is regarded as essential that before becoming too concerned with details relating to the interpretation of test scores, the NAT user should share in certain basic theoretical considerations, and gain a clear understanding of the conceptualization of intelligence underlying the tests.

The far reaching importance of decisions made on the basis of information derived from the individual's performance on an intelligence test, and the potentially damaging effect test scores can have, demand that the test user is well informed about the theoretical assumptions made in the construction of a particular instrument.

Chapter 1 provides a brief and selective survey of major theoretical positions concerning the concept of intelligence that are being reflected in the research literature and that have shaped many of the opinions expressed in professional and public debates at the present time.

Chapter 2 describes cognition and intelligence as conceptualized by the author for the purpose of the development of the NAT.

Chapter 3 deals with the role of the NAT in terms of current assessment conventions. Its applicability in particular situations and its limitations are discussed also.

CHAPTER 1

THE CONCEPT OF INTELLIGENCE

In any discussion of the construct intelligence, particularly when its measurement is contemplated, it is necessary to define as precisely as possible what is meant when the term is used. This and the following two chapters will attempt to do this. These chapters will lead the reader to discover the frailty of the construct and to an appreciation of why, lacking the strength of theory usually assumed to be associated with it, the construct intelligence 'fails to support the elaborate superstructure based on the premise of its existence' (Lewis, 1976, p.1).

Part I of this book is thus expected to leave the reader considering seriously the use and misuse of measures of intelligence in our society.

This first chapter is intended for those who wish to know more about the concept of intelligence and its relevance to intelligence testing. The aim of the chapter is not to provide a description of historical developments, but rather to focus on the factors that led to certain dominant approaches in the measurement of intelligence.

The information presented in this chapter is divided broadly into four sections covering definitions of intelligence, early theories and research, psychometric theories, and modern developments.

Definitions of Intelligence

> It has been suggested that intelligence is one of those concepts that everyone understands and yet no-one can adequately define. (Salthouse, 1982, p.53)

There is a lack of agreement among professionals in psychology, education and other social sciences concerning the meaning of the concept. This is not to say that no definitions have been proposed, but rather that none have proved satisfactory to all parties. There may be almost as many definitions of the term intelligence as there are individuals who have struggled to define and measure it.

In contrast to the lack of definitional consensus, the notion that individuals differ in intelligence and that such differences can be measured and studied scientifically has become a generally accepted idea (e.g. Carroll, 1982).

There is a generally held belief that intelligence

> is relatively easy to measure, and that as a monolithic construct, it is a useful predictor of subsequent human behaviour—is firmly entrenched in the mind of Western man (Lewis, 1976, p.1).

This type of pragmatism shows that there has been little advance in more than 50 years, because Thurstone (1924) suggested

> There is considerable difference of opinion as to what intelligence really is, but we can still use the term as long as it is demonstrably satisfactory for definite practical ends. We use electricity for practical purposes even though we have been uncertain as to its ultimate nature, and it is so with the intelligence test. We use the tests and leave it for separate inquiry to determine the ultimate nature of intelligence. (p.xiv)

Earlier than Thurstone, Binet and Simon (1905) insisted:

> Our goal is not at all to study, analyse and to disclose the aptitudes of those who are inferior in intelligence . . . we confine ourselves to evaluating, to measuring their intelligence in general; we shall establish their intellectual level; and to give an idea of this level we shall compare it to normal children of the same or of an analogous level. (p.193)

While social scientists and other professionals have not been able to find a generally applicable definition of the construct intelligence, people in the street, that is, lay persons in relation to this topic, tend to think that they know what intelligence is. Most people believe that they can recognize intelligence (or the lack of it), particularly in others.

What is meant when the term intelligence is used?

Examples of frequently-cited but limited definitions of intelligence include:

a biological reality (Jensen, 1969)

that which intelligence tests measure (Boring, 1923)

that which is responsible for the score on the test (Underwood, 1974, p.204)

that which qualified observers (peers, teachers, etc.) describe as intelligence on the basis of repeated observations of behavior in many situations (Barron and Harrington, 1981, p.444).

According to the *Oxford English Dictionary* the word intelligence has been part of the English language since the 14th century, and is derived from the Latin *inter legere*, the literal translation of which is 'to bring together'. According to the dictionary its general meaning in English is 'the faculty of understanding'.

Several definitions are similar to that in the dictionary. For example, the psychologist Pieron (1926) defined intelligence as the capacity to understand easily. McNemar's (1964) understanding of the concept includes the fact that individuals differ in their capacity to comprehend and to learn.

According to Binet and Simon (1905) intelligence consists of such dimensions as judgment, comprehension, and reasoning. The following two definitions of intelligence reflect similar conceptions of the processes involved in intelligence:

> Intelligence refers . . . to one's ability to be affected by a wide range of circumstances and to delay reaction to them while the significant elements are selected out and weighted with respect to their bearing on the attainment of any particular end . . . That person is most intelligent who, with a given amount of experience and maturing, is most apt to perceive significant relations and to react discriminately to them as distinct from the numerous irrelevant elements in situations met. (Peterson, 1922, p.388)

> Intelligence may be regarded as the capacity for successful adjustment by means of those traits which we ordinarily call intellectual. These traits involve such capacities as quickness of learning, quickness of comprehension, the ability to solve new problems, and the ability to perform tasks generally recognized as presenting intellectual difficulty because they involve ingenuity, originality, the grasp of complicated relationships, or the recognition of remote association. (Freeman, 1925, p.258)

Other approaches to the definition of intelligence have focused less on the psychological 'content' of the concept, but rather on what intelligence permits an individual to do. Among early definitions of this kind was that of Binet and Simon (1908), who regarded intelligence as the capacity to learn, and Terman's (1921) suggested ability to engage in abstract thinking. Other similar definitions include the ability to deal with novelty (Haggerty, 1921), the capacity to form hypotheses that permit trial and error behaviour (Thorndike et al., 1921; Thurstone, 1923, 1924), and the capability to use symbols (Garrett, 1946).

Stern (1914) equated intelligence with the capacity for adaptation. Wechsler (1939) stated that

> Intelligence is the aggregate of global capacity of the individual to act purposefully, to think rationally, and to deal effectively with his environment. (p.3)

Fischer's (1969) definition reflects both the previous ones.

> Intelligence refers to the effectiveness, relative to age peers, of the individual's approach to situations in which competence is highly regarded by the culture. (p.669)

More recently, Lewis and Brooks-Gunn (1981) pointed out that

> IQ is best considered a set of skills, which is defined by a specified culture and which changes over time—both in the life time of the individual and in the history of the species. (p.235)

Estes (1982) explains

> I shall take intelligence or intellectual performance to refer to adaptive behavior of the individual, usually characterized by some element of problem solving and directed by cognitive processes and operations. (p.171)

For Estes, intelligence is a property of behaviour, which is determined jointly by cognitive function and by motives. This is a view of intelligence quite different from that conveyed by definitions that focus on intelligence as the ability to learn, or intelligence as a set of cognitive parameters determining the performance of an individual.

Perhaps as a reaction to the confusion reflected above, some psychologists have tried to construct very comprehensive, all inclusive, definitions of intelligence. For example, Stoddard (1941) offered the following comprehensive definition:

> Intelligence is the ability to understand activities that are characterized by (1) difficulty, (2) complexity, (3) abstractness, (4) economy, (5) adaptiveness to a goal, (6) social value and (7) the emergence of originals, and to maintain such activities under conditions that demand a concentration of energy and a resistance to emotional factors. (p.255)

Piaget's definition of intelligence is another example of comprehensive definitions. Piaget (1950) suggested that intelligence involves basically the capacity for adaptation, which is gained through the assimilation of increasing abilities. For Piaget, intelligence implies increasingly higher levels of cognitive organization (i.e. increased structural complexity), the capacity to invent trial and error behaviour, and the ability to anticipate consequences.

Some notable clinical psychologists have used the term intelligence without even attempting to define its meaning (e.g. Gathercole, 1968; Rapaport, Gill, and Schafer, 1968; Savage, 1968). Weisman (1968), for example, suggested that it might well be a waste of time to search for a meaning of the term intelligence beyond seeking to determine whether intelligence tests measure what an individual has learnt.

The attempts at definition described above, together with those in the literature in general, show that, in their endeavour to define the construct intelligence, psychologists have tended to confound the processes it involves (e.g. judgment, reasoning, memory, attention, etc.) with the outcome scores obtained from test performance, and with the nature of intelligent behaviour. The latter emphasis is exemplified by Pieron's (1926) thesis,

> Intelligence does not exist, it is only an effect, a functional resultant under certain defined conditions, a behavior value. (p.59)

Again, 20 years later, Chein (1945) pointed out

> No psychologist has ever observed *intelligence*; many have observed intelligent behavior. (p.111) . . . Intelligence is an attribute of behavior, not an attribute of a person. (p.120)

More recently, Horn (1978) discussed another definitional approach, and noted:

> For some . . . intelligence is life achievement, as indicated by earning (or even stealing) money, gaining an education, speaking several languages, or simply 'doing well'. . . There is no necessary reason why individual differences in intelligence as defined scientifically[1] will have much to do with differences in achievement in a complex society such as ours. (Horn, 1978, p.213)

The results of a number of studies suggest that the major differences between people in life achievement, as measured by income, prestige, social standing, and even education, are due more to circumstances and 'luck' than to differences in personal characteristics and attributes, including attributes of intellectual ability (e.g. Jencks, Smith, Acland, Bane, Cohen, Gentis, Heyns, and Michelson, 1972; Lundberg, 1968; Mayeske, Okada, Beaton, Cohen, and Wissler, 1973; Mosteller and Moynihan, 1972; Warren, 1980).

Obviously, this does not mean that individual differences in general and specific abilities are unrelated to achievement in life; rather, it suggests that

> life achievement is not a univocal indicant of intelligence or even the criterion that scientific measures of intellectual abilities necessarily must predict. A science of human abilities must be specified in terms of operations of measurement, and the concepts of theories that adequately account for the essential features of confirmed findings. (Horn, 1978, p.213)

The examples of attempted definitions of the concept of intelligence given above should be enough to indicate that the situation is chaotic. This impression is validated in published surveys of the relevant literature (e.g. Bouchard, 1968; Edwards, 1928; Cattell, 1943; Garrett, 1946; Miles, 1957; Thorndike et al., 1926; Tuddenham, 1963).

However, another way of interpreting the diversity of opinions expressed, and the enormously variable and complex array of behaviours that are regarded as indicative of intelligence, is to suggest that most if not all of the definitions mentioned in the preceding pages capture at least part of an aspect of intelligence, but not the nature of the construct in its totality. One must conclude that intelligence has many different dimensions, a point to which we shall return a number of times in this book.

---

1   By which Horn means psychometrically, on the basis of factor analysis.

Early Theories and Research

Theories of intelligence have existed since the ancient philosophers observed and attempted to explain the superiority of humans over other species. Egyptian hieroglyphics and the writings of Plato (429–348 BC) and Aristotle (384–322 BC) reflect the fact that philosophical theorizing concerning the structure of the human intellect took place at that early stage.

The ancient Greek philosophers sought the key to the human mind in the 'soul'. Aristotle postulated a system of hierarchically ordered multiple souls, the highest of which, 'nous', was reserved only for man. The lowest soul, responsible for purely vegetative functioning, was assumed to be common to all living organisms. It was postulated that animals, in addition to the lowest soul, possess a soul that controls movement.

These theories, only partly transformed by medieval theology and Descartes, have exerted a strong influence on, and shaped the widely held religious attitudes concerning the nature of man in society.

The philosophers of the 17th, 18th and early 19th centuries, for example Hobbes, Locke, Hume, James Mill, and John Stuart Mill, regarded the ability to reason as the guiding force in human intelligence.

The biologists Darwin (1809–1882) and Spencer (1820–1903) associated the increasing size and apparent complexity of the brain of organisms with increases in their behaviour repertoire and their capability of adapting to the requirements of varying living environments. They studied and described the progressive increase in the flexibility and sophistication of behaviour with evolution.

For example, Spencer (1864) postulated that intelligence evolves gradually, as a result of a phenomenon in some species in which basic drives become increasingly differentiated and thus develop into a hierarchy of more specialized capabilities. He postulated that the latter ranged from simple sensory reflex reactions to highly complex and finely tuned cognitive abilities. Modern developmental psychologists tend to suggest that the same kind of development is characteristic in the growing of the human being from infancy to adulthood.

Koehler, the father of Gestalt psychology, sought to explain 'insight', the term he used to describe the capacity shown by members of higher species, particularly apes and humans, to restructure a given situation to their advantage, or to solve a problem by recognizing the relationships and interactions between its components. Koehler and his colleagues postulated that 'insight' is more important than the acquisition of conditioned reflexes or adaptation resulting from trial and error behaviour.

Until the middle of the 19th century, theories focused on how possession of the intellect—manifesting itself in soul, reason, rationality, etc.—sets humans apart from other species. Intelligence was conceived as the most important common characteristic separating members of a higher level species from those of lower ones.

Possible differences in mental ability among members of the highest level species were not considered. Variations of this type between individuals, even if they had not been ignored, would, obviously, have lacked importance in the social organization of feudal societies.

The first experimental studies designed to investigate individual differences in a psychological function were probably the reaction-time experiments conducted by the German astronomer F.W. Bessel (1784–1846). The earliest attempts to quantify observed differences in physical and psychological variables among persons were made by Darwin's cousin Francis Galton (1822–1911), whose *Hereditary Genius* (Galton, 1871) and *Natural Inheritance* (Galton, 1889) are probably the earliest scientifically based reports documenting individual differences in mental abilities.

Galton assumed intelligence to be distributed in the population in the same manner as differences in height, weight, etc. appear to be distributed, that is, as reflected by the normal curve. Together with Pearson, Galton developed the statistical technique of correlation, which was later applied by Spearman in his investigations of general and specific abilities and their interdependency and organization.

Spearman (1904) claimed to have demonstrated that all abilities largely depend on a common factor 'g', and to some lesser degree on a number of specific components he called 's'. Spearman's work will be discussed further in the next section.

The investigation of individual differences in intellectual functioning and the analysis of basic mental processes were quite inseparable at the turn of this century. An understanding of observed differences in human performance was sought in the characteristics (or elements) of mental processes. Thus Galton and his followers, J. McK. Cattell (1890), Sharp (1899), Wissler (1901) and others, studied individual differences in mental functioning on the basis of observations of the variations in the development and association of single sensory and perceptual variables.

Binet

It was Binet who moved the investigation of differences in the intellectual abilities of individuals from elementary to more complex variables. Like his contemporaries, Binet initially thought of intelligence as consisting of distinct simple abilities, which could be evaluated separately but understood as a composite. Binet did not provide any theoretical guidance as to the nature of possible composites and their determinants. What soon became clear to Binet was that the research results coming from the experimental laboratories of German empirical psychology were unable to provide him with the tools required for analysis of the more complex aspects of human mental functioning.

Having been set the task of predicting school success, namely, identifying those children in Paris schools who could not be expected to cope with normal schooling, Binet was forced to abandon theoretically based investigation in favour of practical expediency, that is, an atheoretical determination of apparently relevant measures.

Binet had much the same difficulty as have many psychologists and counsellors today. He was appointed to accomplish a task of assessment. No theoretically based procedures were available to him, so he designed a series of tasks, based on what he had observed his own daughters (fortunately of the same age as the children he had been asked to assess) could accomplish.

Performance on the tasks discriminated between 'those who are inferior in intelligence' and 'normal children' (Binet and Simon, 1905, p.193). Binet thus accomplished his assignment successfully. The tasks were refined, Binet's observations were replicated, and the Binet Scale was published in France (Binet and Simon, 1905), and a few years later in America (Terman, 1916). A success story? The answer to this question would vary depending on the position of the respondent. Binet's success was instrumental in separating, for at least the following 70 years, the measurement of individual differences from the domain of cognitive theory.

Carroll (1982) divides the developmental history of ability testing into two quite separate periods:

> (a) an 'early' or 'developmental' period beginning in the late 19th century, during which the foundations of theory and practice in psychometrics were laid down; and
>
> (b) a 'modern' period starting around 1935 with the founding of the Psychometric Society and its journal *Psychometrika*, during which many refinements were made in the technology of testing and during which testing became a major enterprise. (Carroll, 1982, p.30)

More precisely, Carroll (1982) regards the publication of Galton's *Hereditary Genius* (1871) as the beginning of the early or developmental period. He points out that

> During this time, the science of mental testing has progressed from its crudest beginnings to a stage of high development, leaving only matters of refinement for the period from 1935 to the present. It was during this earlier time that major problems in the study of mental abilities were identified, the basic methodologies were developed, and tests of mental ability came into wide use. (Carroll, 1982, pp.31–32)

While not in total agreement with Carroll's view, the present author certainly supports the latter part of the above statement.

The pragmatic approach of Binet—not to be concerned with the analysis and description of aptitudes but confining himself to their evaluation—was followed by a number of Binet's contemporaries (e.g. Goddard, 1912; Terman, 1916; Yoakum and Yerkes, 1920) and by subsequent developers of ability tests, including Wechsler (1939, 1949, 1958, 1974, 1982), who accepted the sufficiency of measurement in the absence of cognitive theory, that is, the reason for assessment rather than theoretical conceptions of what is being measured. It must be admitted, therefore, that during the past 80 years pragmatism rather than theory has been and still remains the prevalent force in the development of individual and group intelligence tests.

The major contribution made by Binet, namely, his contribution to scaling, tends to be mentioned only rarely. He developed 'une échelle métrique d'intelligence'—an intelligence 'scale'. The scaling (Binet and Simon, 1905) consisted of a series of tasks of increasing difficulty. Each task was seen to represent the typical performance of children at a particular chronological age level. The tasks were highly varied, but most of them relied on the understanding of language and the ability to reason with verbal, numerical or spatial stimulus materials.

In Binet's time, the dominant models available for the explanation of individual differences, especially in personality, were essentially typologies, such as psychoanalytic theories. Binet's scale is based on the assumption of the continuous variation in mental abilities, and is thus an important innovation in the theory of measurement. Another innovation was the idea that the outcome of each task would be binary, that is, the performance on each task would be rated as either pass or fail.

The kinds of tasks employed by Galton, Cattell, and the psychologists involved in the experimental laboratory phase of the testing movement most frequently yielded reaction-time scores, magnitudes of 'just noticeable' differences between stimuli, and other measurements that had the properties of other kinds of physical measurements.

Very few of the scores would thus have had the characteristics of the binary score. As expressed by Carroll (1982):

> What is striking here is the idea of a scale composed of tasks of increasing difficulty, where, in addition, each task corresponds to a different level of ability of 'mental age' (a concept Binet originated). There was nothing like this in the previous history of mental testing (except perhaps the erection of bars of different heights to test jumping ability, or testing minerals for hardness by finding which one of a graded series . . . could produce scratches in them). (p.40)

Group Tests

Soon after the publication of Binet's scale, several American psychologists, including Otis (1918) and Whipple (1910), recognized that many of the tasks included in the scale could be adapted for group testing. A number of subtle but radical changes in the methodology of measurement (in the way performance on the items was interpreted) occurred when the Binet items were adapted for use with groups.

The measurement assumptions made for group tests differ from those for individual tests in the following major ways:

1   First, and most importantly, group tests provide for a method of deriving scores that is completely different from that used for individual tests.

Whereas the Binet scale called on the tester to identify the point or region on the scale of task difficulty that separated generally successful performance of the child from generally unsuccessful performance, thus determining the level of the child's intellectual development or functioning on the basis of the types of tasks he or she was able to complete reliably, group tests require the testee to answer as many items as possible, usually within a set time limit, and the score is computed simply as the number of items correctly answered.

> A group 'test' became an assemblage of items; generally each item or task yielded a binary score (pass or fail). The test score became the number of such items that were passed, and the resulting scale was called a 'point scale'. When the test was given under a time limit, the score became the number of items that the examinee was able to attempt *and pass* within that time limit. (Carroll, 1982, p.41)

Thus Binet's scale of intelligence based on the difficulty of the tasks the testee was able to accomplish became a point scale representative of the numbers of items completed. This is not the place to discuss the implications of this change for test construction, for the consideration of the homogeneity of items, item difficulties, the influence of timing, and such like features. The aim of the present discussion is, rather, to alert the reader to the differences in measurement assumptions that underlie individual and group tests.

The test score obtained on the basis of the number of items correctly answered (with a possible adjustment for guessing made by subtracting a fraction of the number of incorrect answers) is generally referred to as a *raw score*. The meanings of such raw scores are quite arbitrary. Their interpretation is dependent on the knowledge of the characteristics of the test, for example whether the items were easy or difficult for the group. Even a conversion of raw score to *percentage correct* score would help little in conveying the meaning of the score. These difficulties were recognized by the early developers of group tests, with the consequence that elaborate statistical techniques, such as the determination of percentile rank, already foreshadowed by Galton (1885), were worked out for the interpretation of scores with respect to those obtained by certain stated groups on the same test, for example age peers, grade, etc.

The developments described above resulted in the concept of the *normative* interpretation of test performance. Over time, responsible test publishers started to provide quite elaborate norm tables, that is, tables describing the correspondence between scores and percentile ranks of those scores for particular reference groups. Various types of standard scores were used to represent these norms.

Normative interpretations were useful enough when the aim of testing was classification, but they are much less satisfactory if testing is in some way to lead to an improvement in performance. A normative interpretation of test performance does not really characterize the performance of an individual, because it gives little information about either the absolute level of that person's abilities, or about how the particular score came to be achieved.

> The problem of relating mental test scores to absolute or quasi-absolute, levels of abilities was never satisfactorily solved in the developmental period of mental testing; in fact, it is a problem even today, although the technology for solving it is now much more advanced. (Carroll, 1982, p.43)

2 A second important change that took place when group tests were developed was that, whereas Binet-type items usually required a definite answer on the part of the testee (e.g. a definition of a word, or a numerical answer), group tests tended to require merely the recognition of the correct, or most correct answer among several options provided. The literature is not clear on exactly how the multiple-choice type of item came to be developed, but this response format became characteristic of almost all group tests of intelligence.

3 Another contrast between individual and group intelligence tests lies in the fact that the latter are almost exclusively paper-and-pencil tests. Unless the tests include only non-verbal, (i.e. diagrammatic) items, these tests require that the testee is able to read. There appears to be an underlying assumption made by test constructors that all testees can be expected to be equally able to read the stimulus material, and that only their ability to reason on the basis of the presented material is at issue as far as the assessment is concerned. This assumption has led to some of the best founded criticisms of group ability tests.

Criticisms

As noted above, since Binet, the measurement of intelligence has been based on observed differences in individual's performances on a variety of items of knowledge and problem-solving tasks. The general rationale for these collections of tasks, that is, intelligence tests, is based on the usually implicit assumption that the intelligent person has accumulated a considerable amount of knowledge, and is able to solve problems. The tasks making up the intelligence tests are assumed to be somehow representative of the types of information, general knowledge and types of problems to which the intelligent person is expected to have been exposed.

Difficulties facing the designers of traditional intelligence tests have increased as a result of the problem of sampling items that might be representative of the already vast and now exponentially increasing body of knowledge to which an individual may have been exposed. Is it, in fact, still legitimate to talk about a single body of knowledge to which all educated persons can be expected to have had access? The age of the universal genius finished at the beginning of this century, at about the time when the first intelligence tests were published.

Other criticisms of the Binet and other intelligence tests of the traditional type include the comment that scores obtained on them are too strongly influenced by language and memory, by school experience, and by a variety of cultural stimulations restricted to certain cultural, ethnic and socioeconomic levels of society.

On examination of the contents of major verbal intelligence tests, it can be seen that the largest part of their content measures previous achievement. The justification for this lies in the notion that intelligent persons derive greater knowledge from experience and learning than less intelligent individuals. This view may be acceptable, and could even be regarded as appropriate in situations where tests are administered to individuals who have had similar experiences and fully adequate educational opportunities under conditions of reasonably adequate social, emotional and motivational stability. However, for individuals whose environments have been characterized by deprivation of one kind or another, or in cross-ethnic and cross-cultural situations, these tests may produce invalid results.

The enhancing effect of high socioeconomic level on intelligence test performance was noted by Binet and by other early writers (e.g. Yerkes and Anderson, 1915), and its biasing effect has been stressed increasingly in recent times.

Verbal intelligence tests have tended to focus on school-related knowledge and skills. This explains Weisman's (1968) call for periodic revision of both intelligence tests and school curricula so that both represent a wider spectrum of the abilities to which a culture has come to give its priorities. In their traditional form, standard norm-referenced intelligence tests are highly sensitive to the relativity of general philosophical attitudes concerning the nature of human beings, and their roles and expectations in many contexts. 'Such tests do reflect, at least partly, the concept of intelligence current in the culture in which they were developed' (Anastasi, 1958, p.203).

High intelligence leads to social prestige; it is understandable, therefore, that the language, attitudes and information that are perceived to be dominant among persons enjoying high prestige in a society have tended to provide the criteria for the assessment of intelligence. Nor is it surprising that there has been a tendency for the content of such tests to reflect the most frequently rewarded values of the test constructor's own socioeconomic status and political orientation at the time of test construction.

More detailed discussions concerning the limitations of the usefulness of traditional intelligence tests in varying social and cultural contexts are published in the special issue of the *American Psychologist* entitled 'Testing: Concepts, Policy, Practice, and Research' (Glaser and Bond, 1981), and in writings by, for example, Jackson (1975), Kamin (1974), Karrier (1973), Kearney and McElwain (1976), Ogbu (1978), Vernon (1979, 1982) and Warren (1980).

Psychometric Theories

The development of techniques for factor analysis led to the formulation of theories of intelligence, which, though limited, served as a guiding influence both in the conceptualization of the construct, and in the development of intelligence tests during the first 60 years of this century.

Factor analysis is a statistical technique. Its aim is to identify dimensions (i.e. factors) that can account for the correlations found among a large number of items or tests. The number of factors identified in any one analysis could be as large as the number of items or tests on which scores have been obtained, but the usual expectation is that the application of factor analysis will yield a solution consisting of a considerably reduced number of factors. Both the identification of the most relevant number of factors and the inference of the psychological dimensions represented by the factors can involve a certain amount of subjectivity on the part of the investigator. However, despite its limitations, factor analysis still influences the development of tests and the interpretation of large sets of data. The usefulness of the technique continues to be demonstrated in research, and will become obvious in later chapters.

Single versus Multiple Factors

As noted previously, Spearman observed sizeable positive correlations between tests of different abilities. He suggested that these correlations were a reflection of a common or 'general' factor, 'g', underlying performance on all mental tasks—in other words a common intellectual ability associated with all cognitive functioning. On the basis of factor analysis he claimed to have shown that higher abilities, in particular, depend to a large degree on 'g', and much less on a series of, possibly task-specific or response-determined, specific factors 's'. Although some textbook writers refer to Spearman's theory of intelligence as a 'two-factor theory', the emphasis in Spearman's own writings was definitely on 'g' rather than on the 's's. He appears to have made little attempt to account for the number and diversity of the latter.

Spearman's theory was opposed by a number of his contemporaries (e.g. Thomson, 1920, 1939; Thorndike, 1913, 1919, 1924; Thurstone, 1936, 1938a, 1940, 1947;) and later investigators such as R.B. Cattell, J.P. Guilford and J.L. Horn and their coworkers, who denied the existence of a broad general intelligence factor of the 'g' type, and instead identified a number of basic mental abilities.

Thurstone's factor analytic work resulted in the postulation of nine basic factors, which he conceptualized as 'primary mental abilities' as follows:

Verbal comprehension	(V)
Word fluency	(W)
Numerical facility	(N)
Spatial ability	(S)
Reasoning	(R)
Rote memory	(M)
Perceptual speed	(P)
Induction	(I)
Deduction	(D)

Instead of accounting for individual differences in terms of the extent to which different amounts of 'g' contributed to test performance, Thurstone attributed variation in the performance of test takers to differences in these 'primary mental abilities'.

Thurstone's contribution, both in theory construction and in test development, was expanded into a highly sophisticated and influential theory by J.P. Guilford, one of the most active psychometricians. Guilford's (1967) factor analytic 'structure-of-the-intellect' model postulates 120 separate abilities, with 98 factors confirmed (Guilford and Hoepfner, 1971).

Other important early factor analytic contributors to the investigation of intelligence include Carroll (1941); Coombs (1941); French (1951); Green, Guilford, Christensen, and Comrey (1953); Hertzka, Guilford, Christensen, and Berger (1954); Holzinger and Harman (1938); Kaiser (1960); Rimoldi (1951); Smith (1964); Taylor (1947); Wilson, Guilford, Christensen, and Lewis (1954); Wrigley, Saunders, and Neuhaus (1958); and Zimmerman (1953).

More recent studies include the continuing work of French and his co-workers at the Educational Testing Service (ETS), who assembled a number of 'kits' of tests of replicated factors of mental ability (French, 1954; French, Ekstrom, and Price, 1963; Harman, Ekstrom, and French, 1976). In preparation for the production of the third kit these authors (Ekstrom, 1973; Ekstrom, French, and Harman, 1979) published a review of the literature reporting cognitive factors, and concluded that there was sound evidence for the existence of at least 20 factors of mental ability; their third kit (Harman, Ekstrom, and French, 1976) contains tests of 23 factors.

Frequently cited factor analytic studies of mental abilities in non-English language environments include those of Jaeger (1967) from West Germany, Meili (1964) from Switzerland, and Werdelin (1961) from Sweden.

In all the psychometric studies noted above, and in others, the major components of intelligence were identified on the basis of the patterns of the correlations obtained when large collections of ability tests were administered to large groups of individuals, usually adolescents or young adults. Both general and specific ability factors were identified when these matrices were factor analysed. After more than 70 years of controversy concerning the factor analytic structure of the concept of intelligence, the research literature continues to provide support for both theories of single and multiple factors.

Among the most eminent investigators of psychometric intelligence are R.B. Cattell and J.L. Horn and their co-workers. Their work extended the study of the construct intelligence to include the investigation of the relationship of cognitive ability factors and personality traits, and other non-cognitive factors (e.g. Cattell, 1971; Horn, 1968).

The Proliferation of Factors

Whatever notion one might have concerning the meaning of the term intelligence, research using the various techniques of factor analysis has made it clear that intelligent behaviour, wherever it occurs, is complex and multidimensional, and provides considerable support for views such as Guilford's (1967) that there are many 'faces of intellect'.

The proliferation of identified factors of intelligence led to the production of hundreds of tests designed to measure general or more specific abilities.

Unfortunately, the tests do not necessarily measure the same constructs. Factors with similar names do not guarantee similar structures. It soon became meaningless to generalize about an individual's intelligence beyond the performance on the particular test on which the score was obtained.

On the other hand, a remarkable result of research involving these diverse tests is that, with rare exceptions, performance scores obtained on them are positively correlated. This finding remains robust when several tests are administered at one time, and also when the times between test administrations extend over a number of years (with the proviso that the first testing did not take place before the age of approximately eight years).

Also, as pointed out by Horn (1978):

> It is remarkable, too, that these many and diverse test measures usually correlate positively with performances that are said in common parlance to indicate intelligence, performance of the kind indicated in school achievements of a variety of kinds, on-the-job success, money earned, prestige, etc. (p.214)

Horn explains this phenomenon in terms of the operation of an underlying 'g' factor (referred to as 'G' by Horn and his colleagues) in all these situations, and notes further support for his hypothesis as follows:

> Another interesting bit of evidence indicating G among the diversity of abilities is found in results showing positive intercorrelations among the *means* for ability tests in different schools sampled in a fairly representative manner, as in Project TALENT (1962). This evidence can be interpreted as indicating that systematic samplings of children for different schools, or the influences (learnings) produced by schools, operate in respect to a general factor. The correlations in this case are considerably higher than those typically found for the same abilities in sampling over individuals. Humphreys (1962) points out, for example, that the means for Reading Comprehension and Mechanical Information correlate in excess of .9 in samples of schools, but only .3 and .4 in samples of school-age children. The high correlations for schools suggest that influences other than those represented by G (produced by, or producing, G) are relatively weak. (Horn, 1978, p.214)

The proliferation of factors that were identified as representative of dimensions of the construct intelligence created doubts concerning the usefulness of intelligence and its measurement in the minds of increasing numbers of psychologists. Questions raised addressed both the methodology of factor identification and the relevance of the factors. Was the proliferation of factors due to artifacts of a methodology based on correlations, or was it a reflection of the complexity of the human intellect? Other questions were raised concerning the number of factors that could be regarded as being of substantial importance in intellectual development, education, decision making, and in day to day mental functioning (Carroll, 1982). As early as 1941, Ellison and Edgerton had observed that relatively few of Thurstone's primary mental abilities correlated significantly with any kind of scholastic success. Only verbal reasoning abilities were found to have reliably significant correlations with school performance.

Guilford (1967) and Guilford and Hoepfner (1971) explained the proliferation of factors as an indication of the complexity of the intellect. Guilford has developed a three-dimensional model for the summarization and classification of the many factors that he claims to have identified. The model, which he named the 'structure-of-intellect' model, allows for the simultaneous classification of any given factor on the basis of its content, the operations elicited by tests of the factor, and the types of products that result from the operations. The model puts forward a choice of four types of contents of factors, five types of operations, and six types of products.

Attempts to cope with the problem of factor proliferation originated from different directions, representative of the major areas in which concern had been expressed. Methodologists (e.g. Cooley and Lohnes, 1962, 1971; Fischer, 1974; Green, 1966; Linn, 1968; Lord and Novick, 1968; Rasch, 1960, 1980; Wright and Stone, 1979) reexamined and established alternative statistical procedures for the identification of factors.

The Cattell–Horn Model

A different approach to the problem of factor proliferation is implicit in the work of Cattell and Horn. Their theory is that intelligence is comprised of at least two major and different kinds of abilities, *fluid ability* and *crystallized ability*.

These terms were coined by Cattell (1943), who called attention to a possible distinction between basic capacity (fluid intelligence) and abilities that are acquired through education (crystallized intelligence). Cattell (1971) viewed both kinds of abilities as group factors complimenting the general intelligence factor. Both fluid and crystallized intelligence were seen as having associated with them a larger number of factors representing narrower abilities at the level of and similar to Thurstone's primary mental abilities. Extensions of this work were shown to support a hierarchical model of the organizational structure of component abilities such as fluid intelligence, crystallized intelligence, visualization capacity, general retrieval capacity, perceptual speed, and memory, which, in turn were shown to be accounted for by three oblique factors, namely, the original fluid intelligence, ability to concentrate, and school culture (Hakstian and Cattell, 1976). Horn (1976, 1978) presents evidence of the wide applicability of these factors, also across the age range.

Crystallized intelligence refers to the organization and appropriate application of previously acquired skills and knowledge. It develops through experience, and acculturation, particularly schooling.

Fluid intelligence is generally regarded as more 'native' and as developing earlier than crystallized intelligence. It involves the ability to solve new problems that have not been previously learnt or for which no strategies have been taught. This kind of intelligence includes the flexible adaptive facility required for new learning and problem solving in unpractised situations. Fluid intelligence leads to the acquisition, during development, of the knowledge and experience required in adult life. It is represented by abstract and often non-verbal reasoning tasks that require flexible, adaptive problem-solving skills, and is often seen as almost synonymous with reasoning ability (Sternberg, 1977). Fluid intelligence is thought to reach its peak at the stage of early adulthood, and then to gradually decline, particularly with advancing old age.

Horn (1976) described the two kinds of intelligence as follows:
[Crystallized intelligence:]

> Awareness of concepts and terms pertaining to a broad variety of topics, as measured in general information and vocabulary tests, and in tests which measure knowledge in science, mechanics, social studies, English literature, mathematics and a variety of other areas. It is also manifested in the Information, Vocabulary, Comprehension, Similarities and, to a lesser extent, Arithmetic subtests of the Wechsler scales. This is the dimension most likely to be referred to as indicating intelligence. In much British work it is labelled verbal-educational intelligence.

[Fluid intelligence:]

> Facility in reasoning, particularly in figural non-word symbolic materials, as indicated in tests such as letter series, matrices, mazes, figure classifications, and word groupings, as well as Block Design, Picture Arrangement, Object Assembly, and Picture Completion subtests of the Wechsler scales. The dimension also is likely to be referred to as indicating intelligence. Some characterize it as non-verbal intelligence (although verbal tests can

measure it) or performance IQ. In British work it is known as spatial-perceptual-practical intelligence. (Horn, 1976, p.445)

According to the Cattell–Horn theory, fluid intelligence is invested in learning throughout the school years to produce crystallized intelligence. Crystallized intelligence is the kind of ability needed for the successful completion of most tests of verbal knowledge and school achievement. Some investigators regard crystallized intelligence and scholastic aptitude as synonymous (e.g. Snow, 1978a).

As noted above, fluid intelligence tends to reach its peak with the completion of formal schooling. Crystallized intelligence reaches a somewhat later peak, and is thought not to decline appreciably thereafter. One might hypothesize that during the early 20s some slight positive changes in fluid intelligence could occur, namely, continued development if fluid intelligence is thought of as including the ability to find novel solutions to problems, or the beginning of decline, if fluid intelligence reflects the biological influences on the cognitive system and the ability to learn as argued by those adhering strictly to the Cattell–Horn position.

Horn (1978) described dramatic differences in the continued development and extension of crystallized intelligence skills and achievements during the early adult years. Individuals who continued their education or training after the completion of high school showed continued improvement, while those who did not take part in further academic studies or vocational training tended to fall behind their high school peers in academic problem-solving ability. However, individuals not engaged in further education or training might show advantages over their peers in the kinds of problem-solving skills that are encountered in everyday living.

In the case of individuals who do not continue post-secondary education, the crystallized intelligence dimensions that increase most during early adulthood appear to be largely job-related.

An interesting attempt to provide structure for the near chaos created by the proliferation of factors of general and specific abilities is that of Snow (1978a). On the basis of the Cattell–Horn hierarchical model of fluid and crystallized intelligence factors, and adding a visualization factor (closely related to what is commonly called 'spatial ability', and involving the ability to manipulate visual input and images), Snow provided a schematic model of intelligence in which he attempted to distinguish the major components of intelligence and their hypothesized levels of generality. A summary of this model is provided in Figure 1.1.

Various similar models have been provided in the literature (e.g. Lohman, 1979a, 1979b; Smith, 1964) showing differing detail. Snow's (1978) schema, on which Figure 1.1 is based, was chosen to demonstrate this type of factor summarization because it clearly shows major distinctions among many of the cognitive factors and abilities discussed in this book, and makes allowance for several levels of generality.

Figure 1.1 provides one example of how the construct of general ability or intelligence might be broken down into different kinds of intelligence, in this case, to distinguish between crystallized ability, fluid ability and visualization ability. These, in turn, can be divided into more specialized verbal, quantitative, perceptual, spatial, and memory abilities. At the lowest level of the model presented in Figure 1.1, many kinds of specific abilities and skills can be identified. The question marks and boxes made up of unconnected lines are intended to remind the reader that less agreement has been reached concerning the factors constituting fluid intelligence and visualization

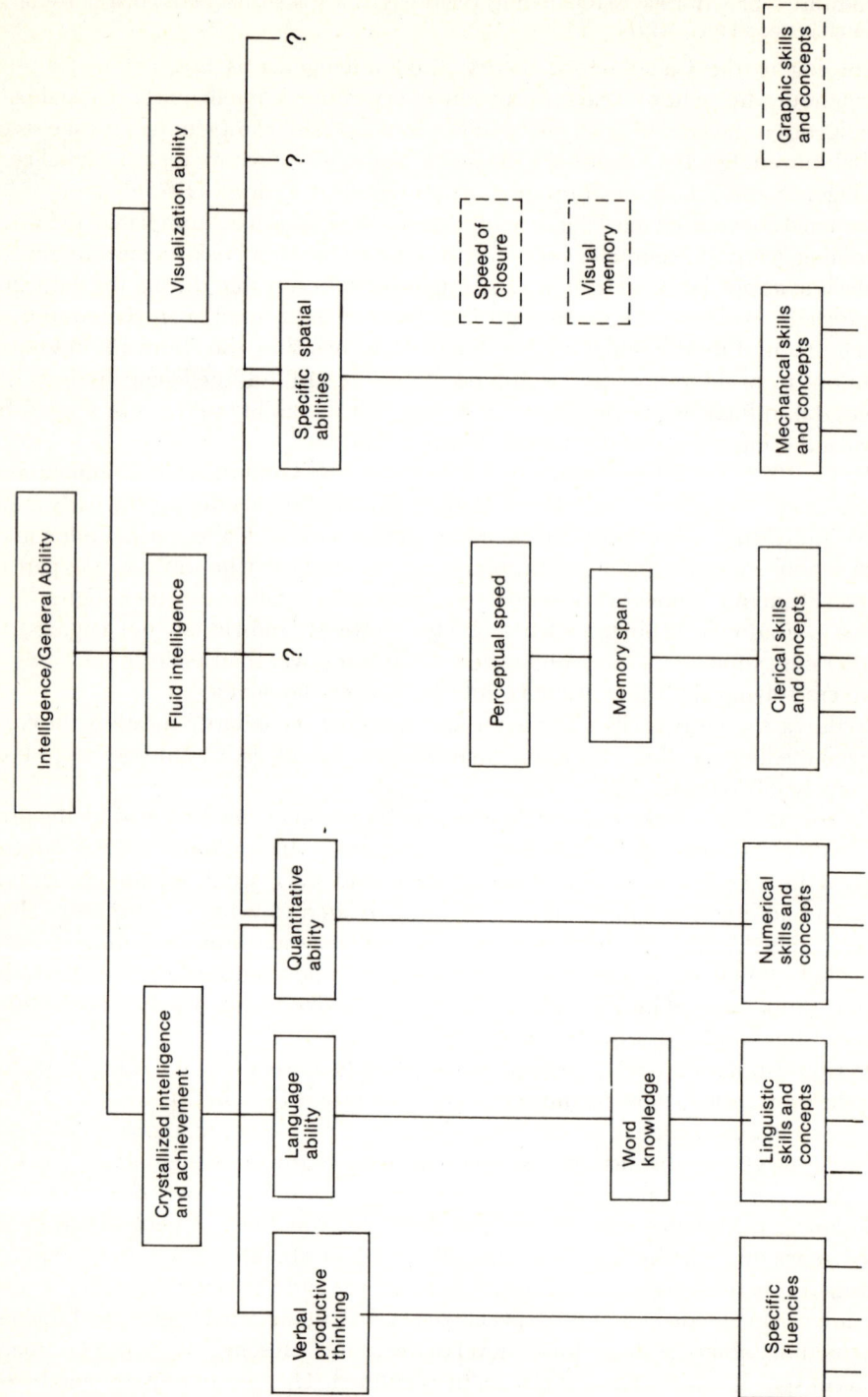

Figure 1.1 A Hierarchical Model of Mental Abilities (after Snow, 1978)

abilities than about other factors describing aspects of general ability. For example, current research suggests that there may be several specific factors reflecting spatial abilities that are unlikely to tie neatly into a gross scheme such as the one presented in Figure 1.1. Rather, there may be subtle connections, including stimulus and environment bound trade-offs within the individual's cognitive functioning between verbal, analytical, and spatial information-processing abilities. Despite this, as pointed out by Humphreys (1962) and others, a simple hierarchy, even though it may simplify the organization of mental functioning, provides a useful taxonomy at a stage when theory is still frail.

The abilities depicted in the model presented in Figure 1.1 are examples of the cognitive factors that have been identified with some consistency across decades of factor analytic research.

Nature–Nurture

Longitudinal and cross-sectional studies have shown that these abilities tend to differentiate with age, at least through childhood and adolescence. This has been viewed by some as resulting from the unfolding and differentiation of the nervous system with maturation (e.g. Garrett, 1946), and by others as the result of learning and transfer of learning among cognitive tasks (e.g. Ferguson, 1954, 1956).

Many psychometricians appear to assume that cognitive factors correspond to rather permanent constitutionally determined traits or attributes of individuals, which originate, at least in part, from genetic sources. An analogy drawn by Carroll (1982) explains this view clearly.

> The tests measuring such factors are assumed to elicit the operations of these traits—somewhat in the way that a weight-lifting task calls on the individual's muscular powers. (p.75)

He emphasizes further that

> Factors can also be looked upon as manifestations of learned competencies. It can be easily demonstrated that if two types of content tend to be learned or practised together (as opposed to not being learned together), tests of those contents will tend to have a positive correlation, giving rise to an underlying factor. (Carroll, 1983, p.75)

Ferguson's (1956) interpretation of factor analytic models is based on the rationale that learning leads to the acquisition of abilities and skills that can transfer to various tasks and can generalize. His theory does not exclude the possibility that individual differences resulting from constitutional and genetic variations may set differential limits on the potential development of the mental abilities in individuals, rather it draws attention to the potential use that can be made of learning processes in attempts to explain factor analytic findings. Carroll (1962), Hunt (1961) and others have investigated this model further, but no comprehensive studies involving a variety of factors obtained in different domains have been conducted to evaluate the consequences of Ferguson's position.

Conclusions

Psychometric research through its methodology of factor analysis tried to organize the emerging knowledge concerning mental abilities, and contributed great refinement to the methodology of mental measurement.

Spearman (1904, 1923, 1927) and Thurstone (1938a), the early pioneers of psychometrics, were emphatic in describing their work as 'prescientific', meaning that they were measuring variables, for which no theoretical explanations were available, and that they were classifying human performance on the basis of constructs that would yet need to be explained by theories.

This insight of Spearman and Thurstone concerning the scientific status of their work appears to have been increasingly ignored by psychometricians, at least until the 1960s. For more than half a century the study of individual differences in mental functioning has centred around the methodology of factor analysis, which continued to lead towards the identification of more and varied factors as the end product of research, but has been less fruitful in explaining ability factors in terms of psychological or educational processes — thus remaining as prescientific as the pioneers of the method were forced to be.

Progress during the past century occurred in the increasing sophistication of statistical procedures. Test theory developed out of the discipline of mathematics, and nowadays is strongly built on technology. It has promoted procedures for increasingly accurate and reliable measurement of individual differences, with little if any consideration of the nature of the variables being measured. Measurement is the prerequisite of scientific theory. 'Whatever exists exists in a quantity', is a quotation assigned to E.L. Thorndike. But the investigation of measurement for its own sake leads to refinements in measurement, not towards a theory of *what* is being measured.

The research on psychometric intelligence has succeeded in establishing, beyond doubt, that individual differences exist, but, despite some of the previously mentioned attempts, it has been unable to explain what the factors mean.

Looking back over the research endeavour of the past 50 years, Carroll (1982), himself a psychometrician, evaluates the state of the art as follows:

> Factor analysis has been concerned with the decomposition of mental abilities into 'factors' . . . Test theory has been concerned with various statistical models and operations designed to produce certain desirable measurement properties in tests or test scores . . . these two types of scientific endeavour have had both productive and counterproductive features. Factor analysis has had at least the potentiality of facilitating detailed understanding of what could be measured, and test theory has promoted the more accurate measurement of whatever could be measured. On the negative side . . . in factor analysis there has been too much interest in the identification of factors as an end product of the research effort, and too little interest in explaining the factors identified in terms of their composition and antecedents. In test theory, there has been overemphasis on desirable measurement properties without corresponding consideration of what exactly was being measured—a pure trait or melange of correlated response tendencies. (Carroll, 1982, p.107)

Modern Developments

Until the previous decade the concept of intelligence tended to be treated as if it had been created by psychometricians. Lay people and professionals alike felt that the proper use of the term was restricted to the domain of psychometrics. The modern era is characterized by a demand by researchers, practitioners and the general public for answers to questions of basic theoretical importance, that is, the construct of intelligence is expected to remain a vital one only if it can be explained as well as measured. Such demands reflect a general acceptance of the view that progress in measurement techniques and statistics used in the assessment of mental development and functioning must be paralleled by the development of adequate theory and an understanding of what is being measured.

Educational and psychological studies conducted during the 1970s have established that individual differences among learners often interact with instructional treatment variables (e.g. Cronbach and Snow, 1977; Snow, 1977b, 1981). This coincides with an increasing emphasis in the delivery of all educational services at the present time on individualization, which implies a need for the identification of psychologically definable strengths and weaknesses in individuals so that intervention procedures can be tailored to the diagnosed needs of individuals. All this has emphasized the need for a deeper, more process-oriented understanding of the nature of the construct intelligence, and the abilities, skills, knowledge and psychological processes it subsumes.

Since the late 1970s, intelligence research has entered a new era, partly in response to the questioning of the power and limitations of the explanatory theories put forward by psychometricians, and partly as a direct result of the evidence accumulating from the experimental analyses of individual differences in information processing.

The concept of intelligence, from its restrictive psychometric definition as a statistically derived factor, has come to include such dimensions as reasoning, problem solving, creativity, the ability to solve novel kinds of tasks, the ability to acquire and reason with new conceptual systems, the ability to learn under conditions of imperfect instruction, planning and other meta-cognitive skills, speed of memory access, etc.

According to Horn (1976), a major focus in intelligence research during the 1970s has been that

> ... of specifying the basic cognitive processes identifying the primary abilities, describing the essential functions (call it what you will) of intellectual performances. This is the task of finding a good way to talk about the ways in which humans process information, form concepts, solve problems, acquire and express knowledge, use language, etc. It is, in part, a problem of finding useful systems for simplifying. (p.438)

Intellectual ability tends now to be viewed as dependent, to a large extent, on the efficiency of the individual's information-processing capacity, and not as the result of a generalized, somewhat 'magical' characteristic, energy or substance referred to as 'intelligence'. In relation to this theoretical orientation, learning difficulties or other manifestations of temporary or lasting cognitive deficits are not necessarily the result of a generalized intellectual weakness, but might be caused by an imbalance in the individual's information-processing skills (e.g. over- or under-utilization of certain cognitive strategies, the use of strategies that do not match task requirements or the cognitive style of individuals, etc.). As a research topic, the field of intelligence is once again included within the domain of research into cognitive processes more generally.

The ground for these developments was prepared initially by researchers who urged interaction and a pooling of research efforts between the fields of experimental psychology and pschyometrics. A number of investigators (e.g. Butcher, 1968; Carroll, 1974; Cronbach, 1957, 1975b; Simon, 1976; Sternberg, 1977) had suggested that research in both areas had been accumulating large but separate sets of knowledge and methodological expertise for too long. They argued that the findings from experimental psychology should be applied in psychometric research in order to produce a better understanding of the meaning of scores obtained on psychometric tests. Conversely, Bouchard (1968); Carroll (1976); Carroll and Maxwell (1979); Hunt, Lunneborg, and Lewis (1975); Resnick (1976); Simon (1975); and others emphasized the potential value of the systematic investigation of individual differences in cognitive processes.

Examples of studies in which some such integration has been brought about include Bruner, Goodnow, and Austin (1956); Rowe (1985a); Sternberg (1977); Wason and Johnson-Laird (1972) and others who used items from psychometric tests as experimental tasks, and characterized individual differences in performance on these tasks through analyses of the response patterns and/or errors.

Whitely (1981) has shown how psychometric latent trait methodology can be combined with an information-processing paradigm to provide new insights into how reasoning components enter into performance on psychometric tests.

Much of the modern research into the construct of intelligence can be characterized by what Pellegrino and Glaser (1979) have referred to as either the *cognitive correlates approach* or the *cognitive components* approach. Both approaches involve the correlation of parameters from information-processing research with scores obtained on psychometric tests of general or specific abilities. The approaches have different goals, and are neither mutually exclusive nor mutually exhaustive.

The aim of the *cognitive correlates* studies is to identify basic cognitive processes that discriminate between high and low scorers on the tests. The tendency in these studies is to correlate the results of performance on simple laboratory-type tasks with scores on psychometric tests. Examples of this research include that of Chiang and Atkinson (1976); Goldberg, Schwartz, and Stewart (1977), Hunt (1978); Hunt, Frost, and Lunneborg (1973); Hunt, Lunneborg, and Lewis (1975); Jensen and Munro (1979); Keating and Bobbit (1978); Keating, Keniston, Manis, and Bobbitt (1980).

The *cognitive components* approach (e.g. Carroll, 1976; Egan, 1979; Pellegrino and Glaser, 1980; Rowe, 1985a; Simon, 1976; Snow, 1980; Sternberg 1977, 1979, 1980) involves the investigation of complex information-processing tasks. Items from traditional intelligence tests are analysed with the aim of identifying components of the processes underlying performance. The most ambitious of these studies to date is probably Sternberg's (1977, 1980b) 'componential analysis' of analogical reasoning.

Two quite outstanding theoretical contributions in the field of intelligence research during the past decade were made by Robert Sternberg and by Glaser, Pellegrino and Lesgold. The advances in the conceptualization of the construct of intelligence resulting from their work since 1977 are comparable only with Newell and Simon's (1972) contribution to methodology and procedure, which revolutionized psychological research, not only research into problem solving but also with respect to any cognitive process.

Sternberg's (1977) componential analyses of analogical reasoning have grown into a broader theory of human intelligence (e.g. Sternberg, 1981a, 1981d, 1984), which uses information-processing components with varying functions and of different levels of generality. His theory is hierarchical and postulates 'lower order performance', that is, acquisition, transfer and retention components, and 'higher order' control processes used for executive planning and decision making during problem solving, and allows for the development of automatic information-processing components.

Glaser, Pellegrino and Lesgold (1977), in their seminal paper entitled 'Some Directions for a Cognitive Psychology', asserted that

> it is strongly recommended that the most significant use of measures of intelligence and aptitude should be not primarily for the purposes of prediction, but for indicating how intellectual performance can be improved. (p.508)

This view constitutes a significant break with the traditional, categorization- and selection-oriented, *raison d'être* of intelligence tests. The rejection of conceptions of a fixed level of intelligence in favour of models in which the assessment of intelligence might provide the basis for adaptive training has become almost universal in modern cognitive research. Support for this statement is found in Resnick's (1981, p.684) article in the *Annual Review of Psychology*, in which she points out that the literature relating to intelligence research during the past 10 years has 'a decidedly new look' (Resnick, 1981, p.684). She notes that traditional psychometric approaches are being replaced by approaches that are aimed at the discovery of cognitive processes that underlie test performance, and suggests that the 'new look' approaches differ in emphasis from traditional approaches in the investigation of intelligence in at least three ways:

- They aim to define intelligence in behavioural terms, rather than to refine its measurement and predict outcomes.
- They require that definitions of the nature of intelligence reflect psychologically valid cognitive processes that underlie 'intelligent' behaviours.
- They focus on the malleability and adaptability of human aptitudes, skills and abilities.

In the light of the profound changes that are taking place in our society as we are entering an age in which human cognitive activity will revolve increasingly around the processing and transmitting of information, the concern to increase intellectual efficiency, that is, to teach information-processing skills, becomes particularly meaningful.

The rapid changes in our society are leading to the development of an increasingly large gap between the opportunities available to a technologically educated 'elite', and the opportunities available to those who have been displaced by automation. Many of the intellectual skills and abilities that are needed for membership of the elite group can be summarized as the 'ability to adapt' to changing situational and task requirements.

Members of our society with less ability will require special training in adaptable skills and abilities to ensure that they have a chance of leading a reasonably satisfactory life. Because humans are now able to build machines that can be programmed to 'behave relatively intelligently', the need for workers of average and below intellectual ability and/or achievement is decreasing rapidly. Machines are taking over the areas in which these individuals had found employment in the past. Research overseas is seeking ways of helping these individuals to acquire the basic skills necessary for success in a technological economy. Experimental compensatory instructional programs, which are aimed at raising levels of information-processing capabilities, range from 'learning to learn' programs to procedural training in areas in which electronic equipment has replaced traditional devices. (For reviews of this literature see Campione, Brown, and Ferrara, 1982; Detterman and Sternberg, 1982; Sternberg, 1982.)

Intelligence is malleable; it has been shown that a multitude of intellectual skills of varying levels and complexity can be developed, increased, and compensated for, by means of guidance, training, and the provision of appropriate experiences. What is required is a description of the intellectual performance of an individual in operational terms, a description that can form the basis for intervention in order to change performance—in other words, to facilitate the increase in intellectual ability.

The type of assessment device that is likely to contribute to improvements in intellectual performance must provide for the interpretation of ability or skills in terms of manipulatable variables that enhance or impede performance. The first step towards the achievement of such assessment is to develop tests that are aimed at analysing individuals' performances with a view to identifying those components of the processes of cognitive performance itself that might be responsible for the outcome differences observed in the performance of cognitive tasks including educational achievement.

> Test scores and other individual-difference parameters need to be conceived of as representing points on curves of individual growth (and decline?), rather than as points on a normal distribution in the population. (Carroll, 1982, p.101)

Even more importantly, the parameters that are assessed must focus on specific and relevant behaviours and skills that are directly interpretable in terms of specific training objectives and goals of performance.

CHAPTER 2

THE MODEL OF INTELLIGENCE UNDERLYING THE NAT

The discussion of the definitional problems and the varied dimensions attributed to the concept of intelligence contained in Chapter 1 could be described as having raised more questions than it might have answered. One would have to agree with the view expressed by Weiner (1976):

> Given available knowledge to date, it is illusory for psychologists to believe they know what intelligence is; any such comfortable position would be naive. (p.129)

And yet, the issue of defining intelligence cannot be brushed aside as an academic or semantic problem. What is meant by the term intelligence determines what *can be expected* from the data derived from measures of intelligence, and *when*, *where* and *how* these data can be used.

More emphatically, the meaning attached to the term intelligence is the core from which the interpretation of intelligence test performance originates, and to which all understanding of mental functioning and achievement is anchored.

Options

The current lack of consensus about a clear and generally useful definition of intelligence allows three major options to the psychologist seriously considering the nature of intelligence.

He or she can give in to dismay and abandon all attempts at assessment, or the psychologist can agree with Thurstone and others that there is such a phenomenon as 'intelligence', the meaning of which will one day be known; and that for the moment, in the absence of definition, it can still be hypothesized that the construct exists and that its effects can be observed and measured.

As a third option, the psychologist can support the notion of the behaviourists, and consider intelligence to be an intervening variable, the outcome of its operation being measured by the intelligence test.

Acceptance of the first option would clearly obviate the remainder of this book. It would also be a retrograde step as concerns present educational practice and requirements. Education (i.e. schooling, and training more generally) and cognitive abilities (i.e. intelligence) do not operate independently but are fundamentally confounded. Adequate intellectual functioning is basically a product of education, and learning and educational achievement are products of intellectual functioning. To meet the educational needs of individual learners requires a combination of the identification of specific strengths and weaknesses in abilities and skills, with teaching, and the evaluation of the match between the two.

The second option was chosen by the developers of traditional intelligence tests, who assumed that there is such a phenomenon as intelligence, which can be examined psychometrically. The third option implies that one is dealing with a mysterious 'force', which can influence behaviour but which cannot itself be measured.

None of these options provide an answer to the psychologist who is required to develop an intelligence test in the 1980s and beyond, and who is expected to provide an instrument that is defensible not only in a psychometric sense, but in terms of a theoretical rationale. It is generally accepted that much more theoretical and empirical research is needed before generally defensible and broadly suitable procedures can be developed. But it is evident that—whether we are ready or not—the assessment of psychological functioning and educational achievement, including disadvantage, and an increasing demand to find valid procedures to improve the opportunities for minorities are growing concerns.

It was in response to these concerns that the author was asked to develop a non-verbal group ability test. As none of the three options listed above proved to be acceptable, the only alternative was to try to develop a rationale for the task in relation to the scientific knowledge that has been accumulated in the psychological literature, particularly in the areas of psychometrics, and experimental, developmental, and cognitive psychology.

As discussed in the preceding chapter, the intelligence test was designed specifically to serve as a device in the selection of people, and in the prediction of potential for training or academic achievment.

Performance on group intelligence tests is interpreted on a normative scale. Whether the test yields a single score, such as IQ, or multiple scores, for example, verbal, numerical, etc., an individual's performance is interpreted by comparing his or her score(s) with those of a reference group, usually a large, representative, stratified sample of appropriate age. The basic information derived from the intelligence test thus relates to the relative standing of the testee based on his or her level of performance on the test compared with the performance of the reference group(s) who provided the norms. It cannot be stressed strongly enough that an individual score on such a test is meaningless in itself, and uninterpretable except in comparison with the distribution of scores obtained from the reference group(s).

Traditional group intelligence tests may have been useful in the context for which they were designed; however, their legitimacy in present-day educational settings is questionable.

In the past, educational decisions tended to be made on the basis of the estimates of intellectual potential provided by the scores obtained on these standardized tests. Intellectual potential was regarded as relatively fixed, and probably genetically determined. In contrast to this, more recent developments in physiological, psychological and educational research emphasize the malleability and adaptive functional development of cognitive skills. This has resulted in an acceptance, by psychologists, counsellors, teachers and other professionals operating in a broad educational area, of the recommendation of Glaser, Pellegrino, and Lesgold (1977):

> that the most significant use of measures of intelligence and aptitude should not be primarily for the purposes of prediction, but for indicating how intellectual performance can be improved. (p.508)

Even if it were possible to produce validly updated versions of traditional group intelligence tests, it is unlikely that such tests would contribute to the aim of improving intellectual performance. Their major limitation in this respect derives from the fact that they do not provide any information about the processes associated with the intellectual performance that results in a particular score. They tend not to provide a means of interpreting general or specific abilities or skills in terms of educationally relevant and modifiable variables that enhance or impede cognitive performance. The interpretation of test results encompasses both test and student characteristics. The interpretation of test scores involves attempts to determine significant aspects of a person's intellectual strengths or weaknesses relative to the characteristics measured by the test. Unless a coherent picture of both the test and the student characteristics evolves, the interpretation is not complete, and may lack validity.

If we accept that intelligence has at least some clearly identifiable components (and the literature in experimental, developmental, educational, and information-processing psychology, as well as that of psychometrics, lends strong support to such a view), the appropriateness of the measurement model underlying traditional group tests as a means for revealing differences in cognitive functioning must be questioned.

Because the traditional model compares average scores obtained by groups, and since low scores on cognitive tests, like low school achievement etc., can be the result of difficulties or deficits in different component abilities in different individuals, the averaging of scores for groups tends to mask (and may even cancel out) individual strengths and weaknesses. In other words, since individuals performing in the same IQ range are not necessarily a homogeneous group, either in their skills or their approach to tasks, strategies, motivation, etc., it is invalid to base the evaluation of their abilities on a measurement model that assumes intra-group homogeneity.

Thus, the traditional approach has obvious limitations when the aim is to describe the performance of an individual in order to intervene and change performance by increasing intellectual efficiency. In order to achieve such an aim it is necessary to produce tests that contain tasks of known functions or behaviours, with a view to identifying the components of performance that might be generating the individual differences generally observed in total score differences.

Psychometric tests identify differences between persons, but describe performance in terms of hypothesized psychological constructs. In contrast to this, designers of experimental and information-processing research into intelligence set out to develop models and theories aimed at providing an understanding of cognitive performance, but tended to disregard individual differences. The dilemma was summarized aptly by Whitely (1977) as follows:

> The different approaches of experimental psychology and psychometrics have resulted in practically important measures of intelligence which are not understood, in addition to cognitive theories which have no practical implications for measuring individual differences. (p.465)

What has been lacking are ability tests that might provide a direct basis for educational intervention that can be tailored to the specific needs of the individuals—this means tests that pinpoint strengths and weaknesses, and thus provide information relevant to the design of procedures that may raise the intellectual efficiency of the individual. A rationale for the development of such tests could be of the kind suggested by Anderson (1976):

> I am proposing a change in our interpretation of what it means to understand the nature of human intelligence. I once thought it could mean unique identification of the structures and processes underlying cognitive behavior. Since that is not possible I propose that we take 'understanding the nature of human intelligence' to mean the possession of a theory that will enable us to improve human intelligence. (p.16)

The Nature of the NAT

For the development of the NAT battery, it was accepted that a major psychological and educational demand currently made of theories and tests of intelligence is that they should provide information that can be used to improve intellectual performance. So it was decided to try to design an assessment device that may place individuals into different score positions in relation to well defined and psychologically relevant dimensions or aspects of general or specific abilities. It is expected that such an approach may provide, in practice, more useful descriptions of individual differences than IQ scores from traditional group intelligence tests when psychological or educational intervention is the aim.

Instruments for the assessment of cognitive development and functioning traditionally focus on two areas, (1) the knowledge acquired by the individual (often referred to as crystallized intelligence) and (2) the availability of cognitive abilities and skills that enable learning and the acquisition and use of knowledge (often referred to as fluid intelligence). The NAT battery focuses on the latter set of skills.

Cognitive activity is a complex part of human functioning, which occurs, for example, during problem solving. Problem solving is a mental activity that, as a minimum, requires the operation of such cognitive processes as preliminary perceptual analysis and synthesis of the task requirements and/or the situation, and the availability, selection and application of cognitive operations that are appropriate to the problem situation.

To investigate cognitive functioning, it is therefore necessary to create tasks or stimulus situations in which the individual has no automatic (i.e. reflex), or previously established response.

Tasks that are to form the basis on which cognitive functioning is to be evaluated must be designed to elicit such processes as the analysis of the task requirements, the identification of essential components, the formulation of hypotheses and/or the development of solution strategies that respond to the perceived demand characteristics of the task. Obviously, these processes are modified by the environment and the execution of solution strategies.

The literature contains descriptions of a large number of possible, but by no means obvious, aspects and dimensions of cognitive performance that can be observed with some consistency across a large number of experimental tasks. The kinds of tasks included in the NAT battery were chosen so as to be unfamiliar to the testee. They are simple enough so that their demand characteristics can be identified by most, and their execution presents little difficulty. The author attempted to isolate basic perceptual, conceptual, memory, and attention processes that, according to the research literature, have been found to distinguish reliably between persons of lower and higher ability.

The subtests contained in the NAT battery are *criterion-referenced*. Each subtest consists of items that tap the particular aspects of general ability on which it is based.

The term 'criterion-referenced' was first used by Glaser (1963) as a label for the type of test that is designed to provide a measurement of stated outcomes of instruction. Criterion-referenced tests were first designed to provide descriptions of student achievement relative to a set of items that reflect the intent of instruction in a particular domain. During the 1970s, which saw an explosion of papers relating to this model (cf. Hambleton, Swaminathan, Algina, and Coulson, 1978), its use was extended to include the measurement of operationally definable characteristics and constructs by tests in which the sum of items directly represented the trait under study.

> Construct validity, by linking test behavior to a more general attribute, process or trait, provides not only an evidential basis for interpreting the processes underlying test scores, but also a rational basis for inferring testable implications from the broader network of the construct's meaning. (Messick, 1975, p.961)

From Messick's perspective, reflected in the above quotation and extensively discussed and supported more recently by Roid and Haladyna (1982) and others, it becomes clear that criterion-referenced methods may be used in either of two contexts, that is, with operational definitions or in relation to construct validity. The former applies to test scores that are interpreted solely on the basis of what the items broadly represent (i.e. there is common agreement that the item and the trait are matched); the latter is based on the underlying meaning of test items as derived from a theory of the relations between a test and variables of the real world.

The questions answered by criterion-referenced tests provide truly diagnostic information, and can thus make a profound contribution to the education and training of individuals. Examples of the types of questions addressed by criterion-referenced measurement are: 'Is a certain individual able to perform a specified task?', 'Has he or she acquired particular (defined) skills?'. As explained by Popham (1980):

> Unlike their norm-referenced predecessors, which rely chiefly on the relative status of an examinee's performance in relationship to the performance of those in a (statistical) normative group, criterion-referenced tests are supposed to tell us what it is that examinees can or can't do. (p.15)

The criterion-referenced approach to measurement was chosen for the development of the NAT for a number of reasons. Firstly, this model is consistent with the author's view, discussed in more detail later in this chapter, that intelligence can be understood as a functional system of essential component abilities and skills. Criterion-referenced measurement allows for the sampling of a broader range of component abilities than the paradigm of traditional IQ test construction. Secondly, criterion-referenced measurement is more likely to provide an understanding of why a particular level of cognitive performance or educational achievement has been reached, as at least some of the determining processes can be identified for individuals. Thirdly, criterion-referenced measurement provides the kind of information necessary for the development of intervention procedures that meet the needs of individuals. This is particularly important in view of the growing acceptance of the idea that intelligence is not fixed but malleable.

To communicate the criterion-referenced information obtained on the basis of test performance, the NAT battery provides an ability profile for each testee. The basic rationale of this method will be discussed later in the chapter.

The Meaning of Intelligence as Assessed by the NAT

Inspection of the subtests makes it obvious that the NAT attempts to measure general ability as reflected by the availability of a number of information-processing skills. The aim of this approach to the description of individual differences is to provide a theoretical framework for the analysis of intelligence by means of the NAT. To the extent that this effort was successful, NAT profiles and scores should be able to provide an account of the nature of important component skills that influence the performance of individuals.

The NAT battery is organized into a series of different subtests so that a number of different aspects of intelligence can be measured, and because a heterogeneous sample of assessed behaviours produces greater validity for the measurement of such a complex phenomenon. Within the field of intelligence testing there is some dispute about whether the various subtests of an intelligence battery are merely different measures of the same kind of intelligence, whether they measure various dimensions of intelligence, or whether they are measures of different kinds of intelligence (e.g. Gardner, 1983). This debate is not of relevance in the present context, as it is based mainly on semantic, definitional differences. The author shares the view of those who believe that it is meaningful to talk about general intelligence, a view that is probably best described in a recent quotation from one of the pioneers of information-processing research:

> The most deeply rooted preconception guiding my theorizing is a belief in the unity of human cognition, that is, that all the higher cognitive processes such as memory, language, problem solving, imagery, deduction and induction are different manifestations of the same underlying system. (Anderson, 1983, p.1)

This position does not deny that there exist many powerful special-purpose systems, particularly for the processing of perceptual information and the co-ordinating of motor performance. However, the author of the NAT believes that these 'peripheral' systems are part of a common cognitive system, the operation of which results in higher level cognitive functioning. Moreover, human intellectual functioning may be a reflection of the operation of the common system, that is, intelligence, while the processes of peripheral systems may not differ too much between humans and other mammals.

Of all the basic theoretical notions in the author's mind, the most important is probably the conceptualization of 'intelligence' as a functional system of component abilities. This idea to some extent reconciles the traditionally conflicting views of those adhering to either 'g' or multiple 's' theories of intelligence.

The term 'functional system' may require explanation. At first, the terms system and functional will be defined separately.

A number of broad meanings have been attached to the term *system*. The following definitions are among those given in the *Oxford English Dictionary* (1967):

A. An organized or connected group of objects

1. An assemblage of things connected, associated or interdependent, so as to form a complex unity. A whole composed of parts in orderly arrangement according to some scheme or plan; rarely applied to simple or small assemblages.
2. (Physics) A group of bodies moving about one another in space under some particular dynamic law of gravitation. . .
3. In various scientific and technical uses: a group, set or aggregate of things, natural or artificial, forming a connected, complex whole.

B. A set of principles, etc., a scheme, method or department of knowledge or belief considered as an organized whole. (p.2115)

Webster's Third New International Dictionary of the English Language (1966) defines a system as

a complex unity formed of many often diverse parts, subject to a common plan or serving a common purpose . . . an aggregation or assemblage of objects joined in regular interaction or interdependence. (p.2332)

All the above definitions imply that the concept of a system may provide a reasonable model when one is thinking about a phenomenon in terms of the interaction and interdependency of its component parts, and of how these work in concert when an objective is being achieved.

A few more definitions are necessary before the usefulness of a system's framework as a model of intelligence can be demonstrated. The simplest system consists of what is usually termed INPUT, PROCESS, and OUTPUT.

INPUT involves all ingredients that enter the system. It consists of all the stimuli that are consciously or automatically responded to and/or transformed into OUTPUT. With respect to the intellectual functioning of individuals, INPUT would include both genetically and environmentally determined variables, the characteristics of the task as well as those of the testee, the procedure, the setting, social and cultural factors, etc.

PROCESS is the part of the system that operates during the conversion or transformation of INPUT to OUTPUT. In a manufacturing PROCESS raw materials (INPUT) are converted into finished products (OUTPUT). During test performance or other problem-solving activity, PROCESS refers to the performance itself, that is, what takes place when the testee works on the task and seeks to find a solution (OUTPUT). During cognitive performance many of the components making up the PROCESS part of the system are probably information-processing and memory variables.

The OUTPUT of a system is its product. When the ingredients making up the INPUT of the system have been processed by the system, OUTPUT emerges. In a most general sense an IQ score can be regarded as the OUTPUT (not the only output, but the most frequently used one) of an individual's performance on an intelligence test.

A system consisting of the three basically necessary parts is illustrated in Figure 2.1.

INPUT → PROCESS → OUTPUT

Figure 2.1 Simplified Model of a System

Obviously, a reasonably valid model of test performance would be much more complex than the simple model shown in Figure 2.1. Such a model would include a number of FEEDBACK LOOPS, which represent more complex relations between the parts of the system, and would probably have to include SUB-SYSTEMS, which, although parts of the overall system, have all the characteristics of a system themselves.

In the author's view intelligent behaviour is mediated by specific component abilities and skills. Component skills are likely to exist in varying kinds of specificity. Some of them are so specialized that performing even the simplest task entails the use of a variety of them. Thus, a given skill or set of component abilities, which under certain conditions contributes to the performance required for a particular task, may be necessary, but not sufficient, to accomplish that task. Only when a number of component skills co-operate, might a given task be performed successfully. A 'functional' system provides a representation of the operation of the pattern(s) of component skills necessary for a given kind (or level) of performance.

Luria (1966a, 1966b) drew attention to different usages of the term *function*. As he pointed out, the same term is used to refer to the specific function of a small component part of a machine, or to the function of the machine as a whole. This dual use of the word has led to considerable confusion in the area of psychological assessment.

With the increasing popularity and use of the term function, and its development into a jargon word in recent years, psychologists, teachers and others began to confuse the function of narrower component skills (e.g. visual discrimination) with the function of more complex abilities such as the perception of visual stimuli. Some came to see visual perception as a function of visual discrimination skills, thus disregarding the fact that perception of any kind is actually the result of complex interactions of many component skills. As in Luria's machine part versus machine as a whole example (in which no part of the machine, whatever its specific function, could achieve the function of the machine as a whole), no one component of a mental process working in isolation can produce intellectual achievement. Instead, a large number of component abilities and skills must co-operate; in other words, they must work as a 'functional system'.

Luria's Model

The idea of a functional system was borrowed from Luria (1966a, 1966b, 1973), who used the model in relation to physiological rather than psychological variables. He applies the term to the interacting areas of the brain, the operation of which must be co-ordinated in order to produce a given behaviour. Luria's theory differs from both brain localization and equipotential theories. The localization theory postulated that each function results from the operation of a single specified part of the brain; for example, the brain was seen to contain a speech area, a walking area, and so on. Equipotential theorists suggested that for all functions all areas of the brain participate on an equal basis, and that no one area relates specifically to a particular behaviour.

In Luria's theory (1966a, 1966b, 1973) no single area of the brain is considered to be responsible for any particular overt behaviour. However, neither are all areas of the brain considered to contribute equally to all behaviours. According to Luria's theory of a functional system, a limited number of brain areas are involved in each behaviour, each in a specific and predictable way within the system. Luria's model may be thought of as a chain, each link of which represents a particular area of the brain. Each link is necessary for the chain to be complete, yet each link plays its own specific role in the overall chain. If any part of the functional system is broken, the behaviour represented by the chain is injured.

Another important concept in Luria's model is the notion of pluripotentiality. This concept postulates that any specific area in the brain can participate in numerous functional systems. If one area of the brain is injured many behaviours are disrupted, depending on the number of functional systems in which the given area is involved. The role of a particular brain area is similar in each system; thus, one area may be involved in a large variety of tasks requiring visual and motor integration. This may sound similar to the usual localization theories in which specific skills are assigned to a particular area of the brain. However, according to the pluripotentiality concept and in contrast to localization theories, Luria postulates that the various areas of the brain cannot operate in isolation. Actual behaviour can only result from the co-operation of several areas.

The final idea of major importance in Luria's theory is the lack of uniqueness of functional systems. Any given behaviour can be the result of the operation of a number of functional systems. This means that, while one system may be deficient or injured, the behaviour can be continued because of the availability of an alternative functional system. Luria and his followers (e.g. Golden, Osmon, Moses, and Berg, 1981; Golden, Hammeke, and Purisch, 1979; Reitan, 1966a, 1966c) have suggested that the number of functional systems available for a behaviour may, in fact, be an index of intelligence. The more functional systems there are, the more the individual can minimize the effects of brain injury. Luria accounts for the severity of the effects of brain injury in young children on the basis of a lack of alternative functional systems, because the children were too young to have developed the neurological circuits needed for those increasingly complex functional systems.

A Translation of Luria's Model

As noted above, the structural components and processes of Luria's model are physiological, neurological, and perhaps biochemical. The present author's interest was not in areas of the brain or in neurological circuits, but rather to describe the psychological processes that are applied during cognitive performance and that can be manipulated through training. However, Luria's conception of the operation of a functional system appeared to provide a very suitable model on which to conceptualize the phenomenon of intelligence.

The model of the concept of intelligence underlying the NAT assumes that intellectual ability and achievement originate not from isolated skills and abilities but from the co-operation and interaction of many component abilities, all of which are somehow necessary but none of which are sufficient in themselves to ensure adequate intellectual functioning. This is true for what tends to be referred to as general ability, and also for more specific abilities and talents.

When one part of the functional system is weak or deficient, the whole system is affected, and if affected strongly enough could be incapacitated. On the basis of assessment with traditional group intelligence tests only the deficiency of the whole system could be inferred. Though it was suspected that 'something' was lacking, it was not possible to ascertain what this something might be. So the tendency was to label persons as lacking in the global 'substance', intelligence.

Further, each set of component skills can be expected to participate in a number of functional systems. The number of systems probably depends on the experience and environments to which the individual has been exposed, including genetic, social, ethnic, educational, and other factors. If a component ability is weak or lacking, one would expect every functional system of which it is a part to be affected.

The examination of deficiences in important component skills would thus lead to the identification of distinct patterns of deficient intellectual functioning. This identification lies at the core of psycho-educational diagnosis. Once a pattern is observed by either teacher or psychologist, deficient component skills can be hypothesized, and such hypotheses validated on the basis of further assessment. Similarly, the identification of deficient component skills can lead to educational intervention and training *before* such deficits affect too many functional systems.

The NAT battery was developed in a way that allows the testing of a number of important component skills in different combinations in a variety of subtests. A relatively restricted set of component skills is measured in each test. When the performance level of an individual differs radically between two tasks in which the required skills differ only slightly, it becomes possible to explore functional systems systematically.

Like Luria's model, the NAT model assumes that more than one functional system may make achievement of a particular type of task possible, as there can be more than one way to accomplish a given task. For example, a solution to an arithmetic problem might be derived by one or more analytical processes, or it could be retrieved from memory after rote learning. The methods would be expected to use different functional systems.

It is generally accepted that deficit or weakness in a particular perceptual, conceptual, or other skill will interfere with the accomplishment of any task that requires this skill. Conversely, behaviours that do not require the skill(s) in which the individual is deficient will be performed normally. This is why, even in the absence of certain essential mathematical reasoning skills, a problem might still be solved through rote learning rather than logical analysis, as in the example above.

One important implication of a definition of intelligence as a functional system is that there is no one-to-one correspondence between any specific component skill and performance on a complex cognitive task. For example, if a child cannot learn to spell and this disability is accompanied by a strong deficit in sequencing ability (a very important prerequisite skill for spelling) the functional system for spelling is impaired in *at least* one aspect and possibly in others. Conversely, the absence of a deficit does not indicate that any particular component ability is intact, but only that some functional system for the achievement of a certain task is intact.

Because there can be multiple functional systems using different (or different combinations of) component abilities, the lack of a deficit does not necessarily yield much information.

On the basis of Luria's model it could be expected that the number of functional systems available for the same kind of task would increase with age. Support for such an expectation might be obtained from research concerned with the development of abstract thinking, and its effects on the operation of the total system of cognitive components.

The increase in the contribution of conceptual factors as determinants of the perceptual processes of humans is the result of the development of formal logical thinking skills and the ability to form and test hypotheses concerning relationships between objects. The growing ability to process perceptual information of increasing complexity is thus related to the development of abstract thinking.

The perceptual skills of young school beginners are basically restricted by a tendency to 'unbiased' experience and observation of 'reality'. In older school children this tends to develop into skills suitable for close and exact observation of detail and high perceptual acuity. The adolescent's perception contains more than the observation of reality. It includes many abstract elements, that is, elements resulting from the process of generalization. As explained by Rubinstein (1973), the specific percept becomes a sample of a general phenomenon or class. It appears as though the adolescent and adult were examining the content of perception, by joining to it an increasingly finely tuned system of knowledge, experience and theory. This widens the percept, but at the same time acts as a filter selectively, so that the unconstrained focus on 'reality' typical of the perception of the younger child, which leads to the previously noted high ability for exact and objective observation, tends to be masked, and is frequently lost (e.g. Nickel, 1975; Rubinstein, 1973; Wolf, 1971).

In conclusion, one might summarize the theoretical position underlying the NAT by citing its major assumption, namely that cognitive development, ability, and intellectual achievement do not originate from isolated skills and discrete abilities, but from the co-operation and interaction of many component skills and processes (some learnt, some innate; some under conscious control, some automatic), all of which are necessary, but none of which are sufficient in themselves to ensure adequate intellectual functioning. This situation is represented by the model of a functional system. When one part of the functional system is weak or lacking, other aspects, and often the whole system, are affected to a greater or lesser degree depending on the pattern of strengths and weaknesses, the availability of alternative functions, and the demands of the task confronting the individual.

The rationale for such a position rests on three major premises, which were derived from a synthesis of the existisng body of knowledge in experimental, educational, and developmental psychology, and from psychometrics.

Premise 1 is that not all individuals operating at the same level of intelligence (i.e. measured IQ) manifest the same pattern of cognitive strengths and weaknesses. Rather they constitute a heterogenous group. The same is true for individuals with learning disabilities, underachievers, low achievers, and high achievers, the talented, the gifted, etc.

Premise 2 is based on the belief that intellectual ability depends to a large extent on the efficiency of the individual's information-processing capacity, and is not the outcome of a generalized 'substance', intelligence.

Under this premise, learning difficulties and other manifestations of temporary or lasting cognitive deficits do not necessarily result from a generalized intellectual weakness, but might be caused by an imbalance in the individual's information-processing abilities, for example over- or under-use of certain cognitive strategies, or the use of strategies that do not match the requirements of the task or the cognitive style of the individual.

The possibility that imbalances in information-processing skills may occur is increased by the tendency in most individuals to use 'preferred', well practised strategies, and to neglect to practise strategies that are new or that come to them less naturally. Less efficient functional systems may well be used as crutches, but their over-utilization could lead to a stunting of development of new component abilities and thus seriously affect general performance. The reported instances of specific learning problems of such eminent men as Leonardo da Vinci and Albert Einstein may well be explained in terms of such imbalances in information-processing skills.

Premise 3 is that intelligence has been shown to be malleable. Delayed intellectual maturation has long been advanced as a major contributing factor to lower-than-expected intellectual functioning, lack of readiness to learn, etc. Maturational lag implies that with proper training learning deficits can eventually be overcome or at least ameliorated. Impressive success of educational intervention focusing on carefully diagnosed deficits has been reported (e.g. Campione, Brown, and Ferrara, 1982; Guthrie, 1978; Lee, Koenigsknecht, and Mulhern, 1975; Rourke, 1975). The training of componential skills of generalizable problem-solving abilities, though still in its experimental stages, is showing promising results (for a review, see Detterman and Sternberg, 1982).

Ability Profiles

The interpretation of NAT performance requires profile analysis as well as the interpretation of observations in a normative framework. The NAT thus allows for a combination of qualitative and quantitative information, which is expected to be more useful than either alone could be.

As a consequence, valid interpretation of the NAT requires at least a working knowledge of those psychological variables contributing to the functional systems that might determine responses to the items constituting the various subtests. It is also important to recognize how the subtests differ in the major component skills they purport to tap and in their relationship to one another. An attempt is made in the later chapters to examine these basic questions, and to provide some tentative answers.

The logic of basing the assessment of general ability on a profile of criterion-referenced tests might be compared with that of using the statistical technique of factor analysis. The aim of both procedures is to find a parsimonious way of representing a unifying entity underlying a set of variables.

The NAT consists of a sufficiently differentiated battery of subtests that combine important component skills of cognitive ability in various ways, so that a pattern of individuals' performances across subtests can be established. Performance can thus be quantified with reference to the shape and the level of the profile as being within normal limits, high or low, without losing the information necessary for an objective pattern analysis and needs-based intervention.

The combination of qualitative and quantitative procedures has a major advantage in that it facilitates the empirical exploration of patterns of component skills (both deficits and high-level abilities), and that it might encourage empirical verification of theoretical predictions. Data collected on the NAT can produce patterns of results that can be validated and interpreted further on the basis of empirical studies of the subtests themselves or similar tasks, and can generate patterns of results that can be matched against clinical or theoretical expectations.

The author's initial research has concentrated on the quantitative aspects of the NAT battery, because the quantification of observations is essential for determining the validity and usefulness of any scientific assessment procedure. However, material on the more qualitative aspects of the battery has been included in each of the relevant chapters, and frequent references have been made to work in the published psychological and educational literature that will lead the reader to more detailed descriptions and explanations of the mechanisms of the component processes of the functions assessed by the NAT. In addition, strong emphasis has been placed on the integration of quantitative and qualitative information.

A number of points of clarification in relation to the assessment procedure advocated for the NAT are in order at this point.

One, it is important to remember that the performance on subtests or items, in fact all cognitive activity, reflects functional systems rather than 'pure' skills. The examiner's assumptions about how the testee may have approached the task and dealt with it are not necessarily reflections of how the task was actually executed. The presence of alternative functional systems must be remembered. There is usually more than one way by means of which a problem can be solved. For example, it is often observed that persons compensate in what tend to be regarded as quite idiosyncratic ways for deficiencies in component abilities. Within the framework of the present model this compensatory behaviour is the result of the operation of an alternative functional system.

Two, because the items of each subtest elicit diverse functional systems, abilities and deficits are expected to produce some elevation or depression of the profile on a number of subtests. Examination of the relative elevations and depressions in the profile is of great importance in the interpretation of NAT performance, just as it is in the case of tests such as the Minnesota Multiphasic Personality Inventory (MMPI).

Three, the evaluation of the profile is only a part of the total process of test interpretation, in which hypotheses that have been generated from an examination of the profile are then checked in analyses of subtest performance, item patterns, and qualitative features of the performance. Individual profile elevations or troughs cannot be interpreted as reflecting specific strengths and weaknesses without reference to the details listed above.

Four, at first sight test users may feel that there are not sufficient items in a given area to justify the measurement of a specific set of skills, and that many items are too easy. Such a view would assume a methodology of strict test homogeneity and weighted difficulty levels, an assumption that is inconsistent with the theoretical framework within which the NAT was developed.

While the number of items assessing a specific set of skills in a given subtest may be limited, items tapping functional systems in which the particular skills play a part exist in other subtests, even though the major emphasis in different subtests may vary. In many instances the component abilities involved in any one type of item are repeatedly involved in other item types across the battery, even though the relationship between tests may not be immediately obvious.

Functionally complex items make it more difficult for the test user to tease out particular strengths or deficits. Also, testees may make use of many different alternative functional systems in their performance on complex items, which might defeat the diagnostic purposes of the assessment. Simpler tasks are more readily perceived as demanding certain specific and often basic skills. Tests made up of complex items are generally more time consuming, yet may not provide much additional information beyond that provided by more simple, straightforward items.

For the reasons discussed above many of the more complex items originally included in the trial tests were excluded from the final version of the battery, in favour of more basic, easily scored items. The latter type of items were found to be more sensitive to specific strengths and weaknesses in the test performance than the more complex tasks, which correlated more highly with the total test score. More basic types of items tend to provide better diagnostic information than complex items, which in turn tend to be more useful when classification is the object of the assessment. This difference in the usefulness of different item types for different purposes might account for the frequently cited observation that the correlation between verbal and non-verbal tasks increases with the complexity of the items.

Item complexity may thus lead to an increase in correlation between different types of performance, but it is unlikely to make an explanation of what is being measured more probable. Examiners who wish to test response to complexity *per se* are advised to use other instruments in addition to or in place of the NAT.

The use of less complex items in the NAT was further supported by the finding that the current subtests discriminate adequately between persons operating at different levels of intellectual functioning and educational achievement.

Overall, current indications are that the quantitative and qualitative evaluation procedures provided by the battery make the NAT a powerful tool for the analysis and description of the *nature* of cognitive and developmental strengths and weaknesses. The assessment of the latter and their interpretation make the NAT useful not only for the determination of educational and vocational prognoses, but, more importantly, for the planning of intervention procedures aimed at the improvement of intellectual efficiency.

CHAPTER 3

THE ROLE OF THE NAT IN THE ASSESSMENT OF GENERAL ABILITY

The purpose of this chapter is to discuss some general points relating to the NAT specifically, and to its nature, role and limitations. Issues relating to methodology, purpose, diagnosis, and test bias are addressed. Questions pertaining to technical matters are omitted, as these are dealt with in the *Manual for the Non-Verbal Ability Tests* (Rowe, 1985c), which accompanies the NAT battery.

Test Content

Critics of intelligence tests often focus on the argument that the items making up such tests lack resemblance to 'real life' problem solving. Some people might regard this argument as particularly valid in relation to non-verbal tests such as the NAT.

What tends to be ignored in this type of argument is that the content of a psychological test item or other stimulus situation is merely the vehicle for its essential function, which is to elicit from the subject the behaviour (cognitive or other) that is to be observed, from which inferences will be drawn. The complex processes elicited in real-life situations, in which intelligence is presumed to be demonstrated, contain many of the same basic components of ability or skills that can be elicited in a simpler and more isolated form in an intelligence test item.

The NAT battery consists of a set of non-verbal, group-administered tests of cognitive abilities; the tests are based on figural and diagrammatic stimulus materials. The tests measure a variety of information-processing components of general ability, and were designed to provide a systematic method by which a step-by-step profile that reflects inter- and intra-individual differences in important cognitive areas can be built. The examiner can thus identify a pattern of cognitive components of the performance as well as the level of intellectual functioning of individuals and groups.

The choice of which aspects of intelligence should be included in the battery was founded on published research, and took cognizance of traditional and of recent research concerned with the psychological components of underlying differences in cognitive performance. The construction of the subtests was facilitated by the availability of published research that identified and described important dimensions of intellectual functioning, and identified the types of tasks that may elicit behaviours reflecting such functioning. An insight into the relevant literature is provided in the chapters contained in Part II of this volume, while an introduction to the theoretical framework within which the NAT has to be considered has been presented in Chapters 1 and 2.

The 18 group-administered paper-and-pencil tests included in this edition of the battery provide a measure of general intelligence that is based on information-processing components relating to perceptual (P), conceptual (C), attention (A), and memory (M) abilities, as follows:

Test 1:   Matching Shape (P)
Test 2:   Matching Direction (P)
Test 3:   Categorization (P)
Test 4:   Picture Completion (C)
Test 5:   Embedded Figures (C)
Test 6:   Figure Formation (C)
Test 7:   Mazes (C, P)
Test 8:   Sequencing (C)
Test 9:   Picture Arrangement (C)
Test 10: Visual Search (P, A)
Test 11: Simple Key Test (P)
Test 12: Complex Key Test (A, C)
Test 13: Code Tracking I (A, P)
Test 14: Code Tracking II (A, P)
Test 15: Visual Recognition (M, A)
Test 16: Auditory Recognition (M, A)
Test 17: Auditory Recall (M)
Test 18: Visual Recall (M, P)

Methodology

From a methodological point of view the NAT differs from other group intelligence tests in three essential ways: (1) it is a non-verbal test, (2) it includes the measurement of attention skills as part of its objective assessment, and (3) it produces an ability profile in addition to an overall score for the description of the performances of individuals.

There are many instances in which valid psychological assessment is masked by the language deficits of the testee, because performance on most intelligence tests is inextricably linked with language performance. It must be remembered, however, that testing procedures that eliminate the requirement for the subject to read or to make a verbal response often yield higher levels of performance than standard verbal tests (e.g. Furth, 1966; Gelman, 1972; Lancy and Goldstein, 1982; Siegel, 1973).

The fact that the NAT is a non-verbal test has many advantages, some of which are noted more specifically in other chapters. The major benefit of a test such as the NAT is that it can lead to a reduction in bias and disadvantage, which are frequently caused by language, social, and cultural variables.

Although there have been frequent suggestions that some persons are more fairly tested by non-verbal rather than by verbal tests, it must be stressed that a complete assessment of intelligence requires the use of both verbal and non-verbal tests. Knowledge of vocabulary, a facility with words and quantitative concepts, and the ability to reason in verbal terms should be assessed. Where linguistic, cultural or other disadvantage is suspected, the purpose of verbal tests is to assist in the assessment of the degree of disadvantage and in the pinpointing of specific weaknesses, their diagnosis, and possible remediation. The discussion contained in Chapter 13 of this book is expected to provide adequate guidance to those who seek to use the NAT in conjunction with other tests.

The contaminating influence of attention deficits on performance of verbal intelligence tests has been widely documented, in particular with respect to the assessment of autistic children (e.g. Freeman and Ritvo, 1976; Kanner, 1943; Lancy and Goldstein, 1982; Rutter, 1978). Definitions of childhood autism tend to focus on such symptoms as the failure to develop social relationships (including rapport during testing!), language retardation, and ritualistic or compulsive behaviours. Most clinicians claim that the intellectual abilities of most autistic children can be considered as 'normal', but that the characteristics of the disorder tend to interfere with the expression of cognitive skills in the manner in which they are assessed in the normal child.

For persons with suspected linguistic and/or attention deficits (for example recent immigrants, autistic children, deaf or aphasic persons), traditional measures of intelligence and cognitive development are inappropriate. The NAT battery facilitates the assessment of many aspects of intellectual functioning by means of a set of non-verbal tasks that require minimum, verbal directions, if any, and no reading or language response. During test trials of the battery there was little evidence of frustration among the testees. Motivation was observed to be high at all age levels. The NAT can thus provide an effective means for the assessment of intellectual functioning and development in groups and individuals who have severe communication problems. Diagnosis-based training methods for individuals so afflicted have increased in recent years. The interpretation of NAT performance can contribute important diagnostic information for such purposes.

On the other hand, language-free tests can present a number of inherent difficulties not only for the test developer but also for the user. The most important difficulty probably derives from the fact that language-free assessment procedures tend not to contain direct means for the communication of misunderstandings and other possible difficulties that may lie outside the test domain. This has important implications for the interpretation of non-verbal tests because the interpretation of results necessarily involves some means of evaluating the adequacy of the processes elicited by the stimulus materials.

For example, apart from the cognitive processes being assessed, the response requirements of a number of the NAT subtests involve motor and visual–motor co-ordination skills that may be relatively complex for certain groups of individuals. Although every effort was made in the construction of the tests to reduce the complexity of the response requirements, some contamination of results could occur. The fact that even individually administered non-verbal tests, such as the Bender Visual Gestalt, the Wechsler Block Design tests, etc., involve highly complex manual and constructive skills is of little consolation.

It is important, therefore, for the examiner to make every effort to ascertain whether apparent deficits, observed on the basis of non-verbal measures, could be a reflection of impairment in the means by which the testee communicates his or her skill, rather than impairment in the cognitive ability itself.

Why Profiles?

Most group intelligence tests are non-diagnostic in nature. This means that the basis for their predictive validity cannot be ascertained readily. In other words some of these tests may be relatively effective as tools for the identification of individuals who are likely to encounter learning or other educational difficulties, but they fail to provide information about the nature of the difficulty.

Developments in theory and technology in education have provided strong evidence for the view that low achievers in school and other intellectual tasks tend to be suffering from varieties of ability and skill deficits, and that maximal progress in the area of remediation can be achieved by matching content and method of teaching to the needs and abilities of individual students. The process of matching needs and programs can be greatly facilitated by the availability of a relatively broad picture of the student's strengths and weaknesses in essential psychological functions.

The interpretation of traditional group intelligence tests relies on the comparison of an individual's score with the scores obtained from a normative sample. If the individual's score is higher than the average score obtained by the reference group, the individual's performance is judged to have reached a higher level in the ability measured than his or her peer group. If the individual's score is lower, his or her performance is judged to be slow or deficient relative to the norms. Although testees are rarely suspected of scoring higher than their true abilities, it is frequently suggested that the psychological test scores of some individuals represent an underestimate of their abilities. This question will be addressed further in the discussion of bias and unfairness later in this chapter.

A single summary score can provide an adequate description of an individual's performance only if his or her component abilities are all more or less at the same level. If appreciable variability in the testee's performance in different component skills is observed, a global score provides only crude, but more often invalid, information about his or her intellectual functioning.

Also, it is not always necessary to evaluate a student's abilities with reference to the performance of a norm group. Knowing that an individual's intellectual functioning might place him or her at the 35th percentile rank in relation to a norm group may focus on the possibility of disadvantage, developmental lag or other problems, but such information does not contribute to the design and operation of diagnosis-based intervention. It is essential, therefore, to ascertain which abilities may be contributing to the performance of the individual, and to investigate the pattern in which different component abilities are organized and related.

An ability profile provides a suitable means of displaying significant strengths, weaknesses, and possible extreme asymmetries of ability, thus allowing a better understanding of the meaning of a total score in terms of the nature of the ability of the individual.

In an attempt to provide a better picture of the individual's ability than that provided by traditional group ability tests, the NAT was designed to provide for at least three methods on the basis of which inferences could be drawn. These methods of inference relate to level of performance, pattern of performance, and to the identification of possible differences between levels of skills in perception, reasoning, memory, attention, and concentration.

The *level of performance* compares an individual's subtest and overall performance with a comparative or normative standard. In this edition of the NAT this standard was provided by a non-referred sample of age peers.

Scores representing level of performance have been widely used by teachers and clinicians as well as by researchers, for several reasons. The relative significance of a low score is fairly obvious, that is, the testee is relatively deficient in the ability to perform the specified task. Level of performance scores are easily analysed by conventional statistics, and the assumption of continuous scaling properties of this measure facilitates comparison and interpretation.

Unfortunately, a number of serious problems arise when level of performance is the only input on which to base inferences concerning the psychological evaluation of a person's performance.

Most importantly, low performance on a test may result from factors other than developmental lag or impaired intellectual ability. Cultural disadvantage, social deprivation, educational deficits, test anxiety, health problems, emotional lability, and many other factors can influence any testing situation, and may prevent the testee from achieving a result that can be regarded as representative of his or her approximate level of ability in relation to the skills assessed by the test.

Also, it is difficult to distinguish between developmental and other temporary difficulties and the possibly more serious intellectual deficits, on the basis of level of performance scores alone. As noted above, similarly low scores of two individuals on the same test may lead to quite different diagnostic inferences. A low score could indicate that a testee was unable to grasp what was required, or that he or she might not be able to execute the motor task adequately, which is a prerequisite for the communication of the solution. The same low score may reflect cultural or developmental disadvantage in a student who may be quite capable of adequate performance, given sufficient time and/or assistance.

The implications of the type of diagnostic distinction noted above can be critical, particularly for the selection of intervention and educational assistance. A child whose development in one or more areas appears to be delayed may benefit from general support, assistance in the learning of special skills, and patient encouragement. A child, who, for reasons of general retardation, cerebral damage, or unidentified causes of general incapacity, may not benefit from straightforward methods of educational remediation or enrichment, may require a different approach to intervention, namely, an approach that focuses, at least initially, on very specific, essential, component skills. (It may also require a modification of the testee's own and/or his or her parents' expectations.)

The *pattern of performance* refers to the configuration of scores, that is, the shape of the profile, and can be of high diagnostic significance. For example, the degree of variability of subscale scores on the Wechsler tests, WAIS-R and WISC-R, is often more significant and meaningful than the summary IQ scores. Brain-damaged and other learning-disabled persons often show a much greater amount of variability on the subscale scores than normal or retarded persons, whose scores tend to be more uniformly depressed. Similarly, patterns in the NAT profile provide important information for test interpretation. A depressed total score may have a range of behavioural, intellectual and educational implications, some of which can be clarified on the basis of the ability profile.

The NAT results can be analysed, not only in terms of overall level and shape of profile, but also in terms of the relative adequacy of *performance in relation to the factors* measured by the battery.

Purpose

Although many aspects of the NAT are based on Luria's (1966a, 1966b, 1973) theoretical work, there are two essential differences between Luria's aims and the aim of the NAT battery.

Luria's aim was to map areas of the brain and to identify operations of the nervous system that might correspond to intellectual dysfunctioning. In contrast, the aim of the NAT is to describe the nature of certain cognitive variables in terms of trainable skills of information processing. Also, contrary to Luria's work the NAT is not intended for the identification of organic brain damage, but for assessment of 'normal' functioning.

The utility of the NAT is not restricted to educational situations. The battery has a useful place in vocational assessment, particularly with low educational achievers and other disadvantaged groups.

However, cognitive ability and performance on intelligence tests predict occupational criteria less well than educational criteria. Matarazzo (1972) estimated that the correlation between general ability and educational attainment tends to be approximately .50, but that between general ability and success in an occupation tends to be only .20 or lower. Other studies have also shown that intelligence may predict success in training for a job but not success on the job (cf. Ghiselli, 1966).

While the predictive importance of cognitive ability differences in job success (once the job has been secured) may be reduced by selection factors, and by the increased role of non-cognitive (e.g. personality and motivational) characteristics in determining success, it is nonetheless apparent that occupational prestige is strongly associated with ability. Matarazzo (1972) reported a correlation of .95 between ability and the independently judged prestige of occupations. The massive career study of Thorndike and Hagen (1959) also made this point, and showed further that differences in ability profiles can be associated with different occupations.

Entry to just about all desirable avenues of life currently depends on some sort of admission or selection procedure. Whether tests, written or telephone applications, or interview methods are used, current selection procedures tend to give greater weight to verbal abilities than to any other characteristic of the individual. Verbal communication, verbal knowledge, reading ability, and other language-based skills provide the essential data on the basis of which selection takes place.

Although the importance of language should not be denigrated, it is necessary for us to be aware of the discriminatory effects of an over-emphasis on language in selection. Research and experience throughout the world have shown that the level of language attained by an individual is not a fixed trait, but that language proficiency up to very high levels is highly manipulatable. Persons of average and above average intelligence can be instructed successfully both to increase their proficiency in their mother tongue, and acquire a foreign language. So, the level of attained language skills may not be a better predictor of intelligence, trainability, etc. than any other measure of educational achievement.

As a consequence of the strong reliance in selection procedures on verbal abilities, the higher levels of secondary schools, colleges and universities contain a very large proportion of students of high verbal ability, irrespective of the importance of this ability for their area of study. It follows that a considerable proportion of individuals whose intellectual giftedness, for one reason or another, cannot be ascertained on the basis of their language performance, are being barred from educational courses and from work opportunities where these abilities could be used and cultivated.

The literature contains considerable evidence for the fact that many types of non-verbal tasks have validity for the selection of candidates for numerous technical, scientific, and artistic courses (this is discussed further in Part II).

For example, Smith (1964) showed in follow-up studies in England that spatial ability alone may contribute to success in the General Certificate of Education examination, and to examinations in mathematics, mechanics, art, and many technical subjects, such as engineering drawing, industrial design, metal and wood work, geometry, etc. On the basis of his painstaking research over more than two decades, and encouraged by the findings of other researchers, Smith suggested that a spatial test should be included in the procedures used to select students for grammar school and that this could increase the validity of the battery used.

The NAT can be expected to yield useful supplementary information in selection situations in which a set of non-verbal tasks tapping general ability, is regarded as appropriate.

Diagnosis

No rational approach to intervention, whether educational, psychological, social or physical is possible if it is not preceded by proper diagnostic procedures. Reliable and accurate assessment should therefore constitute the first step in dealing with any form of learning problem or other suspected intellectual disorder. The NAT is intended not as an aid in classifying or labelling individuals, but rather as an aid in determining some of the variables that may be related to a disability and, for the design of remedial measures or other intervention procedures that are appropriate for the diagnosed needs of the individual.

At this stage, the NAT does not provide sufficient information for *differential diagnosis*. In other words, performance data obtained on the battery in themselves do not allow for a distinction between developmental lag, learning disabilities or brain damage. The collection of further data on the performance of special groups may lead to usefulness of the NAT as an instrument for differential diagnosis at a later stage.

Individuals whose scores on the battery suggest severe deficiencies should be referred for more detailed individual psychological assessment. Differential diagnosis of the above type requires a detailed developmental history of the individual and specialized psychological testing. These must be supplemented by neurological and other medical examinations if organic brain damage is suspected. Possible elements of developmental history that might lead to such suspicion include road accidents and other causes of traumatic brain injuries, infections of the central nervous system (e.g. meningitis and encephalitis), prenatal infections, anoxia or premature birth, prolonged neonatal jaundice, and hard neurological signs such as cerebral palsy and hemiplegia.

None of these developmental or traumatic events are in themselves necessarily a cause of deficient intellectual functioning and/or brain damage. However, when the occurrence of such an event in the history of an individual coincides with persistent failure at school and low scores on psychological tests such as the NAT, it is very important to instigate further investigation.

If an individual's NAT Score is 87 or below and, in addition, performance across subtests is uniformly depressed, a diagnosis of specific learning disability or maturational lag is less likely to be correct than one of a more generalized learning disability or retardation. Such an individual can be expected to require special assistance in all areas of learning.

If a testee's performance shows gross imbalance as reflected in a very uneven NAT profile, specific learning problems or developmental lag may well be the cause. An individual who performs poorly on the visual memory tests, embedded figures, and figure formation, but shows average or above-average performance on auditory memory, sequencing, and the figure matching tests, is reasonably likely to be suffering from lack of skills to cope with tasks in the visual gestalt area.

Average or above-average visual memory but low auditory language and sequencing scores are likely to be related to difficulties experienced in the processing of sequentially presented information.

Caution—The diagnostic signs can vary in individuals. They have been presented here with the sole intention of helping examiners to form diagnostic hypotheses. It is expected that few individuals tested will fall neatly into one subgroup even though assigning them to one or other diagnostic category may not pose a major problem.

In the majority of the pilot studies conducted on the basis of different NAT profiles there seemed to be little doubt as to which type of diagnostic hypothesis might be most fitting in relation to the profile of a particular individual. However, the ultimate test of the validity of any psycho-educational diagnosis is whether individuals diagnosed as belonging to different groups respond differently to different forms of diagnosis-based intervention.

Bias

Test bias has to be carefully distinguished from assumptions about cultural differences and unfairness. If differences are found between individuals, groups or populations, it cannot necessarily be inferred that a test is biased.

A distinction must be made between the test itself and the way in which it is used. We do not infer that the ruler or tape measure is biased because we find that Vietnamese children tend to be shorter in height than their Northern European peers. The important aspect of this measurement of height relates to the decisions made on the basis of the use of the measuring implement. If Vietnamese 5-year-olds were refused admission to school because they were smaller than their peers, the issue would be unfair usage of the results of measurement, rather than unfairness of the ruler or tape measure *per se*.

Much of the opposition to the use of intelligence tests in schools, which has been voiced in the press and in professional and parental circles, has been the result of a failure on the part of those opposing testing to distinguish between the test itself and the use made of the test results. A test is used unfairly in a situation in which it provides irrelevant or misleading information to the decision making to which it is meant to contribute.

The measurement literature has given considerable attention to the concept of *psychometric bias*. This refers to bias resulting from norms, differential validity, and the choice of formulae on which the selection of candidates is based. The interested reader is referred to discussions of this concept by Anastasi (1976); Cleary, Humphreys, Kendrick, and Wesman (1975); Flaugher (1978); and Jensen (1980a). Jensen reviews situational and psychometric determinants of bias in great detail and discusses differences between fairness in the usage of results and inherent biasing elements in obtaining, manipulating and relating test scores to other variables.

Flaugher (1978) discussed various dimensions of test bias, and suggests that

> the ways in which the term is used has many widely disparate aspects frequently stemming from entirely different universes of discourse. (p.671)

Two major aspects of the issue relate to questions of differential validity, and to the items making up the test.

To say that a test is biased as a result of its differential validity means that the predictive validity of the test differs for two or more identifiable groups. Much research has been concerned with this issue, namely, the situation where a test is valid for one group but not for another, amongst ethnic groups in the United States of America. The results of this research have not been unequivocal. (Bartlett, Bobko, and Pine, 1977; Boehm 1977; Flaugher, 1978; Katzell and Dyer, 1977; provide a review of this research.)

Bias from test content occurs when the test contains questions or tasks that are in any sense unfair to some testees. For example, tests that ask for information to which some persons have not been exposed or have not had an opportunity to learn are biased. It appears that a great deal of the discussion on this aspect of test bias stems from a confusion about the functions of testing in particular situations, that is, the reasons for testing and the interpretation of results.

> The test is being given to see how many of these particular items can be answered, and regardless of the reason for the inability to answer them. (Flaugher, 1978, p.674)

Test bias in the NAT was investigated with respect to *ethnic groups* and in relation to sex.

In the absence of an outside criterion against which test bias could be evaluated, the statistical method suggested by Echternacht (1974), which assumes that significant item X group interactions can be regarded as a reflection of test bias, was used.

In the investigation of test bias of the NAT the definition of test bias was thus as follows.

The test is biased for a particular group of persons if it contains items on which the average score obtained by members of the group differs from the average score of other groups by a greater or lesser amount than can be expected on other items of the same test. In other words, the biased item(s) are expected to produce an unusual discrepancy between the performance of members of one group and members of other groups.

The performances of Australian Aboriginal, Australian non-Aboriginal, Greek, Italian, Portuguese, Spanish, Turkish, and Vietnamese students of comparable age were compared with one another in relation to items on Tests 1 to 9, and in relation to subtest scores in Tests 10 to 14. No consistent indications of test bias were detected.

These findings are limited because the samples of individuals were not representative of their national populations, and the comparisons in some national age groups were based on extremely small numbers of individuals. However, it is suggested that the content of the NAT is entirely consistent with Wechsler's view that intelligence test items are valid indicators of individual differences if it can be assumed that the test takers share the 'knowledge' of the item content.

The types of items included in the NAT, like those making up many other non-verbal tests of fluid intelligence, are unlikely to be contaminated by cultural influences, and would thus be expected to avoid the penalty that individuals from minority cultures commonly suffer in relation to traditional, usually heavily verbal, assessment procedures. In fact, it might be suggested that the information-processing skills tapped by the NAT might well transcend the areas in which bias tends to play a role. An important related point is that the lack of 'knowledge' content of the NAT offers students and adults tasks they are not likely to associate with previous academic failures.

Sex differences   Every effort was made to avoid the effect of sex-related differences on test performance in the NAT.

The literature concerned with the assessment of intelligence supports the assumption that there are no sex-related differences in the variable underlying what is being measured in intelligence tests. On the other hand, sex-related differences have been observed in the responses to stimulus material frequently used to describe the latent trait, intelligence. It has been suggested that

> research on sex-related differences, more than most other fields of psychology, suffers from researchers' personal and professional prejudices, sex stereotyping and ethnocentricity. (Dwyer, 1979, p.343)

Fennema (1974) and Dwyer (1979) have suggested that the roots of many prejudices can be found in the tendency to over-generalize sex-related ability differences. The definitions of ability or other latent traits being measured are often too global. These authors suggest that unwarranted generalizations tend to be made from one group (cultural, age, ethnic, ability, etc.) to another.

For example, it is commonly assumed that females perform better on tasks involving language skills while males surpass females on mathematical tasks. Yet, Maccoby and Jacklin (1974), Dwyer (1976) and others have found that males, over a wide age range, consistently achieved higher scores than females on vocabulary tests. In the USA, an investigation of possible sex-bias of item types contained in the Graduate Record examination (Hicks, Donlon and Wallmark, 1976) showed no sex-bias in the overall verbal scores. However, closer scrutiny of individual item types showed that verbal analogies favoured males, while antonyms and reading comprehension items favoured females. Other researchers (e.g. Donlon, 1973; Sternberg, 1977) presented evidence for the assumption that performance in verbal analogies does not differentiate between the sexes.

Other studies (e.g. Dwyer, 1979; King, 1959; Murphy, 1977) have found that males achieved higher scores than females in verbal tests, including reading comprehension, where the context was primarily science, engineering or business related. Females were found to achieve typically higher performances than males on descriptive and imaginative passages drawn from the humanities.

Studies showing that males perform better than females on tests of spatial ability, at least by adulthood, have been summarized by many authors (e.g. Harris, 1978; McGee, 1982). The contrasting view has also been reviewed (e.g. Fairweather, 1976; Newcombe, 1982; Wittig and Petersen, 1979).

From its beginning, the test development plan guiding the production of the NAT called for the elimination of all items shown to favour one sex over the other.

The implications and applications of the NAT are expected to widen with increasing use and research relating to the battery. Psychologists and teachers will find that objective information about the nature of a student's cognitive functioning can make a critical difference to both psycho-educational diagnosis and intervention.

PART II

THE SELECTION AND DESCRIPTION OF THE NAT SUBTESTS

Part II is concerned with general issues relating to the identification of suitable stimulus materials and methods of scaling for the assessment of general and more specific abilities (Chapter 4), and describes the nature and rationale of the tests finally included in the construction of the NAT (Chapters 5 to 8).

Basic interpretations, diagnostic considerations, and—where appropriate—a brief examination of strategies for intervention, have been included in the discussion of the subtests. Also included are suggestions of basic comparisons that should be conducted between the scores obtained on certain subtests of the NAT, and between these and other cognitive tasks.

It must be remembered that the subtests contained in the NAT battery do not constitute item sets measuring unique functions. The subtests are factorially complex. This implies that the same cognitive functions are probably being measured by several subtests, and that the performance on one subtest is the result of the simultaneous operation of several cognitive functions. In short, each subtest measures complex phenomena.

The organization of the material presented in this section into chapters was guided by the results of the factor analyses computed on the performance scores of the NAT. Issues of general importance to all or a number of subtests are discussed when first encountered. For example, a number of general points relating to age-determined deterioration in fluid intelligence and on the NAT are made in Chapter 5, even though they relate to perceptual, conceptual, attention, and memory processes.

A major part of each of Chapters 5 to 8 is devoted to descriptive analyses of the contents and functions of the subtests making up the NAT. More specifically, this involves a discussion of the content of the test, its theoretical rationale, significant underlying skills and abilities it purports to measure, the test's importance as a measure of 'g', and considerations concerning diagnosis and intervention.

Special reference is made to the effects of ageing on the component abilities measured.

PART II

THE SELECTION AND DESCRIPTION OF THE NATURE RESERVES

CHAPTER 4

THE SELECTION OF ITEMS FOR INTELLIGENCE TESTS

> The first problem that confronts anyone attempting to devise an intelligence test is that of deciding upon the tests that should be included in the battery. This task is not a simple one, for, in addition to the necessity for fulfulling certain statistical criteria, there are a number of general considerations which, independent of all other factors, restrict one's choice. (Wechsler, 1958, p.61)

The foremost of these factors is the author's model or theory of the nature of intelligence, which the test is to be designed to measure. Another factor relates to the special purpose for which the test is expected to be used. Certain item types are age bound. Item content that is suitable for young children may lead to a loss in motivation in students and adults. Some items, such as the copying of shapes, are found to be very useful in the assessment of cognitive development at the lower levels. They do not work beyond a certain stage of development, not only because of their limited range, but because of the fact that by increasing the complexity of the stimulus to be copied, the skill measured by the test is altered.

Another important factor is to ensure that, apart from age, the content allows discrimination between different levels of ability. Armchair judgments of ability are often misleading. Tasks of simple sensory discrimination are frequently found to be good, while items demanding abstract thinking are shown to be poor measures. It has been shown that tasks involving tricks, or puzzle-like items, are as bad as questions calling for esoteric knowledge or very specialized skills when the aim is to provide an estimate of general ability or intelligence. Statistical criteria alone do not provide sufficient validity, either. For example, two test items may be of equal difficulty as measured by the frequency with which they are completed correctly or failed, yet they may differ significantly in their validity as measures of intelligence. Statistical parameters must be supplemented by evidence of clinical relevance and validity.

The contents of tests of general ability, especially when they are to be used with adolescents and adults, must have face validity, in addition to meeting empirical and statistical criteria. This means that they must not appear unfair, foolish, irrelevant, crafty, or otherwise inappropriate to the testee.

Returning briefly to the special purposes for which the test might be designed or for which it might be used, this obviously relates to the functions of testing.

In considering the aims and functions of the testing of general or specific abilities, one might start by identifying the major direct participants in the testing process. There are probably three—the test producer, the test user and the test taker. The test producer takes responsibility for the design and content of the test, as well as for its physical appearance, and the details of documentation regarding its rationale, statistical validity, and interpretation. These responsibilities are usually shared by the author of the test and the test publisher. The test user is usually an individual or an institution (e.g. a government department, school, or school system or an employer), who expects to base decisions, at least in part, on test results. The test taker is the testee, that is, the individual for whom the test establishes a particular performance score.

The roles played by these major participants in the testing process appear to be clear, but they are not always distinct, as intended and unintended overlap and competition of functions and benefits occur frequently. The function of the test producer appears to be relatively clear cut. The test producer develops tests either in order to meet specific requirements of a certain user, for general distribution, or for sale.

Tests are developed to sample performance, usually with a view either to establish standards of desired levels of performance, to predict later performance, or—and unfortunately much less frequently—to provide diagnostic information that might lead to intervention. Generally, the work of the test producer is oriented towards the needs (real or perceived) of the test users.

The test user is usually an educational institution, a government department or an employer. The most obvious function of ability testing from the vantage point of the test user is to facilitate decision making. Typically, the decisions to be made relate either to selection or to some type of sorting or classification process.

The expectation is that sound selection will increase the institution's or the employer's productivity or social/professional efficiency, and that it will reward those testees who are, in some sense, most deserving of it. If the aim is to select students who can be given additional help at school, given that the number to be selected has to be limited as a result of the shortage of resources, those who are expected to be able to benefit most from the teaching will be selected.

An employer faced with 60 applicants for three positions in a particular trade, must select; and so must a college or university department with 2000 applicants for 250 first-year places. In all situations where there are more people than places, choices must be made. These choices tend to involve the use of test scores. Other criteria for selection might be order of application, family affiliation, on the basis of references, by height, etc. The use of intelligence or ability tests as a selection tool has gained broad acceptance because such tests are regarded as more objective, valid, relevant, etc. than the criteria listed above, or similar ones. Selection becomes classification, when the desire is to match an individual's skills to particular job requirements, or to an educational program. In this case it becomes important to identify specific skills and abilities that relate to job or training requirements.

Testing for classification and placement takes place in large institutions, such as the armed forces, as well as in smaller ones such as the railways, the State Electricity Commission, etc. and, of course, in schools and other educational institutions. In these last two institutions tests are also used to measure learning and achievement in a variety of ways. They are often used to monitor progress, to pinpoint strengths and weaknesses, to diagnose learning difficulties, and to provide a basis for the design of individualized teaching programs. Another frequent purpose for the use of tests is to assess the effectiveness of training or educational procedures and programs. Such testing focuses on the program, not on the individuals completing the tests.

Although in some instances the prime objective of testing is to serve the needs of the test taker (e.g. in diagnostic testing), it is important to remember that selection, placement, and achievement testing are primarily intended to serve the decision-making needs of the test user or those who have commissioned the testing. This does not mean that there may not also be some direct benefits flowing to the test taker in such situations; for example, on the basis of a particular score, the individual might obtain a sought-after job or educational opportunity. Despite this, tests are all too frequently used for decision making for or on behalf of the testees. Those who administer and/or commission the administration of tests are responsible not only to the test user but also to the test taker. Are the interests of the test taker considered at all times? What happens when they cannot be reconciled with those of the test user?

These two questions relate to the fair usage of tests, which was discussed in Chapter 3. It only need be said here that every attempt was made in the construction of the NAT to avoid areas and items that in one sense or another may have been unfair to an identifiable subgroup of the population of individuals to whom the test may be administered. Where, after test trials, statistical evidence showed that the performance of particular subgroups on specific items differed from that of other groups, these items were discarded.

As noted earlier in this chapter, one determinant of test content, which is at least as important as the perceived function of the test, relates to the test constructor's view of what the test measures, that is, the test constructor's theory or model of ability. Major theoretical models of intelligence were presented in the first chapter, and the author's view of intelligence as a functional system was discussed in Chapter 2. The literature concerned with individual differences in experimental, developmental, educational, cognitive, and information-processing psychology suggests strongly that intelligence has clearly identifiable components. Educational research of the past decade has established that individual differences in learner characteristics often interact with instructional treatment variables (Cronbach and Snow, 1977; Snow, 1978a, 1978b). These findings are paralleled by an increased emphasis on individualization in the delivery of all kinds of educational services. Individualization implies a need to identify psychologically definable strengths and weaknesses in individuals, so that training and other intervention procedures can be tailored to the diagnosed needs of individuals.

In an endeavour to identify relevant variables that could be defined in such a way, the research literature was searched for studies that identified variables that could be assessed. Such variables had to be defensible, not only in a psychometric sense, but in terms of theories of individual differences, developmental and educational psychology, experimental and modern cognitive psychology.

A careful analysis was made also of the contents of various standardized tests of general ability and intelligence that are used at present. These tests were studied with particular attention being paid to the authors' statements concerning what it was their tests were purporting to measure. The validity of the statements was assessed on the basis of the empirical literature.

The review of instruments showed that many tests of general or specific abilities consist of sets of items of considerable homogeneity. In extreme cases, the test is made up simply of repeated trials of the same task. In less extreme cases the items might constitute repeated trials of stimuli eliciting the same cognitive process, but with variations in the parameters of the stimulus. At the other extreme are tests that are made up of a wide variety of different tasks, that is, omnibus intelligence tests, which tend to include sets of verbal, mathematical, and, less frequently, diagrammatic items, the performance of which requires a large variety of unspecified cognitive processes.

The research literature shows that the investigation of individual differences in various kinds of intellectual skills goes back to the beginning of the 19th century (Carroll, 1978 for review).

Exactly what cognitive abilities exist or can be differentiated continues to be a matter of empirical research, which is being pursued with seemingly renewed vigor in recent years.

> Some respects in which wide individual differences—described in very general terms—are observed include the following: abilities to perceive aspects of the physical and social environment; abilities to notice and remember specific events, sequences of stimuli, similarities and differences among stimuli, and relationships. (Carroll, 1983, p.1)

Obviously, this research takes into account the fact that any one task or test item is likely to require more than one ability or skill.

Sometimes, it has been suggested that all tests consisting of visual perceptual stimuli are solely tests of Thurstone's 'K' or 'V' factors (Thurstone, 1944). If this were so, one would not expect any correlation between these tests and tests made up of perceptual stimuli from other than the visual domain. Also, it would be difficult to explain the consistently occurring, sizeable correlations between tests of visual perceptual stimuli and verbal as well as non-verbal conceptual tasks of many varieties.

As early as 1926, Davey had shown that pictorial tests of intelligence involve the same 'g' factor as verbal intelligence tests. Line (1931), Spearman (1933), and Stephenson (1931) confirmed that the same 'g' factor can be identified in verbal as well as non-verbal, that is, visual perceptual tests. Stephenson (1931) had been able to provide evidence for a phenomenon that until then had only been suspected, namely that a group factor of verbal abilities ran through all verbal tests.

A reasonable explanation of differences in the abilities that can be measured by non-verbal as compared with verbal tests might be that performance on non-verbal tests is more indicative of fluid intelligence, and that visual perceptual items are less likely to lead to a valid assessment of crystallized intelligence than items using language.

The distinction between fluid and crystallized intelligence made by Cattell and Horn (Cattell, 1968, 1971; Horn, 1968, 1970; Horn and Cattell, 1966) is similar to Hebb's (1949) differentiation between Intelligence A and Intelligence B. The Cattell–Horn theory is comprehensive and contains dimensions that relate to such issues as the heredity versus environment controversy, differential rates of cognitive development, and the influence of brain damage on intellectual functioning. Aspects of the theory are discussed in various other chapters of the book. Here, it is sufficient to reiterate that crystallized intelligence refers to the intellectual prerequisites for functioning in relation to tasks that call on previous experience, learning, education, and acculturation more generally. Word knowledge tests and items assessing general knowledge and information in a culture are prototypes of tests of crystallized intelligence. Fluid intelligence involves problem solving and decision making when faced with unfamiliar stimuli, and in situations where adaptation and flexibility of thinking are required. In the literature, the Block Design tests are generally regarded as the best examples of measures of fluid intelligence.

An individual from an educationally highly advantaged background, whose environment places great importance on educational achievement, may show greater crystallized than fluid intelligence, that is, high performance in specifically trained areas, but poor ability to cope with the types of tasks that Cronbach (1977, p.287) calls 'intellectual surprises'. The same can be true of a student who achieves school success through excessive effort.

> One cannot discount the possibility that the exceptional school achievement [reflecting high crystallized ability] has been accomplished by intensive, mostly rote, learning in the absence of the development of a flexible understanding of pertinent underlying concepts. (Kaufman, 1979, p.29)

The above discussion is not intended to imply that crystallized intelligence relies totally on learning, and that fluid intelligence has nothing to do with learning. As was indicated in the opening chapters, cognitive development and learning are firmly entwined. A basic premise of all intelligence tests is that they measure what the individual has learnt. However, whereas crystallized intelligence tends to reflect direct and deliberate training, fluid intelligence develops through incidental experiences and learning, gained indirectly through exposure to and interaction with the environment. It is of interest to note that viewed from this perspective the distinction between crystallized and fluid intelligence and abilities ties in well with the theories of left versus right hemisphere specialization. As Luria and Simernitskaya (1977) have shown, incidental learning is primarily a function of the right hemisphere of the brain.

As stated earlier, non-verbal items in intelligence tests assess fluid intelligence, flexibility of thinking, broad visualization (a Cattell–Horn factor similar to perceptual organization) and a number of lesser abilities. The successful completion of virtually all non-verbal items requires the operation of the cognitive processes of judgment and evaluation. However, non-verbal items are far from pure measures of these abilities. In fact, they are no more pure as measures of fluid abilities than verbal tests are of crystallized abilities. For example, the successful completion of verbal items such as those contained in Wechsler's Similarities or Comprehension tests (Wechsler, 1958, 1974, 1981) requires some fluid intelligence in addition to crystallized knowledge. On the other hand many non-verbal tasks, such as visual discrimination items, object assembly, picture arrangement, mazes, etc. measure crystallized intelligence at least to some degree, particularly for individuals who have had much practice in puzzles or maze tracing, that is, in the same or similar tasks.

The aim guiding the choice of subtest areas for the NAT was to assess cognitive development and functioning in a broad range of components of intelligence. With the exception of the auditory memory tests, all subtests of the NAT battery employ visual stimuli, which are either pictorial or diagrammatic. Except in the case of the memory tests, the items were designed to elicit immediate problem solving or task execution, and to rely as little as possible on short-term or long-term memory. Some items require the recognition of familiar objects or spatial characteristics such as direction. These obviously rely more on previous experience than other aspects of the battery. Thus both fluid and crystallized intelligence will play a role in the completion of the tasks contained in the battery, though fluid abilities are expected to be elicited more frequently.

The most obvious requirement for the successful completion of tasks requiring the processing of visual perceptual stimuli is good visual acuity. The size of the stimulus items of the NAT subtests can be expected to ensure that the items are not sensitive to any but the most severe impairment of visual acuity.

Every effort was made to ensure that failure in the tasks cannot be attributed to difficulties in naming function, so often blamed for low performance in both verbal and non-verbal tests of conceptualization.

Individuals with severe motor impairment will not be able to complete the NAT in its most generally administered form. However, although the battery was designed for group administration, it is always recommended that physically or mentally handicapped individuals be tested in one-to-one situations. Motor-impaired testees can thus be asked to point to the appropriate response alternatives. For more severe cases, after presenting the stimulus, the tester can point to each response alternative in turn, and elicit a 'yes' or 'no' (nod, etc.) reaction from the testee. In the development of the test contents, care was taken to ensure that most of the NAT subtests can be administered to any person of reasonable vision, who can communicate a yes/no response in some form.

In addition to the aspects of fluid and crystallized intelligence discussed above, more specific processes measured by the items include purposeful visual and auditory analysis and evaluation, feature detection, scanning, sequencing, analysis and synthesis of meaningful and non-meaningful patterns, reasoning, recognition, and recall.

The tasks themselves were designed specifically for this battery. Their characteristics were based mainly on the findings of studies reported in the literature of experimental, developmental and modern cognitive psychology, and on validity studies conducted on published intelligence tests.

Before a final selection of the tests was made several months were devoted to the preliminary empirical work of trying out various possible types of tests on a number of individuals and groups of known levels of intellectual functioning and other characteristics. On the basis of these procedures, four empirically determined test areas were selected, namely perceptual processing, conceptual processing, memory, and attention.

The data collected in the preliminary empirical studies led to the selection of 18 tests to individually and collectively sample general ability and component abilities in the four areas specified above. These tests were administered to samples from various populations, which are described in the *Manual for the Non-Verbal Ability Test* (Rowe, 1985c), and the scores obtained by these groups form the basis for the scales provided in this edition of the NAT battery. The memory tests were developed with fewer and smaller groups because of the financial constraints into which the project ran in its final stages. Further work on these tests is needed.

Tests requiring the analysis and synthesis of three-dimensional figures were discarded (after having been administered to several hundred subjects) because performance showed large sex differences. Similarly, a pictorial test of social intelligence was discarded because it was very biased against certain ethnic groups. This problem did not generalize to Test 9 'Picture Arrangement'.

Apart from theoretical and certain technical considerations, for example suitability for the paper and pencil method of testing, ease of administration and scoring, suitability for age levels, etc., the final choice of tests was based on the following three premises.

1   That the literature of previous research has shown that the variables measured are relevant and correlate reasonably well with composite measures of intellectual performance.

2   That the NAT subtests as a whole, sample a sufficiently broad diversity of component skills and abilities, so that individuals with special abilities or weaknesses are not penalized.

3   That the nature of the individual's performance across the battery, that is, the strengths and weaknesses observed in relation to the requirements of particular areas or subtests, might have implications for intervention.

The third premise takes account of the fact that individuals performing in the same total score range do not necessarily constitute a homogeneous group, either in their abilities or their approach to tasks, the strategies used, their motivation, etc. Identical scores may be arrived at in completely different ways.

The performance requirements of a single test item are multi-dimensional, and the response given to each item is multi-determined. It is extremely important, therefore, to remember the following:

- Even the most broadly based tests can measure abilities and skills only as they exist at the time of testing. Test scores provide no information about how a testee reached a particular level of performance. An ability test 'yields a sample of what the individual knows, and has learnt to do at the time he or she is tested'. (Anastasi, 1980, p.4)
- Psychological tests consist of stimulus material the administration of which provides an indirect measure from which abilities and skills must be inferred.

In the latter point lies the difference between ability and achievement tests, or between educational and psychological tests, more generally.

With the points made in this chapter in mind, the following chapters in this part of the book will discuss briefly the research pertaining to and the main characteristics of the tests included in the NAT battery.

The individual tests are discussed in four chapters. Each chapter is devoted to one of the previously stated areas covered by the NAT, namely perceptual tests, conceptual tests, tests of attention and concentration, and memory tests. Each chapter provides a general introduction to the area and then discusses those tests the major emphasis of which is judged to be in the chapter area.

Chapter 5, entitled 'Perceptual Tasks', contains discussions of the following NAT subtests:

Test 1:   Matching Shapes
Test 2:   Matching Direction

Test 13:   Code Tracking I
Test 14:   Code Tracking II

Chapter 6, entitled 'Conceptual Tasks', discusses:

Test 3:   Categorization
Test 4:   Picture Completion
Test 5:   Embedded Figures
Test 6:   Figure Formation
Test 7:   Mazes
Test 8:   Sequencing
Test 9:   Picture Arrangement

Chapter 7, entitled 'Tests of Attention and Concentration', deals with the rationale and diagnostic applications of:

Test 10:   Visual Search
Test 11:   Simple Key Test
Test 12:   Complex Key Test
Test 13:   Code Tracking I
Test 14:   Code Tracking II

Chapter 8, entitled 'Memory Tests' discusses:

Test 15:   Visual Recognition
Test 16:   Auditory Recognition
Test 17:   Auditory Recall
Test 18:   Visual Recall.

The Scaling of Performance

Traditionally, intelligence test performance has been reported on the basis of age norms. This practice is based on the assumption that intelligence increases progressively with increasing chronological age, and goes back to the 'mental age' (MA) concept.

The latter concept was used by Binet and his followers to describe the level of intelligence of an individual in comparison with the ability of other individuals of the same age.

More specifically, mental age is defined as the 'level of mental development expressed in units of chronological age for which the mental development is judged normal' (Chaplin, 1975, p.311).

The judgment of 'what is normal' at a given age is based on the calculation of the average score obtained on a particular test by a (more or less) representative sample of children or adults of that age. While the concept of MA has been found to be reasonably meaningful by many teachers and psychologists for dealing with children under the age of 12 years, its value becomes increasingly questionable in relation to secondary school students and adults at average or above-average levels of intellectual functioning. Its meaningfulness is limited even in relation to the performance of retarded individuals.

The use of chronological age as the criterion for the definition and classification of intellectual performance has been criticized mainly on three grounds. The first and foremost is that individuals develop at different rates, and that this individual variation is ignored by the variable of chronological age. The variability between individuals appears to be strongest in the very young, and among adults. Chronological age may therefore be actually less useful for the description of intellectual functioning in the very regions where it appears to be most frequently relied on.

The two other criticisms of the use of chronological age to describe levels of test performance concern the properties of the chronological age variable as a tool for measurement.

The second criticism emphasizes that chronological age is a unidimensional variable. Its use as a scaling device implies that all aspects and components of an individual's intellectual functioning develop (and deteriorate!) at the same rate. In other words, knowledge of an individual's chronological age is assumed to provide information about sensory, perceptual and motor skills, concept formation, reasoning ability, etc., all at the same time.

The evidence of more rapid development in motor skills as compared with some intellectual abilities in young children, for example, or the significantly more rapid decline in sensory and motor abilities as compared with cognitive functioning in elderly people, would challenge the validity of the notion expressed in the above paragraph.

The third criticism is that the scaling properties (i.e. the assumed interval scaling) of the chronological age variable lead to the assigning of the same status to age differences throughout the scale. In other words, intervals of two years are given the same 'meaning' whether they occur between the ages of, for example, 0 and 2 years, 16 and 18 years, 40 and 42 years, or 73 and 75 years, even though the first-mentioned age range is undoubtedly a period of greater psychological and physical development than the other two age-ranges in the example, and even though the first two or three age-ranges are likely to imply growth, while the last tends to imply deterioration.

Among suggested alternatives to the chronological or mental age concepts, the use of the concept of 'functional age' in testing and assessment has gained most support. The coining of the term 'functional age' is generally attributed to McFarland (1953), who used it when faced with the need to consider the ability of individuals to perform certain tasks, required duties, etc., in preference to the use of mental or chronological age in the selection of workers.

Although the notion of a test battery to assess functional age has been discussed in the literature (e.g. Comfort, 1969; Fozard, 1972; Kaplan, 1951; McFarland, 1973; Nuttall, 1972), the only reports of large-scale projects using the concept have been with adults (Dirken, 1972; Glanzer, Glaser, and Richlin, 1958; Heron and Chown, 1967).

According to its advocates, that is, those who would like to see the criterion of chronological age replaced by the functional age measure, the advantage of the latter measure is that it can provide an index representing an individual's relative standing on several measures of performance. A performance-based index of this type would obviously be more sensitive to individual differences, and could have greater diagnostic power and better predictive validity than the chronological age scale.

> Individuals assigned to the same functional age would, by definition, possess equivalent skills and abilities even though their chronological ages might vary considerably. Moreover, the units on the functional age scale would be inherently meaningful since they would be expressed in terms of units presumably closely related to performance potential. (Salthouse, 1982, p.15)

Despite the above described advantages, and the general desirability of better measures and diagnostic and predictive indices than chronological age, measures of functional age have not achieved the status that some of the early advocates had expected. One reason for this is obviously related to the fact that schools and educational systems are continuing to use chronological age as the major criterion for organizational purposes. Chronological age determines the point of entry into formal education, the end of compulsory schooling, and to a large extent, class membership in schools and other educational, cultural and social institutions.

A problem with the functional age concept is that, like the chronological age variable, it provides a single, unidimensional index, thus assuming a relationship in the growth and decline of all abilities and skills it represents. If perceptual and conceptual development occurred independently of one another, no single index, even if it were based on the direct measurement of functioning in both areas, would be found useful in the description of intellectual development.

Another difficulty accompanying the notion of functional age, often mentioned by opponents of the measure, is that tasks in different domains, particularly in different intellectual disciplines and jobs, often require quite different abilities and skills. To be useful, the functions measured would thus have to be fairly specific to the task of interest. In fact, the optimally valid measure of this type would be actual task performance, which allows not only for an application of previous experience, learnt skills and abilities, but for the use of compensatory strategies on the part of the testee. The opponents of functional measures thus argue, correctly, that no such measure would be effective in more than a few related contexts.

The approach taken in the development of the NAT, though not totally free of some of the problems discussed above, is expected to meet them to some degree. It was decided to use a functional profile, in addition to the single NAT Score. An individual's relative functioning can be determined on a number of component variables of reasonably general relevance. Functioning in each component skill can thus be considered in relation to the objects that led to the assessment of the individual.

The addition of a multidimensionsal profile to the unidimensional NAT Score is expected to lead to a minimization of tendencies to assume that an individual can be described by a single score or number.

CHAPTER 5

PERCEPTUAL TASKS

This chapter is arranged in three broad sections. The first contains a discussion of the rationale for the use of perceptual tasks in the assessment of cognitive development and functioning. This is followed by a discussion of the influence of age on perceptual skills. In the last section some of the perceptual tests of the NAT battery are discussed in detail. These tests include:

   Test 1:   Matching Shapes
   Test 2:   Matching Direction
   Test 13:   Code Tracking I
   Test 14:   Code Tracking II

Rationale

Historical Developments

Amongst teachers and psychologists it has been accepted for some time that adequate perceptual development is important both in itself and as a prerequisite for the development of conceptual abilities. A generally acknowledged view in cognitive psychology is that general ability or intelligence is reflected both in a person's acquired knowledge and in some more basic, general information-processing skills, which are not necessarily dependent on the content of the information being processed.

That perceptual tasks may serve in the assessment of intellectual functioning has been a long-standing idea in the history of psychological testing. Perceptual stimulus materials have been included in intelligence tests since their inception early in this century. Their use was justified by a rationale suggesting that inferences about abilities and skills can be made on the basis of the way in which individuals perceive particular stimuli, and by the way in which they structure their stimulus environment, including the relationship between different stimuli.

In a similar manner perceptual tests like the Rorschach, the Bender Visual Gestalt Test, the Thematic Apperception Test (for descriptions of these tests see Buros, 1978) and other clinical instruments were justified. It was suggested that inferences about the personality of individuals can be based on the way in which they perceive particular stimulus patterns.

All this reminds us in some way of the early ideas of Max Wertheimer and his associates Kurt Koffka and Wolfgang Koehler whose work on perceptual phenomena was responsible for the birth and growth of Gestalt psychology. The basic set of empirical statements characterizing the Gestalt movement was published by Wertheimer (1923) under the title *Principles of Perceptual Organization*, the main argument of which is that unique organizing principles inherent in the nervous system influence the way in which external stimulation is transformed into conscious perception.

On the basis of this rationale, Goldstein (1927, 1936, 1939) designed perceptual tasks in his studies of soldiers who had sustained traumatic head injuries during the First World War. He found that the responses of his patients contained such psychological characteristics as figure/ground confusion, perseveration, forced responsiveness to extraneous stimuli, and concrete rather than abstract thinking, above all.

In the mid-1940s Heinz Werner and Alfred Strauss conducted a series of studies in which they compared retarded and non-retarded subjects with and without brain injuries. This research resulted in the listing of behavioural characteristics in response to perceptual stimuli that were said to differentiate between persons with and without brain injuries. Werner and Strauss extended these studies to children, and found that the responses of children to perceptual stimuli could be equally diagnostic as those of adults. The history of the study of perceptual and motor problems in brain-injured, mentally retarded, and other learning-disabled children has been traced by Hallahan and Cruickshank (1973).

While the use of perceptual tasks for assessment purposes was originally restricted to the diagnosis of brain injury, the 1950s and 1960s showed a dramatic and significant increase in this use for the study of children who were experiencing learning difficulties, particularly in the area of reading. According to Hallahan and Cruickshank (1973), all the best known research workers in the area of learning disabilities, and those responsible for the development of the major tests in this area, were at one time or other colleagues or students of Werner and Strauss, or were significantly influenced by their work. William Cruickshank, Samuel Kirk, and Newell Kephart all worked with Werner and Strauss in their early investigations, while Ray Barsch later worked with Kephart at Purdue University. Marianne Frostig, while not a direct associate of Werner and Strauss, has stated that their work had a significant influence on her approach to the early identification and remediation of perceptual disabilities.

Process Theories

The focus in much of the research in modern cognitive psychology has been on the identification of basic sets of abilities and skills used in the processing of information, and on the determination of their relationship to traditional psychometric measures of ability (e.g., Carpenter and Just, 1975; Chiang and Atkinson, 1976; Hunt, Frost, and Lunneborg, 1973; Hunt, Lunneborg, and Lewis, 1975; Keating and Bobbitt, 1978; Lunneborg, 1977, 1978).

The rationale for most of the more recent utilizations of perceptual tasks in the assessment of intellectual and personality variables is based mainly on cognitive style theory and its extensive research applications (Witkin, Oltman, Raskin, and Karp, 1971).

In this context, the term 'cognitive style', for which some writers prefer the label 'cognitive controls' (e.g. Broverman, 1960; Santostefano, 1969; Wachtel, 1972), refers to certain characteristic and self-consistent modes of functioning observed in individuals and groups during perceptual and intellectual activities. Witkin and his co-workers have found that cognitive styles are manifestations in the intellectual sphere of still broader dimensions of personal functioning, which cut across diverse, cognitive and non-cognitive psychological areas.

The emphasis in research concerned with cognitive style has been on its relationship with adaptive functioning aided by cognitive processes in the psychological economy of the individual. This emphasis has led to a search for connections and consistencies from one psychological area to another, and to the finding of formal stylistic similarities across many intellectual and personality areas. The contribution of this research has been to move towards a more integrated holistic view of cognitive processes and of the operations of the human being as a whole.

Broverman (1960) suggested that cognitive style variables provide a profile of mental abilities for each individual. Santostefano (1969) believes that cognitive style variables determine the amount and organization of information available to the individual involved in cognitive activity, and thus his or her cognitive achievement.

Messick (1976) reviewed cognitive style variables and listed 19 different ones. He wrote of cognitive strategies (i.e. styles) as general tendencies in the approach to mental tasks. He compared cognitive styles with abilities by contrasting and by relating them. In this treatise abilities are regarded as unipolar traits while cognitive styles are seen as bipolar. Abilities are assumed to be narrower in scope, because they tend to be measured on the basis of *level* of performance, whereas cognitive styles are measured by *degree of manner* of performance.

In other words, Messick regards the construct of ability as unipolar because it involves the measurement of competencies in terms of outcomes. He also emphasized the directional value of the construct, that is, more ability is regarded more highly than less ability. Cognitive style, on the other hand, implies an emphasis on process rather than outcome, and is usually regarded as bipolar, with each extreme having different implications for cognitive functioning, depending on the nature and the demands of the situation. Also, whereas ability is usually regarded as facilitating functioning in particular content areas, cognitive style is a more pervasive, controlling mechanism.

The cognitive style variables thus exert control over mental functioning while abilities, as measured by tests, do not. Messick points out that as a controlling variable, cognitive style also helps to regulate the direction, duration, intensity, range, and speed of functioning. Implicit in this approach to the relationship between cognitive style and intelligence is that the two are not antithetical but confounded.

Guilford (1980a) found that most of the cognitive style variables discussed by Messick (1976) and by others in the recent literature could be reconciled with his Structure of the Intellect model (Guilford, 1967), but notes:

> It is unlikely that cognitive styles are merely abilities [in the psychometric sense!], for many of them definitely appear to represent directions of preferences in information processing . . .

> Preference for divergent versus convergent production is an example of a choice between two intellectual operations... Among sensory categories there is a style characterized by choices among visual, auditory, and kinesthetic information.... Other cognitve styles appear to involve preferences among different products of information... favouring units versus classes versus relations as items with which to deal (Guilford, 1983, p.731).

The judgment of the relationship between cognitive style variables and abilities obviously depends on the definition of ability. If ability or intelligence is defined solely on the basis of a score obtained on a test regarded as an ability test, style and strategy variables obviously play no direct part, because an IQ or similar score does not convey any information relating to how it was obtained. If, however, ability is regarded as a reflection of the variables underlying performance itself, for example information-processing ability and efficiency, cognitive style and strategy variables as defined by Guilford become part of the functional system of intelligence.

Nineteenth century psychologists regarded perception as an imprint made by external stimuli on a passive organism. Visual perception, for example, was explained as the impression of an environmental stimulus on the retina. The concept of the isomorphism of the structure of an external stimulus with the structure of the excitation of cells in the retina or visual cortex had its strongest proponents among the Gestalt psychologists.

Modern psychology attempts to explain the processes of perception in a less mentalistic way. Luria (1973), for example, regards perception

> as an active process of searching for the corresponding information, distinguishing the essential features of an object, comparing the features with each other, creating appropriate hypotheses, and then comparing these hypotheses with the original data. (Luria, 1973, p.229)

This view of the operation of perceptual processes concurs with that of other distinguished cognitive psychologists, including Broadbent (1958), Bruner (1957), Leontiev (1959) and Vygotsky (1957, 1960, 1962, 1978).

More recent theories suggest that an early stage of perception involves the separation of the perceived stimulus (as received by the brain via the sensory system), into a large number of elements. These elements are subsequently coded, and through synthesis fitted into a dynamic system that is appropriate to the stimulus situation. In other words, meaningful interaction with the environment requires the recognition of patterns through analysis and synthesis. This is illustrated by the fact that basic prerequisites for coping with the world, such as distinguishing the familiar from the unfamiliar, understanding speech, and reading, all require the processing of patterns, and that

> Pattern recognition is not a simple matter of matching sensory input with memories, because the neural signals arising from stimulation undergo many changes on their way from the senses to the brain, and the existence of illusions shows that these changes are determined by internal factors. (Juola, 1979, p.489)

As noted above, pattern recognition involves both analysis and synthesis. The mechanisms of these processes include the search for the important elements of information inherent in the situation, their comparison with each other, the creation and testing of hypotheses concerning the meaning and structure of the information as a whole, and the validation of the hypotheses through comparisons with the salient features of the perceived stimulus.

> This process of selection and synthesis of the corresponding features is *active* in character and takes place under the direct influence of the *tasks* which confront the subject. It takes place with the aid of ready made *codes* . . ., which serve to place the perceived feature into its proper system and to give it a *general* or categorical character; finally, it always incorporates a process of comparison of the effect with the original hypothesis or, in other words, a process of verification of the perceptual activity. (Luria, 1973, p.230)

The theory suggests further that when familiar objects or other stimuli, that is, percepts that are firmly established through past experience, are perceived, the process described above operates but contains a number of short cuts, whereas the perceptual processing of new or complex stimuli proceeds unabridged.

Beyond the purely sensory level, it is believed that individuals differ in the size and complexity of the sample of stimulus characteristics they can take in at a glance. Trabasso and Bower (1968) suggested that such differences might be associated with differences in measured intelligence, and with individual differences in the response to anxiety, particularly in the testing situation.

Information that has been encoded, and that is being held in a sensory register or buffer, is subject to decay after the first few seconds. The rate and the extent of the decay also vary across individuals. This induced state of divided attention is a major non-sensory source of individual differences in cognitive tasks, especially of memory. In fact, it has been suggested (e.g. Baltes, Reese, and Lipsitt, 1980) that the superiority of adolescents and young adults to older persons observed in many perceptual tasks is the result of the difficulties of the older people with divided attention, rather than due to deficits in the capacity or the decay of the sensory system.

Perceptual Factors

Research concerned with the demands of visually presented tasks has shown that at the most basic level these tasks require, among other variables, skills in the encoding, remembering, the ability to transform information, and the ability to match spatial stimuli.

As noted above, the importance of the encoding process is unquestionable. The nature of the processes by which what is perceived is internalized, that is, the internal representation of external stimuli, is likely to set limitations to the encoded information, and may even determine the transformational processes that may be able to operate on this information.

While a large number of perceptual factors have been identified in the literature (for details see Carroll, 1980; Ekstrom, French, and Harman, 1979; Lohman, 1979a, 1979b), three of these are of particular importance in relation to the tests discussed in this chapter. All of them are speed based and they include: speed of closure, that is, the speed with which incomplete visual stimuli are matched with their internal representations; perceptual speed, that is, the speed with which visual stimuli are matched; visual memory, that is, short-term memory for visual stimuli; and kinesthetic speed, that is, the speed with which up/down, right/left discriminations are made.

Other factors such as spatial relations, spatial orientation, and visualization are more important in relation to some of the NAT tests discussed in the next chapter.

The spatial relations factor probably represents individual differences in the speed with which simple visual stimuli are reflected and/or rotated mentally. Spatial orientation is generally regarded as involving the ability to imagine how a stimulus array will appear from another perspective. Historically, the requirement for the presence of this factor was that individuals solved a spatial orientation task by imagining that they themselves were re-oriented in space. Such a factor is difficult to measure, as tests designed to assess performance on the factor are often solved by mentally rotating the stimulus array, rather than by the problem solver's imagined re-orientation of self. Specific aspects of this notion have been discussed by Evans (1980), Hebb (1972), Kosslyn (1980), Pylyshyn (1973), and others in the research literature.

The visualization factor plays a role in most tests of visual perceptual content. The factor is strongly related to 'g'. Specifically, it tends to refer to the ability to manipulate representations of visual objects mentally. Tests measuring this ability load on Guilford's (1969) factor are labelled 'cognition of figural transformation'.

Hunt (1978), Lunneborg (1978), and others have associated differences in the speed of encoding from a sensory percept with verbal ability, suggesting that language may function as a mediator between the percept and short-term memory. Day's (1973) research in the auditory domain suggests further, that some persons are more bound to stimulus details while others integrate stimulation more readily to perceive meaning. Factor analytic studies including those reported by Guilford (1967), Thurstone (1944), and many others suggest that two separable human abilities may be operating in the visual perceptual system. These are generally referred to as *speed of closure* and *perceptual speed*. They are associated with differences in the speed required for the integration of spatially arranged stimuli as meaningful wholes, and with differences in the speed of discriminating between stimuli as same or different, respectively.

It has been suggested (Guilford, 1967; Messick and French, 1975) that there may be abilities comparable to the above, in the auditory system. Also, Thurstone's (1944) factor analysis of perceptual abilities had identified several other individual difference factors, presumably associated with the functioning of perceptual processes.

Three other interesting sets of findings from the literature related to perceptual processes and abilities might have implications for the interpretation of the NAT.

Firstly, individual differences in the speed of solving simple perceptual items were generally found to be independent of scores obtained on more difficult experimental tasks and on verbal reference tests.

Secondly, individual differences in the speed of solving complex perceptual tasks were consistently related to performance on verbal reference tasks. The implication of this finding is that it is possible that individuals solved complex perceptual items using strategies that were not strictly non-verbal.

Some subjects solve complex non-verbal items by using perceptual spatial strategies, others use a combination of spatial and verbal strategies, while yet others show a preference for the use of verbal analytic strategies in all problems. An implication of this finding is that if some subjects solve the items on a carefully constructed non-verbal test or experimental task using verbal strategies, then perhaps spatial ability is not all that important in these situations. Also, verbal and spatial perceptual abilities may be more independent from one another than the literature on mental tests tends to suggest.

Thirdly, performance levels attained on simple perceptual tasks are often highly correlated with scores obtained on more complex perceptual tasks. In fact, there is considerable research evidence for the conclusion reached, after careful review, by Cooper and Regan (1982)

> that basic processes of visual coding, representation, and comparison may contribute more to spatial ability than seemingly more complex operations such as efficiency of mental transformation. (p.144)

Tests of such basic perceptual skills have been shown to be useful as predictors of certain aspects of job performance, technical school success, achievement in calculus and other mathematics courses, and success in engineering (for reviews see McGee, 1979; Smith, 1964).

Mathematics Achievement

The literature contains considerable evidence concerning the importance of perceptual, particularly spatial, abilities in mathematics learning and performance (Bishop, 1973, 1979; Fennema, 1974, 1979; Lin, 1979; Sherman, 1979; Smith, 1964). Some mathematicians, for example Fennema (1979), have claimed that all mathematical tasks demand spatial thinking.

Nearly 50 years ago, the Australian mathematician and psychologist H.R. Hamley (1935) suggested that the major components of mathematical ability are general intelligence and the ability to perceive number and space configurations, and to retain such configurations as mental pictures (McGee, 1979).

Moses (1977), in a study involving 145 year 5 students from an American elementary school, concluded that perceptual abilities are a good predictor of problem-solving performance. In a later study, Moses (1980) investigated differences in spatial visualization, reasoning and mathematical problem solving. She also investigated the effects on these differences exerted by a sequence of visually presented reasoning exercises. Her results supported the findings of Smith (1972) that people with high spatial perceptual skills have a considerable advantage in mathematical learning over those lacking such skills.

However, this does not mean that high spatial abilities are a prerequisite for mathematics achievement for all individuals. Sherman (1979), after a careful study of the effect of spatial ability on mathematical performance in which a number of other cognitive and affective variables were controlled, stressed that the spatial ability factor was one of the main factors, not the main factor, that affected mathematical achievement. Krutetskii (1976), who used clinical methods extensively in his investigation of mathematical achievement, also notes that gifted mathematicians do not always possess above-average perceptual abilities, and that many of them prefer solution methods that make little use of spatial ability. The findings in this area are not conclusive.

Reading

> The ability to read rapidly and with high comprehension is a crucial aspect of 'intelligent' behavior in any literate society. At minimum, reading involves picking up visual information... and processing that information on a variety of levels so as to yield, eventually, understanding of the meaning. (Cooper and Regan, 1982, p.132)

Much research has been devoted to the investigation of relationships between reading achievement and performance on tests of visual and auditory perception. Many of these studies relied on the Illinois Test of Psycholinguistic Abilities (ITPA) (Kirk, McCarthy, and Kirk, 1971) to provide measures for the perceptual skills under discussion. The findings of these studies have tended to be inconclusive. Bruininks (1969), Gallistel, Boyle, Curran, and Hawthorn (1972), Golden and Steiner (1969), and others found significant correlations between various visual and auditory perceptual skills, and reading. However, in other studies (e.g. Bruininks, Lucker, and Gropper, 1970; Kass, 1966; Macione, 1969) it emerged that performance scores on the ITPA subtests did not differentiate reliably between good and poor readers. None of these studies addressed the question of how level of intelligence might affect the relationship between perceptual skills and reading.

Newcomer and Hammill (1975) reviewed ITPA research, and concluded that, although performance on some of the subtests appeared to be correlated significantly with achievement in reading, most correlations drop below 'the established level of significance' (Newcomer and Hammill, 1975, p.735) when level of intelligence is controlled.

Jackson (1978), Jackson and McClelland (1975, 1979), McClelland and Jackson (1978) demonstrated, in a series of elegantly designed studies, the consistency of their finding of very basic visual information-processing differences between average and highly proficient readers. In the interpretation of their findings these investigators concur with the basic premises of a number of information-processing theories of reading (e.g., Estes, 1975; Frederiksen, 1978; Rumelhart, 1977b) that the processing of information during reading occurs at many different levels of perception and analysis, both interactively and simultaneously, and that these levels are likely to be organized in a loose type of hierarchy. It is argued that the reading process (i.e. understanding what is read) involves subprocesses including analysis of visual perceptual stimuli, and recognition of perceptual features and patterns such as letter clusters, words, semantic and conceptual relationships. The output of processing at each level of encoding and analysis may serve as input to the level(s) above, but may in turn also be influenced by output from subsequent or 'higher' levels.

The research by Jackson and his co-workers showed conclusively that highly proficient (adult) readers differ from less proficient ones in the speed with which they can execute certain basic visual information-processing skills, and that this finding is independent of the effects of previous experience and practice in reading. These results would suggest that highly proficient readers bring a set of abilities to the task, which is independent of practice, and also of the word knowledge and language comprehension skills that account for so much of the variance in studies of reading.

Jackson and McClelland (1979) suggest that the set of abilities described earlier may totally account for the often-found association between reading ability and verbal or general ability. Finally, there is the likelihood (well supported in the information-processing literature) that the same information-processing components are, in fact, responsible for the achievement of specific intellectual tasks such as reading, and for what is regarded, more generally, as cognitive development or ability.

As early as 1969, Cohen contended that most visual perceptual measures are more closely related to intelligence, more generally, than to reading.

The Influence of Age

Research has indicated that the abilities and skills required for efficient processing of perceptual information received from the environment weaken with increasing age (Botwinik, 1973; Honzik, 1984; Layton 1975; McFarland, 1968; Panek, Barrett, Sterns, and Alexander, 1978; Salthouse, 1982; Wechsler, 1958).

This decline in information-processing ability is assumed to be the major cause of the observed performance decrements with age on laboratory tasks such as reaction time (Botwinik, 1971, 1972, 1973; Rabbitt, 1965; Welford, 1951, 1977). For example, Salthouse and Somberg (1982) compared the relationship between speed and accuracy on a choice reaction-time task between young (aged 18 to 21 years) and older (aged 60 to 84 years) adults. They found no difference between these groups in the rates of increasing accuracy, but showed that members of the older group were slower in integrating information but not in actual rate of information extraction.

A weakening of performance with age has also been found in relation to selective attention (Broadbent and Heron, 1962; Clark and Knowles, 1973; Craik, 1965), and measures of cognitive styles (Comalli, 1970; Kogan, 1973; Schwartz and Karp, 1967).

In a well designed, cross-sectional study, Panek et al. (1978) investigated the performance of 175 females, ranging in age from 17 years to 72 years, on a large range of information-processing abilities, which previously had tended to have been investigated in separate studies. The findings of these investigators provide strong support for a hypothesis of an overall decline on all information-processing variables, rather than selective deterioration or drop out. They found that the decline becomes most evident in the late forties and early fifties. Simple choice reaction time was a variable that did not follow this trend, but the data for complex reaction time support the findings of other investigators (e.g. Birren, 1965; Rabbitt, 1965; Welford, 1977), who have reported a slowing of psychomotor activity on complex reaction time and/or perceptual-motor tasks from the age of approximately 40 years onwards.

> The fundamental fact that intelligence as assessed by traditional intelligence tests with cross-sectional procedures exhibits more or less continuous decreases across successive age groups beginning at about 25–30, has not been disputed. (Salthouse, 1982, p.81)

A number of psychologists including Spearman (1927) have recognized this phenomenon, and have speculated as to whether beyond the age of 30 years people are, in fact, too old for highly intellectual and creative efforts. However, Wechsler (1958) and others have emphasized that intelligence, as measured on standardized tests, is not the only factor involved in human achievements, but that knowledge, understanding, judgment and wisdom are more dependent on actual experience than on sheer capacity, and experience is usually related to the age of the individual.

> The important question in many evaluations of adults seems to be whether the individual can handle the tasks of interest, rather than the position on the decline function.... Most abilities exhibit gradual decline, such that even at the age of 70 there is considerable residual ability, that may be sufficient for the performance of many activities. (Salthouse, 1982, p.82)

It is important to note two other aspects of this topic. One, intellectual decline resulting from ageing alone is a continuous process rather than a sudden and abrupt event; and two, intelligence, as measured by ability and achievement tests, is not a single, unitary trait. Rather, it consists of a combination of developmentally distinct but functionally interdependent component abilities, which interact with one another. Thus, intelligence should be investigated as a functional system if an understanding of performance is to be obtained. Such an investigation must include the analysis of mechanisms and processes that might be responsible for particular levels of performance.

The literature makes it quite clear that different component abilities of intelligence exhibit quite different trends as far as their development and possible decline across the adult life span is concerned. The differential decline on the subtests making up the Wechsler Adult Intelligence Scale (WAIS), for example, documented by Wechsler (1958) and others, suggests that the answer to the question of whether and for how long intelligence remains stable depends on the particular areas assessed in the intelligence test.

On the basis of the documentation provided by Wechsler (1958) and in view of the Cattell–Horn theory of fluid and crystallized intelligence (Horn, 1967, 1970, 1975, 1978; Horn and Cattell, 1966; and Horn and Donaldson, 1976, 1977, 1980), one would expect that an intelligence test consisting of such subtests as included in Wechsler's verbal tests, particularly Information, Vocabulary and Comprehension, would remain fairly stable across adulthood. On the other hand, one might predict that scores on the performance subtests, such as Digit Symbol, Picture Arrangement and Object Assembly might decrease with increasing age.

The above examples suggest that global measures of intelligence are unlikely to be suitable for investigating changes in the mental functioning of adults with age because the meaning of the global measure is completely dependent on the subtests included, and differential performance in particular areas may well be masked. Neither comparisons of the scores obtained on two different global tests, nor of the same global test at two ages, are meaningful if the same total score can be achieved by various combinations of subtest scores.

> Abandoning the concept of global intelligence in favor of component abilities in discussions of adult development should therefore eliminate much of the confusion and emotionality. (Salthouse, 1982, p.71)

As noted above, the constraints placed on the construction of the NAT, that is, the requirement for a group-administered language-free test, made the battery largely a measure of fluid intelligence. All subtests of the NAT require visual–perceptual ability, and most depend on basic spatial abilities for the encoding and comprehension of the stimulus material.

Early findings that older adults generally perform more poorly on tests of visual and spatial abilities than younger adults (Heston and Cannell, 1941; Weisenburg, Roe, and McBride, 1935; Willoughby, 1927; and others) continue to be confirmed (e.g. Arenberg, 1978, 1982; Berg, Hertzog, and Hunt, 1982; Muhs, Hooper, and Papalia-Finlay, 1979; Salthouse, 1982) on the basis of a number of different psychometric tests.

On most of the NAT tests a performance decrement of approximately 5 per cent per decade beginning about the age of 25 to 30 years has to be expected. This estimate is based on some experimental studies with different groups of adults, and on the findings reported in the research literature relating to similar tests (e.g. Wechsler's Object Assembly, Picture Completion, Picture Arrangement and Block Design). The decline in all of these tests in cross-sectional studies was found to be very similar, namely, approximately 5 per cent. (For review see Salthouse, 1982.)

Somewhat stronger deterioration was found for tests of perceptual–motor speed, which is a prerequisite for the completion of the speed and accuracy tests and the maze tests in the NAT battery.

As noted in other parts of this book, many skills and abilities are required for the successful completion of each one of the NAT subtests. But the tests in which the requirement is to mark as many symbols of a particular set of characteristics in a given time, or in the maze tests, perceptual–motor speed and visual skills are particularly important determinants of the final score.

Symbol substitution tests of the Digit Symbol type (Wechsler, 1958) have been shown to result in an age-related decline in performance of approximately 10 per cent per decade (e.g. Bilash and Zubek, 1960; Goldfarb, 1941; Heron and Chown, 1967; Schaie and Strother, 1968a; Wechsler, 1958; Whiteman and Jastak, 1957).

There are very large individual differences in the rate of change in intellectual abilities, just as there are tremendous differences in the peak levels of these abilities reached by individuals. In fact, correlations between chronological age and raw scores on subtests of intelligence scales seldom exceed .5 (Salthouse, 1982, p.79), which although statistically considered sizeable, indicates that only 25 per cent of the variability in intellectual development and functioning (as represented by the test scores) can be accounted for by the age variable.

Table 5.1 contains the correlations of NAT subtests with age in years, and shows that the scores follow a very similar pattern to that reported in the research literature.

Table 5.1   The Correlation of NAT Subtests with Age

	Test	r	
	1	.24	
	2	.18	
	3	.17	
	4	.17	
	5	.25	
	6	.33	
	7	−.11	
	8	.25	
	9	.25	
	10	.33	
	11	.24	
	12	.36	
	13	.47	
	14	.38	
Mean correlation:	over all tests	.25	$SD = .14$
	perceptual tests	.31	$SD = .11$
	conceptual tests	.19	$SD = .14$
	speed/accuracy tests	.26	$SD = .22$

Also, it has been suggested that the rate of decline in cognitive abilities and skills may be less rapid in initially more intelligent individuals (e.g. Blum and Jarvik, 1974; Foulds and Raven, 1948; Riegel and Riegel, 1972). On the other hand, Baltes, Nesselroade, Schaie, and Labouvie (1972) have presented a rather convincing argument that many of these results might be explained as artifacts of statistical regression.

It is obvious that people vary greatly in their specific patterns of decline with ageing, hence the advice of Salthouse (1982):

> At the present time, then, it is probably not wise to draw any conclusions about differential rates of decline across particular groups of individuals. (p.79)
>
> ... it is just not possible at the current time to characterize the communalities responsible for particular aging trends. (p.80)

On the basis of the findings reported in the literature, and taking cognizance of the increasing variation within and between adults of increasing age, and of the increasing importance of extraneous variables influencing the performance of adults, it was decided not to provide information on age differences among adults.

It is suggested that the inspection of adult NAT profiles will provide considerable clinical insights concerning differential levels of component functioning in individuals. Where the performance of groups of individuals needs to be compared cross-sectionally it is suggested that such comparisons be made on the basis of factor and individual subtest performance only. As noted above, global scores, that is, the NAT scores, are not useful in this respect.

Perceptual Subtests

As noted previously, none of the subtests of the NAT measure unitary skills or abilities. All tests sample performance on multi-dimensional variables, and the items elicit multi-determined skills and behaviours.

Perceptual abilities and skills are elicited by all subtests of the NAT in response to the stimulus material. Therefore it is questionable whether it makes sense to discuss 'perceptual', 'conceptual', 'speed and accuracy', and 'memory' tests in separation. Yet, it might be argued that the contribution of different functions varies in different tests.

To organize the material to be presented in this section, the aim was to base the choice of tests to be discussed in each chapter on the results of the factor analyses conducted to ascertain the construct validity of the battery. However, the investigation of the construct validity of the NAT, reported in detail in Chapters 8 and 9, predominantly showed that all subtests contribute strongly to a substantial 'g' factor, which accounted for over 67 per cent of the variance in the total sample. In age-related samples and other subgroups the amounts of variance accounted for by this factor ranged from 56 per cent to 86 per cent. (Mean variance accounted for 65.34 per cent, $SD = 6.61$ per cent.) These findings support the questioning of firm divisions between the subtests. On the other hand, smaller but consistently occurring factors were identified, the structure of which would justify their definition as perceptual, conceptual, attention (i.e. lack of distractibility), etc.

The division of the tests for discussion in this and the following chapters of this section therefore should be regarded as largely a matter of organizational convenience rather than as a strict indication of specific aims and different contents in the tests. The tests discussed in this chapter are Tests 1, 2 and 10 to 14. The response requirements for Test 1 and Test 2 are similar, as are those for Test 13 and Test 14. The difference between the tests in each of these pairs lies in the increased complexity of Tests 2 versus Test 1, and Test 14 versus Test 13.

Test 1: Matching Shapes

This 10 item, multiple choice test, was designed to assess the testee's ability to judge relatively gross differences in visually presented stimuli (figures), some of which have been rotated. The requirement is to recognize various geometric shapes regardless of size or orientation.

In other words, the test aims to measure the ability to perceive and recognize the form and structure of a stimulus as a whole, as opposed to the ability to perceive details, which is measured in Test 2 and in a number of other NAT subtests. Test 1 also measures form constancy.

Based on careful review of the literature relating to research in perception, Smith (1964) suggests that the ability 'to form a clear impression of a shape or pattern as a whole . . . a form perception factor' (p.203) is a prerequisite for success in most complex perceptual tasks.

> Each test item requires simple categorization, which might be defined as the means by which people decide whether or not something belongs to a simple class (e.g. deciding that a particular object is an instance of the concept 'boy'). (Medin and Smith, 1984, p. 114)

In the present context the example of the concept 'boy' might be replaced by 'square', 'circle', 'triangle', etc. Difficulties experienced by testees in relation to this test and to Test 2 result from the failure to identify the defining properties of the stimulus and/or response.

Test 2: Matching Direction

In this 20 item, multiple choice test, the stimulus has to be matched with respect to both shape and direction. Test 2 thus requires complex categorization, defined by Medin and Smith (1984) in relation to verbal exemplars as

> The means by which people decide whether or not something belongs to a complex class (e.g. deciding that a particular object is an instance of the concept *rich boy*) (Medin and Smith, 1984, p.114).

Examples of the complex class concept in relation to the Matching Direction Test would be 'chairs standing in a certain position', 'leaves dropping in a particular way', 'arrows pointing in a defined direction', etc.

The classification concept used here and in relation to Test 1 is based on the classical point of view, which holds that all instances of a concept share common properties, which are necessary and defining conditions of the concept. Expressed differently, 'The classical view assumes that the defining properties provide the structure that holds a category together' (Medin and Smith, 1984, p.123).

The ability to note significant details is of even greater importance in responses to the items contained in Test 2 than for those in Test 1.

The tasks presented in both tests thus demand not merely a perception, that is, seeing or recognizing a stimulus, but they also require categorization based on accurate perception. The latter demands sequential cognitive action, for example perceptual analysis, perceptual synthesis, integration, and the organization of the response. Thus, an inability to complete the items correctly is not necessarily accompanied by an inability to perceive them. Instead, failure on these tests may be the result of an inability to identify the salient features of the stimulus and/or the response alternatives. Difficulties with these tests may also be related to problems of perceptual integration, or even to the perceptual motor requirements of the mode of response demanded by the tests.

One of the major difficulties faced by those wishing to make diagnostic interpretations of the scores of these and other tests in the area of visual information processing relates to the identification of the strategies used by testees during testing.

Whether in real life or in testing situations, people (prototype or unique) may use a variety of strategies when learning concepts. These strategies range from hypothesis testing (e.g. Kellogg, 1981; Martin and Caramazza, 1980) to memorization of individual instances of the concept (e.g. Kossan, 1981).

While in most situations hypothesis testing is taken for granted as an efficient strategy, non-analytic processes, such as memorization of the presented specific examples of a concept and the classification of new instances on the basis of their similarity to memorized ones, are usually regarded as inefficient.

In the completion of matching tests differences in performance scores are solely the result of differences in overall speed with which the items are completed. While both reaction time and perceptual speed more generally are important components of cognitive development and functioning, and major determinants of intellectual achievement in many societies, they do not provide diagnostic information that might be useful for the design of intervention procedures.

Visual matching tasks, as presented in Tests 1 and 2, can be accomplished in a variety of different ways. The discussion here is concerned with qualitative differences in the performance of testees. Quantitative differences are reported in the size of the score achieved on each test.

Firstly, some testees will perform the required matching tasks by finding instances of the 'same' stimulus. Other individuals will identify the matching stimulus by eliminating instances in which the stimulus is 'different', while yet others may use a combination of both of these strategies.

The literature suggests that, all other things being equal, 'same' oriented strategies require less time than 'different' oriented strategies (e.g. Bamber, 1969; Bindra, Donderi, and Nishisato, 1968; Cooper, 1976; Krueger, 1973), but that the time required by 'different' oriented strategies decreases as the stimuli to be compared become less similar (e.g., Egeth, 1966; Hawkins, 1969; Nickerson, 1969). Testees applying both types of strategies in the same situation would generally be expected to be slower even than their 'different' oriented peers, except in a type of simultaneous or dual-process situation, where the choice between 'same' or 'different' response strategies is affected differentially by a given stimulus manipulation (e.g. Egeth and Becker, 1971; Hock, 1973; Krueger, 1970, 1973), with the result that the time taken to respond may be shorter than in either of the other strategy-choice situations.

Secondly, as noted earlier, some testees will complete the task demanded by the item by comparing each response alternative with the stimulus figure, a one to one correspondence strategy. Others will memorize the stimulus as a whole—with all, some, or none of its relevant features—and will compare each response alternative with this internal representation of the stimulus. The latter holistic process can be contrasted with a more analytical comparison process, in which the testee might hold in memory a representation of the essential features, that is, detail of the stimulus, which is used for more analytical comparison processes.

Which strategies can be expected to lead to most efficient performance depends not only on the characteristics of the test item, but also on the characteristics of the testee. Familiarity with the task, previous experience, even strategy preferences play a role in this regard. Some research workers have hypothesized that observed differences in the approach to visual comparison tasks can be explained by individual differences between subjects; for example, Hock, (1973), Hock, Gordon, and Marcus (1974), and others distinguish between 'structural' subjects and 'analytical' subjects with respect to their approach to these tasks.

Explanatory theories aside, observation, post-test questioning of testees, testees thinking aloud during 'testing the limits', etc., can all provide valuable diagnostic information concerning the way in which a particular score was achieved. This type of information does provide a guide towards an understanding of a particular individual's difficulties with the task, and allows for the design of appropriate intervention aimed at increasing the individual's efficiency in similar information-processing tasks. However, the level to which information-processing capabilities can be trained varies with individuals. (An introduction to literature relevant to this area can be found in a collection of recent papers edited by Detterman and Sternberg, 1982.)

Perceptual Speed and Accuracy Tests

The concepts of perception and attention are confounded. There is a lack of consensus in both the information-processing literature and the differential literature concerning their definition and meaning. A presentation of alternative conceptualizations of the nature of perception and that of attention is beyond the scope of the present discussion. Major approaches to investigation of perception and attention are noted earlier in this chapter and in Chapter 7 respectively.

But it can be said here that some approaches to the conceptualization of perception focus on information that is obtained directly from the environment (e.g. Deutsch and Deutsch, 1963; Gibson, 1966; Norman, 1976), while others view perception as the outcome of a sequence of internal processing stages (e.g. Kahneman, 1973; Rumelhart, 1977a). Some theorists regard attention as a filtering mechanism (e.g. Broadbent, 1958; Cherry, 1953; Treisman, 1964), whereas others emphasize the limited capacity of the set of information-processing resources available to individuals in particular situations (e.g. Norman and Bobrow, 1975). Yet others conceive attention as being a skill that can be modified through practice (e.g. Hochberg, 1970; Neisser, 1976).

The view of the nature of human intellectual functioning adopted in the design of the NAT, namely that intelligence is a functional system for processing and transforming environmental information in which component processes are highly interdependent and interactive, rather than strictly independent and at best sequential, makes difficult the separate analysis of the contribution of perceptual and attentional processes to cognitive performance. In fact, only in carefully designed experimental settings would it be possible to attempt to isolate just where in the information processing (which takes place during performance) the attentional, perceptual, conceptual or memory factors most influence intelligent behaviour.

In common with other speed and accuracy tests, Tests 10 to 14 measure the ability to work fast, accurately, and with concentration. The task requirements for these subtests combine perceptual recognition and matching with speed, accuracy, and memory skills.

These tests, particularly Tests 11 and 12, also assess flexibility in the application of perceptual information-processing skills. Like all speed and accuracy tasks, that is, tasks requiring high concentration, Tests 10 to 14 in the NAT battery load highly on 'g'.

All of the tests require the testee to identify and keep track of a standard stimulus, the characteristics of which are similar to those of the stimuli surrounding it.

In Tests 10 to 12 the sought-after stimulus differs from those surrounding it with respect to detail, not in Gestalt (i.e. content or structure) as is the case in Tests 13 and 14. Tests 10 to 12 have a stronger requirement of visual discrimination skills than do Tests 13 and 14, but the latter tests require a greater amount of perceptual flexibility and short-term memory.

Performance on Tests 10 to 12 may be more amenable to 'diffuse attention' (attention to detail), while Tests 13 and 14 require 'fixative' or 'concentrative' attention (Meumann, 1907; Smith, 1964), which requires the testee to grasp and mentally manipulate figures as wholes, that is, to absorb their structure. In other words, testees who can form and retain a relatively flexible image of a figure with four corners will have no difficulty in finding other such figures in the array. The salient characteristic of the sought-after stimulus, namely, 'four corners', is retained in a fixative model of attention to the task.

Successful performance on Test 12, when following Test 11, depends particularly on the noting of explicit relationships between parts of the stimulus, on perceptual flexibility, and on concentration.

The literature has shown that the most universal processing difference for tasks of this kind (and for tasks of name and letter matching) between individuals of higher and those of lower cognitive ability lies in the speed with which the tasks are accomplished (e.g. Chiang and Atkinson, 1976; Cooper and Regan, 1982; Hunt et al., 1975; Keating and Bobbitt, 1978). Another possible processing ability underlying performance on these tests is the speed with which items can be compared with a memory representation. The applicability of this latter ability would depend on the processing strategies used by the individual testee.

Performance on NAT Tests 10 to 14, namely, Test 10: Visual Search, Test 11: Simple Key Test, Test 12: Complex Key Test, Test 13: Code Tracking I, and Test 14: Code Tracking II can be expected to correlate well with speed of reading. Research has shown that fast readers pick up more from a single fixation than slow readers (Gilbert, 1959; Huey 1908/1968; Jackson and McClelland, 1975), because they have an advantage in visual processing (Jackson and McClelland, 1979). They can process a large amount of test or other visual stimuli per fixation.

As noted previously, the attention and concentration related abilities sampled by these tests are discussed in Chapter 7.

The notion that attentional and perceptual capabilities might determine in significant ways the overall intellectual ability of an individual has been entertained since the early days of systematic intelligence testing (see e.g. Spearman, 1927; Thurstone, 1938a; Wechsler, 1958).

This same view has been one of the seminal premises underlying the recent and much heralded unification of cognitive, information-processing and individual differences approaches to the study of intellectual functioning (Carroll, 1976; Cooper and Regan, 1982).

Many kinds of perception-based individual differences in abilities, skills and underlying psychological processes have been noted in this chapter. Some of these differences appear to be of a more general nature, and refer to component abilities involved in many kinds of intellectual performance. Others appear to be more specialized skills, which are developed and applicable in more narrowly defined situations. While the same comment might be made in relation to all cognitive abilities, the occurrence of component abilities and skills that must be developed in more specialized settings appears to be more frequent in the area of perception.

For the purposes of the assessment and evaluation of general or more specific abilities, the processes underlying perceptional abilities and attention have been defined as basic component processes, which might well contribute to observed performance differences on ability tests such as the NAT.

The NAT battery includes stimulus items that might not traditionally have been regarded as perceptual or attentional. However, they were chosen for inclusion on the basis of their relevance and strengths as measures of such component abilities as demonstrated in the research literature (for recent expositions see, for example, Geissler, Buffart, Leeuwenberg, and Sarris, 1983; and Requin, 1978).

CHAPTER 6

CONCEPTUAL TASKS

The study of conceptual skills is the study of how people think and learn. As noted previously, a prerequisite component of cognition is perception. Most (non-verbal) tasks eliciting conceptual skills are intended to reflect how an individual's knowledge of objects and concept is organized, or to show how he or she operates and organizes objects in space.

Brain-damaged individuals can be expected to display more confusion on these tests than on any other NAT subtests.

The nature, rationale, and diagnostic implications of seven of the NAT subtests are discussed in this chapter. This set of tests consists of:

Test 3:   Categorization
Test 4:   Picture Completion
Test 5:   Embedded Figures
Test 6:   Figure Formation
Test 7:   Mazes
Test 8:   Sequencing
Test 9:   Picture Arrangement

Test 3: Categorization

This test requires skills in classification and concept formation. The term classification as used in this context refers to the ability to recognize class identities and to use them in establishing logical relationships. The individual can sort stimuli on the basis of a unifying functional characteristic or abstract concept, and is able to recognize subclasses and common elements in class identity.

The most common form of a concept attainment task requires the individual to inspect a sequence of stimuli that differ in one or more dimensions.

In the Categorization Test, the testee is confronted with arrays of pictures, all but one of which belong to a particular class. One of the pictures belongs to a class that is mutually exclusive of the set or concept under which the other pictures can be categorized.

The requirement of this test to identify 'the odd one out', in other words to recognize which elements of the stimulus array 'belong together' and to mark the object that does not belong, is an expression of concept formation.

> Picking out the odd item... has a certain intrinsic fascination, and resembles operations known to primitives (e.g. picking out the odd animal from the herd). (Cattell, 1940, p.171)

Categorization and concept-formation activities provide the human being with information about positions and relationships of objects, events and other stimuli making up his or her everyday world. All perceptual input of which we are conscious involves concept formation, because a prerequisite to identifying anything is the ability to determine where it belongs in one's world. Each word used to label an object implies concept formation, mostly automatic.

> Consequently every thought process, the most simple and the most complicated, implies concept formation in the sense that our looking upon, and mode of discerning, thought processes is such that concept formation always appears to be one aspect of them. (Rapaport, Gill, and Schafer, 1970, p.99)

A first step towards solution of a task tends to be based on a concept based on one of the common features of the stimulus set. The conceptual content is then checked against other characteristics of the elements of the stimulus array to see whether it sufficiently excludes them.

> In the determination of the conceptual content of the group, interacting processes of induction and deduction have already taken place. The more homogeneous the group is at first glance—that is, the more familiar and stereotyped its conceptual content—the less consciously perceived these processes become. (Rapaport, Gill, and Schafer, 1970, p.199)

Categorization and concept-formation tests can tap at least three levels of conceptualization. Tests of the first level require the testee to consider stimuli as belonging together on the basis of concrete (often physical) attributes they have in common. The second level requires the grouping of stimuli as belonging together because of the function they share, or because of a common function performed with or on them by people. On the third level, the testee recognizes and expresses or visualizes the essential abstract-conceptual common content in generic terms.

The Categorization Test contained in the NAT battery lends itself to either the first or second level of conceptualization, or both. However, the opportunity for the examiner to identify which level of conceptualization has been reached in a particular task arises only in a situation in which the test can be administered individually, and in which the testee can be encouraged to verbalize his or her thoughts and/or actions during the task, or to answer questions. Such a methodology can provide an indication not only of whether the testee's concept formation is at a concrete, functional or abstract-conceptual level, but will also provide the examiner with an opportunity to assess how rigid and concrete (i.e. narrow), or how fluid, vague and overgeneralizing, the concept formation of a testee is.

> It has been suggested that categorization tests are built upon the assumption that intelligence may be conceived as a means whereby a person is able to deal with his partly unfamiliar present in terms of his better known past. This may be accomplished by an active organization and reorganization of past experience, as well as of the present situation. Hence a person's ability to provide *various* classifications of a given situation might be of crucial importance for his future problem solving behaviour. (Raaheim, Kaufman, and Bengtsson, 1980, p.119)

In other words an ability to classify and to categorize a given stimulus, event or situation requires flexibility, that is, the ability to conceive a stimulus and the relationship between stimuli in more than one way. Mental flexibility is probably a basic necessity for intelligent adjustment, that is, for mental adaptation to the stimulus situation.

According to Goldstein and Scheerer (1941) a characteristic of categorization and concept-formation behaviour is to grasp the essential characteristics of a given whole, to break up a given whole into relevant parts, and to synthesize the parts on the basis of the essential characteristics of the whole. The formation of a concept is thus the outcome of a preparatory, often trial-and-error, process of interchanging inductive and deductive steps, until a balance is reached in the actual content of the formed concept.

The Categorization subtest of the NAT contributes substantially to the 'g' factor. In the factor analysis of the data obtained on the total sample, 52 per cent of the variance in this subtest may be attributed to 'g'. The Categorization Test also contributes significantly to the conceptual factor. Across the entire age range the mean loading of this subtest on the 'g' factor was .62 (SD = .11).

Diagnostic Considerations

It is generally accepted that categorization skills are fundamental to the learning of such basic subjects as reading, spelling and arithmetic (Brainerd, 1978; Inhelder and Piaget, 1964; Weikard, Rogers, Adcock, and McClelland, 1971).

Categorization can be understood as the class counterpart of seriation. In other words, whereas seriation refers to one-dimensional ordering, classification refers to one-dimensional categorization.

Multiple relationships between elements of the situation or stimulus sets have to be recognized and co-ordinated in this type of task. Brain-damaged individuals display difficulties on reasoning tasks such as those included in the Categorization Test. They may cling to practical or technical details. There is a general tendency for brain-damaged individuals to restrict their attention to one or too few aspects of a problem or situation without seeing the correct interrelationships among the parts.

Emotional, motivational, and temporary or more lasting psychological factors can influence the performance of an individual on a test of concept formation. One of the most common examples of inability to complete the items occurs when subjects look for differences rather than for similarities in the pictures reflecting the concept. Adolescents and adults who are unable to understand what the task requires may be of low intellectual ability. Those who understand the task but refuse to comply show negativistic behaviour, the reasons and origins of which need to be further investigated. This behaviour usually manifests itself in the individual's insistence that there is not an 'odd one out', meaning that the majority of elements of the multiple choice response do not have anything in common. A common practice of examiners in such a situation has been to explain to the testee that asking to mark the item that does not belong implies that the other items form a group, that is, that similarities between them exist.

The inability to complete successfully easy concept-formation tasks is most widespread in schizophrenics and depressive psychotics. Normal individuals, even if highly anxious, neurotic, or severely depressed, show few if any failures on easy items.

Experience has shown that categorization and concept-formation skills are among the most frequently affected functions when the results of psychological maladjustment or more severe cognitive difficulties are beginning to exert an influence on intellectual activity and ability.

> Concept formation is one of the main channels through which maladjustment encroaches upon thinking, . . . and in it we may be able to discover early traces of impending maladjustment. (Rapaport, Gill, and Schafer, 1970, p.190)

In other words the effect of psychological maladjustment or damage on intellectual functioning can be discovered earlier in concept formation and categorization than in other aspects of thinking. While in verbal concept-formation tasks, such as the Wechsler Similarities tests, impairment can be disguised by verbal conventions (Wechsler, 1958), which is not possible in non-verbal tasks of the type contained in the NAT Categorization Test.

Rapaport et al., (1970) summarizes the rationale for both verbal and non-verbal tests of concept formation and categorization as follows:

> Concept formation is based on something that transcends formal information and formal logic. Since the item analysis shows that it is not a lack of information or of logic that is the basis of failures and low scores, . . . the examiner can with assurance conclude that, if failures occur, there is a disturbance of the automatic balance in thought processes that allows for good mobilization of attitudes summing up information and logic in an appropriate manner; and that maladjustment is encroaching upon concept formation. This is the true diagnostic significance of concept formation. (Rapaport et al., 1970, p.105)

Observed significant deficiencies in the performance on the NAT Categorization and other concept-formation tests can often be remediated, as the component skills are highly trainable. Depending on the age of the student the teacher may need to begin training by stressing common elements as well as differences on both the concrete and abstract levels. Physical manipulation should be encouraged at the lowest levels of developing concepts from concrete items.

Another version of the categorization task, suitable for younger children or intellectually handicapped persons who are unable to complete the items of the present test, can be created in a one-to-one situation. The testee is provided with a collection of objects (usually about 10 items or more), which belong to two mutually exclusive classes of objects, and is then asked to sort the objects into two categories. For example, toy animals and toy 'people' are presented, and the testee is asked to 'put the things together that go together'.

Component-categorization or concept-development skills that can be practised in the classroom include the comparison, sorting, and combination of objects. Such practice might be introduced in the following approximate order:

1. Identification of items that do not belong to a given set.
2. Identification of objects that are the same in some way.
3. Identification of objects that are the same in some given way.
4. Specification of particular characteristics by which objects are the same or different.
5. Sorting and re-sorting of items according to different criteria.
6. Resorting of sets after new objects have been added.

A useful strategy at a somewhat higher level is for the teacher to encourage students to make lists of similarities and differences, and to make sure that differences between essential and superficial component elements can be distinguished.

Class-inclusion problems can be practised. This involves the development of the ability to recognize subordinate categories of a given category, and the understanding that the elements of the subordinate category are always fewer than the elements of the category to which it belongs. This training will lead to the ability to group objects (and later subtract items) together to form hierarchical systems of categories. For example, roses and carnations can be grouped together under the category of flowers, flowers and trees belong to the category of plants, etc.

At all age levels remediation, namely, the demonstration of similarities, differences and relationships, must proceed from the testee's functional level, and then gradually move to higher levels of concept formation. Thinking in categories needs to be practised. Repetition is necessary to reinforce the learning of all concepts.

Test 4: Picture Completion

The NAT Picture Completion subtest provides a measure of the testee's ability to analyse visual stimulus patterns of varying complexity, to recognize familiar items and to determine missing components that are essential to the item.

> Ostensibly it measures the individual's basic perceptual and conceptual abilities in so far as these are involved in the visual recognition and identification of familiar objects and forms. To be able to see what is missing from any particular picture, the subject must first know what the picture represents. But, in addition, he must be able to appreciate that the missing part is in some way essential either to the form or to the function of the object or picture. (Wechsler, 1958, p.78)

Rapaport et al. (1970) have suggested that the picture-completion task is explicitly one of concentration. 'Judgment and knowledge for the most part do not enter these Picture Completion tasks' (Rapaport et al., 1970, p.121).

The development of the first picture-completion test is generally attributed to Healy (1914). This type of task, which has become generally accepted through its use in all Wechsler tests, was used earlier in this century not only by Binet, but also in the batteries put together by Knox (1914), Pintner and Patterson (1917), and in the Army Beta Test (Yoakum and Yerkes, 1920) and the Grace Arthur Test (Arthur, 1925, 1930).

Wechsler (1958) saw the major importance of his picture-completion tests as measures of the ability to distinguish essential from non-essential details. Reichard and Schafer (1943) saw the tests' major role in the measurement of concentration. Rapaport et al., 1970 emphasized the measurement of concentration by means of an evaluation of the individual's capacity to appraise relationships, and Zimmerman, Woo-Sam, and Glasser, 1973 suggested that the test reflected, above all, accuracy of perception of reality.

Cohen (1952) found the Wechsler picture-completion test to be a subtest that did not reflect a single factor, but measured verbal and non-verbal factors simultaneously. Saunders (1960) suggested that picture completion is composed of three factors, namely, contact with reality, maintenance of perspective, and effect of uncertainty.

In addition to visual altertness, memory, attention to detail, and reasoning, the task requires the ability to recognize a gestalt, to separate essential and non-essential parts from the whole, and other basic perceptual and conceptual abilities.

The task demands virtually no visuo-motor activity; rather, the testee is required to compare a visual pattern with a concept, not with other visual patterns. To do this requires the use of memories of past experience of similar objects.

Performance on picture-completion tasks reflects to a considerable degree attention paid to the environment, and correlates highly with performance on such tasks as map reading, art work, the monitoring of signals and other activities requiring close attention to, and concentration on, detail.

Factor analytic results showed that the NAT Picture Completion subtest makes a significant contribution to the 'g' factor. In the overall analysis 48 per cent of the total variance in this subtest was shown to be attributable to 'g'. In the age-specific analyses the mean loading of the Picture Completion subtest on the 'g' factor was .66 (SD = .09).

Diagnostic Considerations

The Picture Completion subtest tends to be perceived as a non-threatening test. In fact, it can provide relaxation from tension in the testing situation. Many testees enjoy participating in picture-completion activity.

Woo-Sam, Zimmerman, and Rogal (1971) suggested that picture-completion tests are relatively insensitive to brain damage. Wechsler (1958) suggested that the task was particularly useful for the assessment of intellectual functioning at lower levels of educational achievement.

Low scores on the test may be due to lack of attention to detail, inattention to the environment, faulty previous learning, anxiety, negativism, etc. or to a lack of familiarity with the material (rare in our civilization). Defective vision can obviously be a major cause of low performance on a picture-completion task. Most frequently, however, low performance on this test would reflect the testee's inability to distinguish between essential and non-essential components of the stimulus or situation.

When administered in a one-to-one situation picture-completion tasks may also reflect personality traits (e.g. Glasser and Zimmerman, 1967). These authors suggest that finding fault with oneself for not finding missing parts may indicate a guilt-ridden and self-directed orientation. Finding fault with the item, that is, the picture, may indicate projection of blame or other-directedness.

Enriched exposure to the environment, encounter with selected television programs, and the focusing of the testee's attention on functional versus peripheral components of objects, events and situations, will help to raise the level of performance on picture-completion tasks. Lack of concentration will depress scores on this test.

Test 5: Embedded Figures

The identification of embedded, or hidden, figures has become well established as a means of identifying differences in a variety of cognitive and non-cognitive components of human functioning. Embedded-figures tests require the testee to identify a component element in a more complex visual array.

The NAT Embedded Figures Test consists of 22 items. In each item a simple stimulus figure is presented, which the testee is asked to locate within each of three different complex figures. In other words, in the complex figures the testee is presented with a simple geometric design, which is contained within a more complex, organized field. 'What is at issue is the extent to which the surrounding visual framework dominates perception of the figure within it' (Witkin, Moore, Goodenough, and Cox, 1977, p.6).

The test attempts to quantify the extent to which the surrounding organized field has influenced the testee's perception of the stimulus figure embedded within it.

The test measures a construct that has been given a variety of labels. Best known are 'cognitive style', and field-dependence.

> The common denominator underlying individual differences in performance [in the various items] is the extent to which the person perceives part of a field as discrete from the surrounding field as a whole, rather than that embedded in the field; or the extent to which the organization of the prevailing field determines perception of its components; or, to put it in every day terminology, the extent to which the person perceives analytically. (Witkin, Moore, Goodenough, and Cox, 1977, p.7)

The last term above refers to the fact that an organized field might have to be 'broken up', that is, analysed, so that the sought-after stimulus figure can be identified. Thus, analysis is an essential component in the solving of any embedded-figure task.

Because at one extreme of the range of performance perception is strongly dominated by the surrounding field (i.e. the organization of the complex figure), that style of perception came to be known as field-dependent. At the other extreme, where the testee experiences component parts of the complex field as relatively separate elements (i.e. where the sought-after stimulus figure appears to 'stand out' from the surrounding field), the term field-independent is used.

Obviously, this does not imply two distinct types of persons. The scores from any test of field-dependence are assumed to form a continuous distribution. The labels, field-dependence and field-independence, therefore reflect tendencies of varying strength, on the part of the testee towards one habitual or preferred style, or the other.

Individual differences in the detection of embedded figures are marked. For some persons, namely, those extremely field-independent, the stimulus figure sought emerges quickly from the complex design, while individuals at the other extreme, namely persons extremely field-dependent, may not be able to identify the stimulus within the time allowed for search.

Embedded-figure tests are essentially adaptations of the figures of Gottschaldt (1926), which appeared first in Thurstone's early work on perceptual abilities, where this type of test was used as a principal measure of the primary ability of 'flexibility of closure', (Thurstone, 1944).

Thurstone (1949) suggested that the two closure factors, 'speed of closure' and 'flexibility of closure', identified by him in several studies may describe component skills required for the solving of complex tasks. He viewed his speed of closure factor as facilitating the accomplishment of closure in an unorganized field. The flexibility of closure factor referred to the retention of a particular configuration in a distracting field. Both factors have been validated through frequent replication in the literature (e.g. Cattell, 1971; Ekstrom, French, and Harman, 1976; Frederiksen, 1965; French, Ekstrom, and Price, 1963; Hettema, 1968; Messick and French, 1975; Royce, 1973).

Thurstone's model, supported by the research noted above, and other studies, proposes that speed of closure determines the ease with which the testee can separate the stimulus figure from its complex surrounds, while flexibility of closure determines the ease with which he or she can keep the stimulus in mind against distraction. Thurstone's

> first closure factor might be associated with inductive thinking, whereas the second closure factor might be more associated with deductive thinking. (Smith, 1964, p.195)

To increase the likelihood of including the characteristics inherent in both factors in the NAT Hidden Figures Test, the test was designed in such a way that the subject is required to identify the stimulus in three different fields. Only if the stimulus figure has been found in all three complex fields has the item been completed satisfactorily.

Much of the literature has shown that the two factors, flexibility of closure, and speed of closure, tend to combine in more complex perceptual, and in conceptual, tasks (Cattell, 1971; Ekstrom, French, and Harman, 1979). Both constructs have been related to a number of other component abilities, particularly to field-independence and field dependence. The work on the latter constructs by Witkin and his colleagues has generated widespread interest and research. Witkin's earlier work, based on rod and frame tests, stressed the contrast between the subjects' utilization of physical orientation cues relating to the vertical (which, according to his theory, depend on immediate visual perception), and internal proprioceptive cues. Extreme reliance on the former was found to be related to relatively passive and undifferentiated reactions, while the tendency to rely on the latter was interpreted as reflecting more active coping reactions, and an analytic approach towards the environment.

It has been observed that relatively field-dependent persons have a tendency to adhere to the organization of the field as presented. They are likely to resist any restructuring of the field. Field-independent persons are likely to overcome the dominant organization of the field, or situation, and to adapt it to the needs of the task and/or moment.

High correlations have been found between performance on visual embedded-figure tasks and such tasks in the tactile and auditory sense modality. Field-dependent and field-independent styles of information processing have been identified also in persons who were blind or deaf from birth (Fiebert, 1967; Witkin and Oltman, 1968).

As research evidence accumulated, it was shown that these cognitive styles, first identified in perception, in fact manifest themselves also when the individual is dealing with symbolic representations such as thinking and problem solving. It has been found that the person who finds it difficult to perceive an item, object, idea, etc. as separate from the surrounding field, that is, a relatively field-dependent person, is likely to experience difficulties of a similar kind in problem solving, where the solution requires a restructuring of the task, for example the removal of some critical component from the context in which it is presented, and its utilization in another context.

> When it appeared that nonproprioceptive tests such as EFT or Kohs Blocks were good measures of independence, also that differentiation could be demonstrated in problem-solving, memorization, etc., the emphasis shifted to Werner's (1940) theory of development from primitive-global to analytic-differentiated functioning. (Vernon, 1972, p.370)

The concept of a global-analytical continuum of cognitive style can be described as follows: Persons whose scores place them at the field-dependent extreme of the continuum show a tendency to experience an organized field or configuration as given, and to allow it, consciously or unconsciously, to dictate the manner in which that field and its components are perceived and used. When the field is highly structured this leads to difficulty in processing its parts as discrete entities. When the configuration lacks structure, perception of it tends to be global and diffuse. At the extreme of field-independence, there is a tendency for perception to be co-ordinated, even if the field lacks inherent organization and structure.

Witkin et al. (1971) applied the labels 'global' and 'articulated' to these extremes. In his writings Witkin points out considerable similarities between field-dependence/independence, and such constructs as the flexibility dimension of Guilford (1952, 1957), and the flexibility of closure dimension first established by Thurstone (1944).

Basically, what is being measured is the extent to which a person can overcome a restricting context.

> This ability, when developed, makes possible an analytical way of experiencing, and thus an analytical way of dealing with stimuli, whether immediately present in the individual's environment, or represented symbolically. (Witkin et al., 1971, p.3)

During the past 40 years, the use of embedded figures as test stimuli in research and psychological practice concerned with cognitive and non-cognitive behaviour has increased greatly.

In an early example of non-cognitive research with embedded figures, Pemberton (1952) showed that individuals who excelled in flexibility of closure had high ratings on such variables as self sufficiency, independence of the opinion of others, interest in scientific problem and theory, dislike of rigid systematization and routine, etc.

By now, the literature contains a great diversity of studies on field-dependence/independence. The topic areas that have been investigated range from learning and memory (e.g. Goodenough, 1976; Robinson and Gray, 1974), mathematics achievement (e.g Bien, 1974; Buriel, 1978; Vaidya and Chansky, 1980), reading, (e.g Buriel, 1978; Denny, 1974; Eakin and Douglas, 1971; Kagan, 1965; Robinson and Gray, 1974; Santostefano and Paley, 1964), to interpersonal relations (e.g. Witkin and Goodenough, 1977), leadership (e.g. Weissenberg and Gruenfeld, 1966), social conformity (e.g. Witkin, Dyk, Faterson, Goodenough, and Karp, 1962/1974), and cross-cultural differences (e.g. Berry, 1976; Buriel, 1978; Witkin, 1967; Witkin and Berry, 1975).

Individual differences in field-dependence/independence, and in style of cognitive structuring and restructuring have been found at all age levels (Witkin and Goodenough, 1981), beginning as early as kindergarten (Coates, 1974; Coates, Lord, and Jakobovics, 1975). According to Witkin and Goodenough, 'Children who develop rapidly towards field-independence develop greater competence in cognitive structuring' (1981, p.66).

Witkin, Goodenough, and Karp (1967) produced developmental curves for embedded-figure tasks in a sample ranging in age from 8 years to 24 years and showed a marked, continuous increase in field-independence between the ages of 8 years and 15 years. A slowing down of growth was shown with increasing age. After the age of 15 the developmental curves tended to level off. They produced a plateau during early adulthood.

Data obtained from groups of elderly people (e.g. Comalli, 1965; Schwartz and Karp, 1967) indicate a definite tendency to return to greater field-dependence with increasing age. Witkin et al. (1971) suggests that at some point between the age of 24 years and old age, most probably in the late 30s, a process of increasing field-dependence begins.

Concerning cognitive structuring and restructuring, the literature contains a considerable number of studies showing pronounced sex differences in spatial visualization ability (Maccoby and Jacklin, 1974), one of the important component abilities of cognitive structuring. With very young children these differences are in favour of girls (Coates, 1974). During adolescence, a reversal of this effect is observed. Male high school students tend to be less field-dependent than their female peers (Maccoby and Jacklin, 1974). Distinct increases in field-independence are generally observed in students up to year 11 (Wolf, 1971). The overall developmental trends in this ability are difficult to interpret, mainly because of the rapid development of disembedding skills, which are part of human development from kindergarten age to adult. Also, this has led to the use of different tests, which often makes comparison between studies difficult or impossible (Snow and Lohman, 1981). Witkin and Goodenough (1981) summarized the issue as follows:

> On the individually administered EFT [embedded figure test], mean scores typically tend to be higher for men than for women, but sex differences are very small for group forms of the test, and usually significant only for very large samples. . .
>
> In view of the variation in results among tests with adults, and the use of different tests for different age groups, it is difficult to draw any definite conclusions about trends in the development of sex differences in disembedding abilities. (Witkin and Goodenough, 1981, p.67)

A number of studies have found small but repeated sex differences in field-dependence/independence among adults. Some of these differences were observed among young adults, with the young women being more field-dependent than their male peers. However, Witkin et al. (1977) stressed that the mean performance differences between the sexes were quite small in comparison with the variability of scores within each sex group. Statistically, the distributions for men and women show considerable overlap. No significant differences between males and females were obtained in the Australian samples during the development of the NAT Embedded Figures Test.

It is most likely that sex differences, where they can be substantiated, have resulted from differences in the child-rearing methods, training and socialization in general, undergone by boys and girls. Further support for such an explanation is provided by the results of cross-cultural studies, which showed sex differences in field-dependence/independence to be

> uncommon in mobile hunting societies and prevalent in sedentary, agricultural societies—societies which are characteristically different in sex-role training and in the value attached to women's roles in the economy. (Witkin et al., 1977, p.7)

Child rearing practices, training and life experience are likely to play a very important role in the development of many cognitive and non-cognitive dimensions of human personality. Explanations of developmental changes, and reasons for sex and individual differences in field-dependence/independence and other human characteristics, have also been sought in biological and ecological factors.

Many studies have indicated that field-dependence/independence is likely to be a relatively stable, reliable factor throughout childhood and early adolescence, and that there is some consistency in this characteristic in adults even over years (e.g. Bauman, 1951; Faterson and Witkin, 1970; Witkin, Goodenough, and Karp, 1967).

Vernon's (1972) study showed that a major proportion of the reliable variance on the test is accounted for by a general fluid intelligence factor, with field-independence reflecting fluid analytic ability. Boersma, Muir, Wilton, and Rarnahm (1969) found a strong relationship between field-independence and motor sensitivities, and with such personality variables as the development of a sense of separate identity, the development of social skills, and even with career choice. There is some evidence that field-dependence might increase with age (Panek, Barrett, Sterns, and Alexander, 1978; Sims, Graves, and Simpson, 1983).

As more research is accumulating, field-dependence/independence is being more widely regarded as an important dimension of personality. It is most frequently regarded as the component of psychological functioning that describes 'global versus articulated cognitive style' (Anastasi, 1982, p.549), or differentiation in cognitive behaviour more generally (Goldstein and Blackman, 1978a, 1978b; Witkin, Dyk, Faterson, Goodenough, and Karp, 1974).

> In interpersonal situations... the field-dependent tend to have certain advantages in getting along with others. They tend to be more attentive to social cues, more responsive to other persons' behavior, and more emotionally open than are field-independent persons. (Anastasi, 1982, p.595)

Studies focusing on cognitive variables, excluding personality dimensions, tend to suggest that field-independent individuals display greater intellectual curiosity and mental flexibility, and prefer inquiry learning and other active-participant approaches to learning, while field-dependent persons tend to 'sit back'. The latter prefer the material to be presented to them in easily accessible form, and 'they often use "spectator" approaches' (Anastasi, 1982, p.595).

In factor analytic studies 'flexibility of closure' and factors of similar content were repeatedly found to be loading on variables that might be interpreted as reflecting 'analytical problem solving strategies' (e.g. Botzum, 1951; Cattell, 1971; Ippel and Bouma, 1981; Messick and French, 1975; Pemberton, 1952). Witkin and his co-workers based their conception of an 'articulated-global continuum' of individual differences on such factor analytic evidence, which they believed to be linking structuring tendencies to analytical tendencies of the kind involved in field-dependence/independence measures.

> From such evidence it became clear that we were dealing with a broad dimension of individual differences that extends across both perceptual and intellectual activities. Because what is at issue is the characteristic approach the person brings with him to a wide range of situations—we called it his 'style'—because the approach encompasses both his perceptual and intellectual activities—we spoke of it as his 'cognitive' style. (Witkin et al., 1977, p.10)

Vaidya and Chansky (1980), noted that

> a field-independent cognitive style is characterised by an analytic approach to a situation, consisting of the ability to overcome an embedding context while transcending the salient features. In contrast, a field-dependent cognitive style is global. It is determined by the prevailing field or context of a situation. (p.326)

The Embedded Figures subtest of the NAT was found to be among the best measures of 'g' in the NAT battery. As in the case of the Categorization Test, 52 per cent of the total variance in the Embedded Figures Test was shown to be accountable in terms of the 'g' factor. Across specific age groups the mean loading of the Embedded Figures Test on 'g' was .59 (SD = .07).

Diagnostic Considerations

The authors mentioned above, and others (e.g. Bien, 1974; Buriel, 1978), found that a field-independent cognitive style is related to mathematics achievement at all grade levels, especially in the area of the acquisition of mathematical concepts. They argue that field-independence is likely to influence achievement in mathematics because the ability to think analytically required in both areas involves perceptual and conceptual disembedding, and the development of problem-solving strategies that depend on reorganizing and restructuring information.

Wolf (1971) found field-independence to be closely related to the intellectual factors of divergent thinking and cognitive fluency.

As noted previously, similar relationships have been postulated between cognitive style, learning to read, and concept learning and other non-mathematical areas (e.g. Buriel, 1978; Cohen, 1969; Denny, 1974; Robinson and Gray, 1974; and others). For example, children who are in the early stages of learning to read, particularly when phonemic methods of instruction are used, must visually identify discrete vowels and syllables within a larger, more complex word. These children are thus required to perceptually, and conceptually, break up a complex stimulus field into its various component elements, often to arrive at new relations between the components of the field.

These findings have obviously important educational implications. They emphasize the importance of adapting instructional procedures to the cognitive style of individual learners. Witkin, Moore, Goodenough, and Cox, (1977) suggested that a matching of teacher and student in cognitive style is more likely to result in effective teaching, and a better interpersonal relationship between the two, than would mismatching of cognitive styles. The present author doubts whether a match of preferred cognitive style of the teacher with the style of the student is necessary for effective teaching and learning. Rather, it is suggested that those teachers who know how individual differences in cognitive style can affect learning, and who make every effort to identify cognitive styles in their students, will be able to adjust teaching programs to the needs of individuals.

Cohen (1969), focusing on analytical and relational cognitive styles, showed research evidence of the bias and incompatibility that can result from field-dependent ideology and the encouragement, or at least tacit reinforcement of particular learning styles.

> So discrepant are the analytic and relational frames of reference that a pupil whose preferred mode of cognitive organisation is emphatically relational is unlikely to be rewarded in the school setting either socially or by grades, regardless of his native abilities and even if his information repertoire and background of experience are adequate. (Cohen, 1969, p.830)

Brain-injured adults have great difficulty in locating embedded stimuli, and with similar perceptual and conceptual tasks characterized by figure– ground instabilities (Golden, 1978; Luria, 1973; Smith, 1964; Strauss and Werner, 1942). However, as noted before, it must be remembered that almost all studies in this area have found considerable overlap in the statistical distributions of the scores of brain-damaged and control subjects (e.g. Golden, Osmon, Moses, and Berg, 1981; Smith, 1964; Werner and Strauss, 1941).

In summary, it can be noted that the field-dependence/independence concept has generated a great deal of research and has found widespread interest and practical application 'because it seems to provide new and far reaching dimensions of cognition' (Vernon, 1972). What is measured by the Embedded Figures Test, apart from field-dependence/independence, involves many other, widely accepted, parameters of human functioning. In the cognitive domain these include 'g'-type general ability, and creativity (Wolf, 1971); spatial ability (Smith, 1964) flexibility and speed of closure and adaptive flexibility (Guilford, 1967, 1982).

The essential features of the cognitive variables being measured by this test can be summarized as follows:

1   The test measures important component dimensions of what tends to be referred to broadly as general intelligence.

2   What is being measured characterizes the process rather than the outcome of cognitive activity and performance. The test helps to assess and describe individual differences with respect to the question 'How do persons perceive, solve problems, learn, relate to others, etc?'

3   What is being measured can embrace both cognitive and non-cognitive dimensions of psychological functioning, and interactions between both.

4   What is being measured has been found to be relatively stable over time. This does not mean, however, that it cannot be altered through guidance, counselling and training. In fact, some characteristics of cognitive style may be altered easily through appropriate intervention procedures (e.g. Witkin et al., 1977).

5   The results of this test cannot be interpreted in a 'go-no-go', field-dependent versus field-independent category fashion. As with other perceptual and cognitive abilities, there is no implication that people might fall into two distinct groups, for example global versus analytical thinkers. It will be found that scores on the Embedded Figures Test obtained from any reasonably sized group of subjects will distribute the scores of individuals along a continuum.

Test 6: Figure Formation

This subtest of the NAT samples the ability to perceive and analyse shapes and patterns into their component parts, and then to identify the component parts that produce the target shape or pattern. This process is generally referred to as analysis and synthesis.

The task combines visual organization with the comprehension of the structural components of the stimulus, their interrelationship, and memory. In addition to analysis and synthesis, logic, reasoning, planning and non-verbal organization have to be applied in this test of spatial relationships. Figure Formation could thus be conceived as a non-verbal concept-formation task.

Successful performance on this test is largely dependent on the individual's ability to perceive a gestalt, and to analyse it into its component parts. Spatial analysis, logic and reasoning, that is, abstract thinking, are also involved. The individual must be able to visualize the relationship of fragments of the stimulus to the whole. Another component process in the Figure Formation Test is probably visual closure. In some instances testees are unable to visualize the relationship of parts of the stimulus when they are presented in separation.

Concentration, the ability to persist, creativity and flexibility, that is, the ability to change direction, are further important determinants of successful performance on this task.

Traditionally, the best known task of this type used in individual intelligence tests has been the Block Design task. First conceived by Healy and Fenald (1911), its use was increased by Kohs (1920). Block Design subtests were part of the early scales put together by Knox (1914), and Pintner and Patterson (1917); they were part of the Army Beta Test (Yoakum and Yerkes, 1920) and the Grace Arthur Test (Arthur, 1925, 1930), and were used by Cornell and Coxe (1934). Block Design is a subtest of the Binet and of all Wechsler intelligence scales.

Because of the abstract nature of the stimuli making up the NAT Figure Formation Test, performance on this subtest is not directly related to past experience. This makes it possible for figure formation to provide an indication of the testee's logical thinking processes that is not contaminated by the influence of past educational and cultural experiences.

The Figure Formation subtest is the best measure of 'g' among the NAT subtests. The results of the analyses of the performance data obtained on the total sample showed that 72 per cent of the total variance in the performance on this test can be attributed to 'g'. In age-specific analyses the test also contributed substantially to the 'g' factor, with a mean loading of .75.

Diagnostic Considerations

Because of its high loading on 'g' the Figure Formation Test is one of the most valuable subtests of the NAT battery. It can be an indicator of high mental ability that is not contaminated by previous learning and experience, or by other environmental influences.

Performance on the Figure Formation Test can provide a reasonable estimate of the intellectual potential of a person with language or verbal handicap.

Scores obtained on the test need to be carefully evaluated in the light of the testee's current educational achievement, perceptual organization, and educational potential.

Brain-damaged and some very elderly persons have particular difficulty with this type of task. They often cannot cope with the practice examples even after assistance has been given. The difficulties of these individuals appear to be the result of a lack or deterioration in the ability to synthesize information.

They tend to display a deficit or loss of 'abstract ability' in the Goldstein and Scheerer (1941) sense of the term.

In elderly people the inability to perform figure-formation tasks could be the result of a loss in the ability to shift attention. Brain-damaged individuals also tend to lose flexibility in thinking, and may lack the concentration required for this task.

Some individuals have difficulty in attending simultaneously to the whole stimulus and to fragmented parts of it. Others get stuck on certain elements of the array of possible responses, apparently unable to relate them to other parts or to integrate them into the target pattern.

High scores on the Figure Formation Test may be a reflection of well developed skills of perceptual organization, the ability to analyse and synthesize, and/or an ability to adapt quickly to new tasks.

Low scores may be the result of poor visual acuity, poor perceptual skills (including figure/ground disturbance), lack of concentration, distractibility, lack of motivation, anxiety, emotional problems, lack of mental flexibility and creativity, or low cognitive ability.

Remedial activities might include jig-saw puzzles, cutting and pasting, and the taking apart of objects and their reconstruction from parts. Initially, the teacher might do well to stress the relationships between parts and the whole of familiar objects, and then to move on to more abstract stimuli. The most important training task is aimed at making the individual aware of the relationship between shape, size, and spatial arrangement of parts and the whole.

Test 7: Mazes

This test combines perceptual–spatial activity with conceptual (i.e. anticipation, comprehension, reasoning and planning) and motor responses. How strong the conceptual or reasoning component of this test is dependent on the approach taken by the testee to the stimulus requirements, and on the strategies he or she uses in trying to complete the task.

Test items are usually constructed with the assumption that to perform them requires certain cognitive skills. Obviously, the appropriateness of a test as a measure of cognitive ability is limited by the extent to which it addresses the cognitive skills it purports to measure.

In most testing situations, and for that matter in most psychological experiments, a tacit assumption tends to be made that all subjects presented with a particular task will solve that task in much the same manner.

> Idiosyncratic variations in solution strategy are covered—or perhaps obscured—by the error of measurement blanket, even though data averaged over subjects may not represent the performance of all or even any of the subjects in the sample. (Lohman and Kyllonen, 1983, p.108)

Variations in solution strategy rather than being unwanted experimental noise could be a manifestation of individual differences in adaptation to the task requirements, in other words one of the central features of intelligent performance. Research has shown (e.g. Cooper, 1980; Hunt and McLeod, 1979; Kail, Carter, and Pellegrino, 1979; Rowe, 1985a; Snow, 1980; Sternberg, 1977) that important differences in solution strategy can be observed both between problem solvers and within problem solvers over tasks. Often, tests measure different abilities for different testees, depending on how the latter solve the test items. Solution strategy is a function of both the individual and the task.

Irrespective of the approach and strategies used by testees, maze tests are sensitive measures of at least visual attention, spatial organization, motor co-ordination and motor integration.

At the lowest level the NAT mazes consist of trail-marking tasks. They measure visual–spatial scanning ability and motor sequencing skills. Also involved are visual–motor co-ordination, a steady hand, the ability to be flexible in switching between patterns, and sustained attention to the task.

At a higher level of cognitive processing mazes require comprehension, planning, and reasoning skills. As summarized by Glasser and Zimmerman (1967):

> Mazes call first for planning and insight, for attention to instructions such as the request not to lift the pencil, for pencil control and hence visual motor co-ordination, and for speed combined with accuracy. (p.102)

At this level of operation the maze is perceived as a whole, and a solution plan is prepared before the task is begun. Trial and error activity is seldom observed in testees who use such strategies.

The completion of a maze as a psychological test was conceived by Porteus, who first publicized the usefulness of the task at a meeting of the British Association for the Advancement of Science in Melbourne in August 1914. Because the content of the task is essentially culture-free, mazes have been used extensively with cross-cultural groups in both the study of perception and the attempted measurement of intelligence (e.g. MacArthur, 1967; Vernon, 1969, 1982), and in general research (e.g. Ibarrola, 1951; MacCrone 1928; Nissen, Machover, and Kinder, 1935).

The results of early studies have been summarized by Porteus himself (1965), and Porteus and Gregor (1963). David (1974) also provided a historical review.

Porteus (1937) used his mazes in what was probably the earliest study of the perception of African bush dwellers. Jahoda (1969) used Elithorn's (1955) perceptual maze test in Ghana. Porteus's mazes have been used with Australian aborigines (e.g. David, 1967, 1974; Dawson, 1973; Gregor and McPherson, 1963; Pichot, 1967).

The literature contains surprisingly little information concerning preferred structures for maze tests. Apart from the suggestion that the pattern has to be such that it can be perceived as a whole, rather than having to be completed merely by trial and error, and that the performance can be scored equally well on the basis of either errors or time taken, no adequate research that included recommendations for the best design of mazes for testing or experimental purposes could be found.

Two special features were included in the NAT mazes. One, the mazes were designed to be centred from either direction, so that left-handed testees are not disadvantaged. Two, some alternative paths were placed early, to force the testee to consider the maze as a whole.

Factor analytic investigations of the NAT showed that performance on mazes is a less effective measure of 'g' than performance on the other conceptual subtests. In the overall analysis only 21 per cent of the total variance of performance on mazes could be explained by the 'g' factor. The mean loading of this test on 'g' factors in the age-specific analyses was .48 (SD = .09), with a tendency for loadings to increase with age.

In the factor analysis of the data collected on the total sample, mazes contributed substantially to the conceptual factor. In the age-specific analyses the Mazes Test's strongest contribution varied between the conceptual and an attention (speed and accuracy) factor.

In the literature, too, (e.g. Cohen, 1959; Sattler, 1982; Wechsler, 1974) maze tests have not always shown as high a correlation with 'g' as other subtests included in intelligence scales. However, as acknowledged by Porteus (1937), Wechsler (1958) and others, maze tasks are 'intriguing to primitive as to civilized people, and can therefore act as a good "shock absorber" before the more artifical test forms' (Cattell, 1940, p.169).

In the trial testing of the NAT battery, the Mazes subtest was found to be one of the most non-threatening of the tasks administered. Testees of all ages enjoyed the activity, and their relaxation during the task was obvious. Because of this the decision was made to administer the test as a 'shock absorber' before some of the most difficult conceptual tests included in the battery, and roughly in the middle of the total testing session.

Diagnostic Considerations

The demands placed on the individual by this test can be summarized in two groups as follows:
- Attention to the directions, which includes the requirements of locating a route from entry to exit, avoiding blind alleys, crossing no lines, and maintaining the pencil on the paper throughout the task.
- Execution of the task, which involves, apart from self-control, remembering and following the directions, maintaining adequate visual–motor co-ordination and small muscle control; the ability to size up and comprehend the total situation, planning, and resisting the disruptive effects of an implied need for speed.

While performance on mazes is not a direct measure of visual–motor co-ordination or perceptual development, poor performance on the task may reflect deficits in such areas, especially if the latter are also suggested by the scores obtained on other NAT subtests.

High scores on mazes may suggest good visual–motor co-ordination, while low scores may lead to hypotheses such as low visual–motor co-ordination, impulsiveness, lack of planning, etc. As the test is a measure of planning and foresight, scores obtained on it together with those obtained on Tests 6 (Figure Formation), 8 (Sequencing), and 9 (Picture Arrangement) can provide an estimate of the individual's planning ability.

The mazes in the NAT were designed in such a way that a normal individual should make few, if any errors. The inability to remain within the boundaries of the stimulus pattern and an inability to perceive the paths to be traced must be regarded as highly abnormal. Because of this, evidence of repeated failure on this test can be interpreted as a strong indication of visual, visual–perceptual, visual–motor, motor, or conceptual impairment. The test is sensitive to both organic and emotional disorders.

Maze tests have been used to discriminate brain-injured individuals from psychiatric patients at approximately 70 per cent effectiveness (Golden, 1978; Golden, Osmon, Moses, and Berg, 1981; Goldstein and Neuringer, 1966). Qualitatively, psychiatric patients are likely to exhibit bizarre patterns of performance (e.g. Goldstein and Neuringer, 1966). Where motivation and co-operation can be taken for granted, maze tests can provide highly accurate discrimination between brain-damaged and psychiatric individuals.

However, as noted above, it must be remembered that difficulties on this test may be related purely to deficiencies in the organization or execution of the hand movements needed to cope with the response mode. This consideration is particularly important when the test is administered to elderly, motor-impaired, highly neurotic, or very anxious persons.

Although the activity of completing mazes appears to have only marginal, if any, direct educational significance, some aspects of performance on maze tests are related to learning and educational achievement. Attention, concentration, sequencing, and all the other functions involved in this task, have direct applications in the classroom and other situations involving intellectual activity.

Test 8: Sequencing and Test 9: Picture Arrangement

Tests 8 and 9 share a rationale, and interpretations of performance on them exhibit more communalities than differences. For this reason, discussion of both tests has been combined in this section. Differences between the tests are highlighted where appropriate.

The stimuli contained in Test 8, Sequencing, are pictures of single items and symbols out of which a hierarchical series has to be produced. Test 9, Picture Arrangement, requires the sequential ordering of pictures depicting elements of social situations.

Both tests examine the testee's ability to think of a theme or concept, that is, a rule, that serves to combine and unify several pictures or abstract stimuli; and then to sequence the stimuli in the order that depicts the theme logically and correctly with respect to the given response alternatives. The response requirements for this task are thus psychologically highly complex.

Visual analysis and organization, attention, the distinction between essential and peripheral aspects of the stimulus, planning and anticipation, concept identification, comprehension, memory, reasoning, rule induction, sequencing and judgment enter into the performance of both tests.

Although concentration is a prerequisite for all cognitive achievement, the complicated task requirements may cloud its importance in the performance of Tests 8 and 9. Thus, these tests cannot serve as measures of concentration. Special efforts to concentrate during performance on these tasks are usually necessary only in cases where motivation is lacking, or where the testee is unable to comprehend the meaningfulness of the stimulus elements, that is, when salient and peripheral features of the stimulus are perceived as of the same importance. Given sufficient motivation on the part of the testee, the latter situation can be expected to lead to an 'effortful selective search for meaning' (Rapaport et al., 1970, p.129), which would obviously require considerable concentration.

The planning requirement of the sequencing and picture arrangement tasks implies involvement of both attention and judgment. Attention provides the means for the testee to convey to himself or herself the essential features and characteristics of the individual stimulus pictures, and differences between them.

The identification of essential features, anticipation, the formation of hypotheses, etc., are all based on judgment. However, the sequencing aspect of task requirements in these tests is considerably more complex than that of judgment. Sequencing implies an additional *temporal* perspective of judgment and other component abilities.

In addition to the response requirements shared with Test 8, Test 9, Picture Arrangement, requires the awareness and comprehension of a social situation, social planning, the ability to anticipate in social and environmental settings, and a certain amount of humour.

The rationale and method used in the design of the Picture Arrangement Test is very similar to those of the Wechsler tests, which are, however, individually and verbally administered tests. In the latter tests the testee is handed a set of individual pictures, in random sequence, which he or she is required to lay out in a sequence 'making a meaningful story'. The Wechsler picture completion tasks thus allow for trial and error activity, for direct visual comparison between various sequences, and for alterations in all or part of any sequence.

The NAT Picture Arrangement and Sequencing Tests require greater reliance on memory and a stronger capacity for abstract reasoning than the Wechsler picture arrangement tasks do.

The role of planning ability and anticipation can be expected to differ between Tests

8 and 9. There is no doubt that there are differences in planning and anticipation requirements between arranging a series of symbols or relatively abstract single stimuli, and arranging a series of pictures into story sequence of logical events. The latter (i.e. performance on the Picture Arrangement Test) requires an understanding of social situations, and is thus likely to be more highly correlated with planning and anticipation in real life than performance on the Sequencing Test.

Factor analytic studies have also shown that the central structural cognitive component of sequencing tasks is rule induction (e.g. Cattell, 1971; Ekstrom, 1973; Guilford, 1967; Thurstone, 1940). Thurstone and Thurstone (1941a, 1941b) went as far as to suggest that rule induction, as a second-order factor, may well be identical to Spearman's 'g'.

This factor analytic research has been complemented more recently by efforts aimed at identifying the cognitive underpinning of rule induction within frameworks of information processing (e.g. Pellegrino and Glaser, 1980, 1982; Sternberg, 1977; Whitely, 1976).

Viewed from an information-processing perspective, the most likely methods for use in the solution of a sequencing task are: generate and test hypotheses methods, heuristic search methods, and induction methods (Newell, 1963, 1973).

While these three types of methods may differ with respect to their underlying theoretical models of the paths of information flow between components, they agree with respect to a number of broad processes. These include the following.

1   *The detection of relationships*, which involves a scanning of the elements making up the potential series, and the formation of hypotheses as to how one element of the set of stimuli might be related to others.

Only three relationships are required to place a particular element of a sequence into context, namely, focus element, next forward, and next backward. However, the problem is that the elements of sequencing tasks normally exhibit a considerable variety of characteristics on the basis of which such relations could be established. The second basic component of such a task is therefore the following.

2   *The identification of a dimension or scheme* that can provide a basis for classification and ordering.

3   The third, and most complex component of sequencing tasks involves *the identification of hierarchical relations*. This, again, requires the establishment, comparison and evaluation of a number of hypotheses.

4   All sequencing tasks rely heavily on *memory*. The major general components of sequencing ability have been listed in order of increasing requirements of short-term memory availability.

Simon (1972) noted at least four distinct theories proposed during the 1960s to explain how humans process information to produce sequences (i.e. Leeuwenberg, 1969; Restle, 1970; Simon and Kotovsky, 1963; Vitz and Todd, 1969), and pointed out that these and other similar proposed explanations (e.g Glanzer and Clark, 1962; Gregg, 1967; Klahr and Wallace, 1970) can be shown 'to be mild variants of the same theme' (Simon, 1972, p.381). He suggests that the above proponents of theories

> agree in proposing the following: (a) that subjects perform these tasks by including pattern descriptions from the sequences, and (b) that these pattern descriptions incorporate the relations of *same* and *next* . . . between symbols, iterations of subpatterns, and hierarchic phrase structure. (Simon, 1972, p.381)

Factor analyses of the performance data obtained on the NAT battery showed that both the Sequencing, (Test 8) and Picture Arrangement (Test 9) are strong measures of 'g'. In the overall analyses 62 per cent of the total variance in Sequencing and 58 per cent of the variance in Picture Arrangement were explainable in terms of the 'g' factor.

In the age-specific analyses of the NAT data, an average of 44 per cent of the total variances in both tests could be accounted for by the 'g' factor, with standard deviations of 10 per cent and 8 per cent for Test 8 and Test 9 respectively.

Diagnostic Considerations

In studies of information processing, cognitive psychologists have found that rule induction is a critical underlying variable in a number of important intellectual and educational activities. These include concept formation (e.g. Simon and Lea, 1974), reading comprehension (e.g. Greeno, 1978), mathematics (e.g. Holzman, Pellegrino, and Glaser, 1982, 1983) and effective teaching in general (e.g. Norman, Gentner, and Stevens, 1976).

Both tests measure some of the abilities and skills that are generally regarded as prerequisites for the acquisition of reading ability, for example left to right sequencing, fitting parts into a logical sequence, perceptual organization, attention to detail, and, above all, rule induction.

The relevance of the component abilities measured in these tests to reading comprehension is obvious. Reading is not just a matter of perceiving and comprehending each word as a separate entity, and then putting the words together; the first or major word(s) awaken an anticipation in the reader of a sentence structure or pattern that will define his or her integrating, organizing, giving meaning to, etc., the language content of the rest of the sentence. Readers who cannot anticipate, do not comprehend what they are reading.

In mathematical problem solving, too, the individual's achievement is to a large degree a reflection of his or her ability to anticipate the consequences of initial approaches to the tasks, acts or situations, and therefore is a reflection of planning ability.

Disturbances in the ability to anticipate make planning impossible. This is true for performance on the NAT subtests discussed here, for problem solving in educational settings, and for real-life endeavours.

The role played by judgment in the Sequencing and Picture Arrangement Tests was discussed earlier in this chapter. Logically, one might be tempted to assume that as soon as a person's judgment was seriously defective, planning ability would be impaired also.

The literature provided considerable evidence that this is not always the case (e.g. Frank, 1983; Rapaport et al., 1970; Wechsler, 1958). Most of the studies have been conducted on the basis of the Wechsler tests, but the findings have considerable application in the interpretation of performance on both the sequencing subtests of the NAT. For example, psychopaths have been found to have Picture Arrangement scores that are highly superior to their comprehension scores on the Wechsler Adult Intelligence Scale (WAIS). The authors mentioned at the beginning of this paragraph and others have attributed this finding to the superior anticipation ability often found in psychopaths.

Rapaport et al. (1970), explained this finding by making the following interesting and rather plausible suggestion:

> It is possible that planning here becomes scheming and, as in dealing with specific life situations, the psychopath may here be quite shrewd. This is not contradictory to the finding that more general life-planning and long-range anticipations of the psychopath are poor or absent. (p. 130)

High scores on Tests 8 and 9 of the NAT may be attributed to good planning ability, the ability to think logically and sequentially, attention to detail, judgment and (in the case of Test 9) social intelligence.

Low scores may be attributed to such factors as visual or perceptual problems, difficulties in sequencing, lack of ability to anticipate and plan, defective short-term memory, lack of attention, impulsiveness and motivational or emotional problems.

Psychiatric patients and brain-damaged individuals tend to do badly on sequencing tasks. The spatial sequencing and analysis of unfamiliar visual material components of these tests make them sensitive to right-hemisphere damage. The concept-formation aspects of the items make these tests sensitive to left-hemisphere dysfunctions.

Deficiencies in the component abilities measured by NAT subtests Sequencing and Picture Arrangement will lead to difficulties in learning. However, under normal circumstances deficiencies in a considerable number of component skills tapped by these tests can be remediated to some degree.

At lower levels there are a number of commercially produced educational materials available to teachers, which are designed to facilitate training in sequencing skills, left/right order, perceptual organization, and attention to detail.

At a more advanced level, teachers can provide activities that focus on sequencing and the logical development of actions and situations. Emphasis needs to be placed also on step-by-step procedures and on the development of rules. Concepts of time should be stressed. At an even more advanced level, games such as 'Go' and chess provide excellent opportunities to practise anticipation, planning and sequencing skills.

The Influence of Age

Because of the perceptual components and prerequisites of the conceptual tests contained in the NAT, the reader is referred to both the general and test specific discussions of the influence of age on performance in Chapter 5.

The influence of age on specifically conceptual tasks has been investigated in a 21 year longitudinal study of psychometric intelligence in adulthood. The conclusions from this study support the findings of earlier studies (e.g. Heron and Chown, 1967; Honzik 1974; Salthouse, 1982; Welford, 1951, 1976) in suggesting that reliable decline in reasoning and other intellectual abilities resulting from ageing cannot be demonstrated before the age of 60 years. A reliable decrement in all conceptual abilities can be shown, however, by the age of 74 years.

Schaie (1982) and other authors in this area stress that there are vast individual differences in changes of intellectual efficiency across adulthood. Early decrement is observed for some (this is often alcohol related), and maintenance of high intellectual functioning into a very advanced age for others. What then accounts for these differences between individuals in the rate of deterioration in intelligence with age? Schaie (1982) states that a favourable environment, varied opportunities for environmental stimulation, and the maintenance of a flexible life-style are the key factors in any explanation of differential intellectual deterioration with age in healthy adults.

CHAPTER 7

TESTS OF ATTENTION AND CONCENTRATION

This chapter contains a discussion of the rationale for the attention subtests in the NAT battery. The subtests designed as foremost measures of attention and concentration are:

Test 10:	Visual Search
Test 11:	Simple Key Test
Test 12:	Complex Key Test
Test 13:	Code Tracking I
Test 14:	Code Tracking II

Attentional processes are responsible for our sensitivity to particular signals that are part of the total 'chaos' of signals of the normal environment. Attention is a prerequisite for the 'recognition' of certain patterns as being meaningful, and for our response to some stimuli and not to others. Exactly how these processes are accomplished is still not completely understood.

The findings from major psychological research relevant to the area are presented in this chapter. Scientific views concerning attentional processes are changing rapidly as the available data base of research information grows. The aim in this chapter was an attempt to convey the current level of psychological understanding of the concept of attention, by pointing out major lines of enquiry rather than by seeking to provide a theoretical synthesis.

What is important for the purposes of the present discussion is that human beings have considerable control over which stimuli in their external and internal environment are responded to. By deciding on the objects, events, ideas, thoughts or other targets to which they devote their attention, people *decide* what to see, understand, remember, learn, etc. and, to a large extent, how efficient their operations will be.

The information provided in this chapter has been arranged under the following headings: The Nature of Attention, Important Effects of Attention, Theories of Attention, Historical Conceptualizations of Attention, Recent Research, Major Aspects of Attention, and The Influence of Age. A brief summary including some suggestions for the clinical interpretation of the NAT results relating to the ability to attend and concentrate concludes the chapter.

The Nature of Attention

An important assumption made in the decision to include attention tests in the NAT is the *attention is an aspect of cognition* and not a discrete variable influencing cognitive performance.

As noted previously, the model of intelligence underlying the NAT is one of an interactive, functional information-processing system. Attention, concentration, freedom from distractibility—or whatever term is used for the phenomenon that results in the orienting, filtering, focusing or selecting mechanisms involved—is an essential component of this system.

Most psychologists both past and present have viewed the so called 'problem' of attention (Lovie, 1983, p.301) as being central to the study of cognition no matter what the purpose of such a study might be. But they have not regarded attention as an intricate component of the cognitive process itself.

> Although attentional concepts have been central to much psychological research and theory, few phenomena have so consistently defied definition. (Bourne, Dominowski, and Loftus, 1979, p.36)

The suspicion that other, possibly more flexible, aspects of cognitive functioning than purely perceptual and conceptual skills may make substantial contributions to intellectual ability and educational achievement is not new, but dates from the very beginnings of psychology as a scientific discipline (e.g. Kulpe, 1904; Titchener, 1908; Wundt, 1873). Titchener's (1908) book *Lectures on the Elementary Psychology of Feeling and Attention* contains one of the important early statements of the perceived centrality of the concept of attention to psychology:

> The system of psychology rests upon a three-fold foundation: the doctrine of sensation and image, the elementary doctrine of feeling, and the doctrine of attention. Our views of sensation, of feeling, and of attention determine, if we are logical, the whole further course of our psychological thought and exposition (Titchener, 1908, p.8) . . .

> Attention . . . means a redistribution of clearness in consciousness, the rise of some elements and the fall of others, with an accompanying total feeling of a characteristic kind. (Titchener, 1908, p.183)

The notion that people who pay attention and who concentrate more may turn out to be more intelligent, or conversely, that more intelligent people focus their attention more effectively than less intelligent poeple, has considerable appeal at the intuitive level.

William James (1890/1950) speculated at length about the relationship between cognitive ability and attention. In his book *Principles of Psychology* he devoted a whole chapter to the description of the operation of attention, which he defined as follows:

> Everyone knows what attention is. It is taking possession by the mind, in clear and vivid form, of one out of what seems several simultaneously possible objects or trains of thought. Focalization, concentration of consciousness are of its essence. It implies withdrawal from some things in order to deal effectively with others, and is a condition which has a real opposite in the confused, dazed, scatterbrained state which in French is called *distraction*. (James, 1890, pp.403–404)

He suggests that

> What is called sustained attention is the easier, the richer in acquisitions and the fresher and more original the mind (James, 1890, p.423)

and takes the position that highly intelligent persons are able to attend more effectively because of their superior cognitive abilities.

> Geniuses are commonly believed to excell other men in their power of sustained attention—but it is their genius making them attentive, not their attention making geniuses of them. (James, 1890, p.423)

It is of interest to note the direction of causality suggested by James, which is in contrast to modern considerations that individual differences in attention may constitute determinants of differences in ability and achievement (e.g. Baron, 1978; Hunt, 1978, 1980; Sternberg, 1977). Despite this, these references provide an illustration of both the importance ascribed to the concepts of attention and concentration by James, and the surprisingly 'up to date' descriptions and definition they contain.

The essential nature of focus in all normal human experience and behaviour has been emphasized in branches of psychology that are at variance in their interpretation of most other functional processes. These otherwise vastly different branches include psychophysics, behaviourism, Gestalt psychology and psychoanalysis.

Without selective focusing 'experience is an utter chaos' (James, 1890, p.402).

> Millions of items of the outward order are present to my senses which never properly enter into my experience. Why? Because they have no *interest* for me. *My experience is what I agree to attend to.* Only those items which I *notice* shape my mind—without selective interest experience is an utter chaos... It varies in every creature, but without it the consciousness of every creature would be a gray chaotic indiscriminateness, impossible for us even to conceive. (James, 1890, pp.402–403)

Our immediate physical and psychological environment consists of a sea of indiscriminate, diverse, scattered, often capricious events, objects and ideas. To avoid equal confusion, chaos and scatter in our perceptions and other cognitive operations, some control process must be available, which allows for the selection of only a limited number of impressions at any one time, that is, processing only a small portion of the continuous tide of chaos.

In modern descriptions this phenomenon is often referred to as the 'cocktail party phenomenon', first noted by Cherry (1953). At a cocktail party or a similar gathering of people there is a tendency for many conversations to be in progress simultaneously. Usually the individual visitor to such an event follows only one conversation at a time, although his or her attention may shift, focusing first on one conversation, and then moving to another.

The ability to focus and to change focus is found in many animals as well as in humans. However, only man has the capacity to direct focus beyond sensory stimuli to vague, abstract ideas, meanings, images, even day dreams. Stimuli in our external or internal environment that do not fall within the limits or scope of our attention are processed as mere peripheral, and often transient, 'noise'.

At any one moment in normal life situations we are surrounded and bombarded by more stimuli (i.e. events, impressions, ideas, thoughts, memories, feelings, etc.) than our nervous system can accommodate. Consequently, selections have to be made. Some of these occur at the automatic or even reflex level, or they occur automatically as a result of previously learned response patterns that have become habitual. 'Any organized human mental activity possesses some degree of directivity and selectivity' (Luria, 1973, p.256). Most frequently the focusing of attention constitutes, however, a deliberate act. This implies that the individual behaves purposefully, and that he or she is an agent of active choice.

Important Effects of Attention

The adaptive operation of attention is a prerequisite for the survival of animals and humans.

> Its remote effects are too incalculable to be recorded. The practical and theoretical life of the whole species, as well as of individual beings, results from the selection which the habitual direction of their attention involves ... Each of us literally *chooses*, by his way of attending to things, what sort of universe he shall appear to himself to inhabit. (Norman, 1979, p.9)

The immediate effects of our attending to stimuli are to facilitate perception, conceptualization, distinctiveness, and memory. Attention also shortens 'reaction time'.

This facilitation effect with respect to, for example, sensation means that a sensation attended to becomes stronger than it would otherwise be; it may also become clearer, which 'means distinction from other things and internal analysis or subdivision ... essentially intellectual discrimination' (Norman, 1979, p.11).

The relative effectiveness of cognitive behaviour depends on the variation between and within individuals in the ability to focus and sustain attention, to 'time-share' cognitive activity, and to vary the focus of attention purposefully and efficiently.

> Every human information-processing task requires the allocation of some (rather poorly defined) 'attentional resources' for its execution. If less than enough resources have been supplied to a particular mechanistic process, then that process may be able to function but it will do so at a reduced level of efficiency. (Hunt, 1980, p.466)

It is not intended to suggest that attention is a constant capacity within groups or even within an individual over time. To the contrary, the ability to attend and to concentrate expands and contracts as a result of environmental, task, psychological and biological conditions. Health, stress, fatigue, interest and emotion are among the variables that most frequently influence the capacity to attend and to concentrate.

Because of basic limitations in memory and in the capacity for the immediate processing of information, successful learning requires the ability to attend directly to the task-relevant information, with extraneous information receiving only superficial attention.

Theories of Attention

Research has shown that differential demands for 'attentional resources' can be used to explain individual differences in a wide range of tasks (e.g. Hunt, 1980; Hunt, Lansman and Wright, 1979; Lansman, 1978). There is evidence that particular types of mental retardation are accompanied by particular attention deficits (Money, 1964; Warren, 1978). Zeaman and House (1963) suggested that visual discrimination learning in moderately retarded children requires the previous acquisition of a chain of two responses: (1) the ability to attend to the task-relevant dimension of a stimulus, and (2) to use the correct cue of that dimension. Zeaman and House (1963) argue that the difficulties being experienced by retarded individuals in relation to discrimination tasks relate to the first, rather than the second phase, of this dual process. In other words these authors suggest that retarded individuals experience severe limitations in attention and concentration.

Traver and Hallahan (1974) reviewed a large number of studies and concluded that children with learning disabilities have difficulty in distinguishing between relevant and irrelevant aspects of a stimulus situation. The reason for their poor learning performance in school is generally viewed as the result of an alleged failure to filter out (Broadbent, 1958) incidental information. (For reviews of experimental studies with samples from various special populations see Hallahan, 1975; Hallahan and Reeve, 1980.)

Recently, however, these interpretations based on stimulus filter theory (Broadbent, 1958; and others) have been criticized (Douglas and Peters, 1979; Traver, 1981), because it was found that learning-disabled children are no more susceptible to distraction than their non-disabled peers. Several authors (Bauer, 1977, 1979; Pelham, 1979; Traver, 1981; Worden, 1983) have pointed out that the tasks that have traditionally been used to measure attention (e.g. the detection of weak stimuli, recall of irrelevant information, sustained performance over relatively long periods) place—on subjects a variety of complex demands that are additional to those of selective attention.

> Attributing poor performance to lack of attention may be simplistic and unjustified. In fact, there is a growing body of research indicating that specific deficits in learning may be more strategic than attentional in nature. (Worden, 1983, p.134)

The interaction between attentional resource allocation and the choice of strategies has been emphasized by Hunt (1980), and is an intricate aspect of intellectual performance under any model that represents intelligence or ability as a functional system.

Historical Conceptualizations of Attention

Conceptualizations of the phenomenon of attention have varied in popularity in the history of psychology and human learning. Its perceived importance has ranged from the belief that it is absolutely indispensible to the study of human behaviour (e.g. James, 1890; Mueller, 1873; Titchener, 1908) to the view that it is no more than a vague, 'mentalistic' construct. Woodworth and Schlosberg (1954) summed up the state of the art as follows:

> In spite of the practical reality of attending, the status of attention in systematic psychology has been uncertain and dubious for a long time. Early psychologists thought of it as a faculty or power, akin to will... Any such view was strongly opposed by the associationists who wished to recognize as forces only sensory stimulation and association. The Gestalt psychologists also have regarded any force of attention as extraneous to the field forces which in their view are the dynamic factors in human activity. The behaviorists have rejected attention as a mere traditional mentalistic concept. (Woodworth and Schlosberg, 1954, pp. 72-73)

Lovie's (1983) analysis of publications concerned with attention between 1910 and 1960 provides counter arguments to Woodworth and Schlosberg's final sentence. Although the belief that 'the effective stimuli are those to which the subject attends' (Trabasso and Bower, 1968, p.2) has not always been held, the literature contains a large number of individual experimental studies of attention and attention-related phenomena.

For example, three major areas of experimental psychology that became particularly involved with research into the mechanisms and the operation of attention were discrimination learning (e.g. Kendler and Kendler, 1962; Lawrence, 1950, 1952, 1963; Mandler, 1962; Trabasso and Bower, 1968; Zeaman and House, 1963), neuropsychology (e.g. Lindsley, 1957; Luria, 1973), and research into vigilance and rapid information processing in humans (e.g. Broadbent, 1958; Egeth, 1966; Treisman,

1964). Most of this research focused on selective attention. In the 1970s, possibly the most comprehensive statements on attention were those provided in books by Kahneman (1973) and Posner (1978).

Recent developments in technology, and related increases in the sophistication of experimental and theoretical studies, have led to a number of refinements in the definition of attention. For example, the distinction between automatic and controlled processes (Schneider and Shiffrin, 1977) has just about replaced the earlier distinction of voluntary and involuntary processes.

Recent Research

Spearman (1927) believed that some kind of 'mental power' was required to account for the 'g' factor found in most intelligence tests. More recently, Jensen (1979) has restated this argument on the basis of his findings concerning 'mental quickness', meaning that in extreme group designs the groups scoring higher on intelligence tests have faster choice reaction times (after allowance has been made for differences in motor movement) than those scoring lower on the same tests.

Most theories of intelligence allow for the validity of a construct such as attention or concentration (e.g. Burt, 1949; Cattell 1963; Horn, 1979; Vernon, 1950; Wechsler, 1958), but few attempts have actually been made to account for the operation of such a construct as part of their theory.

Psychometrics and information-processing scientists have defined intelligence in terms of many dimensions, all of which are generally regarded as aspects of cognitive functioning. The modern psychometric literature does not make reference to primary factors of attention (e.g. Ekstrom, French, and Harman, 1979; Guilford, 1967; Hakstian and Cattell, 1976; Horn, 1976, 1979, 1980).

Guilford (1980a) showed that his 'Structure of the Intellect' model (Guilford, 1967) can account for different types of cognitive style, but noted that the model does not provide an easy fit for attentional variables. He explains this in terms of his finding that attentional variables can operate in any segment of his model. The latter point emphasizes rather than detracts from the importance of the processes of attention: Stankov (1983) explains Guilford's finding on the basis that 'the pervasive "g" is excluded from his [Guilford's] model' (p.478).

The information-processing literature observes the operation of attention largely on the basis of measures of reaction time. It also regards attention as an important aspect of the central processing system. It is viewed as one of the elements of the set of central events in mental functioning that lead to one course of thought, memory, or action rather than to others. More importantly, it is seen as one of the components of cognitive control—the mechanism that maintains the interacting of the cognitive system.

A number of exceptional attempts to relate the concepts of attention and intelligence are being made by Stankov (1978, 1980, 1983). Stankov (1983) reviews and interprets experimental evidence to show that the demonstrable empirical relationship of the two concepts can be related to the theory of fluid and crystallized intelligence (Cattell, 1963; Horn, 1976, 1979, 1980; Horn and Stankov, 1982).

Major Aspects of Attention

As is obvious from the above discussions there are intra- and inter-personal fluctuations in the influence that the environment exerts on our lives at any given moment. There are different ways in which the effectiveness of a stimulus can vary, and the determinants of this variation influence the probability of a stimulus eliciting a response from an individual at any given time.

The phenomenon of attention as treated in the experimental literature is not a single, unitary concept, either. Moray (1969) listed a number of aspects of attention including concentration, search, selective attention, attention switching, and vigilance.

All the aspects of attention noted above contribute to the successful completion of the attention subtests of the NAT battery.

Concentration

The term concentration, often referred to as 'sustained attention', describes the individual's perseverance with a task, that is, his or her continuous, sustained application of cognitive effort aimed at task completion. Luria (1966, 1973) and others (e.g. Hunt and Randhawa, 1983; Kirby and Das, 1977; Lewis and Baldine, 1979; McClelland and Jackson, 1978; Messick, 1973) placed great importance on this aspect of attention, and emphasized its relationship to high achievement.

This attention process is strongly related to success in problem solving, learning and intellectual achievement more generally. It has a positive influence on all cognitive tasks, but is of particular importance in relation to tasks the performance on which does not 'depend too much on intellectual level' and which does 'depend to as small a degree as possible upon content and knowledge' (Wittenborn, 1943, p.20). Concentration is thus a strong requirement for high achievement on all NAT subtests but particularly for Tests 10 to 14, the attention tests.

The literature has shown that tests of this factor have high loadings on 'g'-type factors. This finding was supported in the analyses of the data collected on the NAT.

Search

In the research literature search behaviour as an aspect of attention is usually observed on the basis of tasks that require the individual to identify a target stimulus among a presented array of stimuli with similar characteristics. Test 10 'Visual Search' provides the purest measure of this variable in the NAT battery.

The process is obviously similar, and might under certain conditions be identical, to the traditional perceptual speed factor, which is described clearly in the following quotation:

> This factor is characterized by the task of finding in a mass of distracting material a given configuration which is borne in mind during the search. This includes the ability to compare pairs of items or to locate a unique item in a group of identical items. In all of these cases a perceived configuration is compared with a remembered one. The tests of this ability are all speeded; in no case is the target configuration so hidden as to cause difficulty if plenty of time were available. (French, 1951, p.227)

The search aspect of attention, which is a prominent response requirement in subtests 10 to 14, loads strongly on the 'g' factor in the analysis of the NAT data, and has been identified 'as a marker of fluid and crystallized intelligence' (Stankov, 1983, p.476).

This factor, which Horn (1972) called 'Perceptual Speed' or 'Search', and which he subsequently labelled 'Clerical Perceptual Speed', was found to be strongly linked to fluid intelligence by Horn (1980).

Selective Attention

While the sensory apparatus facilitating human information processing is capable of registering a vast amount of varying types of stimulation, the stimuli that are the focus of attention are registered with greatest expediency and clarity.

What determines the focus of an individual's attention at any given moment varies, and can be related to peripheral or environmental factors, for example the brightest, loudest, most frequently occurring or otherwise most salient stimulus (e.g. Berlyne, 1958, 1970), or to central factors, such as physiological, motivational or emotional targets. Centrally determined factors of attention tend to make a stimulus similar to one the individual expects or would wish to perceive. The latter process is often referred to as 'voluntary' attention, that is 'the subject attends to stimuli because they are relevant to a task that he has chosen to perform, not because of their arousing quality' (Kahneman, 1973, p.4).

Attention Switching

One of the best examples of a test of the ability to switch attention is the Otis Directions Test, a subtest of the Otis Test of Intelligence. In this test the testee is asked to respond to changing directions. French (1951) had already noted the occurrence of substantive correlations between intelligence test scores and attention in tasks involving rapidly changing instructions.

Moray (1970) argued that all attention processes investigated in the experimental literature can be described in terms of a continuing, rapid switching of attention among different stimuli. Although this description may not cover all types of attention, or for that matter all experimental situations, the ability to attend to relevant signals and to switch attention in an appropriate manner is obviously a basic requirement of successful test performance, and of adaptive functioning in real life.

Performance on tasks requiring the switching of attention and intelligence (measured on tasks not requiring the switching of attention) share a considerable portion of common variance (French, 1951; Stankov, 1983; Wittenborn, 1943).

The variable of switching attention plays a role in NAT subtests 10 to 14, all of which require selective attention to changing stimuli. However, Test 12, if its administration follows directly after that of Test 11, provides the strongest measure of the ability to switch attention in the NAT battery. The combination of Tests 13 and 14 also contributes to this variable, but to a lesser extent than Tests 11 and 12.

Vigilance

Vigilance, often termed alertness or attentiveness, is required for tasks that involve the detection of an infrequently occurring signal or other stimulus, often over a prolonged period of time. A more comprehensive definition, which would be supported also by Mackworth (1970) and others, notes:

> The term vigilance, which is a physiological psychological readiness to respond, has been defined as that behaviour required to attend to relevant stimuli and ignore irrelevant stimuli over a period of time. (Hunt and Randhawa, 1983, p.207)

In a large number of studies conducted during the 1950s and 1960s (for review see Mackworth, 1970), measures of vigilance were generally found not to correlate significantly with measured intelligence. These findings seemed plausible when explained on the basis of the fact that the vigilance tasks used tended to be simple and monotonous.

However, more recent research (e.g. Eysenck, 1966; Stankov, 1983; Welford, 1976; and East European studies described by Stankov, 1983) showed that a substantial correlation between measures of vigilance and measures of intelligence is, in fact, mediated by individual differences in the level of arousal in individuals over time. In these studies successful attempts were made (under conditions of constant task complexity) to observe changes in the correlation between vigilance and intelligence that accompany changes in levels of arousal.

The links between the arousal system and its determining factors and attention are complex (e.g. Dykman, Ackerman, Clements, and Peters (1971); Lewis and Baldine, 1979; Luria, 1966a, 1966b, 1973). As time passes, during vigilance tasks, subjects have been observed to become bored and less alert, that is, they operate at increasingly lower levels of arousal. In his search for an explanation of the processes operating during vigilance behaviour, Welford came to the conclusion that:

> The theory which most adequately explains the main facts obtained in what is now a vast array of experiments is that the monotonous conditions of vigilance tasks cause the level of arousal to fall. (Welford, 1976, p.146)

The same conclusion was reached by a number of East European investigators (reported by Stankov, 1983).

> There is now reasonably good support in the literature that people with higher general ability have comparatively lower arousal levels at the end of 1 Hour's work on vigilance tasks. Consequently, intelligence correlates negatively with vigilance performance. (Stankov, 1983, p.482)

The Influence of Age

As was noted previously, research has shown that there is an age-related decline in the abilities and skills required for the efficient processing of information derived from the environment (Heron and Chown, 1967; Welford, 1977; and others). This includes such processes as selective attention, concentration and other attention processes (e.g. Barrett, Mihal, Panek, Sterns, and Alexander, 1977; Craik, 1965).

Summary

The consideration of perceptual and memory functions is a long standing tradition in the assessment of general and more specific abilities. In contrast, the inclusion of an investigation of the ability to attend and concentrate has only recently been considered (Guilford, 1980a; Horn, 1980; Stankov, 1978, 1980, 1983).

Attention, in this context, refers to the formation of and adherence to a 'set' or attitude of perseverance, freedom from distraction, and application to the task in hand. The efficiency of this process depends ultimately on the motivation of the individual, and on the saliency of potentially distracting cues in the task development.

Intelligence and attention are inextricably confounded:

> They can be defined along similar lines—in terms of coping with a large amount of information. Empirical evidence indicates that a link with intelligence persists for all phenomena considered to be attentional. (Stankov, 1983, p.487)

It may be concluded that there is enough evidence in the literature to support the profitability of assessing attention as a component of intelligence, as defined in the earlier part of this book and as measured by means of the NAT.

The attention tests included in the NAT require the immediate recognition of signals, the ability to scan the page systematically, vigilance, and continuing memory.

Perhaps more than any other segments of the NAT battery the speed and accuracy tests (Tests 10 to 14) and the memory tests are sensitive to difficulties in attention and concentration. However, slow or otherwise deficient performance at any age does not indicate whether the underlying problem is one of motor slowing (i.e. response inhibition caused by physiological or neurological factors), lack of co-ordination, difficulties in visual scanning, conceptual confusion, or poor motivation.

The most common form of psychiatric breakdown, schizophrenia, is generally accompanied by attentional distortions and a breakdown of attentional control. In this condition all aspects of attention can run wild. They can become extremely and habitually over- or under-active. Selective attention, for example may not operate at all or may remain fixed on a single stimulus (perseveration). Attentional focusing can become either highly diffuse or very restricted, so as to render it just about non-functional in either condition. These different results of the breakdown of the processes of attention may be reflected in the performance of so afflicted individuals in a number of subtests of the NAT, but particularly in Tests 11 and 12, and Tests 13 and 14.

Persons of low intelligence, psychiatric patients, brain-injured subjects, emotionally disturbed and very nervous or anxious individuals may perform equally poorly on these tests. Further testing and clinical observation, or referral are needed before the variables responsible for the indications of diminished attentional ability obtained on the NAT can be identified and verified.

CHAPTER 8

MEMORY

The discussions contained in the preceding chapters of this section, particularly those on perception and attention, have emphasized the organization of the components of cognitive behaviour. It was shown that our perceptions do not constitute a mosaic of jumbled, isolated fragments of sensory stimuli, and that the conceptual cues to which we respond are not random. Instead, as a result of the processes of attention, concentration and learning, other cognitive processes operate as an organized, coherent whole, in which every element relates to every other. Intellectual activity is a manifestation of the operation of a functional system of cognitive component processes.

This chapter deals with short-term memory, and it will be seen that organization plays an equally prominent part in this process as in those discussed in the preceding chapters of this section.

Following some introductory remarks, the subject matter contained in the chapter, which deals with various conceptualizations of the memory phenomenon, is presented under the following headings: The Multi-store Model, The Levels of Processing Model, Attention and Memory, Recall and Recognition, Auditory versus Visual Input, Individual Differences, Memory Disorders, and the NAT Memory Tests.

Memory provides the means for the linking of past and present experience.

> Memory is the way in which we record the past and later refer to it so that it may affect the present... Without memory there would be no then but only a now, no ability to utilize skills, no recall of names or recognition of faces, no reference to past days or hours or even seconds... (Gleitman, 1981, p.271)

The processes of memory are a prerequisite for all intelligent behaviour. Memory plays a critical role in all our cognitive functioning. It is required for all types of learning. Such abilities and skills as speaking, listening, reading, writing—even walking around—all require the operation of memory.

Before discussing ways in which memory might enter into manifestations and interpretations of intelligence, a definition of memory might be required. There has been much less debate about definitions of memory than there has been about definitions of intelligence and learning.

> Memory (is) generally recognized to be an abstraction referring to an organism's capability of storing and retrieving information. In the contemporary literature information stored in

memory is conceived as entering into performance by way of such cognitive processes and operations as memory search, comparison between memorial representations and products of perceptual processes, and decision making. (Estes, 1982, p.171)

Throughout this chapter, then, the term memory will be used to refer to structures and processes involved in the storage and retrieval of information.

A short consideration of the most influential theories of how the human memory operates may increase the validity of interpretation of performance on the NAT memory tests, and their diagnostic usefulness.

The Multi-store Model

During the 1970s the dominant view among researchers was that memory, as a human information-processing system, consisted of three separate stores, namely, sensory, short-term and long-term. A simplified representation of this multi-store model, showing the basic characteristics of each memory store, is shown in Figure 8.1. The model, which owes much to the research of Broadbent (1958) and Atkinson and Shiffrin (1968), has guided a large amount of research and continues to be influential.

Figure 8.1   Memory as a Multi-store Model of Information Processing

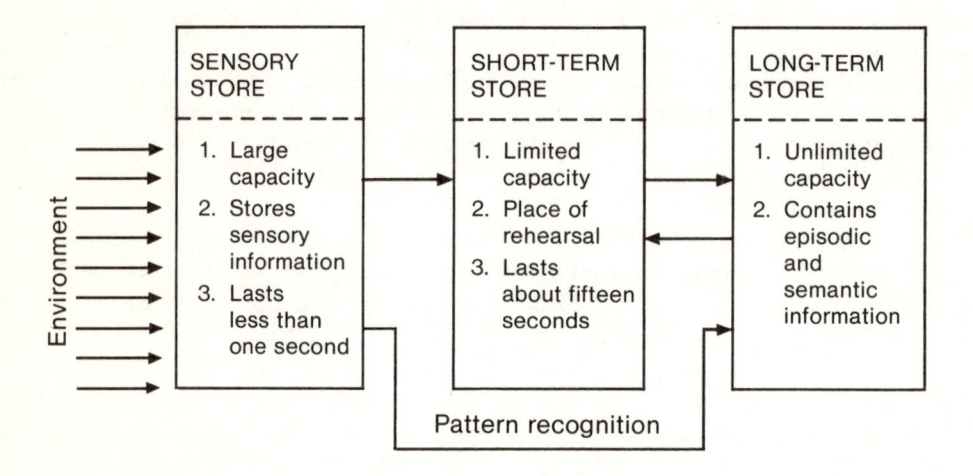

SENSORY STORE	SHORT-TERM STORE	LONG-TERM STORE
1. Large capacity	1. Limited capacity	1. Unlimited capacity
2. Stores sensory information	2. Place of rehearsal	2. Contains episodic and semantic information
3. Lasts less than one second	3. Lasts about fifteen seconds	

Environment → Sensory Store → Short-term Store ⇄ Long-term Store

Pattern recognition

Briefly, according to the multi-store model environmental stimuli are processed in several stages. To begin with, information enters the sensory memory store, which stores it as a row, that is, sensory form. For example, the model assumes that a visual stimulus is stored in sensory memory as a visual representation consisting of such properties as colour, brightness, shape and lines. Similarly, an auditory stimulus is stored in sensory memory as an auditory representation containing such physical properties as loudness and pitch.

The sensory store can contain and handle large amounts of information but the information weakens or decays in less than one second. One of the reasons for this is that information in this store can be replaced by new information. Thus, whatever is stored in sensory memory is forgotten very quickly unless it is transferred into short-term memory.

In order to enter the short-term memory store, the information in sensory memory must be recognized. Pattern recognition involves the matching of information in the sensory store with information in the long-term store, which allows for the assigning of the information of well established, that is, learnt, categories. Sometimes, the process of pattern recognition involves attention to particular pieces of information in the sensory store but not to others. To summarize, the sensory memory store retains large amounts of information briefly, allowing limited time for pattern recognition and attentional processes to take place.

As can be seen in Figures 8.2 and 8.3, a number of current theories of memory identify primary (or immediate) memory and working (or operational) memory as two distinct systems contained in short-term memory. The first processing and registration of stimulus input takes place in *primary memory*. The term *working memory* appears first to have been used by Posner and Rossman (1965), and was explained by Posner (1967) as follows:

> All human information processing requires keeping track of incoming stimuli, and bringing such input into contact with already-stored material. (p.267)

Working memory thus acts as a temporary retainer of 'just-perceived' information while it is being processed further into long-term memory, and at the same time it is regarded as

> an active state, perhaps by a rehearsal or recycling process, information draws either from recent perception or from long-term memory that is actively involved in an ongoing task. (Estes, 1982, p.197)

Many learning and problem-solving situations place heavy demands on working memory. However, 'unattended' information is rapidly lost from working memory.

Information that has entered sensory memory and has been recognized or categorized may pass into short-term memory. The short-term memory store has limited capacity. It can hold about seven pieces of information (plus or minus two) at any one time (Miller, 1956). The pieces of information might be numerals, single letters, familiar words, etc. No matter what the items are there are constraints on how much can be stored. The short-term memory store can retain information for approximately 15 seconds, long enough, for example, to allow me to dial a telephone number that I have just looked up.

As in the sensory memory store, forgetting results both from the gradual decay of information over time, and from the displacement of stored information by incoming information. However, by rehearsing, information can be retained in short-term memory indefinitely.

In summary, unlike sensory memory, short-term memory stores only limited amounts of information, but retains it longer—for approximately 15 seconds—and it stores categorized information that can be rehearsed and thus retained indefinitely. Obviously, the storage of rehearsed information over time will reduce the store's capacity to accept new categorized information.

To counteract this problem, and for more efficient information processing, the information in short-term memory store can be coded into an even more durable form by entering into the long-term memory store. Unlike short-term memory, long-term memory has no limits in capacity and can retain information over long periods of time, often permanently. Despite this, the information in long-term memory can be forgotten, as we are often unable to retrieve a required piece of information that is stored in long-term memory. Such failures to retrieve information can result from interference, as occurs in cases where the recall of a person's name is blocked by the recall of other names. Retrieval failures can also result from the absence of appropriate retrieval cues, for example a person's first name.

The long-term memory store retains many kinds of information, only the two most common being mentioned here. Based on a distinction initially made by Tulving (1968), one kind is referred to as *episodic information*, which is concerned with autobiographical events experienced by the individual at a particular time and place. For example, yesterday's activities, something we read in the newspaper, the memory of what we ate two nights ago, and our last meeting with a particular friend all involve episodic information. Remembering episodic information involves the recall of particular events, their characteristics and the context in which they occurred.

The second common kind of information contained in long-term memory is known as *semantic information*. This includes acquired knowledge of facts and of our broader environment. Knowledge of how to speak, read, write and calculate, of concepts such as time and space, and of the differences between humans and other animals is based on semantic information. Semantic information is sometimes called world knowledge, because unlike episodic information, it is non-autobiographical and pertains to the world, rather than to our personal past experiences (Tulving, 1968, 1972). The information in semantic memory need not be verbal. The term 'factual' used by some theorists (e.g. Estes, 1982) may provide a more easily understood label for this information.

Estes (1982) provided a useful schema to represent the major varieties of memory in combination. This schema is shown in Figure 8.2, in which the rectangle as a whole is meant to encompass memory as a whole, including the varieties or categories that are recognized by different theories at the present time. The vertical line partitions memory approximately in accordance with Tulving's (1968) distinction between episodic and semantic memory.

The horizontal line through the centre of the rectangle in Figure 8.2 represents a partitioning of the different kinds of memory according to duration in time. This line must not be interpreted as providing hard and fast cut-offs in time dimension. Rather, as noted above, short-term memory refers to the individual's ability to maintain for a brief time a relatively rich representation of recent input; in contrast, long-term memory normally retains information over extended periods of time unless interfered with in specific ways. While the information in short-term memory is episodic by necessity, long-term memory can be either for specific events (episodic) or for relations, rules, principles, knowledge, etc. (semantic or factual).

Figure 8.2 represents memory in a static, structural manner. Some of the theoretically postulated inter-relationships among the memory sub-systems shown in Figure 8.2 are illustrated in Figure 8.3. As is implicit in the above discussion, the multi-store model consists not only of three memory stores, but also of a set of processes that accomplish the transfer of information from one store to another. Atkinson and Shiffrin (1968) called these *control processes* because they control the flow of information within the memory system. The control processes of memory are important because

Figure 8.2 Schema of some Major Categories of Memory Recognized in Current Theories (after Estes, 1982)

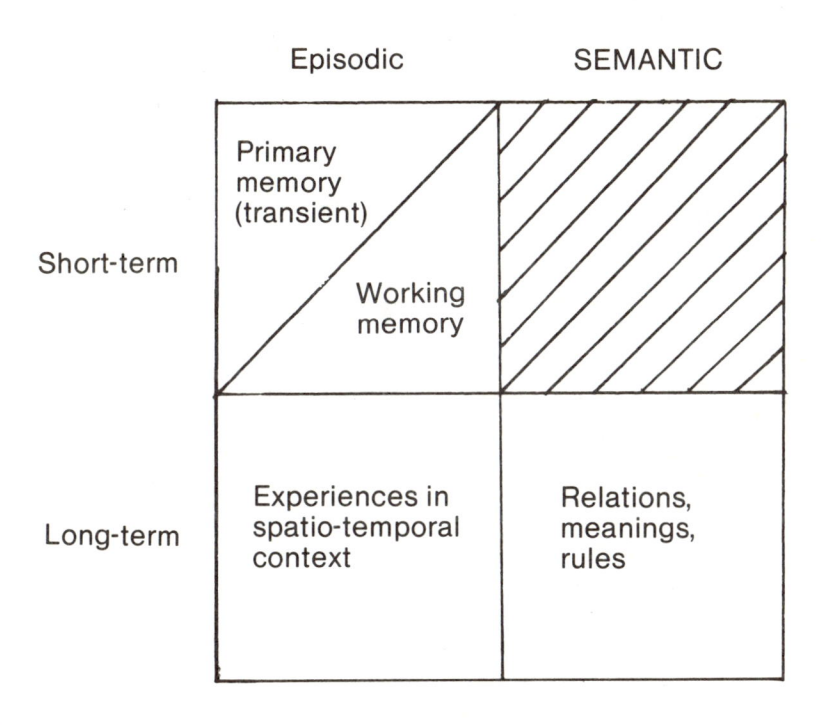

	Episodic	SEMANTIC
Short-term	Primary memory (transient) / Working memory	////////
Long-term	Experiences in spatio-temporal context	Relations, meanings, rules

they govern the encoding, retrieval and manipulation of information in memory. They are also important because the activation of many of them is under the control of the individual. For example, we are using a control process when we deliberately rehearse, practise or attend to pieces of information in an attempt to remember them.

The multi-store model was the prevalent model of memory for over 20 years. Opponents of the model suggested that the multi-store model postulates a greater number of memory stores than necessary (Craik and Lockhart, 1972). In order to provide a simpler account of memory, these theorists began to emphasize the stages and the kinds of processing executed by memory units.

Figure 8.3 Information Plan through Postulated Short-term and Long-term Memory Systems

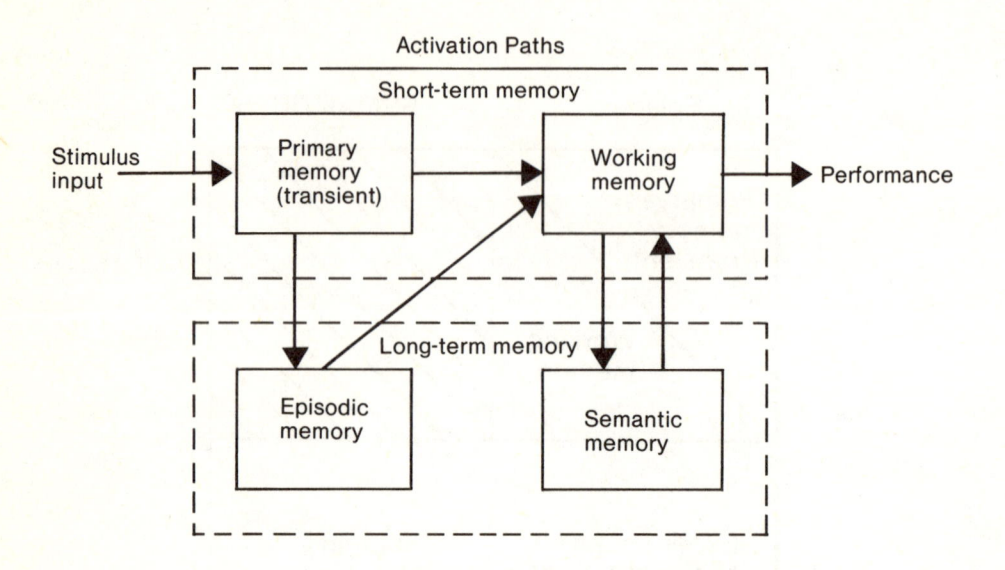

The Levels-of-Processing Model

Craik and Lockhart (1972) argued that memory limitations reflect limitations in processing capacity rather than limitations in storage capacity. Their research has shown that people encode information in a flexible manner. They investigated memory in terms of levels of processing, a concept they introduced initially as a framework to guide research, but which has since been used by many authors as an explanatory account and model. The levels-of-processing model postulates that incoming information is analysed in stages. In the initial stages physical and sensory features are analysed. The intermediate stages of memory allow for pattern recognition and for the classification (labelling) of incoming pieces of information. In this model of memory, information processing takes place in a series of stages or levels, which vary with respect to their depth. Greater *depth of processing* implies a greater degree of conceptual or semantic analysis. Under this model, the semantic level, that is, the level at which naming occurs, is the deepest level of processing in memory. It is regarded as deeper than the level at which physical features are analysed.

As shown in Figure 8.4, these levels can be understood as forming a continuum ranging from shallow, physical analyses, to deep, semantic analyses. The greater the depth of the information processing, the lower is its position on the continuum.

Figure 8.4 The Levels of Processing Model of Memory

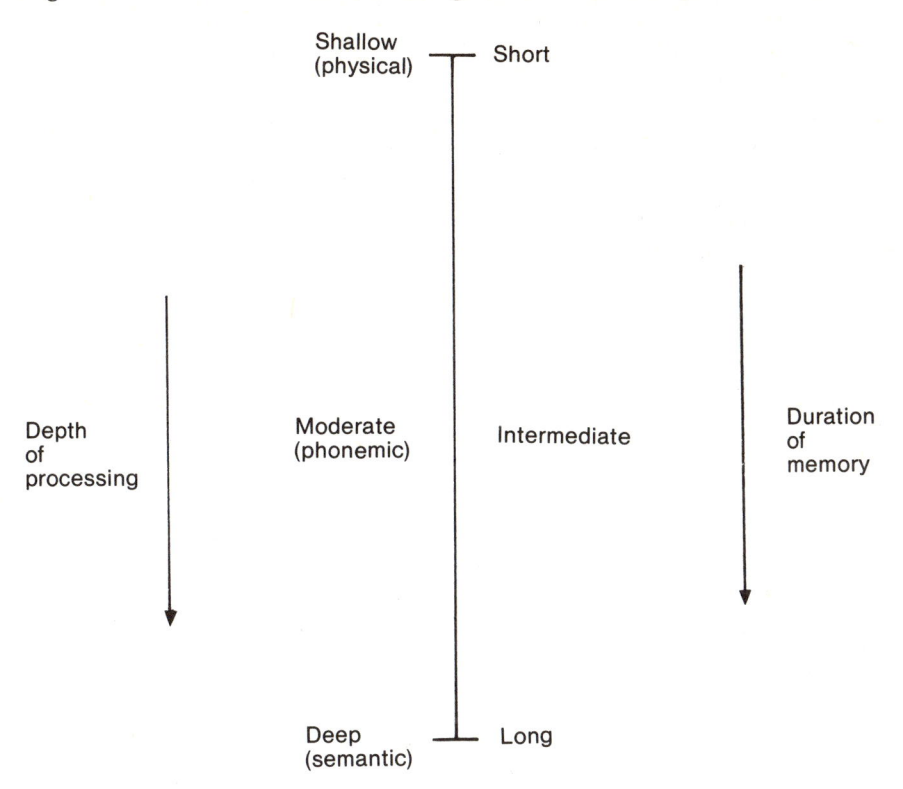

```
                Shallow      ┬ Short
                (physical)   │
                             │
                             │
                             │
Depth           Moderate     │ Intermediate    Duration
of              (phonemic)   │                 of
processing                   │                 memory
     ↓                       │                    ↓
                             │
                Deep         ┴ Long
                (semantic)
```

Perception and memory have long been regarded as closely related processes (Koehler, 1947). The levels-of-processing model of memory reflects this position by postulating that memory is a by-product of perceptual analysis. As shown in Figure 8.4, the deeper the level of processing, the longer the processed information will be remembered. This postulation accounts for the differential retention of phonemic and semantic information in the model in the following way. Phonemic information is remembered for a moderate amount of time because such information has been processed at a moderately deep level. Similarly, semantic information is remembered over long periods of time because it has been processed at a deep level. The model thus accounts for memory without postulating several memory stores.

According to the levels-of-processing model, capacity limitations in memory arise from constraints in our processing capacity, not in our capacity for information storage. The model went through a number of stages of elaboration and refinement (e.g. Craik and Watkins, 1973; Craik and Tulving, 1975; Craik and Jacoby, 1979; Craik, 1979). An important elaboration led to the postulation that in addition to levels of different depths there are two kinds of processing in memory. Type I refers to the recirculation of pieces of information at a particular depth of processing and does not aid retention. Type II processing analyses information at a deeper level and does aid retention. This elaboration of the model allows it to account for the effects of different types of rehearsal.

Further revisions of the model emphasized that retention depends on the elaborateness as well as on the depths of processing. Elaborate processing occurs when incoming information pieces are related to other incoming items or to previously remembered information. Elaborate processing can also occur when a greater number of features of a specific piece of information are analysed, for example by noting different shades of meaning of a word stimulus, greater detail of picture, more potential uses or applications of the stimulus, etc. This type of elaboration may be aiding retention by providing a relatively complete description of the encoded item. In turn, the complete description makes the item more distinctive and thus more easily retrievable. The emphasis on elaborateness of processing avoids the (much criticized) fixed sequence of processing stages while retaining the notion that the manner of encoding determines the level of retention in memory.

Attention and Memory

Much of the discussion in Chapter 7 may have left the reader confused as regards the distinction between the processes of memory and those of attention. Indeed, attention and memory are closely related, so much so that they are indistinguishable in some instances.

> When we attend to an item it becomes part of the immediate present, the currently apprehended chunk of time that seems fresh in our minds and that stands out against the background of the remembered past. (Wessells, 1982, p.96)

The item remains part of the immediate present for a short time only, and during this time it can be recalled easily. To describe the processes occurring at this point, which probably lasts less than half a minute, attention and memory could be regarded in synonomous terms. However, as time passes the item previously attended to fades away or is replaced, that is, it is forgotten, unless active steps are taken to remember it. For example, when I look up the telephone number of a taxi company in a city I am visiting briefly, the number is fresh in my mind initially and easy to recall while I am dialing it. In the absence of rehearsal, however, it fades out of memory just about immediately. As shown by this example, pieces of information on which we focus our attention become memory for a short period of time.

In many everyday life situations, as in the above example, we attend selectively to one task or aspect of a stimulus situation at a time. In other situations we seem to be able to divide our attention between two or more tasks without experiencing interference. For example, while driving along a reasonably familiar route, it is easy to listen to a radio program or to carry on a conversation with passengers in the car. Divided and selective attention have been discussed in Chapter 7. To explain the relationship between memory and attention a model is needed that can show why selective attention occurs under some conditions where as divided attention occurs under others.

One useful model that accounts for both selective and divided attention is the model of *resource allocation*. Kahneman (1973), and Norman and Bobrow (1975), the developers of the model, postulate that man has a limited pool of cognitive resources, which are used in the processing of information. We attend to a task such as memorizing the spelling of a group of words, or learning French vocabulary by allocating resources to that task. The more difficult the task the more of our processing resources are engaged by it, thus leaving fewer resources available for performing another task simultaneously. Performance of a difficult task thus requires selective attention. For example, carrying on a serious debate of a difficult topic might require the allocation of so many available resources that a choice may have to be made between driving and a continuation of the debate. However, if the task is simple, it engages few processing resources, so sufficient resources for the simultaneous performance of other tasks are available. For example, carrying on a casual conversation or listening to light music tend to require few resources and would for most individuals thus not interfere with the simultaneous driving of a car.

> The completion of a mental activity requires two types of input..., a (specific) information input..., and a nonspecific input which may be variously labeled 'effort', 'capacity', or 'attention'. To explain man's limited ability to carry out multiple activities at the same time, a capacity theory assumes that the total amount of attention which can be deployed at any time is limited. (Kahneman, 1973, p.9)

The resource allocation model holds that we use our limited resources in a flexible manner. With reference to the performance of a complex cognitive task, Norman and Bobrow (1975) suggest:

> Up to some limit one expects performance to be related to the amount of resources (such as psychological effort) exerted on the task. If too little of some processing resource is applied (perhaps because processing resources are limited by competition from other tasks being performed at the same time) then one would expect poor performance. As more resources are applied to the task, then presumably better and better performance will result. Whenever an increase in the amount of processing resources can result in improved performance, we say that the task (or performance on that task) is *resource limited*. (Norman and Bobrow, 1975, p.44)

It follows that, for example, if we are dissatisfied with our performance on a task such as speed of memorization of spelling words or vocabulary, reading comprehension, or mathematical problem solving, we can increase our effort, thereby devoting additional resources to the task. The manner in which this is accomplished is dependent, at least in part, on situational or environmental factors. For example, while looking through vocabulary lists in a shop, we might allocate some resources to the words and other resources to the observation of other individuals in the shop. But on the way to an examination we might allocate the bulk of resources to memorizing the words. Similarly, while driving on a freeway in light traffic, I might allocate some resources to driving and others to thinking. If the car in front of me stopped suddenly, I might allocate almost all of my resources to driving. As a result I would have to stop thinking about other matters. These examples are designed to show the flexibility with which cognitive resources can be and are being allocated.

In summary, the discussion contained in this section was aimed to show that the relationship between attention and immediate recall can be explained by the model of resource allocation, which grew out of research concerning selective attention. Selective attention involves the processing of some stimuli and not others at a particular moment. Research evidence (e.g. Craik, 1979; Hirst, Spelke, Reaves, Caharack, and Neisser, 1980; Johnston and Heinz, 1978, Neisser, 1976; Norman, 1979) has provided strong support for the predictions of the resource allocation model, which might be summarized as follows:

1. It is possible to perform two tasks (and at times more) concurrently without interference, provided that the combined demands of the tasks do not exceed the individual's limited cognitive resources.
2. Performance of one task will interfere with the simultaneous performance of another when the two tasks combined demand more processing resources than are available.
3. Individuals can tailor their resource allocation in accordance with the demands of the task and the environment within which they are finding themselves at a particular moment.

Recall and Recognition

Memory retention and retrieval are usually measured in one of three ways, namely, by means of recall, recognition or relearning.

The method of recall requires the individual to report what has been seen, heard or learnt previously. In the method of recognition the individual is presented with the original stimulus embedded in or accompanied by a collection of stimuli that had not been presented originally. In other words, the individual is required to recognize the target information amongst a set of 'distractors'. The method of recognition thus includes direct prompting.

The method of relearning is based on the research findings initially published by Ebbinghaus (1885), and strongly supported up to the present day, that material one has learnt and since forgotten can be relearnt in a fraction of the time that had been needed for the original learning. This method has not been used in the evaluation of memory included in the NAT, and so will not be discussed any further in this context.

When asked whether recall or recognition is easier most students would reply that recognition is easier. In fact, this belief has led to a tendency for students to prefer courses in which performance is assessed on the basis of multiple-choice (i.e. recognition) tests, rather than by means of essays or tests containing open-ended questions (i.e. recall).

This type of argument is based on the assumption that the memory resources required for recognition are less than those required for recall, and that recognition and recall are fundamentally similar memory processes.

This assumption tends to be strengthened further by the accumulated research evidence discussed above, which has shown that forgetting, irrespective of whether it occurs in situations of recall or recognition requirements, is influenced similarly by contextual cues both at the time of encoding and at the time of retrieval. Furthermore, it is influenced by such variables as passage of time (lacking rehearsal), interference, and level and depth at which the information was processed during memorization.

Theorists have evaluated the relationship between recall and recognition by examining whether a particular variable, for example level of processing, has similar effects on these two processes of retrieval. A variable is regarded as having similar effects if recall and recognition involve the same or similar memory processes but not if they involve different processes.

As noted above, many similar effects have been found with regard to forgetting in both recall and recognition experiments. However, a number of variables have been identified, which influence recall and recognition in quite dissimilar, if not opposite, ways. For example, in the remembering of words the frequency with which words occur in the individual's language (as indicated by frequency counts in books, journals, newspapers, etc.) has opposite effects on recognition and recall. In general, rare words are recognized better than common words but recalled less well (e.g. Hall, 1954; Kinsbourne and George, 1974; McCormack and Swenson, 1972). Similarly, rehearsal of stimulus words in a non-elaborative manner often results in an improvement in the level of recognition but has little effect on the level of recall (Mandler, 1979; Woodward, Bjork, and Jongeward, 1973).

Organization is another variable that affects recognition and recall differently. It has been found that highly organized material (i.e. material presented in categories that are meaningful to the learner) tends to be recalled more easily than less organized material. On the other hand, level of organization was found to have no effect on recognition (Kintsch, 1968, 1970). These and other studies suggest that the processes contributing to recall and recognition differ, at least to some extent.

To account for these observations a number of theories postulating that recognition and recall involve both similar and different processes were developed (e.g. Anderson and Bower, 1972; Brown, 1976; James, 1890; Kintsch, 1970; Mueller, 1913). While these models vary in the labels assigned to the hypothesized processes and in other details, they are similar in their major thesis. They propose that two processes underlie recall, whereas only one process underlies recognition. During recall possible candidate items are *generated* by searching through memory, and items that had previously been presented are *recognized* by assessing their familiarity or their contextual associations. Under these models the recognition of items requires the recognition process but not the process of generation. A simple example will demonstrate these differences.

An adult is asked to recall the name of his or her fourth grade teacher. In performing this task many people would start by generating several names of teachers and then attempt to recognize which of the names might be the correct one. The generating part of the process involves searching through memory in a systematic fashion and retrieving potential candidate items. Because of previous school experience, the name of any one teacher is associated with the names of other teachers, and each retrieved name is likely to act as a cue in the retrieval of names of other teachers. As the various names are retrieved from memory, attempts tend to be made to judge their correctness. This recognition process probably occurs as a result of an evaluation of contextual information that may have been retrieved together with each particular name. The recognition process can also occur by assessing the familiarity value of an item. The generation plus recognition process continues until the individual's attempt at recall has been completed or abandoned.

The two-process model of recall and the single-process model of recognition can also account for the previously noted effects of organization during encoding and other variables that have opposite effects on recall and recognition. The model also accounts for the similar effects that some variables have on the two methods of observing retrieval.

When highly organized material is learnt, numerous associations are formed between the items to be memorized. The more highly organized the material, the more obvious are the relations between items, and the stronger are inter-item associations. The thus-established associative pathways between the items improve recall by facilitating the generation process. Organization does not influence the recognition process because the latter does not involve following associative pathways established during learning.

Despite its ability to account for many observations the model described above has recently lost favour. A number of researchers, in particular Rabinowitz, Mandler and Barsalou (1979), and Tulving (1976) have criticized the model on a number of grounds. One of these relates to the fact that it is difficult to measure precisely the generation and recognition phases postulated by the model. This makes it difficult to test the model and its predictiveness. The model also fails to account for the possibility that recall and recognition may be based on different kinds of information (Brown, 1976; Carey and Lockhart, 1973; Underwood, 1972).

An even more important criticism is based on the research of Rabinowitz et al. (1979), who found that subjects do not typically recall words by generating and recognizing them. These researchers suggest that the generation–recognition model of recall may be of limited generalizability, and that generating and then recognizing items may be only one among many strategies used by individuals in their attempts to recall information from memory.

This emphasis on the strategies used by individuals during retrieval places the question of how recall and recognition might be related into a new perspective. If there are numerous appropriate strategies for the retrieval of information, there may be no fundamental relationship between recognition and recall.

Such a view, though in conflict with generation–recognition models, makes sense with respect to the diversity of ways in which recall and recognition may occur. In some instances retrieval from memory seems to require no search process at all, and little evaluation of contextual information. When asked one's name, one does not have to conduct a systematic memory search including the generation of likely names and the recognition of one's own. In contrast, in trying to recall the name of a person, not a close acquaintance, whom one has not seen for years, a generation–recognition search of memory may well be most effective. Similarly, retrieval of the names of distant relatives may well occur on the basis of a familiarity check, with no assessment of contextual cues. However, recognizing persons in photographs may well require a systematic search of memory for information concerning the context in which one might have previously met the person.

Studies that have examined the retention of prose (e.g. Bartlett, 1932; Rubin, 1977) and of episodes such as traffic accidents (e.g. Loftus, 1979; Loftus and Palmer, 1974; Yarmey, 1979) have established that retrieval from memory is often a reconstructive process. Adults tend to recall those aspects of the situation that are most meaningful and fit their expectations best. For example, if the subjects' expectations have changed since the story was first read, then they will distort the story in accordance with their expectations. Research has shown that in some cases subjects actually believed that their plausible reconstructions and their fabrications were correct and accurate. This research has shown that retrieval from memory can also be a highly idiosyncratic process which is guided by plausible inferences made by the individual.

The research discussed in this section provides justification for the assessment of skills of retrieval from memory in the NAT to be based on separate tests of recognition and recall.

A decision whether a multi-store, two-process or strategy model would provide the most feasible explanation of retrieval from memory is not necessary in this context. From a functional point of view these theoretical approaches are highly compatible, and they share the same paradigm, namely recall and recognition, for the assessment of the ability to retrieve previously acquired material.

The assumption that the same or highly similar memory processes operate in the memorization of verbal (including both meaningful stimuli and nonsense syllables) and non-verbal information is based on the work by Ebbinghaus (1885), Bartlett (1932), Carmichael, Hogan and Walters (1932), Hebb and Ford (1945) and others. The early research was aptly summarized by Woodworth (1938) and discussed in relation to the controversy between Gestalt theorists and the behaviourist–functionalist climate of American psychology dominant at the time. A second source is a long review chapter by Riley (1962), which deals with research up to 1960, from a broader perspective.

After 1960, newer approaches began to emerge in memory research. As in other areas of cognitive psychology, these approaches focused more heavily on the processes involved, and provided even stronger support for the operation of highly similar variables with respect to memorization and retrieval of input of different types and in different modalities (e.g. Anderson and Bower, 1973; Crowder, 1972, 1976; Paivio, 1977; Paivio and Csapo, 1969, 1973; Posner and Keele, 1967; Talland and Waugh, 1969).

The role of verbal labels for non-verbal input and imagery for verbal stimuli to facilitate both encoding and retrieval processes as an important and highly efficient strategy was established in this and other research (e.g. Neisser, 1972).

The nature of encoding, that is, the characteristics of the codes formed when the input is first studied, is dependent in part on both non-verbal input and imagery, which occur automatically, and strategies that are under the control of the individual. Thus, some sensory, episodic as well as semantic information is encoded and retrieved automatically as a result of attending to the stimulus. The occurrence of such coding varies with factors such as difficulty, meaningfulness, item familiarity, pronounceability, etc. The individual is able to change the nature of the codes deliberately during study. Often the codes are determined by environmental or other variables which are related to the activities in which the learner engages when the information is first presented. The learner's expectancies regarding the demands of the task (e.g. Mutter, 1980) and differential experience (e.g. Chi, 1976) are likely to modify the variables that determine the choice of code.

Auditory Versus Visual Input

Many years of research have been concerned with the possibility of modality-specific encoding (e.g. Crowder and Morton, 1969; Kahneman, 1973; Murdock and Walker, 1969; Watkins and Watkins, 1973). The search for possible modality-determined differences has taken place particularly in the context of the study of specific learning disabilities. Children who were diagnosed as experiencing specific learning disabilities were frequently found to be deficient in visual short-term memory or in auditory short-term memory. Tests such as the Illinois Test of Psycholinguistic Ability (ITPA) (Kirk, McCarthy, and Kirk, 1968) include subtests to detect such deficiencies.

Although the possibility of modality-specific weaknesses has not been ruled out, the problem is likely to be more complex than previous research had suggested.

One important distinction that has not been made consistently is between the modality of input presentation that resulted in particularly low performance, and the modality in which the deficiency manifests itself most strongly. Most research workers in the area of learning disabilities, and the diagnostic and remediation specialists, appear to have assumed that the modality in which the stimulus has been presented is the same as that in which the deficiency takes place. For example, if a student does poorly on visually presented information, the immediate assumption is that the deficiency is contained in the visual memory system. Yet, the problem might be that the visual information lacks clarity, meaningfulness, etc., or that the visual codes are slow to form or difficult to retrieve, or subject to strong interference.

Alternatively, it has been shown that most individuals presented with information code both visually and auditorily. This recoding from visual to auditory and vice versa may be less efficient in some individuals than in others. The source of difficulty with visual stimuli in such cases would therefore not be the visual system but the mechanisms and strategies by which such recoding occurs, or even in the auditory system.

In a recent experiment Ceci, Lea, and Ringstrom (1980) presented visual and auditory input to three groups of learning-disabled children and to one control group. One of the groups of children with learning disabilities had previously been diagnosed as having visual but not auditory memory problems, another group had auditory but not visual memory problems. Visually and auditorily cued tasks were used. In the visual tasks the cues employed were either colour, location or category names. The auditory tasks used speaker's voice, rhymes or the names of categories. The results of the experiment were surprising. The learning-disabled children had no difficulties in the respective modalities in which they were expected to be deficient. More specifically, those children who had been diagnosed as having deficits in auditory memory performed well on the auditory task when the cues were the speaker's voice or rhymes, but did poorly when the cues were the category names. Similarly, the group experiencing visual impairment performed well on the visual tasks when the cues were colour or location, but performed poorly when the cues were category names. Ceci et al. (1980) interpreted these results as indicating a modality-specific deficit in semantic encoding. In other words, the children who had been diagnosed as having poor visual memories were not translating visual stimuli (pictures) into semantic codes or were not coding them as effectively as they did the auditory stimuli. The reverse situation was observed in the group that had been diagnosed as having poor auditory memories. In other experiments (e.g. Kroll, 1975) it was shown that auditory and visual stimuli were encoded (learnt) with equal ease by subjects with different modality deficits.

What these studies exemplify is how easy it is to misinterpret research results in this area. The fact that converging results concerning individuals' responses to different input modalities are obtained does provide evidence for convergence in encoding and retrieval processes. An experimenter may attempt to control encoding through the choice of stimuli or instructions, or by using meaningless material. Unfortunately, using pictures does not guarantee that only visual code will be employed. Testees may label pictures, sounds, nonsense syllables, etc. for themselves and store the words.

Individual Differences

Impressive success has been achieved, since the beginning of this century, in the assessment and prediction of individual differences in short-term memory. Memory deficits have been found to be highly correlated with low intellectual ability and educational achievement. The correlation between specific and more general learning disabilities, and low performance on short-term memory tests is high, indeed.

Unfortunately, success in the identification and prediction of memory deficits has rarely been accompanied by serious efforts to account for such individual differences in terms of psychological variables and processes.

In the previous sections of this chapter a variety of components and processes that, either singly or in combination, may be responsible for individual differences in short-term memory have been noted. Although it would be of interest to establish whether systematic individual differences can be found in some or all of these components, this is not an aim in the present context. Rather, a more relevant question at this point, in terms of application, is whether systematic individual differences that manifest themselves in a variety of cognitive processes involving short-term memory can be observed. As suggested by Neisser (1982):

> Psychology has followed two routes in the study of memory. Travellers on the high road hope to find basic mental mechanisms that can be demonstrated in well-controlled experiments; those on the low road want to understand the specific manifestations of memory in ordinary human experience. (Neisser, 1982, p.xi)

Studies of the memory deficits of brain-damaged individuals (e.g. Goldstein, 1948; Kinsbourne and Wood, 1975; Luria, 1973; Milner, 1964; Warrington and Weiskrantz, 1970), and the investigation of developmental differences, particularly in relation to the development of encoding and retrieval strategies (reviewed by Dempster, 1981; Halford, 1982; and others) have made important contributions in this respect, as have studies of memory processes in reading and failure to learn to read (e.g. Money, 1966; Stanley, 1975; Vernon, 1960; Young and Lindsley, 1970).

Memory span has been linked with *intelligence* since the beginnings of psychology. Galton (1887) found that memory span tasks accurately distinguished 'normal' from mentally retarded persons. At the same time Jacobs (1887) noted that increases in digit span, to which he referred as 'span of prehension' paralleled the scholastic ability rankings of students in schools. In a review of early research, Blankenship (1938) noted that the importance of memory span as a measure of ability was documented before the turn of this century. More recently, Dempster (1981), Hunt (1978), Hunt, Lunneberg, and Lewis (1975), and others have provided strong evidence for the robust, but not necessarily linear relationship that exists between short-term memory and intelligence.

In an early, comprehensive study (Bolton, 1891–1892) gave short-term memory tests to samples of students ranging from Year 3 to high school. He observed a systematic growth in short-term memory capacity with age, with the function becoming asymptotic by Year 6, at a memory span of approximately 6 digits. A number of more recent studies (e.g. Brown and Campione, 1972; Brown and Scott, 1971; Campione, Brown, and Ferrara, 1982) have shown that young children and adults do not differ in their ability to recognize simple previously presented stimuli. When more complex information is involved (e.g. Dirks and Neisser, 1977; Mandler and Johnson, 1976) developmental differences in short-term memory are observed, but according to

Campione et al. (1982), Mackworth and Bruner (1970) and others, these appear to be related more to acquisition and/or scanning strategies than to differences in the processes or storage involved in short-term memory.

It is generally maintained that high levels of *arousal* have a negative influence on short-term memory (e.g. Craik and Blankstein, 1975; M.W. Eysenck, 1976; H.J. Eysenck, 1967, 1981; and others) have suggested that performance differences between extroverts and introverts, or high and low impulsive persons (e.g. Reville, Humphreys, Simon, and Gilliland, 1980) may be understood in terms of differences in basal arousal or in terms of phase differences in the diurnal arousal rhythm. However, apart from Walker's (1958) theory, work on arousal has proceeded largely independently of theoretical work on short-term memory. According to Walker's (1958) theory, supported by Deffenbacher, Platt, and Williams (1974), Geen (1974), Kleinsmith and Kaplan (1963) and others, a memory trace of a piece of information is laid down during rehearsal or learning. Because formation of memory is not instantaneous, a period of consolidation follows, during which the trace can be accessed only with difficulty. Walker postulated that arousal would increase inhibition during this period of consolidation, with the result that a stronger secondary trace, that is, short-term memory, was formed. Thus, according to Walker's theory, arousal injures retrieval from short-term memory but facilitates retrieval from long-term memory.

Memory Disorders

In addition to the previously mentioned major causes of forgetting through disuse or decay and through interference, both of which are based on the passage of time, a number of other variables can lead to non-pathological forgetting.

Retrieval can be hampered by lack of *availability*. When too much information has been encoded within a short time, memory capacity can be exceeded, and the information lost. When too much time has elapsed between instances of retrieval, old memories can fade. Retrieval can also be hampered by lack of *accessibility*. Attaching inappropriate cues to information, for example inappropriate priority information, may lead to failure to recall the highest priority information; poor attention and very similar cues applied to more than one piece of information can cause interference and confusion during retrieval.

Forgetting due to loss of availability of stored information can occur when too little rehearsal has taken place, or if recently acquired information receives priority over previously learnt material, thus displacing the latter. Another common cause of forgetting is confusion or interference from accoustically or semantically similar stimuli.

Memory disorders accompanying senility often show a clarity in memory for events from the distant past drawn inappropriately into the present. Such inappropriately recalled information when interjected into conversations concerning the present tend to be viewed as unimportant if not trivial, by others, but it has important situational and emotional associations for the person who is judged by others as disoriented with respect to time and/or situation. More severe 'loss of memory' or *amnesia* can be caused by severe emotional shock, physical injury or other assaults to the brain, continued abuse of alcohol and barbiturates. The term *retrograde amnesia* refers to the loss of memory for information that was encoded prior to the trauma. *Anterograde amnesia* refers to loss of memory for events after the trauma.

When amnesia is *localized*, specific information that one might expect to have been encoded approximately around the time of the trauma is unavailable for recall. In cases of *selective* amnesia, which often follows emotional trauma, the individual fails to be able to recall the particular event, for example the death of a spouse, a war experience, a car accident, etc. *Generalized* amnesia is reflected in the inability of a person to recall any life events prior to and surrounding a traumatic event. Finally, failure to recall events around the time of the trauma and into the present is referred to as *continuous* amnesia.

Amnesias vary considerably in severity, ranging from quite transient cases, for example 'football amnesia', to cases of permanent and profound memory disturbance resulting from brain damage.

> In general, amnesia seems to result from an inability on the part of a person to use associative memory structures. This defect influences three separate aspects of the recall process. First, the patient can not bring the appropriate associations to bear when encoding new inputs. As a result, the amnesic's encoding of new input resembles the normal subject's encoding in a distractor task. Second, the patient cannot use retrieval cues to generate potential targets during the generation phase of recall. Finally, even if the patient generates the target, the inability to trace the association between the cue and the target hinders identification. (Glass, Holyoak, and Santa, 1979, p.131)

Special types of memory disorders are encountered by persons who are regarded as mentally retarded. Even after strongly rehearsed motor and elementary cognitive exercises, the memory of these individuals frequently remains very much short-term.

Other special cases of memory disorder are reflected in various *aphasias*. Under such conditions, previously accomplished and frequently practised skills, such as reading, writing and the recognition of pictures or faces, have become unavailable as a result of neurological trauma, which can be brought on by a stroke or other cortical mishaps.

All memory disorders are likely to be the result of faulty encoding of incoming information and ineffective use of retrieval strategies and cues. In both 'normal' and pathological memory processes, encoding and retrieval processes operate in a highly interactive manner.

The NAT Memory Tests

Four memory tests have been included in the NAT battery. These are Test 15: Visual Recognition, Test 16: Auditory Recognition, Test 17: Auditory Recall, and Test 18: Visual Recall. Thus, recognition and recall are measured separately for both visual and auditory input.

Pending the collection of further data, these tasks are being regarded as supplementary tests at the present time. This means that the score obtained on the NAT memory tests has not been included in the derivation of the NAT Score, that is, the total score representing performance on the NAT battery. Obviously, performance on the memory tests can be included on the ability profile. *However, the scaled scores obtained on the memory tests must not at any time be used in the calculation of the NAT Score.*

Before concluding that highly discrepant scores in the memory area of the profile reflect a unique strength or weakness, other possibilities should be considered. The NAT memory tests provide measures of attention as well as of short-term memory. A comparison of the scores obtained on the memory tests, Tests 15 to 18, and the attention tests, Tests 10, 12, 13 and 14, can thus lead to important diagnostic hypotheses.

Both the memory and the attention tests are influenced by distractibility, and the attention tests require short-term memory to some extent. A significant deviation in performance in the attention tests may thus be meaningfully related to high or low performance on the memory tests. The tasks contained in the memory tests require of the individual the ability to retain several items that are not logically related to one another, and that are to be retrieved by either recognition or recall.

Among the subject characteristics influencing performance on the NAT memory tests are short-term memory, attention, mental alertness, freedom from distractibility, sequencing ability and anxiety. The demands of the NAT recall tests have considerable similarity with those made of subjects performing the Digit Span Test contained in the Binet Scale and the Wechsler tests in all their revisions, and in many other individually administered tests (Kubota, 1965; Rapaport et al. 1968; Sattler, 1982).

In Guilford's (1967) 'structure of intellect' classification the NAT memory tests could be classified under 'memory for symbolic systems', that is, the ability to remember the order in which symbolic information has been presented.

As in the case of the Digit Span tests (see review by Batchelder and Denny, 1977) performance on the NAT memory tests can be expected to show only a low correlation with general intelligence, in this case the total NAT Score.

Wechsler (1958) gave serious consideration to the desirability of the continued inclusion of the Digit Span tests in his test batteries. He decided to retain the subtest as an optional test, because be believed that memory span 'though on the whole a poor measure of intelligence, it is nevertheless an extremely good test at the lower levels' (Matarazzo, 1972, p.204). Also, there is impressive evidence that school-related problems such as difficulty in learning to read, problems in arithmetic and other learning disabilities correlate highly with low performance on short-term memory tasks (e.g. Kaufman, 1979; Lutey, 1977; Rugel, 1974; Silverstein, 1968).

Finally, but most importantly, it must be kept in mind that, more than any other ability component, short-term memory is a variable on which a certain minimum level of capacity is required. On the other hand, even extremely high performances in short-term memory tasks seem to contribute little to the general intellectual capacity of the individual (Wechsler, 1958).

The memory tests were found to have low correlations not only with the NAT Score but also with most other subtests of the battery for the reasons just explained.

The NAT memory tests provide a means of indicating, in a language-free setting, whether an individual has the relatively minimal required skills. Obviously, the effectiveness of the tests is entirely dependent on strict attention to the stimuli being presented and on the absence of noise and other distracting stimuli from the testing situation. Anxiety on the part of the testee will have a detrimental effect on performance.

The NAT memory tests are likely, together with the attention tests, to provide a valuable measure of freedom from distractibility.

PART III

THE INTERPRETATION OF PERFORMANCE ON THE NAT

Part II of this book described the content areas on which the NAT subtests are based from a historical and theoretical perspective. The aim of the chapters contained in Part III is to describe the abilities and skills that are measured by the NAT battery as a whole, and the component abilities assessed by combinations of individual subtests. Taken together, the three chapters included in this section should enhance the NAT user's ability to interpret NAT scores and ability profiles both quantitatively and qualitatively.

The dimensions measured by the NAT are discussed empirically and developmentally. Chapters 9 and 10 are largely descriptive. In contrast, Chapter 11 could be called prescriptive, because it suggests quantitative techniques for the interpretation of the NAT profile of performance scores.

The quantitative methods described in Chapter 11 are not merely descriptions of the obtained scores in terms of means and standard deviations, but build on these by adding psychological knowledge to statistics, and offer techniques that permit an understanding of the individual's profile of abilities. Chapters 9 and 10 report on the validity of the NAT for the assessment of cognitive functioning and development.

Chapter 9 begins with a general discussion of major aspects of test validity, and contains a brief non-mathematical introduction to the use of factor analysis in test development and research. This is followed by a description of the factor structure of the NAT.

Chapter 10 discusses the content and structure of major factors from an empirical, developmental and theoretical perspective. The aim in this chapter is to look at the inter-relationship between subtests of the NAT to see whether they group together in ways that add to their explanation and understanding.

Chapter 11 suggests quantitative techniques for the interpretation of the ability profile derived from the scores obtained on individual subtests of the NAT. The chapter proceeds from the discussion of global findings to more precise areas of possible strengths and weaknesses in the testee's performance. Chapter 11 thus begins with the interpretation of the NAT Score, that is the total score obtained on the battery, then discusses perceptual and conceptual abilities, and attention. Finally, an approach to the interpretation of possible significant fluctuations in the individual's scores on specific subtests is discussed.

The quantitative analyses described in the chapters of Part III of this book go beyond the description of obtained psychometric values; these are presented in sufficient clarity in the *Manual for the Non-Verbal Ability Tests* (Rowe, 1985c). Rather, the approach taken is to build on the statistical information, add common sense to psychometrics, and offer a better understanding of the psychological meaningfulness and educational implications of profiles of component skills.

The qualitative interpretation of performance, stressed in Chapters 10 and 11 compliment the statistical procedures, and are a necessary ingredient for the achievement of the goal described above, on the part of the NAT user.

CHAPTER 9

THE CONSTRUCT VALIDITY OF 14 NAT SUBTESTS

This chapter is organized into five sections as follows: The first section recapitulates a number of basic ideas concerning the concept of test validity. The next section provides a brief non-mathematical explanation of the rationale of factor analysis, while the third section describes the findings resulting from the calculation of principal components analysis for the data derived from the total sample. The fourth section discusses the principal components analyses performed on the scores of special groups, including different age levels, and the next section summarizes the findings relating to the construct validity of the test battery, and their implications for the interpretation of the NAT.

Validity

The validity of a test is generally reported in terms of the extent to which the test measures what it is intended to be measuring. Strictly speaking, 'one validates not a test but an interpretation of data arising from a specified procedure' (Cronback, 1971, p.447).

This distinction is of relevance, because it is quite possible for a test to be reasonably valid for the measurement of one kind of characteristic but totally invalid for the measurement of other characteristics. Also, a test can be valid for the measurement of a variable on one group of persons, but entirely invalid for the measurement of the identical variable in another group. It is thus not meaningful to use the term validity in relation to the instrument itself, but rather to apply it to the use of the measuring instrument in relation to the purpose for which it was designed, and for which it is being used.

> Validity is always validity for the measurement of a particular variable. There is no such thing as general validity nor is there absolute validity—we determine the *degree* of validity. (English and English, 1958, pp.574–575)

In the NAT, as in any other instrument used in the assessment process, the term validity refers to the property of the battery that ensures that the obtained scores correctly reflect and describe the variable(s) they are intended to describe.

There are two kinds of approaches to the establishment of validity for the use of a test for a specific purpose or in a particular situation: (1) approaches that compare the content of the test (the subtests or items, whichever is appropriate) with a specified area of knowledge, an area of functioning, set of skills, or other potentially relevant pool of possible test content, that is, *content validity*; and (2) approaches that investigate how the test actually works when given to a sample of the population for which it has been intended and in relation to an outside criterion, that is, *empirical validity*.

Content validity establishes whether a test measures the variables or behaviours that make up the domain under scrutiny. It depends on the degree to which the test content reflects a specified domain of variables. The types of questions that have to be asked in the establishment of content validity include the following. Can the items elicit examples of the kind of performance the test is intended to measure? Collectively, can the items be regarded as a representative sample of the class of performance that constitutes the variable to be measured?

Content validity is particularly useful in the appraisal of achievement tests. For example, in an arithmetic test the items should be chosen in such a way that knowledge of arithmetic and arithmetical skills are the main determiners of performance, rather than, say, reading ability.

There are no well-defined objective criteria of content validity, but a thorough examination of the research literature provided an indication of the types of items that might promise content validity for the measurement of perceptual, conceptual, attention, and memory components of general ability.

> Inevitably content validity rests mainly on appeals to reason regarding the adequacy with which important content has been cast in the form of test items. (Nunnally, 1978, p.93)

Another type of content validity is *face validity*. In its more specific usage the term refers to the extent to which a test is made up of items that on casual inspection seem related to the variables being measured. Anastasi (1976) described face validity as follows:

> It refers not to what the test actually measures, but to what it appears superficially to measure. Face validity pertains to whether a test 'looks valid' to the examinees who take it, the administrative personnel who decide on its use, and other technical untrained observers. (p.139)

The validity described above is hardly sufficient, and is not acceptable as a validity in the measurement sense, although it may contribute to gaining acceptance for an instrument.

Construct validity is probably the most sophisticated form of content validity. According to Popham (1975) it 'attempts, at the same time, to verify both the existence of some hypothetical construct, and a given test's ability to measure that construct' (p.153).

The construct validity of the NAT battery reflects the degree to which each area assessed by the NAT is a sample of the phenomenon or the behaviours defined by the construct in question, that is, cognitive functioning, and the degree to which the tests collectively are representative of the phenomenon thus defined.

The construct validity of the NAT battery was investigated by computing a number of factor analyses, the results of which are reported in this and the following chapters.

The most important empirical validity is *predictive validity*. This provides a measure of the degree to which future performance can be predicted on the basis of performance on the test. Predictive validity is a measure based on the correspondence actually observed for a representative sample of persons between their test scores and their actual behaviour or performance at a given interval after testing. A successful investigation of the predictive validity of the NAT is reported in Chapter 12.

Concurrent validity compares performance on one test with that on others that are accepted as assessing the same variables. Evidence of the concurrent validity of the NAT with other intelligence tests is presented in Chapter 13.

Evidence for the validity of the NAT subtests was thus derived from four quite separate perspectives. The theoretical evidence based on previous published research presented in Part II of this book is independent of the evidence obtained on the basis of factor analytic and predictive studies of the NAT. In addition, the detailed tables, presented in Chapter 13, of the correlations between the NAT and other tests, provide a fourth independent perspective for the validity of the battery.

This approach to discuss the validity of the NAT from several independent aspects, namely, on the basis of separate analyses, has been chosen for several reasons. Most importantly it was recognized that each mode of investigation of the validity of the battery does indeed present a unique view of the tests, their characteristics and interpretation, individually and collectively.

The theoretical background provided in Chapters 5 to 8 dealing with individual subtests offers a consistent and logical theoretical system of information for the understanding of the part played by each test in the comprehensive assessment provided by the NAT. The investigation of the relationship between NAT performance and school achievement, reported in Chapter 12, shows that the NAT is capable of providing a broad estimate of cognitive performance that relates to areas external to the instrument itself. The correlations between tests, discussed in Chapter 13, reveal actual patterns of interaction, which arise either out of their item content or their underlying theoretical structure.

Finally, the factor analyses described in this chapter and in Chapter 10 allow for the grouping of tests in (on the whole) logical combinations that indicate the subtests of the NAT that are most closely related to each other. This makes it possible to identify factor patterns that can describe and explain performance, and provides the possibility of identifying particular areas of strength or weakness in the intellectual ability or skills of an individual.

Factor Analysis in Test Development and Research

The findings concerning the construct validity of the NAT discussed in this chapter and in Chapter 10 were obtained on the basis of factor analyses computed on an initial set of performance scores obtained on the battery by 1135 individuals, ranging in age from 8 years to adult. The scores obtained on the separate tests and part tests were the variables under investigation.

As discussed in Chapter 13 the relatively low intercorrelations between the subtests constituting the NAT battery suggest that fairly distinct component skills are being measured in different subtests.

To analyse the intercorrelations between subtests in matrices of the size of those shown in Appendix B in the Manual (Rowe, 1985c), would be an extremely tedious, and mathematically crude procedure. Therefore, factor analyses were computed in order to ascertain whether performance on the different tests had something in common.

The term factor analysis refers to a set of statistical techniques, each of which makes slightly different assumptions, but all of which make it possible to investigate the internal relationship between a set of variables, for example to interpret scores and correlations between scores from a number of tests.

It is beyond the scope of this book to cover the mathematical basis or the computational procedures of factor analysis. For brief, relatively simple introductions to the field the reader is referred to such texts as Cattell (1978), Child (1970), or Maxwell (1977). More detailed treatments of the methodology of factor analysis can be found in Fruchter (1954), Gorsuch (1974), Harman (1976), and similar sources.

However, an understanding of the use and the results of factor analysis is not dependent on knowledge of the mathematical underpinning or mastery of the computational procedures. What is required is the application of psychological knowledge and understanding. The description of the nature of a particular factor is based on an examination of the tests that load highly on the factor, and on the identification of the types of psychological processes these high-loading tests have in common.

One of the major outcomes of the use of factor analysis in the area of intelligence assessment has been the formulation of theories about the organization of cognitive abilities. In simplest terms, a factor may be understood as a construct for the orderly description of the performance of individuals on a variety of tests. Factors pertain to the inter-relationship between the scores obtained on a number of different tests. For example, if a group of people perform equally well (or badly) on a considerable number of verbal tests, such as analogies, verbal closure, word knowledge, etc., a verbal score might be substituted for the scores obtained on the individual tests. Moreover, if the scores obtained on these verbal tests were to show little, or no correlation with the scores obtained on mathematics, spatial or other types of tests, one might regard the verbal factor as a distinct dimension in terms of which the performance of the individuals can be described. As will be shown, the same can hold for non-verbal abilities.

Qualitative theories concerning the units by which human mental functioning might be represented, or into which the 'mind' might be subdivided, have been proposed ever since philosophers became interested in what it is that sets human abilities apart from those of other animals. The writings of Plato (429–348 BC) and Aristotle (384–322 BC) show that sophisticated philosophical theorizing concerning the structure of the human intellect took place at that early period.

Aristotle accounted for thoughts, dreams and rationality by postulating the existence of multiple souls. The lowest soul, responsible for purely vegetative functions, was regarded as common to all living organisms. In addition to this, animals had a soul that controlled movement. Only man possessed the highest soul, 'nous', which was seen as controlling reason.

However, quantitative studies of the inter-relationship of abilities and other psychological variables have become possible only since the beginning of this century, and since the development of quantitative methods such as correlation and factor analysis.

The basic assumption in the use of factor analysis is that if two or more activities or variables involve a common element, there will be a reasonably sized correlation between them. If two or more tests are taken by a number of persons, the size of the correlations obtained between the scores in the different tests is dependent on the extent to which common abilities or skills constitute the prerequisites for successful completion of the tests. Thorndike (1982, p.277) wrote 'The data provided by test scores are in varying degrees correlated—overlapping and redundant'.

Factor analysis consists of a search for factors that reflect these correlations.

> A factor when found represents the fact that for the persons tested there is an area or region of behaviour within which individuals respond quantitatively in a consistent manner, independently of the particular stimuli. (English and English, 1958, p.199)

A major goal in the application of factor analysis is usually that the smallest number of factors accounting for the largest amount of information contained in the data be extracted.

The rationale for interpretation of the results of any factor analytic procedures is thus based on two assumptions: (1) that tests that have high loadings on a common or a group factor (discussed below) have something in common, and (2) that the individual's performance on each test is due to the weighted sum of a relatively small number of basic underlying abilities. The weighting is likely to differ for each test or task, but the assumption that level of performance is the effect of a summation of abilities remains the same.

The term common factor, used above, refers to a factor on which all variables, in this case tests, load significantly. A group factor is a factor on which some but not all variables load significantly.

What it is that tests loading on the same factor have in common cannot always be determined with certainty. Spearman himself offered only tentative hypotheses suggesting that 'g' might be regarded as the source of general 'mental energy', a concept to be discussed later in this chapter.

American researchers tended to favour multiple factor theories of intelligence, that is, models that recognize 'a number of moderately broad group factors, each of which may enter with different weights into different tests' (Anastasi, 1958, p.325).

The leading exponents of the multiple factor theory of intelligence were Thurstone and his co-workers. Thurstone proposed a 'primary mental abilities' model of intelligence, which was based on about a dozen factors. Those most frequently replicated in Thurstone's own work and in the work of independent investigators (e.g. Ekstrom, French, and Harman, 1976; French 1951; Guilford, 1967; Thurstone, 1938a, 1938b; Thurstone and Thurstone, 1941a, 1941b), are the following:

- *V*   VERBAL COMPREHENSION, that is, the principal factor in reading comprehension, verbal reasoning, verbal analogies, disarranged sentences, proverb explanation, word knowledge, etc.
- *W*   WORD FLUENCY, generally associated with such tests as rhyming, the finding of words with specified characteristics (e.g. cities beginning with the letter A), creativity tests of the type of 'How many uses can you think of for a piece of string?'
- *N*   NUMBER, a factor most closely related to speed and accuracy of simple arithmetic computations.
- *S*   SPACE, that is, a factor that might consist of two distinct factors, one covering the perception of fixed spatial relations, and the other relating to 'manipulatory visualization', in which there is a requirement to visualize transformations, changed positions, directions, etc.

M	ASSOCIATIVE MEMORY, which occurs in tests requiring rote memory for paired associates. Thurstone felt that the evidence was against a broader factor that might have been involved in all memory tasks. Some investigators have proposed other restricted memory factors, such as visual and auditory memory.
P	PERCEPTUAL SPEED, namely, the ability to grasp quickly and accurately visual details, similarities, and differences. It has been suggested that this factor may be the same as the 'speed factor' identified by earlier investigators, and described as 'speed in dealing with very easy materials'.
I (or R)	INDUCTION (or GENERAL REASONING), a factor not clearly defined by Thurstone, who originally proposed an inductive and deductive factor. The latter was best measured by tests of syllogistic reasoning and the former by tests requiring the subject to find a rule, as in the completion of a number series. Evidence for the deductive factor is much more tentative than that for the inductive factor. Other investigators suggest a general reasoning factor, best illustrated by the requirements of arithmetic reasoning tests.

During the 1950s and 1960s a rapid proliferation of hypothesized factors took place. In the above description of some of Thurstone's primary mental abilities, reference has already been made to the possibility of two separate perceptual factors rather than one. Similarly a number of different reasoning factors, verbal factors, and further perceptual factors were identified. For example, Guilford (1964) divided the original verbal fluency factor into factors of associational, ideational, and expressional fluency. Guilford's model accounts for over forty factors, and the author notes further gaps in his model, where he expects other factors to be identified.

The large number of factor analytic studies of intelligence contained in the literature present a bewildering picture. It is difficult to cumulate findings. Studies vary in the type of subjects used, in the nature of the tests, and in the method of statistical analyses. The identification and comparison of factors across studies is almost impossible. Two factors that have been given identical names by different researchers may, in fact, show little if any similarities in content and structure. Conversely, not all factors bearing different names are necessarily distinguishable from one another.

There is a common tendency among test users to assume that an 'IQ' can be interpreted to have the same meaning regardless of the particular test from which it was derived. The above discussion highlights the erroneous nature of such practices.

Such an assumption not only disregards the fact that even the most 'valid' test of intelligence is valid only in relation to the test constructor's personal theory of intelligence, but also ignores that some intelligence tests are largely restricted to the measurement of, for example, verbal fluency or verbally communicated general knowledge, while others draw to a much greater extent on verbal and/or non-verbal problem solving abilities, and yet others focus exclusively on spatial or other perceptual functions.

Even the same test can call into play different and diverse combinations of component skills in different individuals.

Another important consideration in the interpretation of the results of factor analyses is that the correlation coefficients are not totally free from error, and tests with low reliability introduce further chance variation into the analysis, usually in the form of depressed correlation coefficients, and thus depressed loadings on factors.

In the analyses of the NAT, Tests 3 (Categorization), 4 (Picture Completion), and 9 (Picture Arrangement) showed relatively low reliability. This effect becomes very obvious in the pattern of factor loadings provided by these tests. In the present studies the KR20 formula, an estimate of internal consistency, was used as a measure of test reliability. As noted previously, the low reliability of the above tests is the result of their low internal consistency. Obviously, the tests that were internally least homogeneous showed the lowest reliability. Test/re-test reliability would have provided a better reliability estimate, but this could not be obtained within the financial and time constraints of this project. The collection of further data will allow better reliability estimates for these tests, and may thus present a truer picture of their contribution to particular factors. In other words, the estimate made of the contribution of these tests on the basis of the present data is likely to be very conservative.

According to Child (1970, p.1), 'A central aim of factor analysis is the "orderly simplification" of a number of inter-related measures'. More specifically, the aim of the analyses described here was to investigate the overlap of abilities and skills, and to identify an underlying structure that might allow a description of what is being measured by the NAT battery in terms of a smaller number of fundamental dimensions, that is, of component abilities.

Principal Component Analysis

The construct validity of the NAT was investigated on the basis of the factor analytic model of principal components analysis, sometimes also referred to as principal factor analysis. Mathematically, this type of factor analysis extracts principal factors from the correlation matrix with unities as diagonal elements. The extracted factors provide the best least-squares fit to the entire correlation matrix, with each succeeding factor accounting for the maximum amount of variance obtainable from the total set of correlations. The basic assumption is that all the variance contained in the data is relevant. Therefore the main diagonal remains unaltered, that is, it is set to unity, and the procedure attempts to account for all the variance in each test. Principal factors are reported in order of size.

The method of principal components analysis was chosen as a tool in the investigation of the construct validity of the NAT battery precisely because it aims to identify a structure that accounts for *all* the variance in a set of data, instead of restricting itself to the identification of common or shared variance. Factor analyses seeking a structure for the latter use communality estimates in the diagonal cells of the correlation matrix (conventionally, in this type of analysis, a first estimate of communality for each variable is provided by its highest correlation with any other variable—this estimate can later be refined). But the principal components model of factor analysis includes specific and error variance (discussed below) as well as common or share variance, hence using unity in each diagonal cell of the interest correlation matrix.

The major appeal of the principal components model of factor analysis is that it represents the greatest proportion of the variance contained in a set of variables most economically, that is, in the fewest possible dimensions. The first principal component, or the first factor, 'is the best single condensation' (Gorsuch, 1974, p.107) when an efficient condensation of the variables is desired.

The principal components yielded by this procedure are new factors that are generated on the basis of a linear combination of the scores obtained on the subtests.

> The hope is that a small number of such linear composites can incorporate nearly all the information that is provided by the original, much larger set of test variables, and can hence simplify our description of each individual's characteristics. The hope is further, that judicious development of the factors can produce variables that imply a clear and meaningful psychological construct, so that our description of a person is not only simpler but also clearer and more incisive. (Thorndike, 1982, p.278)

The matrix of intercorrelations derived from the scores of 1135 individuals ranging in age from eight years to adult, on 14 subtests of the NAT, is shown in Table B1 in the Manual (Rowe, 1985c). This table shows a set of variables all of which are positively correlated, the correlations ranging from .64 down to .04.

As noted above, from this kind of matrix principal components analysis extracts factors in order of their importance, this being reflected by the amount of variance each factor explains. The first principal component explains the largest amount of variance between the scores. The amount of variance to be accounted for by all other factors is what is left over after the effects of the first principal component have been removed from the intercorrelations. In other words, if the loadings on the first principal component are subtracted from the original correlations between tests, the remainder (referred to as residual variance) represents the amount of correlation between tests to be accounted for by all remaining factors.

Principal components analysis tries to take out as much common variance as possible in the first factor. Subsequent factors are extracted in such a way that each subsequent factor accounts for the maximum amount of remaining common variance, until, ideally, no common variance remains. An advantage of extracting factors in order of their importance is that later factors are usually of little, if any, consequence, and can be ignored.

The size of the loadings on each factor represents the degree to which the tests correlate with a particular factor. The squared loading provides an indication of the proportion of a test's total variance that is explained by the factor.

For example, inspection of Table 9.2 shows that in the case of Factor I, the general ability or 'g' factor, all subtests correlated highly and positively. The highest loading NAT subtests, in descending order, were Test 6 (Figure Formation), Tests 12 and 13 (i.e. attention, speed and accuracy tests), and Test 9 (Picture Arrangement). The proportions of subtest variances accounted for by Factor I in Table 9.2 ranged from 72 per cent (for Test 6 'Figure Formation') down to 18 per cent (for Test 2 'Matching Direction'). On average, 49 per cent of the variances packed into each of the 14 NAT subtests included in the analyses were accounted for by the first factor 'g', the standard deviation being 17 per cent. (The results of the factor analyses will be discussed later in this chapter, present references being for explanatory purposes only.)

The communality (h^2) presented in the last column of Tables 9.2 to 9.8 shows the total shared or common variance of each test, that is, the variance shared in common with other tests contributing to the common factors (which is calculated by summing the squares of the loadings for each test over all factors). The communality does not reach unity for any test because the concern in the analyses described here was to extract common variance. Obviously, each test has some unique variance, namely,

> the part of total variance resulting from the unique properties possessed be the test, and as such would be entirely uncorrelated with other tests in a particular analysis. (Child, 1970, p.33)

The unique variance in a test is, in turn, made up of specific and error variance.

While most uses of factor analytic procedures require the rotation of factors to a more 'meaningful' position, such rotation does not alter the total amount of variance extracted or the number of significant factors. Although the size of each factor might alter during rotation, the total set of new factors produced by rotation will retain the same capacity to reproduce the original data matrix as was found for the initially identified set of principal components. Therefore, both the rotated and the unrotated factors reflect the same correlations with the same degree of accuracy.

In the present study, the factors obtained in the principal components analysis are directly interpretable, without the need for rotation. Prior theoretical information, which guided the selection of the test areas and the design of the items, made it possible to hypothesize that the underlying dimension of interest in the NAT battery would be the factor, determined by the weighted composite of the variances of the tests, that accounts for the greatest possible amount of variance between the tests, that is a general ability factor. Further, perceptual, conceptual, and concentration dimensions were hypothesized. The factors obtained in the analysis were found to be theoretically consistent with those that had been hypothesized. It was possible, therefore, to heed Cattell's admonition, and proceed empirically.

> One must prefer to let data speak for themselves rather than try to rotate factor configurations to fit any arbitrarily conceived set of operations, contents, and products. (Cattell, 1983, p.9)

The decision of how many non-trivial factors could be extracted by the principal components analyses was made on the basis of 'Kaiser's criterion', which was first suggested by Guttman and adapted by Kaiser (1964), Kaiser and Caffrey (1965). The criterion specifies that only factors with latent roots greater than one should be considered as common factors.

Cattell (1966a, 1966b) has pointed out that Kaiser's criterion is likely to be most reliable when the number of variables lies between 20 and 50. He showed that in analyses where the number of variables is less than 20, there is a tendency for the use of this criterion to result in the extraction of a conservative number of factors. Because of this the 'scree test' (Cattell, 1966b) was also applied to the results of the various principal components analyses obtained on the NAT scores.

The basic assumption underlying the scree test is that any set of variables, or any battery of tests, is measuring a limited number of factors well, and a larger number of specific, trivial and error factors much less well. Because of this, the predominant factors account for most of the variance, and are large, whereas the other factors might be quite numerous, but are small. As the principal components model extracts factors by size, the substantive factors will be extracted first, and the smaller trivial and error factors will be extracted later. Since the smaller factors tend to be so numerous, and are taken out in order of size, it can be expected that plotting their roots on a graph would result in a straight line sloping downwards. The dominant factors would not fall on this line, as some of them would probably be much more dominant than others.

The scree test seeks for breaks in the plotted roots, and in this way provides a factor solution based on the minimum number of factors accounting for the maximum amount of variance. At a point where the size of roots drops dramatically, an additional factor would add relatively little to the already extracted information.

In the present study, applications of the scree test and Kaiser's criterion produced equivalent numbers of factors for most analyses. The largest break occurred in all analyses between the first and second factors. The first, common factor thus stood out in the overall analysis and all group-specific analyses. In a few cases the results of the scree test were less clear cut with respect to later factors. It was thus decided to depend on Kaiser's criterion and, in this way, avoid the interpretation of possibly trivial factors. Obviously, the ultimate criterion for the determination of the appropriate number of factors is psychological meaningfulness, which should include taking cognizance also of descriptive efficiency, statistical invariance and usefulness for possible predictive purposes.

The results of the analyses performed on the scores of the NAT battery are summarized in Table 9.1. A principal components analysis of the total sample, based on the performance of 1135 subjects ranging in age from eight years to adult, was followed by analyses for different age groups. Separate analyses were conducted also on the NAT scores collected for a sample of Aboriginal students, all attending schools in non-urban areas of the Northern Territory, and for a group of institutionalized mentally retarded adults.

The obvious discrepancy between the number (N = 1135) included in the overall principal components analysis, referred to in Table 9.1 as the 'Total Sample', and the sum of the number of individuals included in the separate analyses is due to two events: One, the results of the sample of retarded adults were not included in the overall factor analysis, as it was evident, both from previous research and empirical observation in the present study, that different underlying abilities and skills were being measured in the retarded group; and two, not all the results for the 13-year-olds had been processed when the overall analysis was conducted. Because of the already large size of the latter sample, this was not regarded as unduly influencing the overall results of the principal components analysis.

The investigation of the construct validity of the battery in samples of varying age, and in diverse cultural groups provides evidence concerning the appropriateness and fairness of the use of the battery as a means of assessment for different groups. Comparability of factor structures for different groups, that is, a common basis for interpretation of the scores obtained on the tests in different groups, is a necessary condition for validity and fairness in the use of the NAT with persons of different age and cultural background.

Indeed, if a test is not measuring basically the same underlying abilities in different groups, its use with some or all such groups is likely to be inappropriate.

Results from the Overall Analysis of the NAT

The 'g' Factor

The overall principal components analysis yielded a strong common first factor, which accounted for 49.13 per cent of the total variance.

Table 9.1 Summary of Results of Principal Components Analyses on Different Samples

Sample	N	Number of factors extracted	Factor 1	Factor 2	Factor 3	Factor 4	Factor 5	Total
Total	1135	3	49.13	8.75	7.35	–	–	67.29
Aboriginals	90	4	41.17	10.28	8.57	7.27	–	67.29
Retarded adults	47	5	37.94	15.13	9.76	9.08	7.89	79.80
Age 5–7 yrs	46	5	29.81	21.84	13.34	12.46	8.11	85.56
Age 8 yrs	32	4	23.85	20.36	16.20	11.70	–	72.11
Age 9 yrs	36	5	32.31	17.21	10.98	10.16	8.89	79.55
Ages 8+9 yrs	68	5	29.74	15.23	12.61	10.11	8.14	75.83
Age 10 yrs	48	4	31.29	19.37	9.39	8.15	–	68.20
Age 11 yrs	56	4	37.52	14.59	12.60	8.25	–	72.95
Age 12 yrs	190	3	40.00	10.67	8.34	–	–	59.02
Age 13 yrs	346	3	37.05	10.71	8.20	–	–	55.96
Age 14 yrs	84	4	36.83	13.57	10.02	7.48	–	67.90
Age 15 yrs	108	4	36.18	12.84	8.91	8.18	–	66.11
Age 16 yrs	80	3	41.01	10.28	8.80	–	–	60.09
Age 17+ yrs	108	3	45.13	9.82	7.07	–	–	62.02
Mean		3.67	37.19	13.01	9.55	8.43		65.34
SD		0.71	4.71	3.09	1.91	0.99		6.61

The strength of this factor permits the postulation of a general cognitive ability factor, which contributes significantly to the performance on all the tests, and similar intellectual tasks. Conceptually, this general cognitive ability factor might be compared to the 'g' factor proposed by Spearman (1927), and supported by much research (e.g. Burt, 1940; McNemar, 1964; Thomson, 1939; Vernon, 1950).

However, attempts to define and explain the exact nature of 'g' have traditionally relied on various intuitions. Spearman himself offered only tentative hypotheses concerning the nature of 'g'. He proposed that it may be regarded as the general 'mental energy' (Spearman, 1927) of the individual, which provides the fuel for the execution of all other general and more specific intellectual tasks. Spearman regarded tests requiring the identification of semantic relations, for example verbal analogies, as the best measures of 'g'.

The theoretical validity of a general factor of cognitive ability was questioned as early as 1928, when Kelley, in his *Crossroads in the Mind of Man: A Study of Differentiable Mental Abilities* (Kelley, 1928), smoothed the way for other studies searching for group factors.

Kelley argued that the general factor was of relatively minor importance, and was usually attributable to the heterogeneity of the sample, and to the common verbal requirements of the tests employed. He suggested that where the general factor remained after these influences had been ruled out, it would be small and insignificant.

This is not the place to discuss in detail the voluminous literature resulting from the debate concerning single factor versus multiple factor models of intelligence. The interested reader is referred to McNemar's (1964) presidential address to the American Psychological Association, in which he provided a most useful synthesis of the controversial issues. McNemar's thesis is summarized in the following quotation from his paper:

> The concept of general intelligence despite being maligned by a few, regarded as a second-order factor by some, and discarded or ignored by others, still has a rightful place in the science of psychology and in the practical affairs of man. (McNemar, 1964, p.880)

Basically, McNemar's judgment is as valid today as 20 years ago when it was made. This does not imply that the nature of the construct 'g' is well or better understood. Herein lies the challenge for theoreticians and measurement professionals in the 1980s. As was noted in the opening chapters of this book, some progress is being made in this area as a result of the interaction and co-operation between cognitive, information-processing, differential, developmental, and experimental, psychologists and psychometricians.

The concern 'that millions who have been tested on general intelligence tests were measured for a non-existent function' (McNemar, 1964, p.871), while obviously applicable to a considerable number of misuses of intelligence tests, is not universally shared.

McNemar (1964) reminds readers that the American tradition of multifactor rather than 'g' theories of intelligence resulted from Thurstone's (1938b) first application of his centroid method and his subsequently reported failure to replicate Spearman's 'g'.

> As anticipated by some Spearman was not prone to admit defeat. He reworked Thurstone's data and a 'g' was found, plus some group factors. He charged that Thurstone's rotational process had submerged the general factor. (McNemar, 1964, p.871)

A further reason for questioning the conclusiveness of the independence of Thurstone's seven primary abilities is that Thurstone himself (Thurstone and Thurstone, 1941a, 1941b), after finding that—against expectation—his primary abilities were in fact intercorrelated, suggested that a general factor was needed to explain the interrelatedness of the primaries. This is what finally led to the idea of oblique axes, which were regarded as representing the primary abilities as first-order factors, while the general factor pervading the primary abilities was labelled as a second-order factor.

> Furthermore, it could always be said that, in the ability domain, it is less difficult to attribute psychological meaningfulness to first-order than to second-order factors, so why pay much attention to the latter? Thus it was easy for most American factorists to drop the concept of general intelligence and to advocate that tests thereof, despite their proven usefulness over the years, should be replaced by tests of primaries. Hence the emergence of differential aptitude batteries. (McNemar, 1964, p.872)

It remains to remind the reader of Thurstone's officially unexplained decision to allow for the summation of primary mental ability scores on his Primary Mental Abilities Test, so that an IQ-type score can be obtained.

The results of the analyses into the construct validity of the NAT show a strong and persistent 'g' factor, which is due neither to common verbal requirements, nor to the heterogeneity of the sample, as it has been replicated in the age-specific and other groups with special characteristics. Also the strong 'g' factor was obtained in a battery that did not contain any verbal tests.

Verbal reasoning skills are generally regarded as the best measures of cognitive ability. This view is supported by such studies as Cohen's (1957) well known and frequently cited analysis of the WAIS, in which he found just over 50 per cent of the test variance to be accounted for by a single general factor 'g'. The result of the investigation of the construct validity of the NAT is very similar to Cohen's findings, with one difference. In Cohen's study of the WAIS the first factor contained significant loadings from verbal tests, and Block Design emerged as the only non-verbal test shown to be a good measure of 'g'. In the light of this research the results of the analysis of the construct validity of the NAT battery are pleasing, indeed.

Table 9.1 provides a summary of the results of a number of principal components analyses that were performed on the NAT scores obtained by different samples.

The principal components analysis for the total sample yielded three significant factors, that is, factors with latent roots greater than one. Together these factors accounted for more than 65 per cent of the variance packed into the 14 subtests of the NAT battery investigated here.

As can be seen in Table 9.2, all 14 subtests contributed to the first factor, thus defining it as a general factor. All 14 loadings were positive and highly significant statistically ($p < .001$).

As noted previously, the loading of a test on a factor represents its correlation with that factor. The loadings on the 'g' factor ranged from 0.85 to 0.42, the mean and standard deviation of the size of the loadings being $X = 0.69$, and $SD = 0.13$ respectively.

These loadings, and those obtained on the first factors in the age-specific analyses, and in the other special groups presented in Tables 9.3.1 to 9.3.9, 9.4 and 9.5, are high compared with the loadings generally reported in the research literature. Guilford (1964), for example, estimated that 20 per cent of the correlation coefficients in typical analyses of cognitive measures are approximately zero, and that the mean correlation would be only 0.23.

Table 9.2   Results of Principal Components Analysis (Total Sample)

| | Common factor loadings | | | Communality |
Test	Factor 1	Factor 2	Factor 3	h^2
1	64	34	21	57
2	42	69	19	69
3	72	06	36	65
4	69	−01	32	58
5	72	−07	25	59
6	85	−07	01	73
7	46	−57	40	70
8	79	−09	−01	63
9	76	−10	05	59
10	68	20	−17	53
11	53	−47	−22	55
12	80	−07	−28	72
13	80	09	−41	82
14	78	08	−40	77
Latent root	6.79	1.22	1.03	
% Variance accounted	49.13	8.75	7.35	

The analysis accounted for 67.29% of the total variance.

Note: For the sake of clarity and economy positive signs (+) and decimal points have been omitted in the above and all subsequent tables included in this chapter.

Table 9.3.1 Results of Principal Components Analysis (Ages 8 and 9 years)

Common factor loadings

Test	Factor 1	Factor 2	Factor 3	Factor 4	Factor 5	Communality h²
1	22	−02	73	−43	21	81
2	16	20	70	−01	44	75
3	57	32	42	12	−05	62
4	56	57	13	04	−20	70
5	58	13	−15	−41	03	54
6	76	−27	−23	−21	24	81
7	39	68	−13	−07	−41	80
8	61	−36	−34	−15	37	78
9	72	−05	−35	−37	04	78
10	72	14	03	−01	−22	59
11	48	34	−22	61	27	84
12	53	−14	02	65	26	79
13	55	−60	22	17	−38	88
14	42	−68	33	15	−40	93
Latent root	4.16	2.13	1.76	1.41	1.14	
% Variance accounted	29.74	15.23	12.61	10.11	8.14	

The analysis accounted for 75.83% of the total variance.

Table 9.3.2 Results of Principal Components Analysis (Age 10 years)

Test	Factor 1	Factor 2	Factor 3	Factor 4	Communality h^2
1	51	04	60	−01	62
2	67	−25	32	−34	73
3	49	−52	26	05	58
4	63	−50	−13	19	70
5	49	−31	34	41	62
6	69	28	−25	31	71
7	38	−51	−13	33	53
8	51	46	−46	18	72
9	60	35	−01	36	61
10	60	−22	−08	−47	64
11	64	01	−41	−22	63
12	73	00	−20	−43	76
13	41	82	23	−04	90
14	28	81	31	−05	83
Latent root	4.38	2.71	1.31	1.14	
% Variance accounted	31.29	19.37	9.39	8.15	

The analysis accounted for 68.20% of the total variance.

Table 9.3.3 Results of Principal Components Analysis (Age 11 years)

Test	Factor 1	Factor 2	Factor 3	Factor 4	Communality h^2
1	53	45	−44	09	69
2	59	28	−45	21	67
3	67	15	−54	16	79
4	64	−16	−47	01	66
5	71	15	−20	−09	57
6	71	−25	21	−14	63
7	57	−51	08	−06	60
8	68	03	21	−52	78
9	62	−21	−03	−60	79
10	68	−21	26	10	58
11	57	−51	17	50	86
12	66	−16	46	40	83
13	47	68	47	03	91
14	39	74	46	05	91
Latent root	5.25	2.04	1.76	1.15	
% Variance accounted	37.52	14.59	12.60	8.25	

The analysis accounted for 72.95% of the total variance.

Table 9.3.4 Results of Principal Components Analysis (Age 12 years)

| | Common factor loadings ||| Communality h^2 |
Test	Factor 1	Factor 2	Factor 3	
1	54	46	−26	57
2	51	36	−31	49
3	65	27	29	58
4	58	39	−00	49
5	53	05	45	49
6	76	−06	05	58
7	57	−07	61	70
8	70	25	01	55
9	64	12	−23	48
10	62	09	−27	47
11	63	−25	30	55
12	79	−20	−12	68
13	63	−62	−27	85
14	64	−58	−19	78
Latent root	5.60	1.49	1.17	
% Variance accounted	40.00	10.67	8.34	

The analysis accounted for 67.29% of the total variance.

Table 9.3.5 Results of Principal Components Analysis (Age 13 years)

| | Common factor loadings ||| Communality h^2 |
Test	Factor 1	Factor 2	Factor 3	
1	52	−34	34	50
2	27	−68	13	55
3	62	−02	17	41
4	60	05	21	41
5	55	28	28	46
6	74	00	32	65
7	37	65	14	58
8	69	−06	12	49
9	66	02	28	51
10	68	−27	−29	62
11	45	55	−23	56
12	73	08	−26	61
13	72	−08	−48	76
14	71	−13	−46	73
Latent root	5.19	1.50	1.15	
% Variance accounted	37.05	10.71	8.20	

The analysis accounted for 55.96% of the total variance.

Table 9.3.6 Results of Principal Components Analysis (Age 14 years)

	Common factor loadings				
Test	Factor 1	Factor 2	Factor 3	Factor 4	Communality h^2
1	45	62	16	06	62
2	08	75	28	15	67
3	51	58	12	−24	67
4	60	24	−14	−30	53
5	55	39	−41	09	63
6	76	04	−09	−26	65
7	43	−08	−64	33	71
8	66	−33	−34	−22	71
9	74	−08	−25	−06	62
10	56	02	−03	69	79
11	49	−25	26	−25	43
12	84	−23	22	−11	82
13	76	−28	38	18	83
14	65	−29	50	23	81
Latent root	5.16	1.90	1.40	1.05	
% Variance accounted	36.83	13.57	10.02	7.48	

The analysis accounted for 67.90% of the total variance.

Table 9.3.7 Results of Principal Components Analysis (Age 15 years)

	Common factor loadings				
Test	Factor 1	Factor 2	Factor 3	Factor 4	Communality h^2
1	46	10	51	−14	50
2	20	49	62	−16	69
3	51	49	−11	−26	58
4	77	23	−25	19	74
5	62	38	01	23	58
6	78	−04	−27	−18	72
7	53	48	18	24	60
8	74	03	−27	−33	73
9	75	00	−32	−28	74
10	32	13	−14	79	76
11	44	−53	−04	18	51
12	66	−40	10	00	61
13	67	−43	34	11	76
14	62	−49	31	−02	72
Latent root	5.07	1.80	1.25	1.14	
% Variance accounted	36.18	12.84	8.91	8.18	

The analysis accounted for 66.11% of the total variance.

Table 9.3.8 Results of Principal Components Analysis (Age 16 years)

	Common factor loadings			Communality
Test	Factor 1	Factor 2	Factor 3	h^2
1	41	33	30	37
2	39	40	48	54
3	81	−26	06	73
4	77	−20	−06	64
5	63	−01	−50	65
6	78	−19	09	65
7	50	−15	−57	60
8	76	−07	35	71
9	62	−54	34	79
10	34	71	−14	64
11	52	17	−16	32
12	74	05	06	55
13	66	40	−03	60
14	76	09	−19	62
Latent root	5.74	1.44	1.23	
% Variance accounted	41.01	10.28	8.80	

The analysis accounted for 60.09% of the total variance.

Table 9.3.9 Results of Principal Components Analysis (Age 17+ years)

	Common factor loadings			Communality
Test	Factor 1	Factor 2	Factor 3	h^2
1	71	−12	−25	58
2	65	−30	20	55
3	75	−33	−01	67
4	78	00	−09	62
5	66	−16	−15	48
6	76	14	−10	61
7	56	−48	47	76
8	61	−13	−55	69
9	65	12	−44	49
10	57	−12	42	52
11	33	76	17	72
12	74	43	23	79
13	78	22	10	67
14	72	16	−02	54
Latent root	6.32	1.37	0.99	
% Variance accounted	45.13	9.82	7.07	

The analysis accounted for 62.02% of the total variance.

Table 9.4 Results of Principal Components Analysis (Retarded Adults)

Test	Factor 1	Factor 2	Factor 3	Factor 4	Factor 5	Communality h^2
1	58	-04	-01	-42	-51	77
2	79	-18	05	01	-29	74
3	73	32	23	-03	-22	74
4	60	-21	50	29	03	74
5	38	81	10	-20	-26	92
6	22	70	-19	59	-05	93
7	59	-41	24	04	-25	64
8	58	62	-03	-11	29	82
9	25	24	52	-35	56	83
10	72	-08	09	45	04	74
11	68	-26	-15	39	24	76
12	74	-31	11	-24	30	80
13	76	-09	-49	-18	13	88
14	67	-07	-64	-19	14	92
Latent root	5.31	2.12	1.37	1.27	1.10	
% Variance accounted	37.94	15.13	9.76	9.08	7.89	

The analysis accounted for 79.80% of the total variance.

Table 9.5   Results of Principal Components Analysis (Aboriginals)

	Common factor loadings				
Test	Factor 1	Factor 2	Factor 3	Factor 4	Communality h^2
1	56	−28	01	61	76
2	70	−28	−11	37	72
3	74	−28	−26	10	70
4	73	−00	−30	−06	63
5	67	−34	−22	−17	64
6	67	31	−29	−09	64
7	61	−46	06	−34	70
8	62	41	−20	13	61
9	49	40	26	12	48
10	65	−15	03	−46	66
11	46	59	−30	02	65
12	62	28	19	−28	58
13	71	03	55	05	81
14	67	06	60	07	82
Latent root	5.76	1.44	1.20	1.02	
% Variance accounted	41.17	10.28	8.57	7.27	

The analysis accounted for 67.29% of the total variance.

The highest loadings on this first or 'g' factor underlying the NAT were obtained on tests with a large requirement for conceptual abilities, and tests of the ability to concentrate. Research, psychological and educational practice, and general opinion regard both these areas as essential, if not as *the* essential, components of what is generally referred to as intelligence or cognitive ability.

Other Factors

The second and third factors[1] extracted were group factors, that is, they consist of some subsets of the variables measured by the battery as a whole. Both these factors are bipolar, which means that contrasting sets of variables are embodied in them, which is reflected mathematically in the occurrence of both positive and negative loadings on the same factor.

Eight subtests contributed significantly (p;.05) to the second factor, which was easily interpretable as a perceptual factor. In its bipolarity it distinguishes between visual discrimination and judgment (reflected in the positive loadings of Tests 1, 2, 13, and 14), and perceptual speed and accuracy skills (reflected in the negative loadings of Tests 7 (Mazes), and 11 and 12).

Factor III can be interpreted as a conceptual factor. It distinguishes between conceptual skills (reflected in high positive loadings on Tests 7 (Mazes), 3 (Categorization), 4 (Picture Completion), 5 (Embedded Figures), and attention/speed/accuracy/concentration skills (reflected in high negative loadings on Tests 14, 13, 12 and 11).

As noted in Chapter 6, the degree to which Test 7 (Mazes) can be regarded as more strongly relying on conceptual or on perceptual abilities depends on the cognitive strategies applied by the test taker in relation to this task. During testing it was observed, and subsequent statistical analyses bore this out also, that some test takers behaved as though this were purely a speed and accuracy task. No planning, foresight, or attempts to gain an overview of the structure of the maze was observed in these subjects. They appeared to be applying a purely *perceptual* approach. In contrast, other test takers were observed to be examining the maze carefully in its entirety, anticipating and planning before starting on the task, an obviously *conceptual* approach.

The interpretation of the other factors may appear less clear than that of the first, general factor. A reason for this is that in the principal components model of factor analysis the interpretation of factors beyond the first one requires the 'mental removal' of the variance attributable to the first factor from the meaning of each variable. This process of mental removal is not an easy task at any time, and is certainly not straightforward in situations where the first factor accounts for such a large proportion of the variance in the data.

In summary it can be said that in this part of the validation studies of the NAT battery more than 1100 subjects were administered 14 tests. Each individual test taker's performance is therefore described along 14 dimensions, corresponding to the scores

---

[1] The difference in the size of the loadings of Tests 11 and 12 on the perceptual factor is of interest. Considering each on their own, both these tests measure perceptual speed and accuracy, and one would therefore have expected them to show similarly sized loadings on the perceptual factor. However, taken in combination, performance on these tests involves a considerable measure of perceptual flexibility, that is, a *conceptual* skill, and a large measure of concentration ability, that is, the ability not to let the demands of the previous task (Test 11) interfere with those of the subsequent one.

obtained on each of the 14 tests. By applying principal components analysis it was found that three factors accounted for a considerable and statistically sufficient amount of the common variance covered by the 14 tests. It becomes possible, therefore, to substitute these three dimensions for the original 14 in the description of each individual test taker's performance on the NAT battery.

Results from Analyses of Data from Specific Groups

The principal component analyses calculated for specific age groups produced three significant factors (the content of which resembled closely that obtained in the overall analysis) for four age levels, four significant factors for four other age levels, and five significant factors for the youngest age group. The analysis of the scores obtained by the group of aboriginals also resulted in four significant factors.

Age-specific Analyses

The lower half of Table 9.1 reports the results of separate principal components analyses for nine different age groups. On the average, 3.61 factors (SD = 0.71) with latent roots of one or greater were extracted in these analyses.

Across these age-specific analyses the first, second and third principal components accounted, on the average, for 37.19 per cent (SD = 4.71%), 13.1 per cent (SD = 3.09%), and 9.55 per cent (SD = 1.91%) of the variance respectively.

Across the five age groups in which a significant fourth factor was extracted, this factor accounted, on the average, for 8.43 per cent of the variance (SD = 0.99%).

As can be seen in Table 9.1, in cases where a significant fifth factor was extracted, this factor accounted for just over 8 per cent of the total common variance.

The average total variance accounted for in the separate principal components analyses in the nine age groups was 65.34 per cent, (SD = 6.61%).

The average total variance accounted for in the age group in which four factors were extracted (X = 68.49, SD = 2.34) was significantly higher ($p<.002$) than that for the age groups in which only three factors were found to be significant (X = 59.27, SD = 2.19). The importance of the first, general factor, was found to be independent of the number of factors extracted. Differences between the variances accounted for by second and third factors in these groups were not found to be statistically significant ($p<.05$).

The age-specific analyses noted in the upper part of Table 9.1 were exploratory only, the number of subjects in each group having been too small to provide generalizable findings. However, the results are reported here as a matter of interest, because they are suggestive of trends that are obviously in the same direction as the observations in the other age-specific and special group analyses.

In all the principal components analyses conducted for special groups the first factor extracted was a strong common factor with positive loadings from all 14 tests. In addition to this 'g' factor, at least two group factors were extracted in all age groups. The group factors were bipolar, as had been those extracted in the overall analyses. There was a tendency for the second factor to be a perceptual factor, and the third factor to be a conceptual factor. In the younger age groups the conceptual factor preceded the perceptual factor.

In the younger age groups in which four significant factors were extracted a general, a conceptual and two perceptual factors were identified. These factors could be defined as a visualization, namely, visual discrimination, and a perceptual flexibility factor. In the older age groups the fourth factor, where obtained, was an attention factor. The rarely obtained fifth factor is best described as an attention or speed and accuracy factor.

The conceptual factor was defined primarily by high loadings on Tests 3 (Categorization), 4 (Picture Completion), 5 (Embedded Figures), and high negative loadings on tests with a high requirement of speed and accuracy. In judging the size of the loadings on these factors it must be remembered that most of the variance explained by the conceptual tests had been extracted by the strong 'g' factor, which accounted for nearly half of the total variance in the battery, with the strongest loadings on conceptual and attention tests.

In the above analyses an attempt was made to take account of developmental aspects of the organization of cognitive abilities measured by the NAT battery. Carroll (1983) and Guilford (1980a) argued that age has not always been properly controlled in investigations of mental ability factors, and that correlations among test scores obtained on samples that are heterogeneous in age may be spuriously inflated with age variance. Horn and Cattell (1982) presented counter-arguments suggesting that there is no particular kind of variance that necessarily must be eliminated in factor analytic studies; rather that the objectives of the research and theory should 'dictate the kind of variance that a sampling of subjects should introduce into, eliminate from, or reduce in a study' (Horn and Cattell, 1982, p.623). These authors note further:

> In particular, if a common factor is expected to represent individual differences in development, then very possibly, although not necessarily, there should be age variance in the sample of subjects. We say 'very possibly' rather than 'necessarily' because developmental variation is not synonymous with age variation (see Wohlwill, 1970). (Horn and Cattell, 1982, p.624)

Individual differences in maturation and development are often observed among individuals of the same chronological age. For many variables age and development are highly correlated; however,

> eliminating age variance can amount to largely eliminating associated developmental variance. The developmental variance that remains may be too feeble to be detected in a small-rank factor solution. (Horn and Cattell, 1982, p.624)

In the investigation of the construct validity of the NAT battery the same types of factors and a highly similar organization of cognitive abilities were found both when variance attributable to age was excluded, and when it was included.

This shows the stability of the constructs measured, but it does not mean that the factors, as such, are unrelated to age. In fact, the correlations of each of the 14 NAT subtests with age, shown in Table 9.6, range from -.10 for Test 7 (Mazes) to +.47 for Test 13, a speed and accuracy test. The mean correlation with age across the 14 subtests was .27 (SD=.10). On the other hand these correlations are not high enough to suggest that the constructs measured by the NAT reflect no more than a condition of concomitant variation with age.

The question of whether to allow for age variance or not is complex both statistically and conceptually. An extensive literature, mostly from the 1940s, exists on the topic of univariate versus multivariate subject characteristics in selection. Building on this literature, Meredith (1964) demonstrated mathematically the condition under which a factor pattern will be found invariant in subpopulations derivable from a parent pop-

Table 9.6 Correlations of NAT Subtests with Age

Test		Correlation with age
1	Visual Matching	.24
2	Matching of Direction	.18
3	Categorization	.17
4	Picture Completion	.17
5	Embedded Figures	.25
6	Figure Formation	.33
7	Mazes	−.10
8	Sequencing	.25
9	Picture Arrangement	.25
10	Visual Search	.33
11	Simple Key Test	.24
12	Complex Key Test	.36
13	Code Tracking I	.47
14	Code Tracking II	.38

ulation. A major conclusion of his analyses, that the factor pattern in subpopulations will be invariant, but that the correlations between factors can be expected to vary, raises the question of whether the same common variance is being considered under different conditions of selection. This issue is related mathematically to the rank of the factor solution. At the end of his discussion, Meredith (1964) in fact states the proviso that factorial invariance can be expected only if the selection of the subsample from the parent sample does not reduce the rank of the factorial system. The rank of the factor solution that is estimated (to be distinguished from the rank that can be stipulated in pure mathematical theory) is tied closely to the amount of variance that is accounted for by the factors (for details see Horn and Engstrom, 1979). Inspection of the total variances accounted for in all analyses, presented in Table 9.1, suggest that the analyses are comparable. In other words, the similarities in factor patterns can be interpreted as arising from analyses of the same common variance.

The correlations between factors tended to be negative or low, with a tendency for the correlation between the 'g' factor and the conceptual factor to be higher than the other intercorrelations between factors. This pattern, too, was consistent across age groups.

From a conceptual point of view, the literature contains evidence of considerable concern relating to possible changes in the structure and organization of cognitive functioning during various stages of development.

As noted above, many developmental characteristics can be related to age. However, the system of abilities and skills that is required for adequate cognitive functioning in adulthood is being built up and restructured for efficient use by uncountable learning and other experiences to which the individual is exposed over the course of life-span development. Not all development is systematically related to chronological age. There are inter- and intra-individual differences with respect to the fit of developed abilities to the various 'established' age norms. Some factors can be confounded with others at certain developmental stages. This can occur in cases in which little development of a particular component ability may have occurred in a sample of young individuals. Abilities, in common with other human characteristics and attributes, emerge with development and maturation. They cannot be identified, therefore, until whatever prerequisite amount of development has occurred. Thus, 'a factor can be attenuated in samples that are homogeneous with respect to any of the determinants of the factor' (Horn and Cattell, 1982, p.623).

Garrett (1946) summarized early studies in changes of patterns of cognitive development and offered a 'differentiation hypothesis' in which he postulated that during adolescence and adulthood, that is, at college age, an increase in differentiation or fractionalization of general ability into a number of more highly specialized aptitudes and skills can be observed. He suggests that this phenomenon is most probably the result of maturation. Burt (1954) stated a similar hypothesis, which he claims to have proposed originally in 1919, and which contains the suggestion that general intelligence is fairly unified during early childhood, but becomes fractionalized into a more loosely organized set of abilities with age increasing towards adulthood.

Years later, Quereshi (1967), testing 700 children between the ages of 2½ years and 9 years on the Illinois Test of Psycholinguistic Abilities (McCarthy and Kirk, 1963), reported results that

> clearly substantiate the differentiation hypothesis with respect to its three possible deductions: (a) continuous decreases in the percentage of variance attributable to the general factor as age increases, (b) gradual increment in the percentage of variance contributed by group factors with increasing age, and (c) gradual decline in the interdependence of factors in the older age groups. (Quereshi, 1967, p.364)

Garrett's (1946) hypothesis stimulated further research, with varying findings. For example, Swineford (1947, 1948) obtained results of a kind totally opposite to the above. He found that the amount and proportion of variance accounted for by the 'g' factor actually increased with age in children between grades 7 and 10. This finding was supported by McHugh and Owens (1954) in a longitudinal study that showed the general ability factor to increase in prominence in middle and later adulthood.

Doppelt (1950) found that the percentage of variance accounted for by the general factor remained the same for all age levels between 13 and 17 years.

Reviewing research for and against the differentiation hypothesis, though restricted to the first 18 years of life, Anastasi (1958) and Weiner (1964) were unable to provide conclusive evidence in either direction. However, in a study involving a sample of 1400 (700 males and 700 females) equally distributed across an age range between 14 years and 54 years, Weiner (1964) rejected the differentiation hypothesis and affirmed his alternative hypothesis that

> there is no decrease in the prominence of the general ability or intellective factor as a concomitant of increasing age in successive age groups from 14 to 54. (Weiner, 1964, p.586)

The results of the analysis of age-specific data obtained on the NAT battery certainly do not follow the pattern hypothesized by Garrett (1946), Burt (1954) or Quereshi (1967).

The first, general factor tended to strengthen rather than weaken with age. The number of group factors decreased, rather than increased with age, and no decline in the interdependence of factors was observed with increasing age. Substantial-to-high negative intercorrelations were obtained between the first general factor and the perceptual factor. These negative intercorrelations increased with age. Substantial negative intercorrelations between the perceptual and the conceptual factors were obtained in most age groups, but these appeared to be unrelated to age.

It can be seen in Tables 9.3.1 to 9.3.9 that the loadings on the general as well as for the group factors for some of the tests seem notably altered in the age-specific analyses. On the 'g' factor the loadings appear to be increasing with age. Although the mean loadings on the factor were not found to differ significantly from year to year, the difference between young children and adolescents was significant ($p;.05$). The loadings for speed and accuracy and concentration, that is, freedom from distractibility, particularly on Tests 12 to 14 inclusive, were considerably reduced for younger children.

This finding suggests that, in the totality of the components of cognitive functioning indicated by the 'g' factor, the component abilities and skills measured by the above tests are—relative to other measured component processes—the ones that are most severely affected by age-related variables. In other words, speed and accuracy skills, attention and freedom from distractibility are among the skills that best define increases in general cognitive ability as the child proceeds towards adulthood.

The results of the present study tend to support those of Doppelt (1950), Weiner (1967) and perhaps even Swineford's findings of a strengthening of the first principal component with age. However, this last hypothesis needs to be investigated further. The strength of the first principal component certainly must be interpreted in relation to the number of factors that have been extracted.

The present findings of the construct validity of the NAT battery across age groups should be viewed as providing an indication of tendencies, which need to be replicated with more representative samples balanced in size within groups. However, what can be stated with some certainty is that there is no indication of a greater fractionalization of the general cognitive ability construct, as measured by the NAT, with increasing age.

Aboriginals

Sixteen known ethnic groups were included in the various samples used during the development of the NAT. No systematic differences in mean scores and standard deviations within age groups were detected. Because the ethnic groups differed in size, age range, and in the time members had lived in Australia, separate factor analyses of these data were not considered to be appropriate.

The largest and best definable ethnic group was a sample of 110 non-urban Aboriginals from the Northern Territory. To the best of the author's knowledge the age of this sample ranged from 12 years to early 20s.

Ninety of these individuals completed all 14 NAT subtests investigated here.

The principal components analysis extracted four factors with latent roots greater than unity. Together these factors accounted for 67.29 per cent of the total amount of variance. As in the previously described analyses, all 14 subtests provided strong positive loadings to the first factor 'g', which accounted for 41.17 per cent of the variance. The second, third and fourth factors accounted for 10.28 per cent, 8.57 per cent, and 7.27 per cent of the total variance respectively.

The factor pattern obtained in the analysis of the NAT performance by the Aboriginals is very similar to that obtained in the relevant age groups of the rest of the sample. There were six age groups the results of which could be compared with those of the Aboriginal sample.

The average proportion of variance accounted for by the first principal component across the six groups, that is, Age 12 years to Age 17+ was 39.37 per cent (SD = 3.12%) compared with 41.17 per cent in the Aboriginal group. The average amounts of variance accounted for in the perceptual factor and the conceptual factor, were 11.32 per cent (SD = 1.38%) and 8.56 per cent (SD = 0.89%) compared with 10.28 per cent and 8.57 per cent respectively in the Aboriginal group. Only in two of the comparison groups was a fourth factor extracted. Between them they accounted for an average of 7.83 per cent of the total variance (SD = 0.35), compared with 7.27 per cent accounted for by the fourth factor in the Aboriginal sample. The second factor extracted from the data of the Aboriginal sample was a conceptual factor. However, the highest loadings on this factor differed from those on the conceptual factor of the overall analysis. The highest loadings were provided by rule induction, sequencing, figure formation, and concentration tests. High negative loadings on this factor were obtained by mazes, and embedded figures. Factor III could best be described as a speed and accuracy factor, while factor IV is a visual discrimination factor of the type identified in previous analyses.

The correlations between factors did not differ systematically from the trends observed in the other groups. The average sizes of loadings on the general, conceptual and perceptual factors were similar to those obtained in the analyses of the total sample. However, as noted above, the proportional contribution of different subtests varied somewhat.

The loadings on the speed and accuracy tests on the first 'g' factor were considerably lower for the Aboriginal group, but instead a significant speed and accuracy factor emerged in this sample. This suggests that speed and accuracy, freedom from distractibility, and attention may be less connected with general ability *per se* in Aboriginals than in the non-Aboriginal population, aged 12 years and above. This hypothesis would require further investigation. In the meantime the relationship between speed and accuracy and general ability in the general population and in special groups is discussed in more detail in Chapter 10.

Although the overall pattern of the structure of the factors obtained in the Aboriginal sample was very similar to that obtained in the other analyses, the subtests loading most strongly on individual factors varied. Factors that change in their components, and hence in their psychological meaning, cannot be expected to produce comparable information for individuals belonging to different groups. 'The psychometric capriciousness of the factors cannot be ignored', suggested Frank (1983, p.87) in relation to similar problems relating to differences in psychological meaning of WISC-R factors obtained with different samples.

These findings suggest that looking for subtest configurations, when the notion of patterning is based on an assumption of the psychometric independence of subtests, may not be justified for individuals of Aboriginal background. Rather, the assumption should be made that the subtests may not be measuring highly unique factors, but that it is more likely that four factors define what is being measured by the battery.

Retarded Adults

As noted at the beginning of this chapter the groups shown in the second section of Table 9.1 contained too few testees for valid interpretation of the results of factor analyses. In addition, it is suspected that the group of 47 institutionalized adults, considered to be mentally retarded, was a rather heterogeneous group. No background information was available. For some of the individuals, results on some WAIS subtests were available. These are included in Chapter 13.

The exploratory principal components analysis of the scores obtained by the group of retarded adults resulted in the extraction of five significant factors, which together accounted for 79.80 per cent of the total variance.

The first factor, accounting for 37.94 per cent of the total variance, was a 'g' factor. As in the previously discussed analyses, all 14 tests loaded positively and significantly on this factor. However, its loadings, particularly from the conceptual tests were, in general, lower than the loadings obtained by the non-retarded groups. Also, the largest contribution made to this factor originated from tests of visual discrimination and other perceptual skills, rather than from tests of conceptual skills, speed and accuracy, attention, etc., as in the non-retarded samples.

As noted above, as the subtests that load most strongly on this 'g' factor differ from those most dominant in the analyses of NAT scores obtained by other groups, the psychological meaning of this factor differs somewhat from that of the 'g' factors obtained in the non-retarded groups. This matter is discussed further in Chapter 10.

The other four significant factors were bipolar group factors, as had been the factors beyond the first principal component obtained in the other groups. However, again in contrast to the findings in the non-retarded groups, the group factors extracted from the NAT scores of the retarded sample were all *conceptual* factors.

The second strongest factor accounted for 15.13 per cent of the total variance and consisted mainly of the most difficult conceptual tests. In descending order of the size of positive loadings on this factor the tests were Test 5 (Embedded Figures), Test 6 (Figure Formation), Test 8 (Sequencing), and Test 3 (Categorization). The tasks constituting all of these tests were generally perceived as particularly difficult, and must therefore be regarded as unsuitable for intellectually retarded individuals, and for persons with brain damage that has severely affected their cognitive functioning. The other factors were defined by the skills measured by different combinations of a small number, usually two, of the cognitive tests.

Although only exploratory, and therefore highly tentative, these results should provide a caution, not to interpret the performance of retarded persons in relation to the constructs postulated by the NAT for the 'normal' population. The group factors, if replicated, may measure ability components in retarded persons quite different from those in persons not so afflicted. Even the general factor, though more similar to those obtained in the analyses of the data from other groups, may represent a sufficiently different 'intelligence' from that obtained for non-retarded persons. As was noted previously, different levels of the same test may well call into play diverse combinations of component abilities in different individuals.

Summary

Regardless of the age, ethnic background of the test takers, or the nature of the sample the factor analyses computed on the scores obtained on the NAT battery yielded consistent and recurrent results.

The most obvious of these is the finding of a robust first principal component with high positive loadings from all subtests included in the analyses. This factor is a 'g' type factor of cognitive functioning. As noted above, in previous research the 'g' factor tended to load most heavily on verbal reasoning, and other language-based tests. It is gratifying to have been able to identify such a strong and consistent general factor in a totally non-verbal test.

Another consistent finding was the emergence of one conceptual and at least one perceptual factor across all analyses. In some age groups two perceptual factors emerged, the tendency being for one of these factors to focus on visual discrimination, and the other to be defined by tasks with strong visual closure and/or perceptual flexibility components. In some age groups both the latter factors emerged. In addition, a speed and accuracy, and concentration (i.e. freedom from distractibility) factor was obtained in some groups. These variables also contributed strongly to the first principal components across all analyses.

In most of the principal components analyses the perceptual factor emerged before the conceptual factor. However, the relevance of this observation is doubtful in view of the generally small differences in the amounts of variance accounted for between the second and third factors. On the average this difference amounted to only 3.29 per cent (SD = 2.47%).[2]

Implications for Interpretation

The research into the construct validity of the NAT battery, which has been described in this chapter, suggests that the NAT measures the same basic constructs across age groups, and for majority and minority groups.

The consistent emergence of a general ability factor, a perceptual factor, and a conceptual factor, adds considerable information to the interpretation of the NAT battery. It can lead, in particular to an understanding of the NAT ability profile, and to explanations of certain inter subtest fluctuations.

However, while the hierarchical ordering of the subtests that load most strongly on the factors detailed above is not always exactly the same, the analyses described in this chapter must be interpreted as suggesting that the NAT subtests do not measure unique factors, but rather that only three to four factors define what is being measured by the 14 subtests of the battery investigated here.

The subtests thus do not constitute subsets of unique functions. They are factorially complex, with the same cognitive functions being measured by several subtests, and one subtest measuring several intellectual functions simultaneously. As is noted in

---

[2] The size of the standard deviation in relation to the average is the result of the deviance of one age group (age 10 years), where the difference between the amounts of variance accounted for between the second and third factors was close to 10 per cent, that is, the second factor accounted for more than twice as much variance as the third. Excluding the 10-year-old age group the mean difference of amounts of variance accounted for by these factors was 2.54 per cent (SD = 0.80%).

Chapter 11 the model of intelligence underlying the NAT does not encourage users to regard the battery as a collection of 14 or 18 discrete tests each equipped to assess a certain segment of an individual's cognitive functioning. Rather, intelligence is seen as a functional system of component abilities, as discussed in previous chapters. The first step in the interpretation of an individual's performance on the NAT should this not relate to individual subtests. Rather, the profile should first be investigated as a whole, then in relation to the component skills embodied in the perceptual and the conceptual factors. Only in special cases, where satisfactory subtest specificity has been shown to exist, should comparisons between individual subtests be considered.

Subtest Specificity

Following the determination of the factor structure of the NAT battery, the pattern of loadings of each test on the unrotated major factors was examined to determine the relationship of each subtest to general ability. The communality (h^2) of each test was subtracted from its reliability to determine the proportions of common or shared variance, and the proportion of variance that is specific to each test in the battery. The relationship of each subtest to general ability as measured by the NAT, and the specificity of subtests (for method see Cohen, 1959; Kaufman, 1975) were also determined for each age group. This information is required for the valid interpretation of profiles and individual subtests, and is discussed further in Chapter 11.

CHAPTER 10

WHAT THE NAT FACTORS MEASURE

This chapter is organized into six parts. An introductory section is followed by separate sections devoted to the discussion of the meaning and interpretation of the general, perceptual, conceptual and attention factors. The detail and method of presentation selected for each of these sections depends on the nature of the factors. The aim was to present the information in a manner that might lead to the best understanding of what the factors represent. Thus it was regarded as justified to discuss the all-important 'g' factor in greater detail than the other factors which accounted for considerably less of the total variance in the NAT battery. A section focusing on the implications of the meanings of the factors concludes the chapter.

Introduction

Before making any attempt to interpret an individual's profile of scores obtained on the NAT battery, the conscientious tester should consider the meaning of each score. This may be accomplished by answering the following type of questions in relation to each of the subtests:

1. Are there specific skills that are required for successful performance in this area? If so, what are these skills?
2. Do the obtained scores correspond to differences in real abilities or lack of abilities between individuals?
3. Is the meaning of scores the same across the age range, or do developmental changes influence the interpretation of individuals' performances on the NAT?

Question (1) is answered largely in Chapters 5 to 8, where the meaning and theoretical underpinning of individual subtests are discussed. To answer question (2) the information presented in the above chapters should be combined with that provided in Chapters 9 and 11. Question (3) provides the focus for the present chapter.

The empirical findings obtained from the factor analyses at different age levels offered a suitable method for determining whether performance on the NAT corresponds to unitary abilities in the testee, and for the more detailed interpretation of NAT performance at different levels of development.

The developmental issue was also pursued by investigating qualitative changes in the performances of persons of different ages. Nine age levels were used as focal points in the analysis of develomental trends: 8 and 9 years, 10 years, 11 years, 12 years, 13 years, 14 years, 15 years, 16 years, and 17 years and older.

Qualitative differences in test performance at these ages may be interpreted in terms of changes in the level of intellectual functioning as the testee gets older. However, such differences in performance could also be interpreted as changes in the structure of the factors (i.e. in what various subtests measure in combination) at various points in the age distribution.

Details about the theoretical rationale underlying each test were discussed in Part II of this book. In this chapter the four most frequently obtained factors are systematically discussed from the perspective of the component abilities they purport to assess, and within the framework of developmental changes in the structural processes that determine performance, and that may be occurring across the age range.

Factor Analyses

The factor analytic findings discussed in this chapter for each of the major areas assessed by the NAT are based on empirical data gathered and analysed by the author over a two year period. The results of the overall analysis were discussed in Chapter 9. The data for each age group were analysed separately using the statistical technique of principal components analysis, the rationale for which was also discussed in Chapter 9.

The results of the factor analyses provided strong support for the areas chosen for the NAT on the basis of the theoretical and empirical findings published in the research literature.

A 'g' factor, a perceptual factor and a conceptual factor were obtained for all age groups, as well as in the overall analysis. Factors corresponding to each of the four assessment areas, including a separate attention factor, emerged in the analyses of the scores of five out of the nine age groups, in the aboriginal sample, and in the group of retarded adults.

To simplify the initial discussion of the results, *average* factor loadings and standard deviations, and average percentages are used for each subtest rather than separate loadings for each age group.

This summarization of the results does not result in a masking of developmental trends in the performance data reflecting the structure of the abilities measured by the NAT in different groups of individuals. The major, and hence first-discussed, age-related question of interest in this context is at which age a factor emerged for the first and/or last time, rather than the question of specific structure of the factors for different groups.

This approach is justified, because, as noted previously, the same stimulus materials (test items) can elicit different reactions, approaches, strategies, even skills in different individuals, and certainly at different developmental levels.

On the basis of the developmental literature it was expected that somewhat different skills might operate at different points in the age distribution. Such a phenomenon would result in differences in both the size and the hierarchical order of loadings with respect to particular factors emerging with consistency. This matter will be discussed later in the chapter.

As will be apparent in the discussions of the structure of each factor both in this chapter and in Chapter 9, the make-up of the major factors corresponds closely to the composition of the NAT areas themselves. The important implication of this finding is that the scores of each area of the NAT reflect an individual's functioning in a 'real' and meaningful set of component abilities and skills.

The General Factor

The Role of 'g'

As noted previously, the general factor accounted for 67.29 per cent of the total variance in the NAT battery in the total sample of 1135 persons. The same amount of variance was explained by this 'g' factor in the group of Aboriginal students.

In the age-specific analyses an average of 65.34 per cent (SD = 6.61%) of the total variance was attributable to the 'g' factor. Further details of these analyses are contained in Table 9.1.

All tests contributed significantly to the structure of the 'g' factor in both the analysis of the total sample and in the age-specific analyses. The same was found in the analyses of the performance data of the Aboriginal sample, and in a group of retarded adults. The factor loadings obtained are presented in Tables 9.3.1. to 9.5.

The Content of 'g'

Table 10.1 shows the proportional contribution made by each of the 14 subtests to the 'g' factor in percentage terms for the total sample, for each age group, for the group of Aboriginal students and for the sample of intellectually retarded adults.

Inspection of Table 10.1 shows that the contribution of individual subtests to the 'g' factor in the overall analysis ranged from 11 per cent for Test 5 'Embedded Figures' down to 3 per cent for each of Test 2 'Matching Direction' and Test 7 'Mazes'. The average percentage contributed by each subtest was 7.14 per cent (SD = 2.45%).

Although the hierarchical pattern of the subtest contributions to the 'g' factor varied between the retarded and the non-retarded groups, the average percentage of contribution to 'g' across the 14 subtests in the retarded group (i.e. X = 7.20%, SD = 3.51%) did not differ significantly from that obtained in the non-retarded group.

The average percentage contributed by the subtests to the 'g' factor identified in the sample of Aboriginals was significantly lower ($p<.001$) than that for the total group of non-retarded persons. (The scores from retarded persons were excluded from this analysis because the sample of Aboriginals did not include individuals who were regarded as intellectually retarded.)

The average contribution of each of the 14 subtests to the 'g' factors in the age-specific analyses (i.e. X = 7.14%, SD = 0.02%) was equal to that of the overall analysis. The standard deviations of percentages of contributions of the tests for the nine age groups ranged from 1.89 per cent for the 12-year-olds to 4.00 per cent for the youngest age group. The average standard deviation across the age groups was 2.98 per cent (SD = 0.77%).

In the overall analysis a standard deviation of 2.45 per cent was obtained across subtests for their contributions made to 'g'. The standard deviation for the Aboriginal

Table 10.1 Percentage Contributed to the 'g' Factor by Individual Subtests

Test	Total sample	Age 8 & 9	Age 10	Age 11	Age 12	Age 13	Age 14	Age 15	Age 16	Age 17 & Adult	Aboriginal sample	Retarded adults	$\bar{x}$	SD	Excluding retarded sample $\bar{x}$	SD
1 Matching shape	5.96	1.16	5.94	5.35	5.20	5.21	3.92	4.17	2.93	7.98	4.56	6.34	4.82	1.90	4.65	1.93
2 Matching Directions	2.57	0.62	10.25	6.63	4.64	1.40	0.12	0.79	2.65	6.69	7.13	11.75	4.55	4.16	3.75	3.51
3 Categorization	7.55	7.81	5.48	8.55	7.54	7.41	5.04	5.13	11.43	8.90	7.97	10.04	7.73	2.12	7.48	2.07
4 Picture Completion	6.93	7.54	9.06	7.80	6.01	6.94	6.98	11.69	10.33	9.63	7.76	6.78	8.28	1.82	8.44	1.85
5 Embedded Figures	7.55	8.09	5.48	9.60	5.02	5.83	5.86	7.58	6.91	6.89	6.53	2.72	6.40	1.88	6.81	1.45
6 Figure Formation	10.52	13.88	10.87	9.60	10.31	10.55	11.19	12.00	10.60	9.14	6.53	0.91	9.91	3.42	10.90	1.39
7 Mazes	3.08	3.66	3.30	6.19	5.80	2.64	3.58	5.54	4.36	4.96	5.42	6.56	4.66	1.35	4.45	1.24
8 Sequencing	9.08	8.94	5.94	8.81	8.75	9.17	8.44	10.80	10.06	5.89	5.60	6.34	8.31	1.71	8.53	1.65
9 Picture Arrangement	8.41	12.46	8.22	7.32	7.31	8.39	10.61	11.09	6.70	6.69	3.49	1.18	8.00	3.11	8.75	2.11
10 Visual Search	6.73	12.46	8.22	8.81	6.86	8.91	6.08	2.02	2.01	5.14	6.15	9.76	7.03	3.33	6.72	3.38
11 Simple Key Test	4.09	5.54	9.35	6.19	7.09	3.90	4.65	3.82	4.71	1.72	3.08	8.71	5.57	2.34	5.22	2.18
12 Complex Key Test	9.32	6.75	12.17	8.30	11.14	10.27	13.67	8.59	9.54	8.66	5.60	10.31	9.94	2.03	9.90	2.15
13 Code Tracking I	9.32	7.25	3.84	4.21	7.09	9.99	11.19	8.85	7.59	9.63	7.34	10.88	8.05	2.56	7.74	2.50
14 Code Tracking II	8.86	4.25	1.79	2.90	7.31	9.71	8.19	7.58	10.06	8.20	6.53	8.45	6.84	2.86	6.67	2.97
$\bar{x}$	7.14	7.17	7.14	7.16	7.15	7.17	7.11	7.12	7.13	7.15	5.98	7.20				
SD	2.45	4.00	3.07	2.03	1.89	2.96	3.68	3.63	3.30	2.22	1.48	3.51				

sample was 1.48 per cent, and that for the group of intellectually retarded adults was 3.51 per cent.

In summary, it should be noted that the results presented in Table 10.1 and in the above paragraphs suggest that, irrespective of the age of the testees and the type of sample, the structure of the 'g' factor remains constant in terms of the proportional contributions made to its content by the NAT subtests. On average, each of the 14 subtests contributed 7 per cent of the overall content of 'g'.

The observed larger standard deviation of the relative contributions of the subtests to 'g' in the retarded group reflects the fact that a considerable number of the subtests were found to be too difficult for intellectually retarded persons.

The significantly smaller standard deviation obtained in the Aboriginal sample reflects both the smaller range of proportional contributions and the lower variability within the set of subtests in their contribution to 'g'. The latter can be explained by the finding that for the Aboriginal group the loadings of both the conceptual and attention tests on the 'g' factor, though substantial in size and highly significant, were not as high as the loadings of these tests on 'g' obtained in the non-Aboriginal group. The differences in the size of the loadings on 'g' between the conceptual and attention subtests versus the perceptual subtests were less extreme in the Aboriginal group than in the non-Aboriginal samples.

This finding means that it is likely that perceptual abilities play a somewhat more important role in the general ability of Aboriginal students than is the case of their non-Aboriginal peers. An explanation for this assertion, if these findings are replicated, will probably be found in the early experiences and training of Aboriginal children and students. Outdoor living, and physical exercise have a considerable influence in the training of perceptual skills. The fact that the 'g' factor identified for the Aboriginal group accounted for approximately 10 per cent less variance than the 'g' factor in the non-Aboriginal sample may also contribute to an explanation of the differences in the relative variation between NAT subtests in their contribution to the contents of 'g'.

Subtest Variance Explained by 'g'

Another approach to the investigation of the similarity of the meaning of the 'g' factors obtained across various age groups and special samples is to compare the amounts of total variance in the different NAT subtests that can be explained by the 'g' factor for different groups of individuals.

Table 10.2 shows the percentage of the total variance of each subtest that is accounted for or explained by the 'g' factor in the total sample and in a number of separate analyses.

Inspection of Table 10.2 shows that in all age groups factor 'g' explains a proportion of what is being measured for each of the 14 NAT subtests. The general ability or 'g' construct represented by this first general factor is thus a conglomerate of the varying component abilities measured separately and in combination by the individual subtests.

In the overall analysis the largest amounts of variance explained by 'g' were, in order of size: 72.25 per cent for Test 6 'Figure Formation', 64.00 per cent for Test 12 'Complex Key Test' and for Test 13 'Code Tracking I', 62.41 per cent for Test 8 'Sequencing', and 60.84 per cent for Test 14 'Code Tracking II'. Other subtests for which more than

Table 10.2 Percentage of Subtest Variance Explainable by the 'g' Factor

Test	Total sample	Age 8 & 9	Age 10	Age 11	Age 12	Age 13	Age 14	Age 15	Age 16	Age 17 & Adult	Aboriginal sample	Retarded adults	$\bar{x}$	SD	Excluding retarded sample $\bar{x}$	SD
1 Matching Shape	40.96	4.84	26.01	28.09	29.16	27.04	20.25	21.16	16.81	50.41	31.36	33.64	25.64	11.95	24.75	12.32
2 Matching Directions	17.64	2.56	44.89	34.81	26.01	7.29	0.64	4.00	15.21	42.25	49.00	62.41	24.01	21.42	19.74	17.64
3 Categorization	51.84	32.49	24.01	44.89	42.25	38.44	26.01	26.01	65.61	56.25	54.76	53.29	40.93	14.23	39.55	14.37
4 Picture Completion	47.67	31.36	39.69	40.96	33.64	36.00	36.00	59.29	59.29	60.84	53.29	36.00	43.31	11.71	44.12	12.11
5 Embedded Figures	51.84	33.64	24.01	50.41	28.09	30.25	30.25	38.44	39.69	43.56	44.89	14.44	33.28	10.29	35.37	8.36
6 Figure Formation	72.25	57.76	47.67	50.41	57.76	54.76	57.76	60.84	60.84	57.76	44.89	4.84	51.03	16.78	56.17	4.50
7 Mazes	21.16	15.21	14.44	32.49	32.49	13.69	18.49	28.09	25.00	31.36	37.21	34.81	24.61	8.40	23.47	8.05
8 Sequencing	62.41	37.21	26.01	46.24	49.00	47.61	43.56	54.76	57.76	37.21	38.44	33.64	43.30	9.81	44.37	9.77
9 Picture Arrangement	57.76	51.84	36.00	38.44	40.96	43.66	54.76	56.25	38.44	42.25	24.01	6.25	40.89	14.12	44.73	7.59
10 Visual Search	46.24	51.84	36.00	46.24	38.44	46.24	31.36	10.24	11.56	32.49	42.25	51.84	35.63	14.95	33.82	14.66
11 Simple Key Test	28.09	23.04	40.96	32.49	39.69	20.25	24.01	19.36	27.04	10.89	21.16	46.24	28.40	11.18	26.41	9.82
12 Complex Key Test	64.00	28.09	53.29	43.56	62.41	53.29	70.56	43.56	54.76	54.76	38.44	54.76	51.90	11.51	51.59	12.17
13 Code Tracking I	64.00	30.25	16.81	22.09	39.69	51.84	57.76	44.89	43.56	60.84	50.41	57.76	42.55	15.39	40.86	15.30
14 Code Tracking II	60.84	17.64	7.84	15.21	40.96	50.41	42.25	38.44	57.76	51.84	44.89	44.89	36.72	17.12	35.82	17.93
$\bar{x}$	49.05	29.84	31.24	37.60	40.04	37.20	36.69	36.10	40.95	45.19	41.07	38.20				
SD	16.81	16.66	13.41	10.64	10.60	15.38	18.99	18.43	18.95	13.99	10.16	18.65				

50 per cent of total variance could be accounted for by the 'g' factor were Test 9 'Picture Arrangement', Test 3 'Categorization', and Test 5 'Embedded Figures'. The tests for which 'g' accounted least in this analysis were Test 2 'Matching of Direction' (17.64 per cent), Test 7 'Mazes' (21.16 per cent), and Test 11 'Simple Key Test' (28.09 per cent).

The general factor 'g' thus explains the majority of variance in tests requiring conceptual, that is, reasoning and problem-solving abilities, and in tests where attention and concentration are essential. In relation to both these areas, the 'g' factor showed enough importance to be regarded as a dual factor. However, under a model that views general ability as a functional system, it would be expected that the factor representing general ability would be constituted by separate and interacting abilities that may well be originating from different domains.

Attention, that is, the ability to cope efficiently and appropriately with information, and to resist distractions, and the ability to reason through induction and deduction, account for the largest part of the content of 'g'. Visual discrimination, probably the strongest common factor in the three tests with the lowest loadings on 'g', while a prerequisite for the successful completion of many cognitive tasks, would be expected to be of less relative importance to general intelligence than the component abilities measured in the tests with the highest loadings on 'g', noted above.

However, the reader is reminded that these deliberations are relative only. All the 14 NAT subtests loaded substantially and significantly in statistical terms on the 'g' factor. It is unusual in the literature to find a 'g' factor of the strength of that found for the NAT battery. In general, loadings of the size obtained by the lower loading tests in the present analysis match those obtained for 'g' factors in group intelligence tests.

In the Aboriginal sample the 'g' factor also contributed most to the explanation of the variance in reasoning and attention tests. However, as can be seen by comparing the percentage figures presented in Table 10.2 across groups, the importance of the perceptual tests as measures of 'g' is increased in the Aboriginal sample, while the prominence of the attention component is somewhat reduced. As was seen in Table 9.1 the 'g' factor for the Aboriginal group accounted for approximately 8 per cent less of the total variance in the NAT than in the total sample, and a separate speed and accuracy factor (Factor III) emerged in addition to a conceptual (Factor II) and a perceptual (Factor IV) factor. The size and patterns of the intercorrelations between the factors obtained in the two groups did not differ significantly.

The differences in the structure of the 'g' factors discussed above and the number of factors extracted for the Aboriginal and non-Aboriginal groups do not carry the implication that the NAT battery should be regarded as unsuitable for the assessment of persons of Aboriginal or similar ethnic background. To the contrary, the results of the analyses into the construct validity of the NAT would suggest that the battery could actually be particularly sensitive to the assessment needs and NAT-based suggestions for intervention for such groups. What should be remembered, however, is that the NAT Score alone should not be used as the sole index for decision making. The NAT profile itself must be examined for each candidate so that the areas of strength and possible weakness from which a particular NAT score resulted can be identified, and where possible, remediated. These matters are further discussed in Chapters 11 and 13.

In the age-specific analyses a tendency was found for the first factor to strengthen with increasing age. This was accompanied by an increase in the amounts of variance in the reasoning tests accountable by the 'g' factor with age.

The factor explained less variance in the attention tests in the case of the younger age groups than in the case of the older students and adults. The role of the perceptual tests in relation to the meaning of the 'g' factor in different age groups is difficult to ascertain from the data. It is possible that the contribution of perceptually dominant as against conceptually dominant tests depends on the strategies individuals use when they are working on the tasks. Fluctuations across age groups in the amounts of variance accounted for by 'g' in relation to subtests with strong categorization and concept formation requirements could be the result of large intra-group differences in the development of these abilities. As noted previously, chronological age is only a very coarse measure of intellectual development. Developmental differences between individuals of the same age can often be as large as differences between age groups.

In the younger age groups in which more than three significant factors emerged, these included a separate attention factor. In addition, in the youngest age group a perceptual flexibility factor emerged.

Thus, with younger children, the NAT Score is primarily a measure of early development in information-processing skills. Perceptual and concrete reasoning abilities are prerequisite skills for success. With increasing age the NAT Score becomes more a measure of the level of the individual's conceptual development combined with his or her ability to attend and concentrate. The ability to think abstractly also enters into the picture.

In the sample of retarded adults the largest amounts of variance explained by 'g' occurred in tests of perceptual skills and in the attention tests.

In relation to the performance of intellectually handicapped persons similar to that demonstrated by the sample of retarded adults in the present study, the NAT 'g' factor becomes a measure of availability or lack of availability of basic perceptual and information-processing skills, memory, and the ability to attend to a task for a period of time.

The intercorrelations between the factors obtained in the analysis of the data provided by the group of retarded adults are negative and low, but not as low as those obtained in the non-retarded groups. An explanation for this finding may lie in the often made assumption that abilities and disabilities are less differentiated in intellectually handicapped persons. Again, such an explanation would be in keeping with a theoretical view of general ability as a functional system. Under such a model, deficits in one or more areas would be expected to delay or prevent the development of adequate skills in other areas. Thus a low general level of achievement across the areas measured would be expected.

The results of the statistical analyses conducted on the NAT data showed that the 'g' factor obtained in the sample of retarded adults was not sufficiently different to preclude its use in the interpretation of the performance of retarded adults on the NAT battery. However, in the assessment of persons with suspected intellectual handicap it becomes even more important to investigate both the qualitative and the quantitative aspects of the performance, and to attempt to ascertain, in terms of the performance on individual subtests, what a particular individual with a very low overall NAT Score is capable of achieving, and which functional processes might be less affected by the handicap(s) demonstrated in previous intellectual and educational achievement.

To summarize, it can be stated that the factor analyses of results from many different groups, which were summarized in Chapter 9, yielded the same pattern of the structure of the abilities measured by the NAT with striking consistency. Irrespective of age, background and level of intellectual functioning the 'g' factor measured by the NAT battery provides a comparable, broadly based, language-free measure of general ability or intelligence.

The factor is constituted by similarly sized contributions from the 14 NAT subtests investigated. The factor accounted for substantial but varying portions of the total variances of all subtests. Apart from the fact that it has been derived totally from the cognitive performance on language-free stimulus materials, the 'g' factor, structurally, bears a clear resemblance to Spearman's 'g'.

The Perceptual Factor

As noted previously, a perceptual factor was identified in all age groups. In five age groups this factor emerged as the second factor, and in the remaining four it was the third factor. In the analysis of the total sample the perceptual factor was the second factor, and in the analysis of data from the Aboriginal group the perceptual factor was the fourth and last significant principal component extracted.

In the total sample and in the Aboriginal group the perceptual factors accounted for just under 9 per cent and just over 7 per cent of the total variance in the NAT battery respectively.

Across the age range the perceptual factor accounted on the average for 10.87 per cent of the total variance of the NAT (SD = 2.37%). In the group of retarded adults no specifically perceptual factor was identified. It must be remembered, however, that the 'g' factor in this group loaded most significantly on perceptual tests.

Structurally, and in terms of the sizes of the loadings from specific tests on them, the perceptual factors obtained in the total sample and in the Aboriginal group were found to be very similar indeed. In the age-specific analyses the similarity between factors showed a tendency to increase with increasing age.

The subtests most frequently and significantly contributing to the perceptual factors were Test 1 'Matching Shapes', Test 2 'Matching Direction', and Test 10 'Visual Search'. In some age groups Tests 11 and 12, the 'Key Tests', or the Code Tracking Tests (Tests 13 and 14) also contributed significantly to this factor.

A basic response requirement for the successful completion of the perceptual tasks is a facility to perceive detail even when it is buried among perceptual distractors.

Visual discrimination, visual closure, visual flexibility, the ability to distinguish essential from non-essential characteristics of the stimulus, the understanding of part/whole relationships and short-term memory are among the most important component abilities measured by the tasks that load most strongly on the perceptual factor. Speed of responding is a less crucial element in these tests than in many other perceptual tasks.

However, in age groups in which any or all of Tests 11 to 14 contributed significantly to the perceptual factor, a perceptual speed variable was obviously operating.

More detailed information concerning the component abilities that could be required for successful performance in the perceptual area is provided in Chapter 5. This information is provided to guide the NAT user in the derivation of hypotheses to explain the performance of individuals. What must be remembered at all times is that no list of component abilities is complete, and that any given individual tested on the NAT may succeed or fail on some subtests as a result of abilities, strategies or other variables that are unique to him or her.

In young children and in intellectually severely handicapped persons the performance on the perceptual tests may be largely a reflection of visual–motor co-ordination. Individuals in these groups tend to achieve poor scores on tests requiring conceptual and reasoning ability. With age and normal development, logical reasoning assumes a much greater role even in the determination of the individual's scores on perceptual tests. Thurstone's assertion that 'the interpretation of the factor is made largely in terms of the thinking that is involved in doing the tasks' (Thurstone, 1938b, p.1), is certainly supported by the NAT performance of older students and adults. With age, perceptual organization and reasoning become more important aspects of the perceptual factors than visual discrimination.

Perceptual–motor co-ordination, *per se*, is not a major factor in the performance on the NAT of non-retarded persons within the age range recommended for the test battery.

The Conceptual Factor

All analyses yielded a conceptual factor. In the overall analysis of the data from the total sample the conceptual was the third and last significant principal component. It accounted for 7.35 per cent of the total variance in the NAT battery. In the Aboriginal sample the conceptual factor was extracted in second place, accounting for 10.28 per cent of the total variance of the NAT within that group.

In the age-specific analyses the conceptual factor emerged as the second principal component in four, and third in five age groups. The average amount of variance accounted for by this factor across the range of ages analysed was 11.69 per cent, (SD = 3.74%).

In the younger age groups the conceptual factor showed considerable similarity with the 'g' factor identified for older students and adults, structurally and in terms of the relative sizes of the loadings. This is not surprising when one remembers that the 'g' factor in the younger age groups tended to explain a greater amount of variance in perceptual rather than in conceptual tests.

The correlations of the factor loadings of the conceptual factors between the different age groups tended to be statistically significant, but were smaller than those observed between the perceptual factors in most of the age groups. Within age groups the intercorrelation between the conceptual factor and the general factor tended to be larger than intercorrelations between other pairs of factors.

The tests loading most frequently and significantly on the conceptual factor were Test 3 'Categorization', Test 4 'Picture Completion', Test 5 'Embedded Figures', Test 7 'Mazes', Test 8 'Sequencing', and Test 9 'Picture Arrangement'. A significant finding is that Test 7 'Mazes' contributed consistently to this rather than to the perceptual factor, except in the Aboriginal group where Mazes emerged with a substantial but negative loading on both the conceptual and the perceptual factors, and did not load significantly on the speed and accuracy factor.

Concept formation, anticipation and planning, reasoning and evaluation, the distinction between salient and peripheral characteristics of the stimulus, and other variables discussed in Chapter 6 can be expected to contribute to success on tests loading on the conceptual factor.

The Attention Factor

A separate factor, which could be labelled as an attention factor, emerged in the analyses of five out of the nine age-specific analyses, in the group of retarded adults, and in the Aboriginal sample. In this last group, the factor was the third principal component extracted and accounted for 8.57 per cent of the total variance of the NAT performance of this sample. In the Aboriginal group only Tests 13 and 14, the Code Tracking tests, which are pure speed and accuracy tests, had high loadings on the factor.

In all other groups the attention factor was not a pure factor. High loadings on attention tests, usually Tests 13 and 14 together with Test 10 'Visual Search' and/or Test 11 'Simple Key Test', occurred in combinations with high loadings on either perceptual or conceptual tests. These loadings can be interpreted as perceptual or conceptual speed, that is, the ability to come to terms with the requirements of a task and to attend to it.

Whether this dual factor combined attention with perceptual or conceptual skills appeared to depend to some degree on whether the perceptual or the conceptual factor had been extracted just prior to the attention factor. Wherever the perceptual factor had been extracted as the factor preceding the attention factor the latter showed prominence with regard to the conceptual tests. Where the conceptual factor had been the factor extracted just prior to the attention factor the structure of the latter factor was more influenced by the perceptual tasks. An explanation of these variations can probably best be found in the basic statistical procedures inherent in principal components analysis. As noted in Chapter 9, the interpretation of principal components beyond the first one require the 'mental removal' of the variance already explained by preceding factors. As the attention factor tended to be the third or fourth factor the amounts of variance—pertaining to individual subtests in which a considerable proportion of variance had been explained by previously extracted factors—left for interpretation might be quite small.

The above deliberations do not change the meaning of this factor, namely, the ability to speedily and accurately identify the requirements of the task and to attend to them efficiently. Factors with very similar structures have been identified and reported in the literature. Depending on the orientation of the researchers these factors tend to be referred to as 'perceptual speed' e.g. Ekstrom et al., 1979; Neisser, 1967; Pawlik, 1966), 'figure identification' (Cattell, 1971,) 'cognitive style' (e.g. Royce, 1973), 'perceptual accuracy' (e.g. Hoepfner and Guilford, 1965; Hoffman, Guilford, Hoepfner, and Doherty, 1968), etc.

A number of researchers have suggested that this factor may be representing different levels of an automatic process factor (e.g. Ekstrom et al., 1979). Other studies have found a strong relationship between factors similar to the NAT attention factor and mathematics performance factors (e.g. Strowig and Alexakos, 1969) and with the performance on well known ability tests such as the GATB (e.g. Droege and Hawk, 1970; Singer, 1965, Weiner, 1964).

In the NAT analyses in which no separate attention factor emerged, the subtests eliciting attention and concentration skills most strongly provided high loadings on the first or 'g' factor. There is nothing surprising about the finding that 'g' is a complex composite of conceptual, perceptual and attention dimensions.

As was noted in Chapter 7, which is devoted to a discussion of the mechanisms of the process of attention and the major variables investigated in the literature, the ability to attend has only recently been investigated in combination with other processes affecting cognitive performance (e.g. Guilford, 1980a; Horn, 1980; Stankov, 1980, 1983). The structure of the 'g' factor underlying a large proportion of the NAT performance shows that perceptual, conceptual and attention skills are inextricably confounded. The development of cognitive abilities and efficient cognitive functioning result from their interaction.

Conclusions

The consistently emerging strong 'g' factor, to which all subtests of the NAT battery contribute and which accounts for a large part of the variance of the majority of the subtests, shows the NAT to be, first and foremost, a test of general ability.

While, intuitively, one would expect a 'g' factor to represent a synthesis of various forms or dimensions of cognitive skills, the 'g' factor underlying the major part of NAT performance is in fact made up of all the component skills and abilities assessed in the battery, including attention and concentration.

Although the 'g' factor accounted for nearly 50 per cent of the variance in the test battery, two to three additional clear factors tended to emerge, namely, a visual perceptual factor, a conceptual factor and an attention factor.

The general factor bears a clear resemblance to Spearman's 'g'. The correspondence between factors and the NAT areas, though not identical in all samples, is close enough to justify the assignment of a principal role in the NAT interpretation to the 'g', perceptual, conceptual and attention areas, and to consider the scaled scores obtained on tests in these areas as good estimates of the individual's general ability, and specific ability in these three areas.

Finally, to answer the three questions posed for consideration in the introduction to this chapter:

1. Are there specific skills that are required for the successful performance on the NAT subtests?

A large number of specific skills involved in all subtests of the NAT were discussed in Chapters 5 to 8. The diagnostic implications of particular NAT profiles and the planning of intervention procedures would be based on the identification of common component skills assessed in sets of subtests in which the individual has obtained high, average and low scores. However, in this context it must not be forgotten that different individuals may use different sets of skills. The identification of these and their importance will be assisted by the investigation of the communalities in abilities in the configuration of high, average and low achievement in NAT subtests for individuals.

2 Do the obtained scores correspond to differences in real abilities or disabilities between individuals?

The consistency of the results obtained in the factor analyses computed for the total sample and for various subgroups, that is, the thus-demonstrated construct validity of the battery, the results of the study of the criterion validity of the NAT reported in Chapter 12, and the concurrent validity discussed in Chapter 13, all support an answer to this question in the affirmative. The NAT scores do correspond to differences in real abilities or disabilities in individuals.

3 Is the meaning of scores the same across the age range, or do developmental changes influence the interpretation of scores?

The results of the various factor analyses yielded the same pattern of the abilities measured by the NAT with striking consistency. The meaningfulness and robustness of the first factor in particular for all individuals in the age range is thus strongly established. Cross-validation with an Aboriginal sample again produced very similar results.

The meaning of general ability, 'g', as represented in the NAT Score is thus the same across the age range and for the special groups investigated in these analyses.

Developmental changes may influence the interpretation of area scores, that is, perceptual, conceptual, memory, and attention, because younger individuals and persons with severe intellectual handicap must be expected to compensate for component abilities that are not, or not yet, available to them. Because of this, caution is recommended in the aggregation of scores into area scores, this book and the manual accompanying the tests do not provide for the comparative use of such scores. Rather, it is recommended that the NAT Score be used in the first instance, and that its diagnostic meaning be determined by means of an analysis of the profile of subtest performance as discussed in detail in Chapter 11.

CHAPTER 11

THE INTERPRETATION OF THE NAT SCORE AND THE ABILITY PROFILE

This chapter begins with a discussion of the role of the NAT Score and its interpretation. This is followed by some remarks concerning ability profiles and their advantages versus a single-score approach to assessment. Guidance in the interpretation of NAT ability profiles and the appropriate use of scores on single tests is provided.

The NAT Score

Meaning

The major implication of the information provided in the two preceding chapters is that the NAT is undoubtedly and above all a test of general ability or intelligence. The NAT Score might thus be regarded as a type of IQ, with one important difference—the NAT Score represents a set of clearly definable component skills of information-processing aspects of the usually undefined construct of intelligence.

Because of the unfortunate connotations that have become associated with the term IQ, and because of the many misinterpretations of the concept, the term is not being used in relation to the NAT battery. However, the author admits that the choice of the term 'NAT Score' instead of IQ reflects largely a semantic distinction rather than a conceptual one.

Research and clinical experience have shown that the IQs derived from different tests do not represent descriptions or representations of identical constructs. Different IQ tests often yield quite discrepant results for the same individual. For example, it is not uncommon for 'gifted' children to score approximately one standard deviation higher on the Stanford–Binet than on the WISC-R (e.g. Kaufman and Kaufman, 1977; Zimmerman and Woo-Sam, 1970, 1972). Conversely, children from a disadvantaged language background and who, therefore, obtain much higher scores on non-verbal than on verbal tests, will gain a considerably higher overall IQ on the WISC-R than on the Stanford–Binet. The following quotation from two eminent psychologists shows how this dilemma is dealt with at present.

> The existence of these well known differences between the Binet and the Wechsler tests for certain individuals or groups do not cause psychologists to claim that one IQ is 'better' than the other; whichever battery is used simply becomes the criterion for intelligence, regardless of the different IQs that might be yielded by group intelligence tests or by other individual tests. (Kaufman and Kaufman, 1977, p.23)

The possible observation of differences between the level of NAT Scores and IQs obtained on other intelligence tests thus does not imply that the NAT is not a test of intelligence. Rather, such findings might suggest that what is meant by 'intelligence' might differ between tests. An IQ can not be interpreted in separation from its definition, i.e. from the defined validity, for a particular test. The term NAT Score was used in preference to IQ to avoid confusions of interpretation.

The NAT Score is an index of an individual's overall performance on the NAT battery, and does not refer to the performance on any other test. It is a measure of intelligence or general ability as defined for the NAT. Chapters 5 to 8 provided logical, and Chapters 9 and 10 empirical, evidence for the assertion that performance on the NAT merits being regarded as a criterion of intelligence.

Scaling

The NAT Score's mean of 100 and standard deviation of 10 are comparable with the parameters of the Wechsler IQ, which has a mean of 100 and a standard deviation of 15, and the Stanford–Binet, which has a mean of 100 and a standard deviation of 16. The various numerical values that the NAT Score can take on are thus immediately meaningful to any person experienced in the use of such psychological tests.

To non-psychologists, the meaning of the NAT Score like that of an IQ is more easily communicated by its translation to a descriptive scale, a percentile rank, or stanine. Such translations provide a more meaningful explanation of an individual's level of cognitive functioning than does a standard score such as the NAT Score. Each of these options are treated below.

The *descriptive scale* suggested for the interpretation of general cognitive functioning or ability in the NAT is highly similar to and comparable with the descriptive categories used for the description of IQ levels by Terman and Merrill (1973) and Wechsler (1955, 1974, 1981).

A NAT Score of 93 to 106 is described as Average; 107 to 112 is High Average; 113 to 119 is Superior; and 120 and above is Very Superior. Below-average scores are described as follows: A NAT Score of 92 down to 87 is described as Low Average; 86 down to 80 is Borderline; and NAT Scores of 79 and below are described as Deficient.

It is suggested that the above descriptive terms be used to translate the individual's NAT Score into a probable level of intellectual functioning. But it must be noted that it is not legitimate to use the above labels for more than purely descriptive purposes, since it would be highly improper to classify an individual into a specific diagnostic category or educational stream on the basis of a single score. Thus, the term 'Superior' is not necessarily synonymous with the diagnostic label 'gifted', and the term 'Deficient' does not equal the clinical judgment of 'mentally retarded'. Individuals with certain information-processing deficits may obtain low NAT Scores, but may score in the Borderline or Low Average range of a verbal test, the Binet or a Wechsler test. The descriptive categories suggested for the NAT are not diagnostic in themselves, and can thus not be used as labels for diagnostic findings.

Percentile rank (sometimes referred to as centile rank) is probably the type of score most frequently used in reporting the relative standing of individuals on standardized tests.

The term percentile refers to any one of the 99 points that would divide a frequency distribution into 100 segments or groups of equal size. The percentile rank of a person's performance on a particular test is defined with respect to the performance of a norm or reference group of persons on the same test. The percentile rank of a score thus reflects the percentage of persons in a norm group who have obtained an equal or lower score on the same test. For example if 70 out of 100 persons in the relevant norm group obtain a score of 18 or below on Test A, and 75 out of 100 persons obtain a score of 18 or below on Test B, the score of 18 is assigned a percentile rank of 70 on Test A and a percentile rank of 75 on Test B. If John receives scores of 18 on both tests, his performance can be described as follows: on Test A John received a score that was equal to or higher than the scores obtained by 70 per cent of his peers. Only 30 per cent of his peers would be expected to receive a higher score than John. On Test B John's performance was equal to or higher than that of 75 per cent of his peers. In other words 75 per cent of the norm group received equal to or lower scores than John, and only 25 per cent would be expected to receive a higher score.

Percentile rank equivalents for all possible NAT Scores are provided in Table A3 in the Manual (Rowe, 1985c). The test user should consult this table to determine the percentile rank of an obtained NAT Score. As explained above, the advantage of the use of percentile rank for the reporting of test performance is that percentile rank translates directly into the percentage of the relevant reference group the performance of which is equal to or lower than a particular score. Some individuals derive little meaning from test scores, be they raw scores or standard scores; they may find a statement of the following content more meaningful. 'Janet obtained a NAT Score of 119, thus surpassing the NAT performance of 97 per cent of her peers, that is, only 3 per cent of Janet's peers would be expected to gain a score equal to or higher than that obtained by her.'

Stanines are normalized scores that are represented by one digit only. They thus range from 1 to 9, have a mean of 5 and a standard deviation of approximately 2. The difference between adjacent stanines is about 0.5 of a standard deviation. A major advantage of stanines is that their distribution is approximately normal and that they involve only one number. Stanines preclude the user from making fine discriminations, but they provide a useful scale for purposes of initial screening. The relationship between NAT Scores, stanines, percentile ranks, cumulative percentages and z-scores is shown in Table A3, in the Manual (Rowe, 1985c). This table allows for easy transformation of NAT Scores into a number of other commonly used standard scores.

Ability Profiles

Problems of differential diagnosis have been of concern to psychologists since the introduction of the first standardized tests. The history of the attempts to measure intelligence, and traits of personality, is filled with examples that demonstrate the difficulty of defining valid and reliable subgroups of individuals who have some common characteristics.

Many methods have been used in attempts to summarize and describe the similarity among individuals in their responses to certain tasks and other measurable behaviour. Much of the assessment literature is concerned with finding the communality of those variables that have been measured. A variety of multivariate statistical techniques have been used, including factor analysis, cluster analysis, regression analysis, and discriminant analysis, mainly in an endeavour to determine the *unique* features of groups of persons with common background, learning experiences, or psychological symptoms.

In the areas of personality research, organizational psychology, and child neuropsychology a variety of these methods have been used to identify profiles that may be characteristic of the behaviour and/or abilities of particular groups of persons.

The usefulness of the findings from such research is still a matter of some controversy. For the most part, the research results are quite inconsistent. Some of the inconsistencies can be explained by the fact that, although investigators have found statistically significant differences between groups, they have failed to demonstrate that the group differences in particular variables, that is, the group profiles, were distinctive enough to differentiate between groups with specified characteristics. In other words, differential patterns that were statistically significant in terms of a traditional conceptualization of the construct of validity of the tests have been identified, but have been found to lack clinical utility. (For an in-depth discussion of the distinction between classical validity and clinical utility see Wiggins, 1973.)

Most of the published research in the area relied on the grouping of individuals on the basis of previously decided-on diagnostic labels, a practice that must be regarded with considerable suspicion. As pointed out by McDermott (1980), and verified by him in an empirical study of the congruence and types of diagnoses in school psychology,

> The research literature is replete with examples of definitive studies pointing to the lack of diagnostic congruence among clinical psychiatrists, clinical psychologists, mental health workers, and special education placement teams. (McDermott, 1980, p.21)

Why Profiles?

Most group ability tests describe the performance of individuals on the basis of a single global score, such as an IQ or the NAT Score. As was noted previously, the understanding of an individual's approximate level of ability (relative to the ability measured in a reference or normative group) is of limited usefulness. It may suffice for classification and other purposes of global comparisons, but it provides little, if any, information about the nature of the aptitudes and abilities of the testees.

Two persons attaining the same total score may present very different ability profiles, when their performances on specific component tasks are analysed. For the planning of educational intervention, in vocational guidance, and for the evaluation of a person's skills in relation to the requirements of a particular job, it is of the utmost importance to pinpoint and understand the strengths and weaknesses of individual testees in areas that can be operationally defined.

It is generally accepted that in comparative studies of ethnic, cultural, social or age groups, the use of global scores may obscure or distort differences in particular component abilities and skills.

What is recognized less readily is that a similar danger of distortion exists for any group. Individuals performing in the same IQ range do not necessarily form a homogeneous group either in their abilities and aptitudes, or in their approach to tasks, their motivation, etc. *A low score on an intelligence test*, that is, *a low IQ or NAT Score, like low educational achievement, may be the result of difficulties and deficits in different component skills in different individuals.* The use of global scores could mask (cancel out) individual strengths and weaknesses; in fact, it could hide all details providing descriptive information concerning the differential abilities of the individuals assessed.

It must be remembered that the same test can call into play diverse combinations of component skills in different individuals.

The crux of intervention-oriented ability assessment is not to derive information that is based on any absolute comparison of an individual's performance with that of a normative group, but relates instead to the determination of an individual's relative strengths and weaknesses for purposes of remediation or compensatory training. This involves the making of comparisons with reference to both the individual's own level of performance in different areas—the individual thus becomes, in effect, his or her own norm—and comparison with the levels of performance reached by relevant reference groups.

Only if an individual's component abilities are more or less at the same level (i.e. when equal or close to equal scaled scores have been obtained in all subtests) does a single summary score provide an adequate description of his or her performance. If appreciable variation in the individual's level of achievement in different component abilities is obvious, then a global score provides at best crude, but most frequently misleading information about his or her intellectual functioning.

It is essential, therefore, to ascertain the extent of variation within the individual's performance across subtests, and to investigate the pattern in which different component abilities are organized and related for a particular testee.

A performance profile provides a suitable means of displaying significant strengths and weaknesses, extreme asymmetries of observed abilities, and thus allows for a better understanding of the meaning of the total score in terms of the general cognitive ability of an individual.

Because the NAT Score adequately describes the individual testee's level of functioning in a norm-referenced sense, effective profile interpretation might well use this level as a point of departure, and then seek to determine the more specific areas of component abilities that are well developed or poorly developed in relation to the testee's overall level of functioning, summarized in the NAT Score.

The observation that an average or below-average functioning individual's relative strengths may not measure up to a very superior individual's relative weaknesses is irrelevant for profile analysis.

At this point it may be useful to consider the distinction between individual and group profiles. Group profiles do not reflect the abilities and deficiencies of specific individuals. For example, the fact that a group of children with reading disabilities have a characteristic profile on a particular test does not mean that each reading-disabled child's performance (even on the same test) will result in virtually the same profile. Such an expectation would imply unidimensionality for both reading disability and the profile of each person.

A suggestion of unidimensionality in either set of characteristics is obviously absurd. There is no single applicable, generally valid definition of reading disability. The problem is multidimensional and multidetermined, that is, it can be caused by many and diverse factors in the ability, personality, neurological, educational, social, cultural, or other environmental domains. Similarly, persons with reading disabilities can have widely different age–educational, ethnic, social backgrounds, etc., all of which can be expected to affect their test profiles, thus rendering them a unique reflection of the abilities and opportunities of the total person, rather than just the skills relating to a single, isolated aspect of intellectual functioning.

In addition, a group profile tends to mask characteristic profiles of individuals. As noted previously, a major basic assumption of traditional psychometrics is that individuals whose performance on intelligence tests places them in the same IQ range are a homogeneous group as regards their intellectual abilities and skills. For each group of individuals to be assessed the examiner has to ask the question: Is such an assumption valid? Is it, in fact, possible that these individuals might constitute a homogeneous group in their abilities, their approach to tasks, motivation, etc.?

If we accept that intelligence has clearly identifiable components (and the literature concerned with individual differences in experimental, developmental, educational and information-processing psychology would certainly justify such a view), the appropriateness of the model of measurement traditionally used to reveal differences in cognitive functioning must be questioned. Because this model compares average total test scores obtained by groups, and since high or low intellectual achievement may be the result of strengths or deficits in different component skills in different individuals, the averaging of scores for groups would tend to cancel out individual strengths and weaknesses. The evaluation of the abilities of individuals on the basis of a measurement model that assumes the intragroup homogeneity described above must therefore be regarded as lacking in validity.

> Characteristic group profiles are like a significant difference found in an experimental study of handicapped versus normal children . . . No one would interpret this significant difference in an all-or-none fashion (i.e. that every handicapped child has a poor long-term memory) . . . Like significant research findings, characteristic profiles of groups can be regarded as tendencies or trends that become more likely as outcomes for individuals in that group. (Kaufman, 1979, p.205)

An individual test profile is a set of scores that reflects a unique pattern of the performance of an individual on a variety of tests or measures of other characteristics. More specifically, the term 'profile' used in this context refers to a graphical representation of test results, in which a line connects all adjacent scores (in this case the scores of each one of the NAT subtests) on a scale. The line itself is the profile.

The technique of representing a set of test or subtest scores as a profile has several advantages for the interpretation of the results of the test performance.

Most importantly, the technique facilitates examination and evaluation not only of the level of performance, but also of the pattern of abilities and possible weaknesses. The importance of not relying solely on one outcome score describing level of performance, for example IQ, in psychological assessment has been stressed for the past 15 years.

Both in guidance and in research relating to cognitive development and learning, the differences in the component characteristics leading to a particular categorization of performance, or to a diagnosis, are of utmost importance. However, these differences are often subtle, confusing, and difficult to quantify. It has been suggested that the profile approach may be more sensitive to the variables underlying such differences than other methods of psychological and educational measurement.

Another advantage often associated with the use of profiles is that they provide a clear visual representation of what might be quite a complex pattern of performance. Many psychologists and teachers prefer a profile of test scores or other student characteristics, because the relative concreteness of this manner of representation allows a more configural interpretation of performance as a whole, than would tabulated results.

The view that a particular configuration of the pattern of scores across subtests may be of diagnostic significance is not new. For example, the degree of variability of subtest scores on the Wechsler Adult Intelligence Scale (WAIS) and the Wechsler Intelligence Scale for Children (WISC), and their revisions WAIS-R and WISC-R, has often been found to provide more significant and meaningful information than the summary Full Scale IQ scores obtained from these tests.

Brain-damaged and other individuals with intellectual and learning problems often show a much greater amount of variability in their scores on different subtests than do both individuals who are not handicapped in this way, and mentally retarded persons. The scores of the latter tend to be more uniformly depressed.

NAT Profiles

Patterns in the NAT profile can lead to important considerations in interpretation. An elevated or depressed score on a particular test, or set of tests, may have a wide range of implications for problem solving, learning, and achievement, depending on the rest of the profile and other observations.

Where deficits are detected, the examiner has to analyse their nature as completely as possible. A first step is to relate the areas of weakness to other aspects of performance, and to ascertain their implications for possible disturbances in other areas of cognitive functioning and achievement, as well as for intervention.

It is important to distinguish between two methods of assessing factor and subtest differences. One method would be to assess the observed differences in subtest scores in terms of the proportion of normative population in which the same or a larger difference was observed. Another method is to compare the observed difference with the range of differences attributable to the estimated errors of measurement of the tests involved in the comparison. The nature of the problem must decide which method might be more suitable. In the absence of norms, for the time being, the latter method was used in the preparation of Table 11.1. However, in situations where sufficient subjects have been tested to establish local norms, or where other norms are available, the former method might be used, *if* the aim is a normative comparison rather than a diagnostic description of performance.

Profile Interpretation

The aim of this section is to facilitate interpretation of the NAT profile.

Because the theoretical model underlying the NAT represents intelligence as a functional system rather than as a set of discrete component skills, the interpretation of the scores obtained on the battery cannot be based solely on isolated subtests, or on the comparison of two or more subtests at a time.

The consistent emergence in the factor analyses, described in Chapters 9 and 10, of a perceptual and a conceptual factor as well as of a strong general factor, adds information to profile interpretation, and may well lead to explanations of certain subtest fluctuations.

Test users whose examination of the NAT profile begins with pairwise comparisons of apparently high- and low-scaled scores, and who rush to compute the significance of seemingly large differences between the scaled scores obtained by the test taker on two subtests, are ignoring the results of the factor analyses.

NAT users who take account of the fact that a strong 'g' factor and perceptual and conceptual factors were found to exist for test takers of all ages and populations sampled will approach the interpretation of individual profiles by keeping in mind the following considerations:

1. The most likely determinant of the testee's total NAT performance, as reflected in the NAT Score, is a complex multidetermined interaction of his or her performance on all subtests, that is, a general ability of the 'g' type.
2. The most likely determinant of an individual's score on any subtest with a strong perceptual bias are his or her perceptual abilities (e.g. perceptual organization, visual discrimination, perceptual flexibility, etc.) and not the unique component abilities associated with one or other individual subtest.
3. The most probable determinant of a particular score on a test eliciting conceptual skills is the individual's conceptual or reasoning ability.
4. Fluctuations within either or both the perceptual or conceptual sets of tests should be treated as chance deviations until statistical analyses show that they are not.

An appropriate method of analysis of the NAT scaled score profile is a direct extension of the above considerations.

Instead of treating each subtest as an isolated set of skills, the NAT Score, that is, the scaled score representing overall performance on the NAT battery, should be compared with the scaled score obtained on each subtest.

Some examiners will prefer to use average scaled scores across all subtests for these comparisons instead of the NAT Score. The two major advantages of using the average of the scaled scores obtained on the completed NAT subtests are (1) that they relieve the examiner from the need to prorate the scores obtained by individuals to whom not all NAT subtests have been administered, and (2) that the standard deviation obtained as part of the averaging procedure provides a simple indication of the clinical significance of the variability of the individual's subtest performance.

The standard deviation of the scaled scores in the NAT subtests is 10. A standard deviation of ±10 obtained for an individual thus reflects a variation between component skills that can be expected to occur in over 68 per cent of the population. A standard deviation of ±20 or more would occur by chance in only 6 per cent of the population as a whole.

Similarly, instead of treating each subtest as an isolated set of skills, or relying mainly on comparisons of subtests in pairs, the scaled score of each perceptual test should be compared with the test taker's own mean perceptual score. Then the scaled score obtained on each conceptual test should be compared with the individual's mean conceptual score to determine which, if any, of the observed fluctuations are due to chance. Useful information can be obtained from a comparison between the mean scaled score across all subtests and the mean perceptual, conceptual, and, where appropriate, attention scores.

The following procedure for profile analysis is therefore suggested when the aim is to evaluate differences between component skills measured by the battery:

1. Work out the individual testee's own mean scaled score across all subtests, and the standard deviation between the scaled scores.
2. Work out the individual's own mean scaled scores across the perceptual tests (Tests 1, 2, 13 and 14) and the conceptual tests (Tests 3 to 9 inclusive) separately. Where relevant to the objectives of the assessment, the mean and standard deviation of the scaled scores of the attention tests (Tests 10 to 14 inclusively) should also be calculated.
3. Then compare the scaled score obtained on each perceptual subtest with the mean scaled score obtained by the subject across all perceptual subtests.
4. Compare the scaled score obtained on each conceptual test with the testee's own mean obtained across all conceptual tests.
5. Compare the mean scaled scores obtained on the perceptual, conceptual and attention tests with one another and with the average score across all subtests or with the NAT Score.
6. Next, compare the scaled scores for each subtest with the subject's own mean score across all subtests (i.e. a convenient estimate of the individual's general ability as long as the standard deviation between tests is not too large).

Where tests of statistical significance are not required, the representation of the comparative scores in terms of percentile ranks will provide a useful means of interpretation for the observed differences.

If most of the above suggested comparisons are, in fact, due to chance, little or no attention should be paid to apparent fluctuations in the profile. Although an individual's scaled scores on two tests (e.g. a score of 105 on one subtest and a score of 85 on another) may differ significantly from one another, this finding is trivial, and could even be misleading, if one or both of these scores do not differ significantly from the individual's own mean. Only when subtest scores differ significantly from the individual's own mean is it proper to speculate about strengths and weaknesses in component abilities, that is, abilities that are less global than the construct measured by the NAT battery as a whole, perceptual, conceptual or attention ability.

The method of test interpretation suggested here is based on the results of the factor analyses reported in Chapters 9 and 10, which showed clearly the importance of a dominant first factor 'g' (with high positive loadings supplied by all subtests of the battery), and a perceptual and a conceptual factor, thus relegating the analysis of single subtests to a position of less importance.

The profiles obtained by some testees will show that, for example, the perceptual/conceptual, the conceptual/attention or perceptual/attention dichotomies do not hold for a particular individual. However, the factor analytic results obtained in the analyses of the NAT justify that profile interpretation for all subjects should begin with the assumption that a particular dichotomy is valid for all testees, even if subsequent analysis leads to a rejection of this hypothesis for a particular individual.

Davis (1959) developed formulae, based on the standard errors of measurement of component tests, that permit statistical comparisons of single subtest scores with mean scores. Davis's procedures have been strongly recommended by others (e.g.

Kaufman, 1979, 1982; Sattler, 1982) and were thus used here in the derivation of the precise scaled score differences required for statistical significance from the mean score obtained by an individual across the whole battery. These differences are provided in Table 11.1, for both the 15 and 5 per cent level of significance. Davis's procedure makes it possible to estimate the probability that a given scaled score difference is a chance deviation from a true difference of zero.

Psychologists, accustomed to using significance levels of $p<.05$, and $p<.01$, may feel that .15 sets a rather lenient level for the two-tailed testing of null hypotheses. It has been found that in practical assessment, differences between test scores large enough to have a probability of occurring by chance in 15 cases out of 100 are well worth interpreting. Both the revised Wechsler tests (i.e. the WAIS-R and WISC-R) and the British Ability Scale (Elliott, Murray and Pearson, 1978) are following this practice.

Any setting of a level of statistical significance is arbitrary. The chosen level results from an attempt, on the part of the researcher or test developer, to find a balance between the acceptance of differences as significant (i.e. attributable to variables other than chance) when, really, they are not, and the acceptance of differences as non-significant (i.e. attributable to chance), when they are not. Davis advocates the .15 level of significance in the determination of significant differences between test scores, and makes two points supporting his view:

> First, scores derived from most achievement and aptitude tests are sufficiently unreliable as to make their practical utility doubtful if only differences among individual scores significant at a stringent level (such as .01) are interpreted. Second, the penalty for accepting a difference as owing to something other than chance when, in fact, it is a chance deviation from a true difference of zero is not usually great, because test results are ordinarily only one of several factors entering into the making of any important decision. (Davis, 1959, p.162)

Table 11.1[1] provides, for each subtest, the precise differences from the subject's own mean score required for significance. For most purposes, however, it would seem reasonable to round off the given difference to the next integer. In many circumstances the use of a difference of ±7 scaled score points from an individual's mean to denote a significant discrepancy for any of the 14 tests may provide a sufficiently stringent measure.

This latter suggestion is based on the practice of profile interpretation used in the Wechsler tests, particularly in the WISC-R (Kaufman, 1979). The error introduced by the use of a constant difference for all tests might be counterbalanced by the reduction of the need for the examiner to refer to the table for the interpretation of each profile, and the resulting simplication of the clerical procedure required for the interpretation of the battery.

Table 11.2 contains, for each test, precise scaled score differences that are required for the determination of significant differences between mean perceptual, conceptual and attention test differences and single tests loading on these factors.

---

[1] It should be noted that tests with low reliability introduce considerable chance variation into all analyses. As pointed out in Chapter 9, low reliability tends to depress coefficients of intercorrelations with other tests. In Table 11.1 the tests with relatively low reliability, i.e. Tests 3, 4, and 9, require a larger discrepancy from mean total scaled scores than the other tests. Because the reliability coefficient used in the present analyses was KR20, i.e. a measure of internal consistency, the tests with the least internal consistency showed the lowest reliability. Obviously test/re-test reliability would have been a better reliability estimate for these tests, but this could not be obtained within the financial and time constraints of the present project. The collection of further data will allow better reliability estimates for these tests.

Table 11.1 Differences between Mean Scaled Score and Scaled Scores of Individual Subtests at the 15 per cent and 5 per cent Levels of Confidence, and Estimated Standard Errors of Difference between an Average Subtest Scaled Score and Each Individual Subtest Scaled Score

	14 Tests		9 Tests		
Test	15%	5%	15%	5%	SEM Diff.
1	5.13	7.17	5.23	7.31	2.45
2	5.45	7.62	5.51	7.70	2.64
3	11.56	16.16	11.16	15.60	6.08
4	12.42	17.37	11.98	16.75	6.56
5	8.02	11.21	7.86	10.99	4.12
6	3.02	4.22	3.40	4.75	1.00
7	4.78	6.69	4.92	6.88	2.24
8	4.78	6.69	4.92	6.88	2.24
9	13.25	18.52	12.74	17.82	7.00
10	8.64	12.08			4.47
11	7.36	10.28			3.74
12	8.84	12.36			4.58
13	10.13	14.16			5.29
14	8.24	11.52			4.24
Average	7.97	11.15	7.52	10.52	4.05
Standard deviation	3.12	4.35	3.54	4.95	1.79

Table 11.2 Differences between Mean Scaled Scores on the Perceptual, Conceptual, Speed and Accuracy and Memory Tests and Scaled Scores of Individual Subtests at the 15 per cent and 5 per cent Levels of Confidence; and Standard Errors of the Difference between an Average Subtest Scaled Score and Scaled Scores on Individual Subtests

Component	Test	15%	5%	SEM Diff.
Perceptual	1	5.64	6.71	2.60
	2	5.88	6.99	2.71
	10	8.44	10.04	3.89
	13	9.70	11.53	4.47
	14	8.09	9.62	3.73
Average		7.55	8.98	3.48
Standard deviation		1.74	2.07	0.80
Conceptual	3	11.80	14.04	5.44
	4	12.65	15.04	5.83
	5	8.48	10.09	3.91
	6	4.30	5.11	1.98
	7	5.66	6.73	2.61
	8	5.66	6.73	2.61
	9	13.41	15.94	6.18
Average		8.85	10.53	4.08
Standard deviation		3.77	4.48	1.74
Speed/Accuracy	7	5.38	6.40	2.48
	10	8.44	10.04	3.89
	11	7.36	8.75	3.39
	13	8.59	10.22	3.96
	14	8.09	9.62	3.73
Average		7.57	9.01	3.49
Standard deviation		1.31	1.56	0.61
Memory	15	8.42	10.01	3.88
	16	8.27	9.83	3.81
	17	7.05	8.39	3.25
	18	8.27	9.83	3.81
Average		8.00	9.52	3.69
Standard deviation		0.64	0.75	0.29

One commonly held assumption relating to ability profiles is that similar sets of strengths or cognitive weaknesses, such as visual perceptual difficulties, sequencing problems, or certain types of memory deficit, will manifest themselves in a relatively constant ability profile, that is, similar patterns of strengths and weaknesses will be reflected in similar profiles irrespective of age. For example, it is assumed that the ability profile of the child who presents with a particular set of intellectual difficulties at school at the age of 9 years will be relatively similar to the profile of a student, aged 14, who presents with a similar set of learning difficulties. The ability-profile approach is based on the assumption that the characteristics of behaviours represented by the profile reflect measurement of a common set of variables, as provided by the tests or subtests making up the components of the profile.

For the NAT battery it was established that a highly similar set of characteristics is, in fact, being measured at different age levels. The results of separate principal components analyses for each age level are presented and discussed in Chapters 9 and 10. These analyses showed that the same factors emerged at all age levels and in all groups investigated, even though the specific contribution of particular tests to the major common factors varied somewhat with age.

The manipulatibility of intellectual skills and abilities, and the plasticity of the human brain, particularly in children, make the determination of totally consistent age/skill relationships difficult.

The use of the NAT battery for the development of stable profiles for specific diagnostic subgroups of persons must be preceded by considerable numbers of research studies with a variety of groups with known characteristics. Although there appears to be general agreement amongst practitioners that there are identifiable groups of individuals who respond to particular teaching methods and curricula, attempts to define consistent, unique patterns of abilities and deficits have, up to now, remained tentative even in clinical psychology and special education.

Until such unique patterns can be described, only tentative statistical comparisons are possible.

In conclusion it is stressed that the interpretation of a given NAT profile is based on both the level of the profile, and on its shape. The relative highs and lows of performance scores on the different subtests can help in the identification of possible causes of low intellectual performance and/or achievement. When this information is combined with background and developmental information, school results and other psychological test data, a valid interpretation of intellectual performance becomes a likelihood.

In general, NAT profiles can be expected to produce a limited number of overall patterns, each of which can vary from mild to extremely debilitating. The major patterns examiners should learn to recognize include the following:

1 Overall good test performance with no significant variations in the shape of the profile.
2 Average or above average performance in one or a few areas, but impaired performance in others.
3 Low performance in all or most areas, usually with some subtests yielding lower scores than the rest.
4 Equally diffuse, low performance across all subtests.
5 Scattered deficits, but performance on other subtests within the average range.

The Interpretation of Single Subtests

The components of the NAT battery attempt to measure both different aspects of intellectual functioning, and a more generalized level of ability. This section will deal with the interpretation of the performance on single subtests of the NAT.

As discussed in Chapter 2, the model of intelligence underlying the battery is that of a functional system. This explains the overlap between different subtests, which was intentional. The amount of overlap varies. Further details are provided in Chapters 9 and 10, which deal with the results of the factor analyses, and the chapters contained in Part II, which discuss the rationale underlying individual tests.

The items making up each subtest can be thought of as eliciting the utilization of different major component skills, of what we generally refer to as general ability or intelligence.

In cases in which significant discrepancies between individual or groups of subtests and the subject's own mean score or NAT Score are found, the performance on individual subtests can be incorporated in the overall interpretation of the test taker's performance on the NAT battery.

Examination of the scores on the different tests, that is, the ability profile, enables th level of development of different component abilities to be inferred as well as strengths and weaknesses that may be contributing to the intellectual performance of individuals.

However, it is important to recognize that no single test provides a *pure* measure of any simple or complex intellectual skill. All subtests require a certain level of development and the availability of several abilities and skills, of which some are more prominent than others. This is supported by the fact that in the factor analyses described in Chapters 9 and 10, no unique factors, that is, factors on which only one single subtest loads significantly, were identified.

Weaknesses or deficits in any of the component skills assessed in the NAT battery can lead to deficiencies in intellectual and educational performance and achievement. It is thus important to be aware of the range of abilities involved in the performance on a given subtest, and to attempt to understand these factors thoroughly before attempting more complex analyses of the performance data, that is, subtest scores.

There is another prerequisite to profile analysis in terms of single subtests. Before the scores on individual tests of the battery are interpreted, it is necessary to assess whether the subtest does, in fact, contain sufficient *subtest specificity* to make its interpretation, in isolation from the more global assessment provided by the NAT, legitimate.

The term subtest specificity refers to that proportion of the variance packed in a single subtest that is both reliable and unique to the particular component abilities being assessed by the subtest. The scores on a subtest that does not have an adequate amount of unique variance, or the specificity of which is smaller than its error variance, should not be interpreted as reflecting unique abilities or skills.

This caution is valid for any test consisting of subtests, but has not always been heeded by test users. For example, Cohen (1959) showed in a large empirical study that most subtests of the WISC failed to contain sufficient specificity to warrant their interpretation in isolation from the WISC battery as a whole. As the huge literature related to WISC profiles testifies, Cohen's finding did not deter either researchers or clinicians from making subtest-specific interpretations for all WISC subtests. Fortunately, most subtests of WISC-R allow the interpretation of unique skills (Kaufman, 1979; Silverstein, 1976).

To compute the proportion of specificity or uniqueness for a particular subtest, the subtest's common or shared variance is subtracted from its total reliable variance, that is, the test's reliability coefficient. The remainder, which represents the subtest's reliable, unique variance or specificity, is then compared with the proportion of estimated error variance for the subtest (i.e. one minus the reliability coefficient).

There is some conjecture about the most appropriate estimate of a subtest's reliable shared variance. Cohen (1959) suggested as the best estimate of reliable shared variance the subtest's communality (i.e. its shared or common variance, which is calculated by summing the squared loadings of the subtest on all factors) derived from factor analysis. This convention was followed in the present study. The communalities (h^2) for all subtests and age groups were presented in Table 9.2.

Silverstein (1976) argued for the use of multiple correlations instead of communalities as estimates of common variance. Kaufman (1975, 1979) has used both in different studies.

As there is no formal statistical criterion on which to base the decision concerning the amount of specific variance required for the interpretation of single subtests, investigators have tended to follow Cohen's (1959) suggestion that unique variance of a subtest should only be interpreted if it accounts for 25 per cent or more of the total variance, and if, at the same time, it exceeds the error variance estimated for the subtest.

Calculation of the subtest specificities of the NAT subtests for each age revealed some fluctuations between age groups, but these fluctuations seemed basically random, and not systematically related to developmental variables.

Table 11.3 shows the amounts of specificity contained in each subtest estimated for the total sample, and for each age group. Obviously, subtests with relatively low reliability show less reliable variance and higher error variance than more reliable subtests.

It is evident from Table 11.3 that a considerable number of subtests of the NAT battery have a sufficient amount of specificity. These subtests are printed in italics in Table 11.3. Entries in Table 11.3 in normal print are regarded as containing insufficient specificity for individual interpretation. Note that under this criterion the interpretation of single subtests would rarely be available for children under the age of 10 years.

Whenever consideration is being given to the interpretation of unique variance, Table 11.3 should be consulted. The subtests with considerable specificity can be interpreted when the test taker's scaled score differs from his or her mean scaled score by the number of points required for significance (see Table 11.1) in either direction, or by plus or minus seven. Caution is suggested for subtests the specificity of which is sufficient in a few age groups only.

To summarize, the following points should be considered by test users wishing to interpret scores obtained on individual NAT subtests in relative isolation:
1. As noted earlier in this chapter, the emergence of a strong common 'g' factor, and of the consistent group factors of perceptual and conceptual types, should

Table 11.3 Amounts of Reliable Specific Variance Contained in each Subtest of the NAT for the Total Sample and for each Age Group

Test	Total sample	8+9	10	11	12	13	14	15	16	17+	Retarded adults	Aboriginals
1	.37	.13	.32	.25	.37	.44	.32	.44	.57	.36	.17	.18
2	.24	.18	.20	.26	.44	.38	.26	.24	.39	.38	.19	.21
3	-.02	.01	.05	-.16	.05	.22	-.04	.05	-.10	-.04	-.11	-.07
4	-.01	-.13	-.13	-.09	.08	.16	.04	-.17	-.07	-.05	-.17	-.06
5	.24	.29	.21	.26	.34	.37	.20	.25	.18	.35	-.09	.19
6	.26	.18	.28	.36	.41	.34	.34	.27	.34	.38	.06	.35
7	.25	.15	.42	.35	.25	.37	.24	.35	.35	.19	.31	.25
8	.32	.17	.23	.17	.40	.46	.24	.22	.24	.26	.13	.34
9	-.08	-.27	-.10	-.28	.03	.00	-.11	-.23	-.28	.02	-.32	.03
10	.27	.21	.16	.22	.33	.18	.01	.04	.16	.28	.06	.14
11	.31	.02	.23	.00	.31	.30	.43	.35	.54	.14	.10	.21
12	.07	.00	.03	-.04	.11	.18	-.03	.18	.24	.00	-.01	.21
13	-.10	-.16	-.18	-.19	-.13	-.04	-.11	-.04	.12	.05	-.16	-.09
14	.05	-.11	-.01	-.09	.04	.09	.01	.10	.20	.28	-.10	.00

emphasize more global interpretations of NAT performance, and should place the interpretation of single subtests into the background.
2 The proportion of common variance exceeds that of specific variance in most subtests. In fact, for a number of tests the common variance is more than three times larger than the specific variance.
3 The fact that most of the tests with a sufficient amount of specific variance contain much more common variance than unique variance should impel those interpreting scores obtained on the NAT to seek hypotheses based on shared variances of component tests to explain strengths and weaknesses in the cognitive performance of individuals, rather than to be satisfied with highly specific single-test explanatory hypotheses.
4 Only after common-variance-determined hypotheses have been rejected should subtest fluctuations be interpreted in terms of the unique variance of the test.
5 Except in the case of Tests 5 and 10, specific test variance should generally not be interpreted in children under 10 years of age. Obviously, this rule would not apply to profiles that show intertest performance differences of 2 standard deviations and above.

The performance data provided in this first edition of the NAT battery must not be regarded as norms. Rather they reflect the performance of specific groups. It is expected that they will be useful in providing guidelines for the interpretation of test performance until norms for the test battery can be supplied.

Another way of interpreting the NAT performance of individuals is for examiners using the tests with large, defined samples, to produce their own norms. This is relatively simple and guidelines for the production of local norms are provided in Appendix C. Most textbooks concerned with educational measurement will be found equally useful.

Comparisons among Subtests

Finally, it cannot be stressed enough that the interpretation of the performance itself on any given test may vary from testee to testee because of the multiple abilities and other subject characteristics that may affect the gaining of a particular score. As a result, careful comparison of scores becomes an important requirement for the evaluation of test performance, and for the identification of relative strengths and weaknesses in the performance of the testee.

Comparison of performance patterns on the various subtests of the NAT should thus be accompanied by comparison of the NAT profile with various other indicators of cognitive ability. This can be accomplished in many different ways. School achievement, teachers' reports, parent interviews, and performance on other, cognitive tests are only some of the numerous options available. Most profitable would be a comparison of NAT scores with the results obtained from an administration of WISC-R or WAIS-R.

An important point to be remembered is that the NAT profile, and for that matter the results obtained from any non-verbal test or test battery, no matter how broadly based, provide part only of the total assessment of an individual's cognitive development or intellectual skills. Verbal reasoning, word knowledge and other abilities involving language have to be included in the assessment in most circumstances.

The NAT profile may be found useful as a means of backing up and validating results from other psychological or educational assessment. It may also serve as an initial source of hypotheses for the interpretation of observed general and/or specific intellectual weaknesses in individuals with or without language problems.

Intervention

The author believes that finding ways of increasing the individual's intellectual efficiency is a more important task of assessment than finding a label to describe his or her performance.

One of the main strengths of the NAT is that it provides an individual profile, which can be used to develop an appropriate intervention program.

The NAT Score can serve as a single, short-hand, *initial* index of the individual's level of performance. The profile of an individual's performance on tests of a variety of component abilities of general intellectual functioning describes his or her status in several more specific domains, namely, perceptual, conceptual and attention skills.

Because the educational goals for children and young adults, no matter at what level of cognitive functioning they are operating, always include training in the above domains, the ability profile derived from the NAT provides a basis from which a program of training can be developed.

This enterprise may be of crucial importance to many children, as, especially in many classes for students with learning disabilities and in schools for the mildly intellectually handicapped, the aim has not been to assist the individual to develop beyond his or her demonstrated level of ability, but rather to adjust teaching and learning to the level of the assessed deficiencies. Consequently, in such instances, the degree to which an extensive training program of individualized instruction in information-processing skills such as those assessed in the NAT might alter the individual's abilities and the expectations of his or her teachers and parents for success can never be known.

As teachers, counsellors and parents collaborate in the training of such individuals, it should be kept in mind that intervention procedures must be truly individualized, that is, that children with similar profiles may require quite different programs.

When the teacher or counsellor considers a student's NAT profile and its implications for intervention, they can view the information thus provided as a representation of an individualized set of descriptors. The subtests within each domain specify a set of educational objectives that can be accomplished for most individuals during their years of development.

The NAT Score and the scores obtained in specific areas, when compared with the scores of a norm group, indicate how well individuals are functioning in relation to the functioning of others. When a score in a particular area is lower than would be expected for a particular individual, reference to his or her level on each of the individual tests comprising that area would suggest a set of instructional or learning objectives that could form the basis of an individualized plan for intervention.

PART IV

PRACTICAL APPLICATIONS

The preceding three parts of this book were concerned with the NAT battery exclusively. Part IV looks at the scores obtained from the NAT in relation to data derived from other sources. Since the comprehensive assessment of an individual usually involves more than the administration of one test, the ability to interpret NAT scores in the context of the overall investigation of an individual would appear to be essential for competent use of the battery.

Chapter 12 describes a research study into the relationship between NAT performance and school achievement. This study can be regarded as a modest attempt to ascertain the predictive validity of the NAT. In addition to the description of performance characteristics on the NAT of high, average, and low achievers in school mathematics and science, the results presented in this chapter provide the basis for an attempt to further investigate the theoretical structure of the abilities assessed by the NAT battery.

Finally, Chapter 13 relates the NAT to other assessment procedures. It discusses essential supplementary measures and observations that might provide sources of desirable information to complete the assessment process. Important prerequisites for the validity of intervention-oriented assessment, and for the intervention itself, are noted.

CHAPTER 12

SCHOOL ACHIEVEMENT AND NAT PERFORMANCE: VALIDATION OF THE THEORETICAL MODEL

The present chapter contains two types of material. First, it describes what could be termed a study of the predictive validity of the NAT battery, which was conducted on a sample of Year 7 students. The second part provides an initial attempt to investigate the fit of the theoretical notion of intelligence as a functional system with NAT performance.

More specifically, the purpose of the pilot studies reported in this chapter was to investigate the abilities assessed by the subtests of the NAT in high, average and low school achievers, as determined on the basis of school results in mathematics and science. A further purpose was to conduct an initial examination as to whether a systems model of intelligence would, in fact, fit these data better than an assembly model.

Although such terms as 'high ability', 'low ability', 'outstanding achievement', 'underachiever', 'slow learner', etc., have been used extensively to describe individuals whose test performance and/or school achievement differed in certain observable ways, little attempt has been made to investigate in detail the manner and extent to which the cognitive performance itself of individuals categorized under such different labels does, in fact, vary.

If we accept that intelligence has at least some clearly identifiable components, the appropriateness of the traditionally used model of analysis to reveal differences in cognitive ability must be questioned. The traditional model of ability assessment compares the results of an individual's or a group's performance on omnibus or other tests of heterogeneous item content with average scores of groups. Because low intellectual and educational achievement, or low scores on cognitive tests can be the result of deficits in different component abilities or skills in different individuals, the procedure of averaging scores obtained by groups would tend to mask the specific strengths and deficits that, in fact, led to a particular score on the test.

In other words, since individuals whose performance on an IQ test places them in the same IQ range are not necessarily a homogeneous group, either in their approach to the items, motivation, etc., or in their strengths and weaknesses with respect to particular component skills involved in the test performance, it would seem unjustified to base the evaluation of their ability on a measurement model that assumes such intragroup homogeneity.

To avoid this masking effect, and to provide an opportunity for a more extensive description, in operational terms, of individual and group differences, the measurement model chosen for the NAT battery was one that might be described provisionally as a profile of a functional system of components, that is, important component skills of intellectual ability that might describe the nature of an individual's performance.

The aims of the present chapter were (1) to describe the extent to which individuals of similar level of educational achievement, as judged by their teachers for end-of-year school assessment, might show a similar and distinctive pattern in their performance on the subtests of the NAT battery, that is, to assess the battery's predictive validity, and (2) to attempt a first evaluation of the NAT model on the basis of the data obtained from the same group.

The Predictive Validity of the NAT

Method

Subjects This study was conducted with 90 students from seven classrooms. Forty-three of the students were defined as high achievers, 26 as average achievers, and 21 as low achievers. The achievement groups were established on the basis of end-of-year school results, that is, teacher assessment based on examination results and class tests, in mathematics and science. All 90 students had been part of a sample to whom the NAT had been administered approximately 10 months earlier, at the beginning of the same school year.

The group of high achievers had obtained a grade of A in both subjects in their end-of-year assessment, the criterion being a score of above 80 per cent as an average across four school tests in each of the two subjects.

The average achievers had obtained test results ranging between 50 per cent and 60 per cent across all assessments in both mathematics and science, while the group of low achievers included the lowest scoring students across the seven classes. None of these students obtained more than 40 per cent in their school assessment.

The mean ages for the groups of high and average achievers were 12 years 3 months (SD = 6.05 months), and 12 years 4 months (SD = 5.44 months), respectively. The mean age for the group of low achievers was 12 years 7 months (SD = 6.73 months). None of the age differences between the groups were statistically significant.

The mean IQ levels obtained by the three groups on the Jenkins Non-Verbal Test were as follows: 121.52 (SD = 8.07) for high achievers, 103.87 (SD = 11.88) for average achievers, and 96.22 (SD = 13.42) for the low group. None of the differences in IQ were statistically significant.

Procedure The test performances on the three groups were compared by computing an analysis of variance, which was supplemented by Duncan's New Multiple Range Test (Duncan, 1955).

Results and Discussion

A 3 × 14 analysis of variance was computed in order to assess the relationship between reported school achievement and performance on each of 14 subtests of the NAT battery. The results of this analysis of variance are summarized in Table 12.1.

Table 12.1 Summary of an Analysis of Variance of High, Average and Low Academic Achievers Based on 14 Subtests of the NAT

Source of variation	SS	df	MS	F	p
A—Achievement levels	310.64	2	155.32	131.63	<.001
B—Tests	165.50	13	12.73	10.79	<.001
A × B	912.81	26	35.11	29.75	<.001
Within cell (error)	1417.68	1200	1.18		

As can be seen in the table, the difference between the three groups was highly significant ($p<.001$) for both main effects, that is, the achievement groups and the NAT subtests.

The significant difference between the achievement groups shows that performance on the NAT battery does reflect differences in school achievement. This was to be expected as the components of intellectual ability measured by the NAT were assumed to be of general importance.

The significant difference between the students of different levels of school achievement obtained in this analysis suggests that the results obtained by the students as a result of their performance on the NAT at the beginning of the school year, all other things being equal, could have predicted level of achievement as measured by the end-of-year school results for these students.

The significant effect for tests obtained in the analysis of variance reflects variations in test difficulty even for members of the same achievement group. This finding provides strong support for the previously emphasized need for measurement models that are not based on an assumption of intragroup homogeneity of performance processes, but for models that make explicit the individual differences, in terms of strengths and weaknesses experienced by individuals in component skills, within groups presumably operating at the same level of intellectual ability.

The significant interaction effect between achievement groups and tests showed that there were differences between the groups in the adequacy with which they performed the different tests. In other words, the similarities and differences in the performance patterns of the three groups were not entirely constant with respect to the 14 tests. Some subjects performed more adequately on some tests than on others. This finding is totally reconcilable with the conceptualization of intelligence as a functional system. The tests that were perceived as more difficult than others did not vary systematically between groups.

The mean scaled scores obtained on each test for each of the three groups of students are presented in Figure 12.1.

For a number of tests a fairly consistent trend can be observed. The group of high achievers obtained the highest scores on all tests, while the group of low school performers tended to obtain the poorest scores on the NAT subtests. Table 12.2 shows

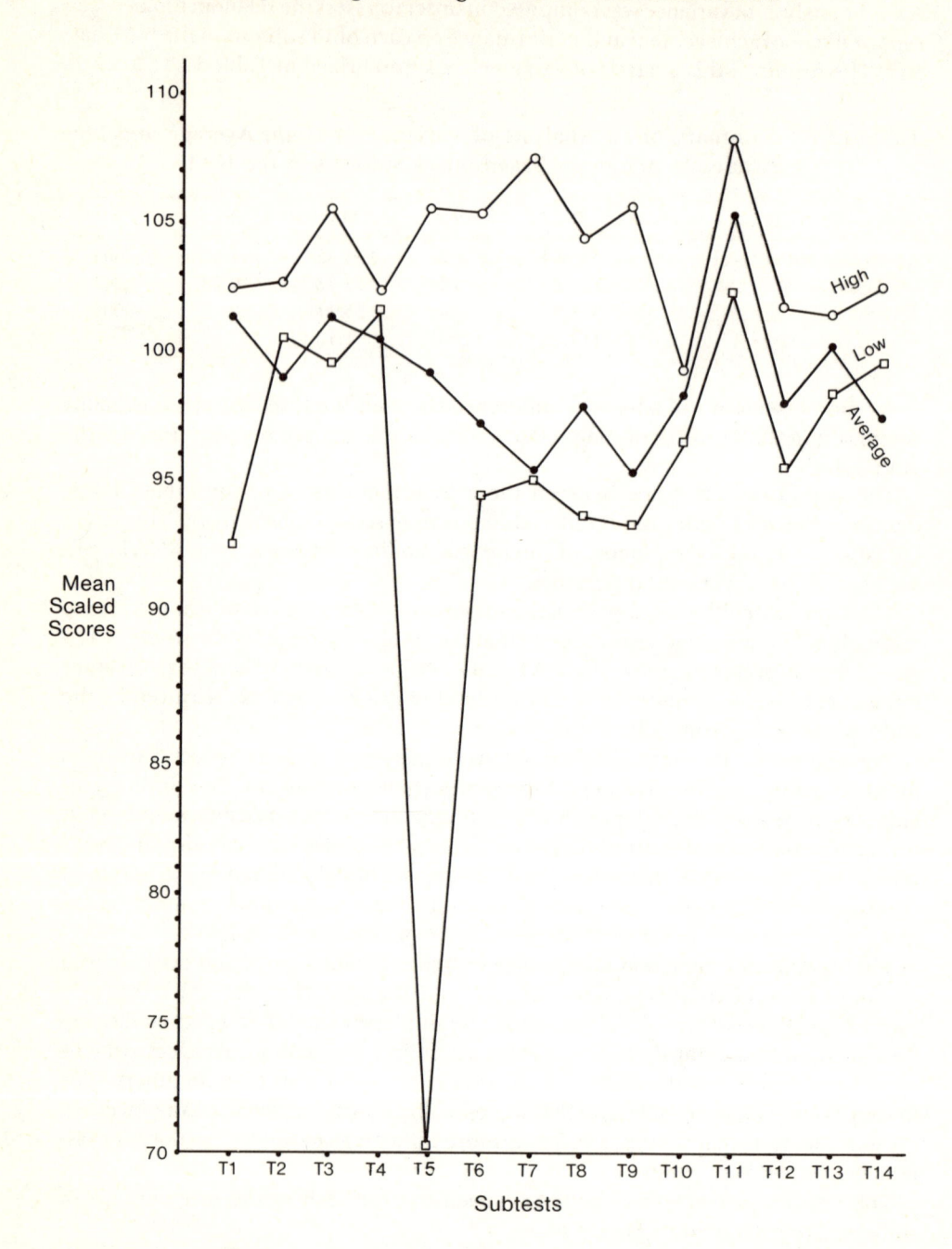

Figure 12.1 Graphic Representation of Mean Scaled Scores Obtained by Groups of High, Average and Low School Achievers

which trends and specific differences between subtests reached statistical significance on the basis of Duncan's New Multiple Range Test (Duncan, 1955).

Table 12.2 Probability Levels Resulting from Comparisons of Differences in Mean Values for the High, Average and Low Achievement Groups

Test	High versus low p$\leq$	High versus Average p$\leq$	Average versus low p$\leq$
1	.05	NS	NS
2	NS	.05	NS
3	.01	.05	NS
4	NS	NS	NS
5	.01	.05	.01
6	.01	.01	NS
7	.01	.05	NS
8	.01	NS	NS
9	.01	.01	NS
10	NS	NS	NS
11	.01	NS	NS
12	.01	.01	NS
13	NS	NS	NS
14	NS	.01	NS
Total NAT score	.01	.01	.05

Whereas Figure 12.1 shows the comparative levels of performance on the 14 NAT subtests for the three groups of students of varying school achievement, Table 12.2 contains details concerning the probability that differences between pairs of means for any two of the three groups might be attributed to chance. It is apparent that the group of high achievers performed at a higher level than either of the other groups in most tests. Differences between the average and low achievers reached statistical significance in one test only. The mean differences in total NAT Score were significant in all pair-wise comparisons.

The overall consideration of the results of the analysis of variance and the subsequent trend analyses may well allow certain generalizations. Low achievers in school mathematics and science seemed to be consistently and significantly less able to cope with the range of component skills assessed by the NAT battery. Considered within the framework of the theoretical model of the battery, they are likely to have developed fewer functional systems.

The subtests that discriminated best between the performance of high and low achievers related both to conceptual and perceptual skills. High and low achievers also displayed significant differences in their ability to attend and concentrate. Significant differences between high and average achievers tended to be restricted to the subtests focusing on conceptual skills, with some suggestion of a difference in flexibility of attention, that is, moving from one set of task requirements to another. Performances on individual NAT subtests by the three groups will be discussed further in the second section of this chapter.

The analysis described above has shown that the evaluation of intellectual ability does not have to be restricted to comparisons between global scores, but that valuable information can be gained by investigating the component skills involved in the process of performance itself, that is, the ability profile.

Remembering that the reported differences in school achievement in mathematics and science of the three groups investigated here were, in fact, not accompanied by significant differences in IQ level, as assessed on the basis of the Jenkins Non-Verbal Test, the results of the present study support a measurement model which allows for heterogeneity within IQ groups as discussed earlier in this chapter. School achievement and the NAT battery appear to be more sensitive to differences in cognitive ability than the Jenkins Non-Verbal Test.

Research workers, psychologists, teachers, parents, employers and others have often been baffled by the apparent discrepancy between the results of performance on group intelligence tests and school performance, ability to learn, trainability and performance in the work place. These discrepancies can be positive in either direction, and might well be explained by the fact that most intelligence and ability tests used at present make the assumption of homogeneity in ability structure and performance processes within ability levels. They therefore tend to mask the real and important differences between individuals, which they purport to assess.

It was demonstrated that the NAT battery of tests was able to differentiate between individuals of high, average and low school achievement in mathematics and science. Further studies are required not only to replicate the above findings, but to compare individuals with different types of abilities and scholastic difficulties, also to establish whether the results of the study reported here could be replicated with different age groups.

Evaluation of the NAT Model

For several decades there has been a controversy as to whether intelligence is a unitary trait of the type of Spearman's 'g', or whether it is made up of a number of separate abilities, as conceptualized, for example, in Thurstone's primary mental abilities or Guilford's model. The idea of a functional system, as explained in Chapter 2, may reconcile these divergent views to some extent.

As was shown in Chapters 9 and 10, on psychometric grounds the NAT would certainly be regarded first and foremost as a test of general intelligence of the 'g' type. The nature of the 'g' assessed by the battery is reflected on the basis of a set of component skills of an information-processing kind, which are assumed to be operating as a functional system.

Like other psychometric tests the NAT yields a measure of the level of an individual's performance relative to the performance of others, but unlike most other psychometric tests it also attempts to account for differences in ability and cognitive performance in terms of components of the performance itself. It thus provides a description of both the level and the nature of an individual's intellectual functioning.

Except where the aim was one of educational or institutional placement, intelligence tests have not, in the past, been used extensively for diagnostic purposes. Rather, the approach tended to be to compare 'underachievers', that is, individuals whose achievement at school was significantly lower than might have been predicted on the basis of their IQ scores, and normal achievers, on a considerable number of educational and psychological tests, and thus to attempt to identify possible causes of underachievement in particular students or groups on the basis of correlations between such tests. This was done by locating areas of testing in which the performance of normal and underachieving students appeared to differ significantly.

This approach was found to have merit in some cases and situations. The problem is that it depends on the assumption that an average or high achiever possesses an assembly of discrete, possibly autonomous skills, which develop independently, and which are necessary prerequisites for adequate intellectual functioning. Also, the approach assumes that an underachiever or low achiever is likely to be deficient in one or more cognitive skills, and capable of at least average performance in others.

From an *information-processing* point of view, at least two highly plausible types of models of the components of cognitive processes involved in intellectual activity and achievement can be proposed.

Models of the first type aim to account for the ways in which components of intelligence, such as perception, memory, verbal association, etc., interact during problem solving, reading, and other higher cognitive activities. There is a tendency for this type of model to attempt to describe temporal relationships between the variables that appear to be relevant to a particular cognitive activity, (e.g. Newell and Simon, 1972; Singer and Ruddell, 1970).

While models of this type seek to describe relationships between variables, models of the second type tend to focus on the component or subskills in terms of their necessity and contribution to cognitive activity and achievement. Within the framework of this second type of model, it is highly probable that one component skill may be made up of many processing variables, and that one processing variable may occur in many different component skills. The reader will recognize that the notion of a functional system, discussed in detail in Chapter 2, which provides the theoretical basis for the NAT battery belongs to the second type of model.

A model of the first type would propose general ability or intelligence to be a set or assembly of independent components. For the purposes of this chapter models of this type will be referred to as assembly models. Models of the second type would view ability or intelligence as a system of associated components. Hereafter, these models will be referred to as systems models.

The components of the assembly model can be regarded as independent, since each of them may be present in varying degrees of strength in the case of a given individual. The only expected relationship among the components is that during cognitive activity they occur or are capable of occurring in close succession.

The implicit use of this type of model for the investigation of cognitive processes has been widespread in education. For example, based on this model is the view that children develop component abilities of intellectual functioning, such as visual discrimination abilities, auditory discrimination, visual memory, auditory memory, and different linguistic skills, etc., independently. Further to this, the model provides support for the possibility that the problems of slow learners, poor readers, and other underachievers may be the consequence of only one, or a few of these abilities having failed to develop normally. The child's performance could thus be impaired as a result of one specific shortcoming, even if the other component skills have developed to normal or superior levels.

Much of the research into problems in the acquisition of reading skills, and into other reading disorders has been conducted within the framework of an assembly model of cognitive skills. Bateman (1966) surveyed 11 such correlational studies, each of which aimed to isolate the causes of reading disability by attempting to identify cognitive skills, the availability and strength of which might distinguish normal from disabled readers. In all these studies it was assumed that the skills investigated were independent of one another, and that a deficit in any of them or in similarly discrete other processes may be the cause of reading disability.

The popular notion that it is possible to isolate subgroups of disabled learners who may be classified as visual or auditory learners relies on the assembly model. Bateman (1969), Myklebust (1967), Strang (1969) and others assert that some children with reading difficulties have inferior visual skills, which impair reading, but that the auditory skills of these children are not impaired, and can thus be used as the major vehicle for instruction.

Contrary to these views based on assembly models, a systems model assumes that a cognitive process or skill consists of interactions between component processes or subskills that are not identical in function or strength, but are interdependent in both their development and operation.

For an individual and task situation these components may contain different degrees of strength, but the cognitive skill or process as a whole does not increase in strength more rapidly than the component with the slowest rate of development. The strength of a cognitive skill is thus influenced highly by its weakest component or subskill, that is, the weakest link in the chain.

The NAT was conceptualized as an example of a systems model. The cognitive ability or intelligence the battery purports to measure is viewed as a complex functional system. This system is operational as a result of the working together of a whole set of different component activities and skills. Each of these components is assumed to make its own contributions, but no component is viable on its own when the individual is faced with complex cognitive tasks. The reader is referred to Chapter 2 for a more detailed discussion of the theoretical notions relating to the NAT.

While considerable additional research is required before the interdependencies, redundancies and compensatory mechanisms among the component skills of intelligence can be described satisfactorily, a review of the literature of the past decade suggests that it is more probable that the components of intelligence conform to a systems rather than to an assembly model.

The subtests making up the NAT battery do not just provide different measures of the same singular ability. It will be observed that differences in content and difficulty among the subtests are marked, and that the correlations between the subtests are moderate only. Rather, the subtests of the NAT measure defined components or sets of functional elements of a more complex system of skills, which, as a whole, may be viewed as ability, intelligence, or some similar, previously barely defined concept.

In the systems model the components of the system, collectively, can serve to define its operation.

The NAT profile is designed to provide information concerning the individual's ability, readiness or capability to cope with educational and other intellectual tasks.

For example, one of the most basic intellectual tasks in our society is that of reading. Goodman's (1967) model suggests that the reading process requires the individual

> to (a) sample visual cues from the array on the printed page, (b) form a perceptual image, (c) search memory for psycholinguistic cues related to the perceptual image, (d) convert the perceptual image to a unit of new meaning, and (e) integrate the new meaning with previously established meanings. (Guthrie, 1973, pp.10–11)

As discussed in the preceding chapters, the non-linguistic skills required to perform the above subtasks are covered in single or a combination of NAT subtests.

It is apparent that the component skills measured by the different subtests of the battery are qualitatively different. Consequently it can be expected that different levels of development or strength may be observed in the performance on these tests. However, since the performance of complex cognitive tasks requires the working together of many component skills, the overall level of achievement will depend on the availability and strength of individual component skills in relation to particular tasks.

For example, in the model of the reading process noted above the temporal sequence during reading is most probably (a) to (e). The occurrence of (e) depends on the occurrence of (a). Since (e) is likely to be strengthened with use, the strength of (e) will depend partly on the strength of (a). Also, a high level of strength in (d) may facilitate the occurrence of (a). In this way the interdependencies among the subskills would prevent several of them from developing to adequate levels if one or more were severely deficient, unless compensatory functional systems for the acquisition of reading that do not include the defective component were available.

Experimental evidence supporting systems models of higher cognitive processes may be derived from the literature. Jensen (1971), for example, reported high correlations between memory span for digits, presented in the visual and the auditory mode. When corrected for attentuation, these correlations were unity.

Jensen's findings support earlier studies (e.g. Gates, 1916; Golden and Steiner, 1969; Rystrom, 1970), all of which suggest that basic intellectual skills that may be related to higher cognitive processes are closely related to each other.

An assembly model of the concept intelligence, as measured by the NAT, would hold that intellectual achievement requires a set of component skills that develop independently. All other things being equal, if this model were to hold for high, average and low achievers, one would expect that low achievers would show average development in most component skills, and would show low performance on only a small number of subtests. The component skills measured by the latter subtests might then be among those preventing normal school achievement. Similarly the difference between the test performances of high and average achievers would be revealed in a small number of subtests, which, in turn would be regarded as measuring the component skills that prevent average students from 'high' scholastic achievement.

A systems model contends that component abilities are inter-related. Development and competence in one component ability may depend on competence in another. Facilitation and transfer, possibly both positive and negative, may occur between components.

If a systems model were to obtain, it would be expected that the performance of low school achievers, compared with that of average and above-average students, would be deficient in many, perhaps all, component skills. Similarly the performance of high achievers, other things being equal, would be expected to be higher than that of the students of average ability, in a considerable number of component skills.

This suggestion may be an oversimplification. A systems model would not necessarily propose a similar relationship between average and low, and high and average achievers because certain skills may have been fully achieved by the average achiever. These skills would then have no part in the discrimination between component processes utilized by high, but not by average students.

The above point does not affect the assumption, under a systems model of intelligence, of more generalized deficiency in low academic achievers. Two explanations could be offered for this more wide ranging deficiency.

Under a systems model a deficit in one or two specific component skills would influence, possibly prevent, the development of other component skills to average expected levels, because, under such a model, component skills are interdependent.

A second explanation is that the source of the observed low performance could lie in a lack of interdependence among component skills for the low achievers. In such a case component skills might be acquired by the individual at a normal rate for an initial period of time. However, the absence of positive feedback, transfer or other types of mutual facilitation among the component skills could prevent the development of other component skills to an average or above-average level of strength.

The criteria for the evaluation of the two models in the present study were as follows. If the tests of component skills yielded little, if any, intercorrelation, an assembly model of overall ability would gain support. If an assembly model appeared to fit the performance of average and high achievers, it could be expected that the NAT scores of low achievers would be average, in keeping with age expectations, on the majority of component skills, and low on a minority of subtests.

Support for a systems model would be gained, if scores on tests measuring component skills appeared to be related, particularly in the case of low achievers. Under a systems model one would predict that low achievers would show lower performance than individuals in the other two groups in the majority of component skills. The conceptual model underlying the NAT was investigated as described below.

Method

Subjects The subjects who contributed the data to this study were the same 90 students who co-operated in the predictive validity study, and who were described on page 200.

Procedure Mean scores, standard deviations and intercorrelations between the scaled scores of 14 NAT subtests were computed for the total sample, and for each of the three groups, namely, high, average and low achievers, separately.

In this study the results of only 14 of the 18 subtests of the NAT battery were analysed. These 14 tests comprised all but the 4 memory tests (Tests 15, 16, 17 and 18), which were omitted because not all subjects in the group were present when these tests were administered. Also, as noted previously, these tests had not been sufficiently investigated in the trial sample as a whole, and are, as discussed in Chapter 8, regarded as optional extras at the present time.

Results and Discussion

Mean differences Table 12.3 shows the mean scores and standard deviations for each of 14 NAT subtests, and for the total NAT Score for the three achievement groups.

Table 12.3 Mean Scores and Standard Deviations for each of the 14 NAT Subtests, and for the Total NAT Score for Three Groups of Varying School Achievement

	High (n=43)		Average (n=26)		Low (n=21)	
Test	$\bar{x}$	SD	$\bar{x}$	SD	$\bar{x}$	SD
1	103.16	5.25	102.15	6.48	93.00	23.32
2	103.45	7.49	99.54	5.22	101.31	6.75
3	106.44	5.33	102.24	7.21	100.90	9.85
4	103.17	6.78	101.31	5.70	102.00	6.58
5	108.69	5.35	99.85	21.33	70.38	46.43
6	106.33	6.96	97.92	6.49	94.90	7.78
7	109.05	19.61	96.15	20.94	95.48	20.55
8	106.42	3.17	98.58	21.15	94.48	23.12
9	107.09	6.97	95.92	20.07	94.19	22.64
10	100.67	7.48	99.08	7.10	97.38	7.72
11	109.37	5.78	106.11	7.39	103.57	10.01
12	102.58	4.39	98.69	4.05	96.24	5.01
13	102.72	6.76	101.23	8.10	99.00	7.37
14	103.51	6.81	98.38	5.44	100.33	10.89
Total NAT score	108.56	5.16	99.64	8.74	91.81	11.91
Mean Score across 14 tests	105.24	3.00	99.79	5.18	95.62	6.87
SD across 14 tests	7.78	1.71	9.72	7.05	16.38	11.30

Inspection of Table 12.3 shows that the differences in total NAT Score between high and average ($t = 4.73, p<.001$), and between average and low achievers ($t = 2.52, p<.05$) were statistically significant. This finding is important, especially as the obtained differences in Jenkins Non-Verbal IQ between the groups were not significant. Table 12.3 also reports for each of the three groups the mean of the mean scores obtained across 14 NAT subtests calculated for each member of each group. These scores together with the total NAT Scores provide information about the average levels of the NAT profiles, while the mean standard deviation across the 14 tests describe tendencies in the regularity, that is shape, of the profiles of individuals. The differences in average mean scores obtained across the 14 tests were significant between the high and average ($t = 4.89, <001$), and average and low groups ($t = 2.30, p<.05$).

The difference between the mean standard deviations across the 14 tests was not significant for the high and average group, but highly significant when the low group was compared with either the high or average groups. This result supports long standing and frequently replicated findings in the research literature and in clinical practice concerning the greater intra-individual variations in cognitive performance in groups of low achievers in school and on intelligence tests.

Inspection of the mean scores obtained on individual tests by the different groups showed significantly lower performances ($p<.05$) of the low achievers than the high achievers in 9 out of the 14 tests. The differences observed between high and average achievers were significant in the case of 8 out of the 14 tests, while the differences between average and low achievers were statistically significant only in the case of one test, namely Test 5, the Embedded Figures test.

This test showed significantly different mean differences between all groups. The most frequently observed significant differences occurred in those tests measuring conceptual rather than perceptual components of general ability. The least number of significant differences were observed in the speed and accuracy tests.

The fact that in the comparisons of single subtests only one difference of means between average and low performers was significant can be explained by the possible lack of real ability difference between these groups. As was noted above the differences in Jenkins Non-Verbal IQ between the three groups did not reach statistical significance. It thus may have been more profitable to compare the performances of high and low achievers only. However, because the school performance of most students is rated as 'average' by their teachers, it was decided to investigate whether NAT subtests would reflect differences in any or all of these groups.

It may be of relevance, at this point, for the reader to be reminded of the fact that the literature reports correlations ranging from 0 to .4 only between teacher assessment and examination and test results for students in lower secondary school.

With regard to the profiles it could be shown that the group of low achievers would tend not only to produce the lowest profile with respect to level, but that, on the average, the profiles of the low achievers showed the greatest amount of both inter and intra-individual differences.

Subtest intercorrelations   These were computed for the total sample of 90 students, and are presented in Table 12.4. These correlations ranged from .01 to .64 with 51 (i.e. 56 per cent) of the correlations significant beyond the .05 level, and 41 (i.e. 45 per cent) significant beyond the .01 level.

When the three achievement groups were analysed separately, a different picture emerged. The intercorrelations between subtests for the high, average and low achieving groups are presented in Tables 12.5, 12.6 and 12.7 respectively. The range of intercorrelations between subtests and the number of significant intercorrelations for each group are shown in Table 12.8.

The low achieving group exhibited a pattern different from those for the average and high achieving groups. The high achievers showed the fewest significant intercorrelations between subtests, and the average achievers did not differ much from their high achieving peers in this respect. The low achieving group showed the highest proportion of significant intercorrelations.

Table 12.4 Correlations Among 14 NAT Subtests for 90 High, Average and Low School Achievers

Test	2	3	4	5	6	7	8	9	10	11	12	13	14	$\bar{x}_r$	SD_r
1	30	13	15	27	25	19	41	37	12	18	22	25	17	23	09
2		15	03	19	33	36	31	23	45	54	48	45	37	32	14
3			15	20	30	06	14	29	19	11	22	16	15	17	07
4				11	20	02	05	10	05	02	08	16	09	09	06
5					52	27	36	41	19	36	46	27	01	28	14
6						37	47	56	17	33	53	25	08	34	15
7							26	34	14	27	34	16	07	22	12
8								54	20	21	37	26	10	28	14
9									10	35	42	14	05	30	17
10										53	36	59	50	28	18
11											64	42	25	32	18
12												36	20	36	15
13													63	32	16
14														20	19

Table 12.5 Correlations Among 14 NAT Subtests for the Group of High Achievers

Test	2	3	4	5	6	7	8	9	10	11	12	13	14	$\bar{x}_r$	SD_r
1	02	02	14	−05	−11	29	16	06	06	−08	−17	07	−00	09	08
2		25	−24	19	18	33	26	08	35	58	40	46	21	27	15
3			23	07	16	−10	24	12	04	13	14	15	−03	13	08
4				11	−04	−22	09	−13	−15	−14	−08	06	−04	13	07
5					21	08	23	06	11	28	34	24	04	15	10
6						31	15	13	−19	11	34	−10	−31	18	09
7							09	28	03	04	20	05	06	16	11
8								34	04	26	06	11	06	16	10
9									−14	20	16	−11	−15	15	08
10										37	18	48	41	20	15
11											55	41	15	25	17
12												13	−04	21	15
13													64	23	20
14														16	19

Table 12.6 Correlations Among 14 NAT Subtests for the Group of Average Achievers

Test	3	4	5	6	7	8	9	10	12	13	14	15	16	$\bar{x}_r$	SD_r
1	45	09	10	03	−13	07	62	41	−24	−29	−12	04	13	21	18
3		−16	23	17	39	08	70	23	44	32	28	24	40	31	16
4			01	−08	05	−20	20	31	19	06	16	13	10	13	08
5				−16	34	19	45	19	15	−13	19	17	29	20	11
6					15	11	06	−13	−04	12	30	38	45	15	13
7						−01	35	23	19	09	37	40	29	23	14
8							13	−26	−00	−02	21	26	24	14	09
9								66	28	03	34	41	29	35	22
10									86	−12	05	28	−05	29	23
12										61	46	43	43	33	24
13											46	25	29	21	18
14												51	51	30	15
15													55	31	15
16														31	15

Table 12.7 Correlations Among 14 NAT Subtests for the Group of Low Achievers

Test	3	4	5	6	7	8	9	10	12	13	14	15	16	$\bar{x}_r$	SD_r
1	57	14	21	14	38	05	28	43	30	39	39	45	25	31	15
3		13	28	10	28	42	−29	06	73	77	74	73	65	44	27
4			09	09	21	07	−24	08	23	−10	−08	08	16	13	06
5				25	41	09	−46	26	29	26	07	36	07	24	13
6					37	16	06	43	09	31	20	−07	−42	21	13
7						44	21	76	24	41	28	26	−02	33	17
8							25	45	21	59	31	14	−02	25	18
9								32	−15	02	20	−13	−19	22	11
10									11	57	42	06	−10	31	22
12										60	41	85	63	37	25
13											77	50	21	42	24
14												41	08	33	23
15													75	37	28
16														27	25

Table 12.8 Range of Significance of Intercorrelations for High, Average and Low School Achievers

		$p<.05$		$p<.01$	
Group	Range of r	n	%	n	%
Total	.01 to .64	51	56	41	45
High	.00 to .64	19	21	9	10
Average	.00 to .86	22	24	8	9
Low	.02 to .85	28	31	14	15

Corrigendum

Rowe, H.A.H. *Language-free Evaluation of Cognitive Development.*

p. 214: The column headings and row labels for Tables 12.6 and 12.7 were misprinted. The tables should be replaced with those given below.

Table 12.6 Correlations Among 14 NAT Subtests for the Group of Average Achievers

Test	2	3	4	5	6	7	8	9	10	11	12	13	14	$\bar{x}_r$	SD_r
1	45	09	10	03	−13	07	62	41	−24	−29	−12	04	13	21	18
2		−16	23	17	39	08	70	23	44	32	28	24	40	31	16
3			01	−08	05	−20	20	31	19	06	16	13	10	13	08
4				−16	34	19	45	19	15	−13	19	17	29	20	11
5					15	11	06	−13	−04	12	30	38	45	15	13
6						−01	35	23	19	09	37	40	29	23	14
7							13	−26	−00	−02	21	26	24	14	09
8								66	28	03	34	41	29	35	22
9									86	−12	05	28	−05	29	23
10										61	46	43	43	33	24
11											46	25	29	21	18
12												51	51	30	15
13													55	31	15
14														31	15

Table 12.7 Correlations Among 14 NAT Subtests for the Group of Low Achievers

Test	2	3	4	5	6	7	8	9	10	11	12	13	14	$\bar{x}_r$	SD_r
1	57	14	21	14	38	05	28	43	30	39	39	45	25	31	15
2		13	28	10	28	42	−29	06	73	77	74	73	65	44	27
3			09	09	21	07	−24	08	23	−10	−08	08	16	13	06
4				25	41	09	−46	26	29	26	07	36	07	24	13
5					37	16	06	43	09	31	20	−07	−42	21	13
6						44	21	76	24	41	28	26	−02	33	17
7							25	45	21	59	31	14	−02	25	18
8								32	−15	02	20	−13	−19	22	11
9									11	57	42	06	−10	31	22
10										60	41	85	63	37	25
11											77	50	21	42	24
12												41	08	33	23
13													75	37	28
14														27	25

Conclusions

These results may be compared with the predictions made earlier in this chapter. The results show that the intercorrelations between subtests are higher for the low achieving group than for the students whose school achievement had been rated by their teachers as average or above, thus suggesting a more generalized deficiency in functioning among the low achieving group. The weaknesses experienced by subjects in certain component skills may have inhibited development and ability in other areas and would thus be expected to influence cognitive performance more generally. This outcome provides support for a systems model of component skills of intellectual functioning, and casts doubt on an assembly model.

It had been predicted that if an assembly model were to hold, the performance of low achievers would be lower than that of their average and above-average peers in a few subtests only. It was predicted that under an assembly model the scores of low achievers would not differ significantly from that of their more academic peers.

It was predicted further that, if a systems model were to be supported, the performance of the low achievers would be lower than that of their more highly achieving peers in a majority of the subtests. Inspection of Table 12.3 shows the accuracy of the latter prediction. A considerable number of subskills had not developed to normal levels of strength.

Not only were the low achievers inferior in level of performance, but they showed greater within-subject and within-group variation than either of the other sets of subjects. Greater scatter between scores on tests of various component abilities have been observed among children and adults of low intellectual achievement.

Another way of interpreting the correlational results of the low achievers might be to suggest that the subskills measured are more similar in this group or are mediated by a common latent trait. However, since the component skills were found to be less intercorrelated in the other groups, in fact least correlated in the high achievers, their independence gains support. It is likely that the components of general ability are more highly integrated in children whose intellectual development has been delayed or restricted for one reason or another. A systems interpretation of the processes involved in the test performances observed here can thus be distinguished from a simple approach, which would maintain that the higher correlations between subskills in low achievers reflect the fact that the skills measured are more similar in low achievers than in their more highly achieving peers.

The obvious variation in difficulty of component skills for the low achieving group reflected in the mean scores, the greater dispersion of scores within subtests, and the considerably greater unevenness of their profiles would negate the above argument. The present data would certainly be better explained by a systems model, which would propose that the skills in low achievers, as measured by the NAT, appear to be more integrated because inabilities in basic skill areas have affected cognitive development more generally, and have thus tended to influence performance as a whole. Support for a functional systems model can be derived from the fact that alternative functional systems were obviously not available to these students.

The similarly low correlations between the component skills in high and average achievers might, at first sight, suggest that an assembly model of intelligence would fit the performance of these groups better than a systems model. However, a brief inspection of the mean of the correlation coefficients obtained for each test (the last two columns of Tables 12.5, 12.6 and 12.7) shows a striking similarity in the average correlations between tests for the groups of low and average achievers. In view of the previously mentioned fact that there was no significant difference in IQ between these groups, and in view of the fact that average and high achievers differed significantly in their performance not just in one or two subtests, but in the majority of the tests, an assembly model does not appear to be supported.

The possibility of a mixed model would have to be investigated in a more tightly controlled study of more extreme ability groups. It is possible that, once basic cognitive skills operate at an efficient level so as not to mutually inhibit development, further growth in specific component skills, that is, growth leading to the manifestation of particular talents, might use processes of a more discrete nature.

The important insight gained from the results of the study reported in this chapter relates to the fact that low achievers display wide ranging, often generalized cognitive difficulties, which are likely to be the result of retarded development or other deficits in important component skills of intellectual functioning. A considerable number of the component skills are at a very basic level, and most of them can be expected to be trainable or compensatable through the assisted development of alternative functional systems.

The NAT battery provides a starting point for the description and evaluation of component abilities, deficiencies in which may be inhibiting the intellectual performance and achievement of individuals.

Although the findings reported in this chapter have to be regarded as tentative, the present initial attempt to evaluate the wider validity of both the measurement and the theoretical model of the NAT has shown that, pending replications with other samples representative of different age groups and other characteristics, the NAT battery can be regarded as a valid non-verbal tool for the description of both the level and the nature of the general ability it purports to be measuring.

CHAPTER 13

USING THE NAT AS PART OF A LARGER TEST BATTERY

The aim of this chapter is to enable those responsible for more comprehensive psychological or psychoeducational assessment rather than the administration of just one test, and who are working under conditions that permit the administration of several tests, to integrate an individual's NAT scores with his or her performance on other tests.

It happens all too frequently that, after several tests have been administered to an individual, these tests are interpreted in complete isolation from each other. What is forgotten in such instances is that, no matter whether concerned with general ability, educational achievement, language skills, perceptual development or conceptual ability, virtually all tests share certain communalities with all other tests in the cognitive domain, that is, there is some overlap in what they measure.

The type of tests that might usefully supplement the information provided by the NAT is discussed in this chapter. Suggestions are made for the selection of additional measures based on hypotheses generated from the individual's performance on the NAT. The use of selected parts of the NAT to serve as supplements, when a different intelligence test, such as the WAIS-R, WISC-R, Standford–Binet, or a verbal group test is chosen as the basic measure of intellectual ability or cognitive development is also discussed.

Finally, quite a few tests are mentioned in this chapter. As the topic of this book revolves around the NAT, the characteristics of the other tests are noted rather than critically evaluated. Potential users are reminded to consult the relevant editions of Buros' *Mental Measurement Yearbook*, *Tests in Print*, and such reference works as *Advances in Psychological Assessment* (McReynolds, 1981 for volume 5), as well as the test manuals pertaining to the tests under consideration, to determine the suitability of any particular instrument for a specified purpose. On the judgment of the author of this book, the psychometric properties of all tests mentioned in this chapter are at least adequate for their use as suggested below.

It is acknowledged, however, that there are very few tests that are completely acceptable technically. For diagnostic use some imperfections in tools often have to be tolerated. It is up to the person interpreting the results and their significance to take such imperfections into account. 'Some schools of thought avoid this dilemma by insisting on achieving a valid score, even when its information value is trivial' (Gathercole, 1968, p.90). Those responsible for comprehensive clinical assessments have to decide for themselves whether a valid trivial finding contributes more than an observation of a clinical kind, the validity of which cannot be established statistically. Obviously, only experienced professionals should move from simple and quantitative assessment into complex qualitative areas.

Relevant Intervention-oriented Assessment

The aim of relevant psychological assessment is to facilitate (1) the development of skills and abilities in those assessed, and (2) informed and valid decision making. To be effective with regard to both these purposes requires assessment to be compatible, even interlinked, with intervention activities, thus creating a system in which assessment-based diagnosis leads to diagnosis-directed intervention, with the outcome of intervention procedures in turn being evaluated through assessment.

For optimal value and efficiency, so that specific and useful information can be obtained, the diagnosis–intervention procedures should

- focus on characteristics that are relevant to the hypothesized developmental or problem domain, or area in which a decision is to be made,
- focus on behaviours and skills that can be manipulated, that is, improved through training,
- be continuing.

The major use of tests should be for the improvement of instruction—for diagnosis of learning difficulties and for prescribing learning activities in response to learning needs. They must not be used in any way that will lead to labelling and classifying of students. (National Education Association, 1973, pp.36–37)

Criterion-referenced measures may best achieve the above purposes. They tend to focus on specific and relevant behaviours and skills, which are directly interpretable in terms of specific goals of performance and teaching.

The NAT is a battery of criterion-referenced tests, which by concentrating on the evaluation of defined components of intelligent behaviour can be expected to provide the psychologist and teacher with quite exact information as to what the individual can or cannot do easily. The NAT profile thus increases the validity of intervention procedures, and monitors the development of important cognitive abilities.

Fair Assessment

The literature contains reports of the identification of many methodological factors and assumptions that can constitute obstacles to fair assessment, particularly in the assessment of individuals in cross-cultural and cross-ethnic situations. It is generally recognized that there is a need for much more theoretical and empirical research before substantial gains can be expected in the validity of such procedures. In the meantime the following points and suggestions relating to assessment procedure, situation, and professional responsibility should be kept in mind.

The choice of method of assessment should be preceded by an evaluation of the purposes and the potential consequences of the assessment. Potential examiners should seek to answer (for themselves) questions such as the following.

- What is the specific purpose of this assessment?
- Who has requested the assessment?
- Exactly what information is being sought?
- To whom and how will the results be communicated?
- Who will benefit from the assessment, and how?
- What are the potential side effects for the testee and others?
- What alternatives are available at this point, for obtaining the required information?

The purpose of the assessment will, obviously, determine the comprehensiveness, depth, and content of testing. Is its primary focus to be on the individual's present status, that is, his or her present strengths and/or weaknesses in specified areas, as required for purposes of differential diagnosis? Or should the focus be on a process, for example the adjustment to a new school, work place, etc.?

Both status and process orientations must allow for the inclusion in the assessment procedure of ways of establishing criteria for future or ongoing evaluation of progress. In other words, status assessment must allow for the evaluation of the efficacy of intervention procedures, while process assessment includes the task of setting up a monitoring system to assess the utility of training methods that are aimed at helping in the process of adaptation.

Naturally, the choice of the tests themselves depends on the purpose for testing, and the special needs of the potential testee. The validity of a test for a particular purpose depends not only on its contents but on the professional competency of the tester. Test results are no more than samples of an individual's performance. They are often expressed in terms of statistical models of measurement, which have to be interpreted.

In as far as cultural variables are expected to influence the behaviours sampled, test results can show variations between individuals, and from one group to another. In general, the more incongruent the cultures of the testee and the test producer are, the more likely is it that a confused, if not invalid, picture might evolve. However, quite frequently sharp differences in performance patterns between groups or individuals can alert the teacher or psychologist to problems of communication and adjustment. But subtle, culture-based performance differences might go unrecognized, or be misinterpreted.

It must be kept in mind that cultural factors influence not only the performance of the testee, but also that of the tester. Where cultural or ethnic variables affect the understanding and interpretation of test results, testers may vary in what they perceive, and in how they interpret the test results. In many situations it is impossible to eliminate cultural or ethnic bias. The task of the professional becomes, therefore, to gather the necessary cultural knowledge and understanding, and to evaluate and interpret the testee's performance in relation to this knowledge.

Non-verbal tests are less culture-bound than verbal tests, personality questionnaires, and interview procedures. Yet, even in the case of tests like the NAT the appropriateness of the stimulus material and procedures needs to be evaluated in relation to the needs of individual testees and groups. With some ethnic groups the tester may have to depart from the standard method of presentation. Where possible, the tests should be scored both for the standard and non-standard, for example 'testing the limits' (to be discussed later in this chapter). Obviously, all deviations from standard procedures, and any observations of behaviour and/or reactions relating to cultural differences should be noted by the tester.

Finally, there is a temptation among professionals to advocate the banning of all tests 'in fairness', because tests have been shown to provide misleading results, and some have resulted in unfair discrimination. Those tempted to reason in this way need to consider the alternatives to testing.

Lennon (1964) suggested that to consider abandoning all testing would be like trying to burn down the barn to catch a mouse. If testing were to be abandoned, the needs it presently serves would have to be met in other ways. It is likely that the use of subjective appraisals would increase, and with it the likelihood of strong bias and discrimination. In short, 'the social consequences of not testing . . . are potentially far more harmful than any possible adverse consequences of testing' (Ebel, 1963, p.143).

A test is biased against members of a particular group of people if it contains items on which the average score obtained by members of the group differs from the average score of other groups by a greater or lesser amount than can be expected on other items of the same test.

Would the alternatives to ability testing be less likely to lead to biased assessment, damaging labels in the community and to self-fulfilling prophesies? Drenth (1977) argued that in certain developing countries the grades obtained in school achievement tests may predict school performance less well than ability tests. Responsibly interpreted and used, test scores tend certainly to provide more and more reliable information than interview impressions and other subjective reports alone. This view is supported by Messick (1982, 1983), Samuda (1975), Wechsler (1966), and others. However, as stated by Ebel, 'One cannot hold a test accountable for the ways in which it is used' (1968, p.385).

In other words valid test usage depends on reliable, conscientious, methodical informed choice, examination and interpretation of test scores.

> Many comparisons depend upon tests, but they also depend upon *our* intelligence, our good will, and our sense of responsibility to make the proper comparisons at the proper time and to undertake proper remedial and compensatory actions as a result. The misuse of tests with minority group children, or in any other situation, is a serious breach of professional ethics. Their proper use is a sign of professional maturity. (Fishman et al., 1964, p.144)

Limitations and Role of the NAT

The results obtained on the NAT, or for that matter of any non-verbal test, no matter how broadly based, provide part only of the total assessment of an individual's cognitive development or intellectual skills. Verbal reasoning, word knowledge, and other abilities involving language have to be included in most cases. Even in the case of instruments containing a language component, more complex issues of diagnosis for intervention, special placement, the selection of training programs that are tailored to the assessed needs of the individual, etc., would usually demand the use of several instruments.

However, the fact that complex diagnosis and remediation require the use of multiple tests does not imply that the NAT must be supplemented by other instruments as a matter of routine. The dimensions covered by the NAT as a measure of general ability and as a broad profile of component abilities are quite sufficient for many testing purposes. The NAT, on its own, certainly serves as an initial source of hypotheses for the interpretation of observed intellectual performance in individuals with or without known or suspected language deficits. Also, the limitations in permissible testing time, and the number of individuals to be assessed often restrict the tester to the use of one instrument.

Where a language-free instrument is required for the testing of groups or individuals, the NAT provides good value as regards breadth of coverage in just over one hour of testing.

Psychoeducational Diagnosis

> The breadth of knowledge and skills needed for effective assessment practice is not always understood by persons new to the field, who often anticipate that assessment primarily involves learning how to give, score and interpret a number of specific tests. (Helton, Workman, and Matuszek, 1982, p.1)

While the skills noted in the above quotation are, in fact, prerequisites of effective assessment practice, psychoeducational assessment is a much broader and more complex endeavour. In addition to the above mentioned skills, it requires knowledge of a number of topics (including theories of intelligence and cognition, child development, and the basic principles of psychological and educational measurement), a good understanding of the variables making up the social context in which the assessment takes place, and the acceptance of the fact that assessment involves the integration of all available information.

This last requirement includes the knowledge that all test results represent a sample only of the individual's abilities and of the observations that could have been made in relation to his or her functioning in a particular area. How valid and appropriate (i.e. representative, predictive, reliable, etc.) the sample of tested abilities or skills might be for a particular assessment depends largely on the purpose of the assessment, and has to be judged for each individual case by the professional responsible for the assessment.

Purposes of assessment Typically, psychoeducational assessment serves two purposes: (1) the classification and categorization of testees according to their level of ability or handicap in relation to a particular set of tasks, and (2) to aid decision making on the basis of the identified needs or general characteristics of individuals. The latter purpose would include the design of intervention procedures to meet individuals' needs that have been identified by means of testing.

At first sight, these two purposes of assessment would appear to be complimentary to each other. Unfortunately, the assessment literature and practical experience have shown that this is rarely true. Instead, a number of difficulties face those attempting to achieve each purpose separately, and major obstacles appear to be encountered in integrating the two.

For most professionals responsible for the assessment of individuals, *categorization* involves deciding whether the testee fits a particular label such as 'mentally retarded', 'deaf', 'speech impaired', 'visually handicapped', 'emotionally disturbed', etc., or as having 'specific learning disabilities', being 'gifted', and so on.

Historically, such labels have, in many instances, led to the testee being given access to special clinical or educational services. In other words, the classification or categorization function of psychoeducational assessment identified *who* might profit from the provision of special services.

However, the categorization of individuals in terms of handicapping conditions alone does not lead to effective intervention, because it cannot specify the educational or training content of the special services that might meet the individual's needs most effectively.

Labels referring to handicapping conditions have been shown to be largely irrelevant to the teaching of a curriculum (Bardon and Bennett, 1974; Duffy, Salvia, Tucker, and Ysseldyke, 1981; Hallahan and Kaufman, 1976; Hobbs, 1975a, 1975b, 1980), since they provide little, if any, specific guidance for the development of needs-based programs for those who have been labelled. Labels can be linked with decision making only in situations where the decision relates to the institutional placement of an individual. Labels provide no information to those faced with decision making in relation to the training of an individual, or when remediation or other types of intervention are required.

Models of non-categorical assessment, in which the performance and other characteristics of the testee are described rather than labelled, have long been suggested as an alternative to traditional educational and psychological classifications (e.g. Gillung and Rucker, 1977; Payne, 1972; Reynolds and Balow, 1972). The obvious advantage of such an approach is that it provides the possiblity of improving the effectiveness of services to individuals experiencing temporary or more lasting handicaps and other difficulties by focusing on the specific contents of the services they need in order to function more successfully.

In the school setting a discontinuation of labelling is likely to reduce the negative bias on educational placement decisions and thus increase the opportunity to learn.

Many psychological tests not only focus mainly on characteristics that cannot be changed easily within the school context (e.g. IQ, personality variables, etc.) but have few if any curriculum or teaching implications. This means that many data collected on children have no impact on their educational experience. On the other side, teachers, curriculum consultants, educational psychologists and others concerned with what goes on in the classroom, are attempting to develop curriculum-related procedures and materials that offer the opportunity to adjust teaching to the learning needs of individuals. Such developments have forced psychologists to recognize that, ideally, assessment ought to be carried out by those who can both collect and make use of the data in the classroom. This approach would also allow teachers to recognize that improved teaching and increased accountability can result from the use of objective data obtained from the administration of educational and psychological tests.

Supplementing the Information Obtained on the NAT

An additional 20 to 30 minutes testing time, and some additional scoring time, can validate, strengthen and extend the picture of an individual's ability that emerges from an administration of the NAT. Wherever appropriate and feasible, the NAT should be supplemented at least with tests of verbal reasoning and word knowledge, and where relevant with tests of social knowledge and educational achievement. In the final count, however, the choice of supplementary tests will depend on the kind of evidence sought.

Tests of Verbal Reasoning and Word Knowledge

Numerous verbal tests are available. The most useful among them for the purposes of a comprehensive assessment of cognitive development or general ability are probably the Wechsler tests, namely, the Wechsler Intelligence Scale for Children—Revised (WISC-R) for ages 6 years to 16 years 11 months (Wechsler, 1974); and the Wechsler Adult Intelligence Scale—Revised (WAIS-R) for the age range between 16 years and 75 years (Wechsler, 1981) or the Revised Stanford–Binet Intelligence Scale (3rd revision, 1960), age range 2 years to adult.

The areas covered by Wechsler's verbal scales are described below.

Information   The tests consist of a variety of items of increasing difficulty, testing general knowledge, for example 'How many weeks are there in a year?', 'What is a hyroglyphic?'

Comprehension   These are tests of logical thinking, in which the testee is required to explain why phenomena occur, and why certain actions take place, for example 'Why should a promise be kept?', 'Why are laws necessary?' Responses are scored according to their quality and the degree of generalization attained. The reasoning assessed in these tests strongly overlaps with what is frequently referred to as 'social intelligence', that is, social maturity and social judgment.

Arithmetic   These tests contain a series of simple to difficult arithmetic items, which have to be solved within a given time limit, and without the aid of pencil and paper. The tasks range from the simple manipulation of concrete materials, to complex story problems. The content of these tests is closely related to skills of number manipulation learnt in primary school. Tests of numerical reasoning also require concentration, and short-term memory.

Similarities   The tasks in these tests require the identification of likeness between different objects. Scoring takes in the level of abstraction and concept formation reflected in a response. Examples: 'In what way are an apple and an orange alike?', 'In what way are first and last alike?'

Digit span   The tasks consist of the immediate recall, that is, verbal reproduction, of series of digits of increasing lengths. The requirement in the first part of the tests is to repeat the digits in the same order in which they have been presented by the tester. In the second part of the tests the digits have to be repeated backwards. For example, when the tester says '7, 4, 3', the testee should respond '3, 4, 7'.

Vocabulary   These are tests of word knowledge in which the testee is required to define stimulus words, the frequency of use of which ranges from very common to rare for the different age groups. Again, scoring takes the level of the testee's response into consideration. 'The general rule for scoring is that any recognized meaning of the word is acceptable . . . While elegance of expression is disregarded, "poverty of content" is penalized . . . If a subject seems to know only vaguely what a word means, his response is credited with but 1 point' (Wechsler, 1974, p.98).

The areas assessed by the tests just described overlap with those assessed in the verbal items of the Stanford–Binet. Of the seven cognitive areas covered by the latter, the following six contain verbal items.

Language This area is covered by tests relating to the quality of word knowledge (through tests of abstract words, rhymes, word naming, and definitions), extent of vocabulary (number of words that can be defined) and comprehension of the relationship between words.

Memory These tests consist of meaningful and non-meaningful visual and auditory stimuli, which are assumed to assess visual, rote auditory, and ideational memory as well as attention span.

Conceptual thinking This area is concerned with categorization and classification, with abstract thinking, and the ability to make predictions.

Reasoning Foremost verbal measures of reasoning in the Binet include the absurdity tests, which have become a prototype for similar items in subsequent ability tests, especially for children.

Numerical reasoning This area is covered by arithmetic reasoning problems, similar to those presented in Wechsler's arithmetic tests. The tests assess school learning in this area, and provide an indication of an individual's ability to concentrate (freedom from distractibility), and to make abstract judgments on the basis of numerical data.

Social intelligence Similar to the comprehension sections in the Wechsler tests, this area overlaps strongly with the area of general reasoning. Social maturity and judgment in social situations are required for the successful completion of the items measuring social intelligence.

In the case of children (aged 5 to 10 years), and when ample time for testing is available, the Illinois Test of Psycholinguistic Abilities (ITPA) (Kirk, McCarthy, and Kirk, 1971) sometimes merits being chosen as a supplementary instrument. This individually administered diagnostic test is purported to identify specific strengths and deficiencies in psycholinguistic functioning. Three types of communication processes (receptive, expressive and organizing), two levels of language operation (representational and automatic), and two channels of language input and output (visual–motor and auditory–vocal) are assessed in the 12 subtests to obtain a profile of psycholinguistic abilities and/or a composite psycholinguistic age quotient.

Another easily administered test is the Peabody Picture Vocabulary Test (Dunn and Dunn, 1981). In this individually administered test of receptive vocabulary, a series of stimulus words are presented orally, and the testee indicates which of four pictures best illustrates the meaning of each stimulus word. The test can be administered in 10 to 20 minutes, and is suitable for testees aged between 2½ years and 40 years.

Where there is no possibility of individual testing, such tests as the Mill Hill Vocabulary Scale for ages 14 years to adult, the ACER Tests of Learning Ability

(TOLA) (ACER, 1977) for ages 8 years 6 months to 13 years 2 months, the ACER Higher (13 years to adult) or Intermediate (10 to 15 years) tests, the Otis Higher (13 years to adult) or Intermediate (9 to 14 years) tests might be used.

The Mill Hill Vocabulary Scale (Raven, 1947; Raven, Raven, and Court, 1982) consists of two types of verbal tasks, one requiring the subject to select a synonym from a set of six words to match a stimulus word, the other involving word definitions.

The other group tests listed above consist mainly of items of verbal and arithmetic reasoning. Verbal items tend to include word definitions, classification of concepts, analogies, and proverbs, while the numerical items consist of number series and arithmetical problems.

The difficulty with these group intelligence tests and with tests of word knowledge is that they rely mainly on word knowledge and on school learning appropriate in particular cultural settings. Hence, these tests tend to discriminate strongly against members from minority groups. They are also often biased against older persons, because the test content is influenced strongly by the knowledge regarded as important at the time at which the test was developed. The norms of most group intelligence tests, which have been standardized or restandardized in recent years, are most valid for persons of school age, or for individuals attending institutions of higher education because they were normed on samples from these populations.

Also, these tests describe the performance of individuals by comparing the level attained by them with that of their peers. In other words, no matter whether a normative test yields a single score or multiple scores, a testee's score is interpreted relative to the scores obtained by a reference group, usually a large, representative sample of appropriate age. Thus, it cannot be stressed enough that an individual score on a norm-referenced intelligence test is meaningless in itself, and uninterpretable except in comparison with the distribution of scores obtained from the reference group.

Norms are based on average scores obtained by reference groups. However, since low intellectual achievement, for example at school, or low scores obtained on intelligence and other cognitive tests may be the result of deficits in different component skills in different individuals, the averaging of scores across groups tends to mask or even cancel out possible strengths and weaknesses characterizing the performance of individuals. As noted previously, since individuals attaining the same score on a test, or individuals performing in the same IQ range, are not necessarily a homogeneous group, either in their ability or in their approach to tasks, motivation, etc., it is invalid to base the assessment of their intelligence on a measurement model that assumes intragroup homogeneity.

Measures of Social and Cultural Knowledge

Individuals of all ages, who are members of minority groups, are penalized in their performance on most intelligence tests, because the tests include socially oriented, and thus culturally loaded, items. Irrespective of whether such items are presented verbally, in writing or pictorially, they may cause the IQ or other descriptors representing the performance of an individual to be very much reduced. For example a score derived from such inappropriate tests or subtests might wrongly suggest that a person's potential may be below average, borderline, even mentally deficient, only because the individual did not have an opportunity to acquire certain facts—deemed important by the test constructor—from his or her environment, or because of culturally determined differences in social customs.

In relation to the above, it is advantageous that performance on the NAT is not heavily dependent on social and cultural knowledge. On the other hand the failure of the NAT to measure sociocultural knowledge and skills does leave a gap in the examiner's understanding of the individual's total spectrum of cognitive functioning. The problem may be remedied by administration of the comprehension subtests of the Wechsler tests. The Stanford–Binet tasks measuring social intelligence might be useful also. Wechsler's Information subtests can be a good measure of acculturation as regards general knowledge.

Another means of measuring social knowledge is to administer the Vineland Social Maturity Scale (Doll, 1965), or the Bristol Social Adjustment Guides (Scott, 1974). The former scale ranges from infant to adult. It provides quotients of maturity and a social quotient, which are derived in a way similar to that used to derive the Binet IQ. The scale consists of descriptive items, answerable either by the testee or a caretaker, which describe progression in the capacity of individuals to look after themselves, and participate increasingly in activities that ultimately lead towards adult independence. Areas assessed include: self-help, self-direction, locomotion, occupation, communication, and social relations.

The Bristol Social Adjustment Guides suitable for children and young people aged 5 years to 15 years consist of a checklist relating to the testee's usual response in a variety of situations and environments, which is completed by a teacher, social worker, or other adult familiar with the child.

A rather important bonus obtained by using separate sociocultural measures together with the NAT is that, while adding a great deal to the information obtained from the NAT, these measures do not influence the estimate of intellectual ability or cognitive development yielded by the NAT. The same is true, of course, for the supplementation of the NAT assessment by language and other verbal tests of ability and/or achievement.

The advantages of administering any of these tests or subtests in conjunction with the NAT go beyond the gaining of an impression of the levels of social or cultural skills attained by individuals. The NAT is a non-verbal test, and it is also fairly limited in its assessment of evaluatory skills (Guilford, 1966).

The completion of most social and cultural items requires both language and evaluation. Consequently, the administration of selected portions from other test batteries as suggested above can enhance the examiner's understanding of the individual's cognitive functioning in several key areas at the same time.

Measures of Educational Achievement

Educational achievement and intellectual development or ability are closely related. They operate interactively. Certain levels of cognitive development are prerequisites for educational achievement. Schooling, like any other educational experience, increases the probability of better coping with problem solving in real life, and of higher scores on educational achievement and cognitive ability tests. However, high performance on intelligence tests is not always an indication of high educational achievement. While the cognitive variables in both areas can be expected to overlap to a large degree, there are many non-cognitive factors that operate differently in these situations.

Despite the long history of assessing scholastic achievement in children, the problems in this area are seen by some (e.g. Helton, Workman, and Matuszek, 1982; Holt, 1970; Savage, 1968) as in some ways equally if not more intense than those relating to the assessment of intelligence.

> The contribution of subjectivity in assessment by teachers, the problems of relating attainment in one school to that of attainment in another are extremely difficult issues to unravel. In addition to this, we have the major issue of cultural differences in educational procedures which make the international use of psychometric techniques of educational attainment an even more difficult problem than for the so called 'cultural free' intelligence tests. (Savage, 1968, p.41)

Though we do not speak of 'culture free' intelligence tests these days, Savage's point is clear. Whatever methods are used, teaching and learning in school is culture bound. Except in the case of ethnic schools, what is taught and how it is taught are highly influenced by the majority culture of the country in which the school is situated. As with all measurement, the real problem in the assessment of scholastic achievement concerns the validity of relating the performance of a particular individual on a single factor, or on several factors, to that of other individuals.

However, despite all their inherent difficulties, measures of educational attainment should be included in a comprehensive intervention-oriented assessment of an individual. Educational measurement can be extremely valuable in itself. It can become even more enlightening when its results are related to those obtained from tests of cognitive functioning, and also, where possible, to descriptions of the behaviour, personal characteristics and other non-cognitive and environmental variables relating to the particular child.

For example, it may be found that a student's school results place him or her in the top 25 per cent among his or her age- or year-level peers. At first sight one might evaluate these results as suggesting that this is an able student who is doing well at school. If, however, assessment of intellectual functioning places this same student's performance in the top 2 per cent of the population, one might entertain a hypothesis of underachievement at school. The evaluation of such a hypothesis and the establishment of causal factors in underachievement are difficult tasks, which might best be tackled by an interdisciplinary team, which should include the student, and where at all possible a parent. Underachievement may be related to educational opportunity, personality factors, motivational variables, social environment, ethnicity and many other dimensions, and interactions between any or all of them.

The important point exemplified in the above example is that educational underachievement or deficits are relative to the individual, and are related to his or her own intellectual level and educational achievement. They are also dependent on the particular level at which the individual is functioning at a given time. For many years the concept of underachievement or educational retardation included only those students whose performance placed them 'at the bottom of the class'. This tended to be accompanied by the tacit assumption that underachievers have low IQs and show comparably low school attainment. The use of psychological tests has shown that one can just as meaningfully speak about educational retardation when the level of educational achievement is quite high. We shall come back to this point later in the chapter, when methods of evaluating the relationship between educational achievement, intellectual level, and certain non-cognitive variables relevant to the problem of underachievement are discussed.

One important consideration in the use of measures of educational attainment is to determine the age at which their valid use might begin. In an educational system like ours, where children start school at the age of 4½ or 5 years, it often takes some time before one can attempt to measure adequately what has been learnt. In practice, it has been found that measurement of educational achievement (in contrast to measures of developmental skills, readiness tests, etc.) should not usually be undertaken until the child has attended school for several years. The problems are, in fact, similar to those discussed in relation to the assessment of intelligence, where it is generally seen as inadvisable to attempt formal testing before the age of 7 or 8 years.

Apart from teacher-made tests, which in most cases will provide the preferred instrument for the assessment of scholastic attainment, a number of standardized educational attainment tests are available, for various subject areas and different ages. The advantage of the standardized achievement tests lies in the fact that performance scores on these tests can be transformed into standard scores so that the performances of students from different schools, backgrounds, etc., can be compared. The National Foundation for Educational Research in Great Britain (NFER), the Australian Council for Educational Research (ACER), and similar national bodies have prepared, and make available, a considerable number of such tests.

The most frequently required standardized educational tests are in the areas of number, that is, arithmetic or mathematics, and reading or English for students between the ages of 7 years and 15 years. Examples of some of the most popular measures will be described briefly, and their uses will be discussed in the next section.

Reading and English   Educational achievement in these areas has often been based on the Schonell Attainment and Diagnostic Tests of Reading and English (Schonell and Schonell, 1960). The four reading attainment tests in this set consist of a word recognition test (i.e. an individually administered test for ages 5 to 15 years) and three tests of reading comprehension (group administered, and appropriate for ages ranging from 6 years to 16 years). The three diagnostic tests included in the series are aimed to investigate whether or not any or all of a large number of specific language-processing difficulties are operating in a particular individual's performance. The contents of the three tests are concerned with auditory and phonic elements of word recognition, directional attack on words, and the perception of visual patterns of words, respectively. Schonell's books contain chapters on the interpretation of the complex factors that may be underlying the difficulties revealed in the test performance. Although not all-embracing or totally conclusive, these discussions are useful for those concerned with clinical diagnosis. The tests by themselves provide a convenient and reliable instrument for the teacher or counsellor who is experienced and sensitive.

The Schonell Diagnostic English Tests (Schonell and Schonell, 1960) are particularly concerned with usage of the English language. They cover such areas as capital letters, punctuation, vocabulary, sentence construction and composition. The tests are normed for age groups ranging from 9 years to 15 years. Profiles of the English attainment and diagnostic inventories of educational difficulties in English can be recorded for individuals on the basis of their performance on the tests.

Another very useful series of measures in this area are the Standard Reading Tests (Daniels and Diak, 1960). The battery consists of 12 tests each of which measures a specific set of functions including perceptual development, eye–hand co-ordination, visual and auditory word recognition, silent reading comprehension, graded spelling, and vocabulary related to reading experience.

The Neale Analysis of Reading Ability (Neale, 1966) consists of three parallel forms of graded oral reading passages and three accompanying diagnostic tests. The assessment includes reading and comprehension as well as auditory discrimination, diagnostic sound production, and the recognition of syllables. The tests are intended for 6 to 13 year old children.

Number The Schonell Arithmetic Attainment and Diagnostic Tests (Schonell and Schonell, 1960) assess mechanical and problem arithmetic skills in children between the ages of 7 and 15 years. The first four subtests cover basic number combinations in addition, subtraction, multiplication and division. Subtest 5 covers more difficult combinations in the above processes. Subtests 6 to 11 contain very carefully graded steps in the above four mathematical operations, and Subtest 12 consists of 40 items of mental arithmetic.

A word of caution regarding the use of standardized achievement tests in mathematics may be in order at this point. The rapid succession of changes in the approach to teaching mathematics in schools during the past 20 years appears to be continuing. Those responsible for assessment must therefore take very special care to make sure that the test measures are valid, before scores are interpreted. This caution applies to both norm-referenced and diagnostic tests. Tests built on a particular approach to teaching do not provide diagnostic information in relation to the performance of students who were taught using a totally different approach. Achievement tests are valid only if they measure what has been taught. There is no achievement without prior learning!

Non-cognitive Measures

Assessment in this area would use measures of personality and motivation. They are outside the normally accepted boundaries for the assessment of intellectual functioning and so will not be discussed in detail here. They are mentioned, however, to stress the importance of their contribution to the understanding of the cognitive and educational achievements of the individual as a whole. The use of non-cognitive measures is restricted to psychologists with special training in personality assessment and in the development and maintenance of behavioural components. Such professionals should be consulted where a comprehensive assessment of personality traits and motivational variables is to be included in the assessment. Certain behaviours are elicited only by certain stimulus materials or in certain interview situations. The clinical psychologist is best equipped to select the appropriate tests for each individual case.

Evaluation of Diagnostic Hypotheses

The question of which tests might best supplement the information obtained from the NAT can be answered in some cases on the basis of the testee's age, the reasons for assessment, and the limitations of the NAT. Often, however, the choice of supplementary tests, whether to be administered formally or informally, that is, in total or in part, can only be made after the client has been observed in the testing situation, and after his or her NAT performance has been evaluated. Additional observations may be needed to follow up hypotheses concerning the testee's functioning that have been generated by a clinical hunch, or by the NAT score or profile.

Mostly, two types of hypotheses require systematic evaluation: (1) hypotheses that are related in some way to the validity of the assessment of the individual, and (2) hypotheses that have implications for diagnosis and intervention, including educational remediation or compensatory training.

Hypotheses of the first type tend to be generated when the person responsible for the assessment believes that a testee's (high or low) score on one or more subtests may be due to factors other than (high or low) ability. Alternative explanations of low performance would include poor environmental conditions, temporary lack of good health in the candidate, extreme test anxiety or other emotional disturbance, uncooperative or disruptive behaviour, impulsiveness, lack of motivation, sensory deficits such as difficulties in visual and/or auditory perception, problems in the comprehension and speaking of the English language, and failure to understand the directions accompanying the tests.

The second type of hypotheses may be related to apparent strengths and weaknesses that have educational implications, or to diagnostic considerations such as suspected educational underachievement, emotional disturbance, mental retardation etc. Such hypotheses should be followed up by diagnostic instruments that aim to measure aspects of the individual's intellectual functioning not covered by the NAT (e.g. language and numerical abilities, scholastic achievement, skills of adapting, personality, etc.). In these cases the administration of supplementary tests may be a necessary prerequisite to permit competent diagnosis. Hypotheses that have implications for intervention should also be pursued as far as possible, if they are to form the basis for decision making in relation to the contents of programs.

To interpret differences between scores obtained on supplementary tests and the NAT, the whole NAT profile as well as background variables should be taken into consideration. Unusually high or low scores on verbal and/or sociocultural measures may be a function of social or cultural factors, but they could also be related to an individual's language or reasoning abilities. Competing hypotheses must be investigated systematically by the examiner before conclusions are reached concerning the testee's sociocultural knowledge. If an examination of the NAT profile reveals adequate general ability and adequate perceptual and conceptual skills, but the performance on supplementary verbal tests is poor, the best explanation for the latter depressed scores is probably that they might be the result of the individual's linguistically disadvantaged or culturally different environment. An individual who does well on the NAT, relatively well on tests of word knowledge and language comprehension, but badly in socioculturally biased tests, shows that he or she has shown potential despite limited exposure to information that is socially and/or culturally relevant to the testing situation.

High scores in verbal and sociocultural tests combined with low NAT performance is also of interest, especially when not accompanied by equally well developed problem solving and verbal reasoning skills. This type of performance may be suggestive of the effects of a highly enriched, socially aware environment, a high need for achievement, and, in children, strong pressure from parents.

The standard scores utilized in different tests and test batteries tend to differ from each other in their means and standard deviations.

To compare an individual's level of functioning on a number of different tests a common metric has to be used. Table A3, in the Manual (Rowe, 1985c), was developed to facilitate direct comparisons. This table includes Wechsler IQs, Z-scores, percentile ranks, and stanines to enable NAT users to compare an individual's level of functioning on a variety of measures. The score obtained on each test is just converted into one of the standard scores noted above.

In most situations, however, consultation of Table 13.1 may provide the desired comparative information. This table contains comparable standard scores for a number of frequently used psychological tests. To compare the level of functioning on two or more different tests, the individual's score on each test is entered into the table, and the scores converted to a common metric such as percentile rank, or the number of standard deviations from the mean. As a reasonable 'rule of thumb', it is suggested that scores on two tests (expressed in a common metric) should lie more than one standard deviation apart before the difference between them can be considered to be psychologically or educationally significant.

Testing the Limits on the NAT

The use of supplementary tests is not the only method for following up a hunch or a hypothesis. In many cases a thorough investigation of the individual's cognitive development and functioning can be made by testing the limits of the NAT. It is important to remember that any such procedure should be performed only after the entire NAT battery has been administered under standard conditions, namely, according to the directions for administration included in the *Manual for the NAT* (Rowe, 1985c).

The technique of testing the limits originated in clinical psychology. It refers to the administration of test items under altered conditions so that greater insight can be gained into the testee's abilities. The method itself, which is also referred to as 'extension testing', has been described for various psychological tests (e.g. Glasser and Zimmerman, 1967; Kaufman and Kaufman, 1979; Sattler, 1982; Taylor, 1959). What is of interest in the testing of the limits is the psychological meaningfulness of qualitative records of behaviour that the method allows to be observed. Typical modifications of the directions for administration used in testing the limits include the following:

- allowing extra time so that the test can be finished
- giving additional cues to see whether, and under what circumstances a correct response can be elicited
- restructuring the task to allow the testee to respond at a more elementary level
- (in verbal tests) changing the wording of an item to see whether failure was due to the testee's lack of understanding of the question

- direct questioning or using other means (e.g. asking the testee to 'think aloud' during problem solving) to infer the testee's method of solving an item.

Some modifications of the directions for administration serve to show up the severity of the individual's difficulties in particular areas, while others are specifically designed to help pin point the cause of a deficiency. For example, a testee can be shown a variety of correct and incorrect responses to the Embedded Figures Test, or any other test in the NAT that lends itself to such modification, to see whether he or she can perceive adequately, even though they may not be able to mark the correct figures. The Picture Completion Test could be altered into a multiple choice test to test the limits of a person with a suspected expressive communication problem.

All these and other techniques of testing can help the examiner to derive and follow up hypotheses. However they should *not* be used to give the testee credit for passing items under conditions of modified administration procedures. Testing the limits can provide the examiner with valuable *qualitative* rather than with additional *quantitative* data. Examiners who wish to quantify the clinical observations they have made by testing the limits of the NAT are strongly advised to follow the above procedure by selecting supplementary tests of appropriate contents and difficulty level after testing the limits of the NAT.

Testing the limits often suffices as the only means of following up hypotheses. At other times it serves as a link between the NAT and possible supplementary tasks.

Using the NAT to Supplement Other Tests

Up to this point the content of this chapter has been based on the assumption that the NAT is the featured test in the assessment of an individual's cognitive development or ability. However, in many situations a group verbal test, one of the Wechsler tests or the Stanford–Binet may be the featured intelligence test in a battery.

Because it assesses 'g' and a number of major components of general ability on the basis of entirely language-free tasks, and because it can provide scores on 18 perceptual, conceptual, and concentration tests, the NAT is a valuable source of supplementary tasks for examiners who have basically used verbal tasks, which may have introduced a considerable amount of bias in a particular assessment. Several of the conceptual tests, or even the perceptual tests, would provide a valuable supplement to the information yielded by verbal IQ tests.

Various separate parts of the NAT can be administered to follow up hypotheses based on information yielded by an intelligence test, just as tasks from such tests may be used to pursue hypotheses generated by an individual's performance on the NAT. For example, an individual whose performance on the Digit Span Test, or on the similarly brief memory tasks included in other batteries, suggests a weak memory, may be given some or all of the NAT memory tests, which provide separate measures for recognition and recall of both visual and auditory input. Similarly, apparently high or low performance on verbal reasoning tasks, sequencing or conceptual thinking in verbal tests can be verified or disputed by administering the pertinent NAT subtests.

Hypotheses generated from WISC-R or WAIS-R profiles may be followed up in the same way. For example the generalizability of the non-verbal skills of an individual earning a very high or very low Wechsler Performance IQ may be explored by administering some or all of the NAT, the contents of which are quite different from the tasks included in the Wechsler tests.

A frequent component in neuropsychological assessment is the information evaluation of specific perceptual and/or conceptual skills. Often the items used for this purpose are poorly designed, unstandardized, or even developed on the spur of the moment. This statement is not intended to curtail the individual psychologist's creative efforts in developing tasks for specific assessment needs. However, in many situations the availability of suitable tasks such as the ones constituting the NAT might fulfil the immediate demands of the situation, and thus save the psychologist time and effort that could be used in other ways and directions.

Prerequisites for the Validity of Intervention-oriented Assessment

As stressed previously, the foremost prerequisite of the ability to interpret test results and other observations obtained during a comprehensive assessment procedure is the understanding of cognitive, psychometric, and related theories of human intelligence, and the overlap and differences between major theories in these domains.

The various theoretical approaches have been well articulated in the general psychological literature (e.g. Cattell, 1963; Guilford, 1967; Jensen, 1979; Luria, 1966a, 1966b; Sternberg, 1977, 1984).

It is imperative that psychologists and other users of the NAT battery understand each of these approaches, if they wish to function as professionals rather than as 'stimulus bound technicians' (Hartlage and Reynolds, 1981, p.355).

As noted previously, many see the field of psychological and educational measurement as a set of tests and techniques for the quantification of performance. Moreover, many believe that to function in this field no more than mastery of the technical skills involved in the administration and scoring of tests is required. Such oversimplication borders on fallacy.

The offer of a set of assessment techniques ranks as a relatively minor contribution of measurement specialists. Of far greater importance is their provision of a paradigm for the evaluation and interpretation of the scores derived by means of assessment techniques.

Without a strong paradigm, psychological and educational measurement could not have progressed to the level of applicability and utility they have reached. As in other areas of scientific enquiry several competing paradigms exist in the field of educational and psychological measurement. For the investigation of a given case and problem, the use of one pradigm might be regarded as more appropriate than that of any of the others.

Most teachers and psychologists are familiar with a variety of testing methods. However, they are not always aware of the fact that several paradigms for both the quantification of observations and for their interpretation have been developed.

Obviously, these paradigms are strongly linked with particular theoretical models.

> Without the foundation of theory, even as imperfect as our theories are at present (we are) limited to working with only the empirical experience generated from trial-and-error

methods or the reading of case examples. Thus, when encountering an individual with a fresh set of problems and nuances of behavior and psychometric data, there is little basis for developing any sort of therapeutic or remedial effort. The same is true for other areas (of psychology). A psychologist could certainly not function as a behavior therapist without extensive comprehension of operant and classical conditioning theories. (Hartlage and Reynolds, 1981, p.355)

For the purposes of intervention and remediation, such as the choice or construction of an individualized educational program, the assessment of an individual's intellectual strengths and weaknesses is maximally useful only when certain prerequisites are being met.

The first prerequisite for valid intervention-oriented assessment is that a majority of the individual's cognitive abilities, information-processing skills, and educational or other intellectual achievements that are relevant to the purposes of the assessment, have been evaluated in a quantifiable, replicable, and valid manner.

This requires the person who is responsible for the interpretation of test results, and for the investigation as a whole to be well grounded in major theories of cognition, individual differences, measurement, and information processing.

The second requirement is that the findings from such an investigation can be translated into a meaningful, relevant, and valid intervention procedure.

In order to be meaningful, the translation of test results into recommendations for intervention procedures must be based on a theoretically sound, defensible rationale. To be defensible, a rationale underlying the tests would usually need to be in agreement with (or at least not contradictory to) current educational, and psychological knowledge. Again, this requires that those responsible for making the translations from the test results have considerable understanding of the knowledge that has accumulated in core areas of educational, developmental, and cognitive psychology.

For a recommendation to be relevant, there must be a logical, as well as a theoretical, relationship between what might be suggested on the basis of the test results, and operations that are feasible for those who will carry out the intervention procedures, for example the teacher, or a school system.

The third prerequisite is that both the assessment and the recommended intervention procedures must be valid. There are many kinds of validity (Cronbach, 1970; Thorndike, 1971), a number of which may be relevant in this context.

Only the two most important types of validity for the present purposes will be noted here. The most obvious of these refers to the probability of the success of the recommendations for intervention based on the test results being better than chance probability. The other most important validity in this context is construct validity.

Construct validity is a complex concept. In this context it might be described best as providing: (1) an indicator of whether the test results have been translated correctly into recommendations for intervention, and (2) a means of evaluating whether the measurement model guiding the translation is valid for the purpose.

As noted previously, the field of educational and psychological measurement contains many theories. Currently, one of the most comprehensive and prestigious models of intellectual functioning, in terms of brain–behaviour relationships, is Luria's neuropsychological model of human information processing, and its various adaptations. This model is certainly not adequate for all clients and purposes of assessment, nor are the models underlying the Illinois Test of Psycholinguistic Abilities (Kirk and Kirk, 1971), or even the WAIS and WISC models (Wechsler, 1955, 1974, 1981).

Individual differences between testees, and the varying purposes of testing indicate that an eclectic approach, that is, the use of a variety of theoretical and measurement models, may provide the best means for the description of the intellectual strengths and weaknesses of particular individuals. It is up to the professional who is responsible for the assessment to 'play detective' in available models of testing and test interpretation, as suggested by Kaufman (1979).

A further important requirement for assessment of any kind is that the procedure used should be efficient in terms of the time and effort demanded for its administration and interpretation. Ideally, testing should sample the relevant abilities without unnecessary overlap or redundancy. In the design of the NAT battery every effort has been made to meet this requirement.

The fourth prerequisite relates to the validity of the interpretation of test scores.

As noted previously, in addition to considerable psychometric sophistication, the accurate and reliable determination of an individual's cognitive strengths and weaknesses requires a thorough knowledge of psychological theories.

Knowledge of the psychometric methodology necessary for the evaluation of a single individual's score, and for the decision whether fluctuations in performance represent real differences in abilities and processing skills, or whether they are simply due to the random variation inherent in all test results, where tests have less than perfect reliability, can be obtained from a variety of basic texts, and more specialized discussions such as Allen and Yen (1979), Field (1960), Kaufman (1979), Kaufman and Kaufman (1977), Payne and Jones (1957), Reynolds and Gutkin (1982) and Sattler (1982).

It is essential, for example, to be conversant with the differences between ipsative and normative test score interpretation, and their interaction in cognitive profiles, in which the determination of special areas of strength and weakness includes the consideration of general ability level. The references listed above will provide a useful entry to the literature relating to this topic.

The fifth prerequisite concerns the validity of the intervention procedures. This requires, for example, that there be no undue emphasis on observed deficits. The professional literature contains considerable criticism of the lack of meaningfulness of many translations of test results into recommendations for intervention and/or remediation (e.g. Hammill and Larsen, 1974; Weiner, 1976; Ysseldyke, 1973; Ysseldyke and Mirkin, 1982).

The strongest challenges in the educational domain have been directed towards the deficit model of remediation. Under this model, training, based on previously identified areas of deficit or weakness, focuses on the area of the student's greatest weakness (e.g. Ayres, 1974; Bannatyne, 1980; Kephart, 1963; Kirk and Kirk, 1971; Vallett, 1967). The strongest argument against the deficit model relates to the stress and anxiety it might elicit in the individual, when the focus is on his or her areas of poorest performance, that is, the areas in which failure has been experienced most frequently in the past.

Table 13.1 The Comparison between NAT Scores and Standard Scores Yielded by Other Tests

Percentile rank	NAT score	Wechsler V, P or FS IQ	Wechsler scaled score	Binet IQ	ITPA scaled score	TOLA IQ age 13 years	OTIS intermed. IQ	OTIS higher IQ	Peabody SS equiv.	SD from mean
99.9	130	145	19	148	54	129			139	+3.0
99.8	129									+2.9
99.7	128	141		144	52					+2.8
99.6	127	140	18							+2.7
99.5	126									+2.6
99.4	125	138		140	51					
99.3										+2.5
99.2	124									+2.4
99.0	123	135	17	136	50	127	135	135	133	+2.3
98.9	122									+2.3
98.6	121						133			+2.2
98.2	120	130	16	132	48	126	130	130	130	+2.1
98	119					125	128		128	+2.0
97	117	126	15	128	46	124	126	125	126	+1.9
96	116	125				123	124		125	+1.7
95						122	123		123	+1.6
94	115	122		124	45	121	122		122	+1.5
93	144					120	121	120	121	+1.4
92	113	120	14	120	44		120		120	
91		119				119	119		119	+1.3
90	112					118	118		118	+1.2
89	111					117				
88	110	115	13	116	42	115	117	115	117	+1.1
87	109						116		116	+1.0
86	108						115		115	+0.9
84		111		112	40	112	114		114	+0.8
82	107	110	12				112			
79							111	110	111	+0.7
77	106					111	110			
76						110	109			
75	105	108		108	39	108	108		108	+0.6
73										+0.5
70	104	105				107	107		107	+0.4
69						106	106		106	

62								+0.3
60	103						104	+0.2
58	102	104			104		103	+0.1
54	101							0(Mean)
50	100	100			100	103	100	−0.1
46	99					101		−0.2
45				38		99	98	−0.3
42	98						97	−0.4
40		96	11		96	97	96	−0.5
38	97	95	10	36				−0.6
37		92			92		95	−0.7
34	96			34		94	94	−0.8
31	95	90	9					−0.9
27	94			33		91		−1.0
25		89				89		−1.1
24	93		8	32	88		89	−1.2
23		85				88		−1.3
21	92		7	30	84	87	86	−1.4
18	91						85	−1.5
16	90	81	6	28	80	82	84	−1.6
14	89	80				81	83	−1.7
13	88	78		27	76	80	82	−1.8
12						79	81	−1.9
11	87	75	5	26	72	78		−2.0
10		74				77	80	−2.1
9	86	70	4	24	68	76	79	−2.2
8	85	65	3	22	64	75	78	−2.3
7		62		21	60	74	76	−2.4
6	84					73	75	−2.5
5	82	59	2	20	56	72	73	−2.6
4	81					71	71	−2.7
3	79	55	1	18	52	69	68	−2.8
2	76					66	62	−2.9
1	75					65		−3.0
0.6	74					64		
0.5	72							
0.3	71							
0.2	70					65	61	
0.1								
Mean	100	100	10	36	100	100	100	1
SD	10	15	3	6	16	15	15	0

It is argued that such an inherently unpleasant focus in, for example, a remedial program, cannot be in the student's best interest. Rather, to be relevant, and to increase the probability of success, a

> remedial approach to a child's learning problems needs to be based on abilities that are sufficiently intact in the child, so as to promote successful accomplishment of the steps in the educational program. This way the interface between the strengths (rather than the weaknesses) determined from the assessment and the intervention strategy is a cornerstone of meaningfulness for the entire diagnostic-intervention process. In the language of Luria, it is necessary to locate an intact complex functional system capable of taking over and moderating the learning processes that are necessary for acquiring the academic skills in question. (Hartlage and Reynolds, 1981, p.358)

Of course, there are situations in which there exist no alternatives, and where focus on weakness is the only available strategy. Also, there are individuals, usually adults, whose specific weaknesses are debilitating not only because of their nature, but because of the individuals' attitude of concern. In such cases intervention procedures that focus on identified weaknesses may well serve to be more anxiety reducing, and hence more successful than procedures that emphasize strengths, and may allow the client to feel that nothing is being done about the areas of his or her specific concern.

Where test scores have to be interpreted for the benefit of others, for example when recommendations for intervention and remediation are being made, a number of potential problems should be kept in mind.

The relevance and practicality of suggested steps of intervention, for example, educational recommendations based on test data, could pose special difficulties for counsellors and other advisors who serve a number of schools or other institutions. The psychologist may not be aware of the availability or lack of availability of special support services in a school or other institution, and specific management problems experienced by the teacher or others responsible for the execution of the intervention recommendations. Resources would include the possibility of obtaining supplementary teaching materials as well as the availability of support staff.

In the types of situations described above, the recommendations are best preserved by the provision of relatively broad guidelines for intervention, which use the testee's intact processing skills, and capitalize on observed intellectual strengths, while at the same time limiting the influence of debilitating weaknesses.

The choice of specific sets of stimulus materials and programs is best left to the person taking charge of the intervention program, who is likely to be more knowledgeable in the area of curriculum materials than the psychologist or school counsellor.

The validity and reliability of the interpretation of test performance, and its translation into valid and relevant recommendations is important not only for the welfare of the testee, but also for maintaining good rapport with teachers and others involved in the intervention process.

Predictive validity of both the assessment and the recommendations is probably the strongest safeguard for the maintenance and continuation of a good working relationship. However, a certain amount of face validity in both assessment and recommendations may be necessary for the sake of those who have to follow through on recommendations, and for the motivation and perseverance of the testee.

REFERENCES

Allen, M.J. and Yen, W.M. *Introduction to Measurement Theory.* Monterey, California: Brooks/Cole Pub. Co., 1979.

Anastasi, A. *Differential Psychology: Individual and Group Differences in Behaviour.* (3rd ed.). New York: Macmillan, 1958.

Anastasi, A. *Psychological testing.* (4th ed.). New York: Macmillan, 1976.

Anastasi, A. *Psychological Testing.* (4th ed.). New York: Macmillan, 1976.

Anastasi, A. Abilities and the measurement of achievement. *New Directions for Testing and Measurement*, 1980, **5**, 1–10.

Anderson, J.R. *Language, Memory and Thought.* Hillsdale, N.J.: Lawrence Erlbaum Associates, 1976.

Anderson, J.R. *The Architecture of Cognition.* Cambridge, Mass.: Harvard University Press, 1983.

Anderson, J.R. and Bower, G.H. Recognition and retrieval processes in free recall. *Psychological Review*, 1972, **79**, 97–123.

Anderson, J.R. and Bower, G.H. *Human Associative Memory.* Washington, D.C.: Winston, 1973.

Arenberg, D. Differences and changes with age in the Benton Visual Retention Test. *Journal of Gerontology*, 1978, **33**, 534–540.

Arenberg, D. Estimates of age changes on the Benton Visual Retention Test, *Journal of Gerontology*, 1982, **37**, 87–90.

Arthur, G. A new point performance scale. *Journal of Applied Psychology*, 1925, 9, 390–416.

Arthur, G. *A Point Scale of Performance Tests.* New York: Commonwealth Fund, 1930.

Atkinson, R.C. and Shiffrin, R.M. Human memory: A proposed system and its control processes. In Spence, K.W. and Spence, Y.T. (Eds), *The Psychology of Learning and Motivation.* Vol.2, New York: Academic Press, 1968.

Australian Council for Educational Research. Operations Test. Mathematics Profile Series. Hawthorn, Australia, 1977.

Ayres, A.J. *Sensory Interpretation and Learning Disorders.* Los Angeles: Western Psychological Services, 1974.

Baltes, P.B., Nesselroade, J.R., Schaie, K.W. and Labouvie, E.W. On the dilemma of regression effects in examining ability-level-related differentials in ontogenetic patterns of intelligence. *Developmental Psychology*, 1972, **6**, 78–84.

Baltes, P.B., Reese, H.W. and Lipsitt, L.P. Life-span developmental psychology. *Annual Review of Psychology*, 1980, **31**, 65–110.

Bamber, D. Reaction times and error rates for 'same'—'different' judgements of multi-dimensional stimuli. *Perception and Psychophysics.* 1969, **6**, 169–174.

Bannatyne, A. Neuropsychological remediation of learning disorders. Paper presented at the NATO, International Conference on Neuropsychology and Cognition, August, Georgia, September, 1980.

Bardon, J. and Bennett, V. *School Psychology.* Englewood Cliffs, N.J.: Prentice Hall, 1974.

Baron, J. Intelligence and general strategies. In Underwood, G. (Ed.), *Strategies in Information Processing.* London: Academic Press, 1978.

Barrett, G.V., Mihal, W.L., Panek, P.E., Sterns, H.L. and Alexander, R.A. Information processing skills predictive of accident involvement for younger and older commercial drivers. *Industrial Gerontology*, 1977, (4), 173–181.

Barron, F. and Harrington, D.M. Creativity, intelligence and personality. *Annual Review of Psychology*, 1981, **32**, 439–477.

Bartlett, C.J., Bobko, P and Pine, S.M. Single group validity: Fallacy of the facts? *Journal of Applied Psychology*, 1977, **62**, 155–157.

Bartlett, F.C. *Remembering: A Study in Experimental and Social Psychology.* Cambridge, UK: Cambridge University Press, 1932.

Batchelder, B.L. and Denny, M.R. A theory of intelligence: T. span and complexity of stimulus control. *Intelligence*, 1977, **1**, 127–150.

Bateman, B. Learning disorders. *Review of Educational Research*, 1966, **36**, 93–120.

Bateman, B. Reading: A controversial view—research and rationale. In Tarnopol, L. (Ed.), *Learning Disabilities.* Springfield, Ill.: Charles C. Thomas, 1969.

Bauer, R.H. Memory processes in children with learning disabilities. Evidence for deficient rehearsal. *Journal of Experimental Child Psychology,* 1977, **24**, 415–430.

Bauer, R.H. Memory, acquisition, and category clustering in learning disabled children. *Journal of Experimental Child Psychology,* 1979, **27**, 365–383.

Bauman, G. The stability of the individual's mode of perception, and of perception–personality relationships. Unpublished doctoral dissertation. New York: New York University, 1951.

Berg, C., Hertzog, C.K. and Hunt, E. Age differences in the speed of mental rotation. *Developmental Psychology,* 1982, **18**, 95–107.

Berlyne, D.E. The influence of complexity and novelty in visual figures on orienting responses. *Journal of Experimental Psychology,* 1958, **55**, 289–296.

Berlyne, D.E. Attention as a problem in behaviour theory. In Mostofsky, D.E. (Ed.), *Attention: Contemporary Theory and Analysis.* New York: Appleton Century Crofts, 1970.

Berry, J.W. *Human Ecology and Cognitive Style: Comparative Studies in Cultural and Psychological Adaptation.* Beverly Hills, Calif.: Sage, 1976.

Bien, E.C. The relationship of cognitive style and structure of arithmetic materials to performance in fourth grade arithmetic. Doctoral dissertation. University of Pennsylvania, 1974. *Diss. Abstr. Int.,* 1974, **35**, 2040–41. University microfilms No. 14–22, 809.

Bilash, I. and Zubek, J.P. The effects of age on factorially 'pure' mental abilities. *Journal of Gerontology*, 1960, **15**, 175–182.

Bindra, D., Donderi, D.C. and Nishisato, S. Decision latencies of 'same and different' judgements. *Perception and Psychophysics*, 1968, **3**, 121–130.

Binet, A. and Simon, T. Methodes nouvelles pour le diagnostique du niveau intellectual oles anormaux. *L' Annee Psychologique*, 1905, **11**, 191–244.

Binet, A. and Simon, T. Le development de l'intelligence chez les infants. *L' Annee Psychologique*, 1908, **14**, 1–94.

Birren, J.E. Age changes in speed of behavior: The central nature and physiological correlates. In Welford, A.T. and Birren, J.E. (Eds), *Behavior, Aging, and the Nervous System.* Springfield, Ill.: Charles C. Thomas, 1965.

Bishop, A.J. Use of structural apparatus and spatial ability: a possible relationship. *Research in Education*, 1973, **9**, 43–49.

Bishop, A.J. Visualizing and mathematics in a pre-technological culture. *Educational Studies in Mathematics*, 1979, **10**, 135–146.

Blankership, A.B. Memory span: a review of the literature. *Psychological Bulletin*, 1938, **35**, 1–25.

Blum, J.E. and Jarvik, L.F. Intellectual performance of octogenarians as a function of education and initial ability. *Human Ability*, 1974, **17**, 364–375.

REFERENCES

Boehm V.R. Differential prediction; a methodological artifact. *Journal of Applied Psychology*, 1977, 62, 146–154.

Boersma, F.J., Muir, W., Wilton, K. and Rarnahm, R. Eye movement during embedded figure tasks. *Perceptual and Motor Skills*, 1969, 28, 271–274.

Bolton, T.L. The growth of memory in school children. *American Journal of Psychology*, 1891–1892, 4, 362–380.

Boring, E.G. Intelligence as the tests test it. *The New Republic*, 1923, 34, 35–36.

Botwinick, J. Sensory-set factors in age differences in reaction time. *Journal of Genetic Psychology*, 1971, (119), 241–249.

Botwinick, J. Sensory-perceptual factors in reaction time in relation to age. *Journal of Genetic Psychology*, 1972, (121), 173–177.

Botwinick, J. *Aging and Behaviour: A Comprehensive Integration of Research Findings*. New York: Springer, 1973.

Botzum, W.A. A factorial study of the reasoning and closure factors. *Psychometrika*, 1951, 16, 361–386.

Bouchard, T.J. Current conceptions of intelligence and their implications for assessment. In McReynolds, P. (Ed.), *Advances in Psychological Assessment*. Palo Alto, Calif.: Science and Behaviour Books Inc., 1968.

Bourne, L.E., Dominowski, R.L. and Loftus, E.F. *Cognitive Processes*. Englewood Cliffs, N.J.: Prentice Hall, 1979.

Brainerd, C.J. *Piaget's Theory of Intelligence*. Englewood Cliffs, N.J.: Prentice Hall, 1978.

Broadbent, D.E. *Perception and Communication*. London: Pergamon Press, 1958.

Broadbent, D.E. and Heron, A. Effects of a subsidiary task on performance involving immediate memory by younger and older men. *British Journal of Psychology*, 1962, (53), 189–198.

Broverman, D.M. Dimensions of cognitive style. *Journal of Personality*, 1960, 28, 167–185.

Brown, A.L. and Campione, J.C. Recognition memory for perceptually similar pictures in pre-school children. *Journal of Experimental Psychology*, 1972, 95, 55–62.

Brown, A.L. and Scott, M.S. Recognition memory for pictures in pre-school children. *Journal of Experimental Child Psychology*, 1971, 11, 401–412.

Brown, J. An analysis of recognition and recall and problems in their comparison. In Brown, J. (Ed.), *Recall and Recognition*. New York: Wiley, 1976.

Bruininks, R.H. Auditory and visual perceptual skills related to the reading performance of disadvantaged boys. *Perceptual and Motor Skills*, 1969, 29, 179–186.

Bruininks, R.H., Lucker, W.G. and Gropper, R.L. Psycholinguistic abilities of good and poor reading disadvantaged first-graders. *Elementary School Journal*, 1970, 70, 378–386.

Bruner, H.J., Goodnow, J.J. and Austin, G.A. *A Study of Thinking*. New York: Wiley, 1956.

Bruner, J. On perceptual readiness. *Psychological Review*, 1957, 64, (2), 123–152.

Buriel, R. Relationship of three field-dependence measures to reading and mathematics achievement of Anglo-American and Mexican American children. *Journal of Educational Psychology*, 1978, 70, 167–174.

Buros, O.K. *8th Mental Measurements Yearbook*. Highland Park, N.J.: Gryphan Press, 1978.

Burt, C. *Factors of the Mind*. London: University of London Press, 1940.

Burt, C. The two-factor theory. *British Journal of Psychology II*, 1949, 151–179.

Burt, C. The differentiation of intellectual ability. *British Journal of Educational Psychology*, 1954, 24, 76–90.

Butcher, H.J. *Human Intelligence: Its Nature and Assessment*. London: Methuen & Co., 1968.

Campione, J.C., Brown, A.L. and Ferrara, R.A. Mental retardation and intelligence. In Sternberg, R.J. (Ed.), *Handbook of Human Intelligence*, Cambridge, UK: Cambridge University Press, 1982.

Carey, S.T. and Lockhart, R.S. Incoding differences in recognition and recall. *Memory and Cognition*, 1973, 1, 297–300.

Carmichael, L.C., Hogan, H.P. and Walters, A.A. An experimental study of the effect of language on the reproduction of visually perceived form. *Journal of Experimental Psychology*, 1932, **15**, 73–85.

Carpenter, P.A. and Just M.A. Sentence comprehension: a psycholinguistic processing model of verification. *Psychological Review*, 1975, **82**, 45–73.

Carroll, J.B. A factor analysis of verbal abilities. *Psychometrika*, 1941, **6**, 279–307.

Carroll, J.B. Factors in verbal achievement. In Dressel. P.L. (Ed.), *Proceedings of the Invitational Conference on Testing Problems, 1961*. Princeton, N.J.: Educational Testing Service, 1962.

Carroll, J.B. Psychometric tests as cognitive tasks: a new structure of intellect. In Resnick, L.B. (Ed.), *The Nature of Intelligence*. Hillsdale, N.J.: Lawrence Erlbaum Associates, 1976.

Carroll, J.B. 'How shall we study individual differences in cognitive abilities?'—methodological and theoretical perspectives. *Intelligence*, 1978, **2**, 87–115.

Carroll, J.B. *Individual Difference Relations in Psychometric and Experimental Cognitive Tasks*. Report No. 163. Chapel Hill: University of North Carolina, April 1980(a).

Carroll, J.B. Remarks on Sternberg's factor theories of intelligence are alright almost. *Educational Researcher*, 1980(b), **9**, 14–18.

Carroll, J.B. The measurement of intelligence. In Sternberg, R.J. (Ed.), *Handbook of Human Intelligence*. Cambridge: Cambridge University Press, 1982.

Carroll, J.B. Studying individual differences in cognitive abilities: Through and beyond factor analysis. In Dillan, R.F. and Schmeck, R.R. (Eds), *Individual Differences in Cognition*, Vol.1., New York: Academic Press, 1983.

Carroll, J.B. and Maxwell, S.E. Individual differences in cognitive abilities. *Annual Review of Psychology*, 1979, **30**, 603–640.

Cattell, J.M. Mental tests and measurements. *Mind*, 1890, **15**, 373–381.

Cattell, R.B. Culture-free intelligence test intelligence. *Journal of Educational Psychology* 1940, **31**, 161–179.

Cattell, R.B. The measurement of adult intelligence. *Psychological Bulletin*, 1943, **40**, 153–193.

Cattell, R.B. Theory of fluid and crystallized intelligence: a critical experiment. *Journal of Educational Psychology*, 1963, **54**, 1–22.

Cattell, R.B. *Handbook of Multivariate Experimental Psychology*. Chicago: Rand McNally, 1966(a).

Cattell, R.B. The scree test for the number of factors. *Multivariate Behavioral Research*, 1966(b), **1**, 245.

Cattell, R.B. Are IQ tests intelligent? *Psychology Today*, 1968, **2**, 56–62.

Cattell, R.B. *Abilities: Their Structure, Growth and Action*. Boston: Houghton Mifflin, 1971.

Cattell, R.B. *The Scientific Use of Factor Analysis in Behavioral and Life Sciences*. New York: Plenum Press, 1978.

Cattell, R.B. The clinical use of different scores: Some psychometric problems. *Multivariate Experimental Clinical Research*, 1983, Vol.6(2), 87–98.

Ceci, S.J., Lea, S.E.G. and Ringstrom, M.D. Coding processes in normal and learning disabled children: evidence for modality specific pathways to the cognitive system. *Learning and Memory*, 1980, **6**, 785–797.

Chaplin, J.P. *Dictionary of Psychology*. New revised edition. New York: Dell Publishing Co., 975.

Chein, I. On the nature of intelligence. *Journal of General Psychology*, 1945, **32**, 111–126.

Cherry, E.C. Some experiments on the recognition of speech with one and with two ears. *Journal of the Acoustical Society of America*, 1953, **25**, 975–979.

Chi, M.T.H. Short-term memory limitation in children: capacity or processing deficits? *Memory and Cognition*, 1976, **4**, 559–572.

Chiang, A. and Atkinson, R.C. Individual differences and inter-relationships among a select set of cognitive skills. *Memory and Cognition*, 1976, **4**, 661–672.

Child, Dennis. *The Essentials of Factor Analysis*. London: Holt, Rinehart and Winston, 1970.

Clark, L.W. and Knowles, J.B. Age differences in dichotic listening performance. *Journal of Gerontology*, 1973, (28), 173–178.

Cleary, T.A., Humphreys, L., Kendricks, S.A. and Wesman, A. Educational uses of tests with disadvantaged students. *American Psychologist*, 1975, **30**, 15–41.

Coates, S.W. Sex differences in field independence among preschool children. In Friedman, R.C., Richart, R.M. and Van de Wiele, R.L. (Eds), *Sex Differences in Behavior*. New York: Wiley, 1974.

Coates, S.W. Field independence and intellectual functioning in preschool children. *Perceptual and Motor Skills*, 1975 (Aug), Vol.41(1), 251–254.

Coates, S.W., Lord, M. and Jakovorics, E. Field dependence–independence social–non-social play and sex differences in preschool children. *Perceptual and Motor Skills*, 1975, **40**, 195–202.

Cohen, A.S. Studies in visual perception and reading in disadvantaged children. *Journal of Learning Disabilities*, 1969, 2, 498–503.

Cohen, J. Factors underlying Wechsler–Bellevue performance of three neuropsychiatric groups. *Journal of Abnormal Social Psychology*. 1952, 47, 359–365.

Cohen, J. The factorial structure of the WAIS between early adulthood and old age. *Journal of Consulting Psychology*, 1957, 21, 283–290.

Cohen, J. The factorial structure of the WISC at ages 7–6, 10–6 and 13–6. *Journal of Consulting Psychology*, 1959, 23, 285–299.

Comalli, P.E.Jr. Life-span changes in visual perception. In Goulet, L.R. and Baltes, P.B. (Eds), *Life-span developmental psychology: Research and theory*. New York: Academic Press, 1970.

Comalli, P.F. Life span developmental studies in perception: theoretical and methodological issues. Paper presented at a symposium: *Research. In the Cognition Processes of Elderly People*. Atlantic City, N.J.: Eastern Psychological Association Meeting, 1965.

Comfort, A. Test battery to measure ageing rate in man. *Lancet*, 1969, **297**, 1411–1415.

Cooley, W.W. and Lohnes, P.R. *Multivariate Procedures for the Behavioral Sciences*. New York: Wiley, 1962.

Cooley, W.W. and Lohnes, P.R. *Multivariate Data Analysis*. New York: Wiley, 1971.

Coombs, C.H. A factorial study of number ability. *Psychometrika*, 1941, 6, 161–189.

Cooper, L.A. Individual differences in visual comparison processes. *Perception and Psychophysics*, 1976, 19, 433–444.

Cooper, L.A. Spatial information processing: Strategies for research. In Snow, R.E., Frederico, P.A. and Montague, W.E. (Eds), *Aptitude, Learning and Instruction*. Vol.1. Hillsdale, N.J.: Lawrence Erlbaum Associates, 1980.

Cooper, L.A. and Regan, D.T. Attention, perception and intelligence. In Sternberg, R.J. (Ed.), *Handbook of Human Intelligence*. Cambridge: Cambridge University Press, 1982.

Cornell, E.L. and Coxe, W.C. *A Performance Ability Scale*. New York: World Book, 1934.

Craik, F.I.M. The nature of the aged decrement in performance on dichotic listening tasks. *Quarterly Journal of Experimental Psychology*, 1965, (17), 227–240.

Craik, F.I.M. Human memory. *Annual Review of Psychology*, 1979, **30**, 63–102.

Craik, F.I.M. and Blankstein, K.R. Psychophysiology and human memory. In Venables, P.H. and Christie, M.J. (Eds), *Research in Psychophysiology*. New York: Wiley 1975.

Craik, F.I.M. and Jaccoby, L.L. Elaboration and distinctiveness in episodic memory. In Nilsson, L.(Ed.), *Perspectives on Memory Research: Essays in Honor of Uppsala University's 500th Anniversary*. Hillsdale, N.J.: Lawrence Erlbaum Associates, 1979.

Craik, F.I.M. and Lockhart, R.S. Levels of processing: a framework for memory research. *Journal of Verbal Learning and Verbal Behavior*, 1972, **11**, 671–684.

Craik, F.I.M. and Tulving, E. Depth of processing and the retention of words in episodic memory. *Journal of Experimental Psychology: General*, 1975, **104**, 268–294.

Craik, F.I.M. and Watkins, M. The role of rehearsal in short-term memory. *Journal of Verbal Learning and Verbal Behavior*, 1973, **12**, 599–607.
Cronbach, L.J. The two disciplines of psychology. *American Psychologist*, 1957, 12, 671–684.
Cronbach, L.J. *Essentials of Psychological Testing*, (3rd ed.). New York: Harper and Row, 1970.
Cronbach, L.J. Test validation. In Thorndike, R.L. (Ed.), *Educational Measurement* (2nd ed.). Washington, D.C.: American Council on Education, 1971.
Cronbach, L.J. Five decades of public controversy over mental testing. *American Psychologist*, 1975(a), **30**, 1–14.
Cronbach, L.J. Beyond the two disciplines of psychology. *American Psychologist*, 1975(b), **30**, 116–128.
Cronbach, L.J. and Snow, R.E. Aptitudes and Instructional Methods: A Handbook for Research on Interaction. New York: Irvington, 1977.
Crowder, R.G. Visual and auditory memory. In Kavanagh, J.F. and Mattingly, I.G. (Eds), *Language by Ear and by Eye: The Relationship between Speech and Reading*. Cambridge, Mass.: MIT Press, 1972.
Crowder, R.G. *Principles of Learning and Memory*. Hillsdale, N.J.: Lawrence Erlbaum Associates, 1976.
Crowder, R.G. and Morton, J. Precategorical acoustic storage (PAS) *Perception and Psychophysics*, 1969, **5**, 365–373.
Daniels, J.C. and Diak, H. *The Standard Reading Tests*. London: Chatto and Windus, 1960 and 1972.
Davey, C.M. A comparison of group verbal and pictorial tests of intelligence. *British Journal of Psychology*, 1926, 17, 80–92.
David, K.H. Effect of verbal reinforcement on Porteus maze scores among Australian Aborigine children. *Perceptual and Motor Skills*, 1967, **24**, 986.
David, K.H. Cross-cultural uses of the Porteus maze. *Journal of Social Psychology*, 1974, **92**, 11–18.
Davis, F.B. Interpretation of differences among averages and individual test scores. *Journal of Educational Psychology*, 1959, **50**, 162–170.
Dawson, J.L. Tonne-Arienta hand/eye dominance and susceptibility to geometric illusions, *Perceptual and Motor Skills*, 1973, **37**, 659–667.
Day, R.S. Digit-span memory in language-bound and stimulus-bound subjects. *Journal of the Acoustical Society of America*, 1973, **54**, 287.
Deffenbacher, K.A., Platt, G.J. and Williams, M.A. Differential recall as a function of socially induced arousal and retention interval. *Journal of Experimental Psychology*, 1974, **103**, 809–811.
Dempster, F.N. Memory span: sources of individual and developmental differences. *Psychological Bulletin*, 1981, **89**, 63–100.
Denny, D.R. Relationship of three cognitive style dimensions to elementary reading abilities. *Journal of Educational Psychology*, 1974, **66**, 702–709.
Detterman, D.K. and Sternberg, R.J. *How and how much can intelligence be increased* ? Norwood, N.J.: Ablex Publishing Co., 1982.
Deutsch, A., Fishman, J.A. and Kogan, N. Guidelines for testing minority group children. *Journal of Social Issues*, 1964, **20**, 127–145.
Deutsch, J.A. and Deutsch, D. Attention: Some theoretical considerations. *Psychological Review*. 1963, **70**, 80–90.
Dirken, J.M. *Functional Age of Industrial Workers*. Groninger: Wolters–Noordholf, 1972.
Dirks, J. and Neisser, U. Memory for objects in real sciences: The development of recognition and recall. *Journal of Experimental Child Psychology*, 1977, **23**, 315–328.
Doll, E.A. *Vineland Social Maturity Scale*. Circle Pines, Minn.: American Guidance Service, 1965.

Donlon, T.F. Content factors in sex differences on test questions. Research Memorandum 73–28. Princeton: ETS, 1973.
Doppelt, J.E. The organization of mental abilities in the age range 13 to 17. *Teachers College Contributions to Education*, 1950, **962**, 1–86.
Douglas, V.I. and Peters K.G. Towards a clearer definition of the attentional deficit of hyperactive children. In Hale, G.A. and Lewis, M. (Eds), *Attention and Cognitive Development*. New York: Plenum Press, 1979.
Drenth, P.J.D. Prediction of school performance in developing countries: school grades or psychological tests? *Journal of Cross-Cultural Psychology*, 1977, **8**, 49–70.
Droege, R.C. and Hawk, J.H. A factorial investigation of non-reading aptitude tests. *Proceedings*, 78th Annual Convention, American Psychological Association, 1970, pp.113–114.
Duffy, J., Salvia, J., Tucker, J. and Ysseldyke, J. Non-biased assessment: A need for operationalism. *Exceptional Children*, 1981, **47**, 427–434.
Duncan, D.B. New multiple range test. *Biometrics*, 1955, **11**, 1–42.
Dunn, L.M. and Dunn, L.M. *Peabody Picture Vocabulary Test*—Revised Edition, Form L and M. Circle Pines, Minn: American Guidance Service, 1981.
Dwyer, C.A. Test content and sex differences in reading. *The Reading Teacher*, 1976, **29**, 753–757.
Dwyer, Carol A. The role of tests and their construction in producing apparent sex-related differences. In Wittig, M.A. and Petersen, A.C. (Eds), *Sex-related Differences in Cognitive Functioning* New York: Academic Press, 1979.
Dykman, R.A., Ackerman, P.T., Clements, S.D. and Peters, J.E. Specific learning disabilities: an attentional deficit syndrome. In H. Myklebust (Ed.), *Progress in Learning Disabilities*. Vol.2. New York: Grure and Stratton, 1971.
Eakin, S. and Douglas, V.I. Automization and oral reading problems in children. *Journal of Learning Disabilities*, 1971, **4**, 31–38.
Ebbinghaus, H.E. *Memory: A Contribution to Experimental Psychology*. New York: Dover, 1964 (originally published 1885, translated 1913.)
Ebel, R.L. *Measuring Educational Achievement*. Englewood Cliffs, N.J.: Prentice Hall, 1963.
Ebel, R.L. (Ed.). *Encyclopedia of Educational Research*, (4th ed.). New York: Macmillan, 1968.
Echternacht, G. A quick method for determining test bias. *Educational and Psychological Measurement*, 1974, **34**, 271–280.
Edwards, A.S. Intelligence as the capacity for variability of response. *Psychological Review*, 1928, **35**, 198–210.
Egan, D.E. Testing based on understanding. Implications from studies of spatial ability. *Intelligence*, 1979, **3**, 1–15.
Egeth, H. Parallel versus serial processes in multidimensional stimulus discrimination. *Perception and Pschophysics*, 1966, **1**, 245–252.
Egeth, H. and Becker, D. Differential effects of familiarity on judgements of sameness and difference. *Perception and Psychophysics*, 1971, **9**, 321–326.
Ekstrom, R.B. *Cognitive Factors: Some Recent Literature*. Princeton, N.J.: Educational Testing Service, 1973.
Eskstrom, R.B., French, J.W. and Harman, H.H. *Manual for Kit of Factor-referenced Cognitive Tests*. Princeton, N.J.: Educational Testing Service, 1976.
Ekstrom, R.B., French, J.W. and Harman, H.H. Cognitive factors: their identification and replication. *Multivariate Behavioral Research*, 1979, **79**, 3–84.
Elithorn, A.A. A preliminary report on the perceptual range test sensitive to brain damage. *Journal of Neurology, Neurosurgery and Psychiatry*, 1955, **18**, 287–292.
Elliott, C.D., Murray, D.J. and Pearson, L.S. *British Ability Scales*. Slough: NFER/Nelson Publishing Co., 1978.

Ellison, M.L. and Edgerton, H.A. The Thurstone primary mental abilities tests and college marks. *Educational and Psychological Measurement*, 1941, **1**, 399–406.

English, H.B. and English, A.C. *A comprehensive dictionary of psychological and psychoanalytical terms.* New York: Longmans, Green & Co., 1958.

Estes, W. The locus of inferential and perceptual processes in letter identification. *Journal of Experimental Psychology: General*, 1975, **1**, 122–145.

Estes, W.K. Learning, memory and intelligence. In Sternberg, R.J. (Ed.), *Handbook of Human Intelligence*. Cambridge: Cambridge University Press, 1982.

Evans, U. Thinking: Experimental and information processing approaches. In Claxton, G. (Ed.), *Cognitive Psychology—New Directions*, London: Routledge and Kegan Paul, 1980.

Eysenck, H.J. On the dual function of consolidation. *Perceptual and Motor Skills*, 1966, **22**, 237–274.

Eysenck, H.J. *The biological basis of personality*. Springfield, Ill.: Thomas, 1967.

Eysenck, H.J. *A Model for Personality*. Berlin/New York: Springer Verlag, 1981.

Eysenck, M.W. Arousal, learning and memory. *Psychological Bulletin*, 1976, **83**, 389–404.

Fairweather, H. Sex differences in cognition. *Cognition*, 1976, **4**, 231–280.

Faterson, H.F. and Witkin, H.A. Longitudinal study of development of the body concept. *Developmental Psychology*, 1970, **2**, 429–438.

Fennema, E. Mathematics learning and the sexes: A review. *Journal for Research in Mathematics Education*, 1974, **5**, 126–129.

Fennema, E. Women and girls in mathematics—equity in mathematics education. *Educational Studies in Mathematics*, 1979, **10**, 389–401.

Ferguson, G.A. On learning and human ability. *Canadian Journal of Psychology*, 1954, **8**, 95–112.

Ferguson, G.A. On transfer and the abilities of man. *Canadian Journal of Psychology*, 1956, **10**, 121–131.

Fiebert, M. Cognitive styles in the deaf. *Perceptual and Motor Skills*, 1967, **27**, 319–29.

Field, J.G. Two types of tables for use with Wechsler's intelligence scales. *Journal of Clinical Psychology*, 1960, **16**, 3–7.

Fischer, C.T. Intelligence defined as effectiveness of approaches. *Journal of Consulting and Clinical Psychology*, 1969, **33**, 668–674.

Fischer, C.T. *Einfuehrung in die Theorie Psychologischer Tests*. Bern: Huber, 1974.

Fishman, J.A. et al. Guidelines for testing minority group children. *Journal Social Issues Supplement*, 1964, **20**, 129–145.

Flaugher, R.L. The many definitions of test bias. *American Psychologist*, 1978, **33**, 671–679.

Foulds, G.A. and Raven, J.C. Normal changes in the mental abilities of adults as age advances. *Journal of Mental Science*, 1948, **94**, 133–142.

Fozard, J.L. Predicting age in the adult years from psychological assessments of abilities and personality. *Aging and Human Development*, 1972, **3**, 175–182.

Frank, G. *The Wechsler Enterprise: An Assessment of the Development, Structure and Use of the Wechsler Tests of Intelligence*. Oxford: Pergamon Press, 1983.

Fredericksen, J. The role of cognitive factors in the recognition of ambiguous visual stimuli. ETS Research Bulletin 65–23. Princeton, N.J.: Educational Testing Service, 1965.

Frederiksen, J.R. *A Chronometric Study of Component Skills in Reading*. (Report No.3757(2)). Prepared for the office of Naval Research by Bolt Beranek and Newman Inc., January 1978.

Freeman, B.J. and Ritvo, E.R. *Autism, Diagnosis, Current Research and Management*. New York: Spectrum, 1976.

Freeman, F.N. What is intelligence? *School Review*, 1925, **33**, 253–263.

French, F.N. The description of aptitude and achievement tests in terms of rotated factor. *Psychometric Monographs*, 1951, No.5.

French, J.W. *Kit of Selected Tests for Reference Aptitude and Achievement Factors*. Princeton, N.J.: Educational Testing Service, 1954.

French, J.W., Ekstrom, R.B. and Price, L.A. *Manual and Kit of Referenced Tests for Cognitive Factors.* Princeton, N.J.: Educational Testing Service, 1963.

Fruchter, B. *Introduction to Factor Analysis.* New York: Van Nostrand, 1954.

Furth, H. *Thinking is about Language: Psychological Implications of Deafness.* New York: Free Press, 1966.

Gallistel, E., Boyle, M., Curran, L. and Hawthorn, M. *The Relation of Visual and Auditory Aptitudes for First Grade Slow Readers Achievement under Sight Word Systematic Phonic Instruction.* Minneapolis, Minn.: Research Development and Demonstration Center in Education of Handicapped Children, University of Minnesota, ERIC: ED 079-714, 1972.

Galton, F. *Hereditory Genius.* New York: The Macmillan Co., 1871.

Galton, F. Some results of the Anthropometric Laboratory. *Journal of the Anthropological Institute,* 1885, 14, 275-287.

Galton, F. Notes on prehension in idiots. *Mind,* 1887, 12, 79-82.

Galton, F. *Natural Inheritance.* New York: The Macmillan Co., 1889.

Gardner, H. *Frames of Mind: The Theory of Multiple Intelligences.* New York: Basic Books, 1983.

Garrett, H.E. A developmental theory of intelligence. *American Psychologist,* 1946, 1, 372-378.

Gates, A.I. The mnemonic span for visual and auditory digits. *Journal of Experimental Psychology,* 1916, 1, 393-404.

Gathercole, C.E. *Assessment in Clinical Psychology.* Harmondsworth, Middlesex, England: Penguin Books Inc., 1968.

Geen, R.J. Effects of evaluation apprehension on memory over intervals of varying lengths. *Journal of Experimental Psychology,* 1974, 102, 908-910.

Geissler, H.G., Buffart, H.F., Leeuwenberg, E.L.J, and Sarris, V. *Modern Issues in Perception.* Amsterdam: North Holland, 1983.

Gelman, R. Logical capacity of very young children: number invariance rules. *Child Development,* 1972, 43, 75-90.

Ghiselli, E.E. *The Validity of Occupational Aptitude Tests.* New York: Wiley, 1966.

Gibson, J.J. *The Senses Considered as Perceptual Systems.* Boston: Houghton Mifflin, 1966.

Gilbert, L. Speed of processing visual stimuli and its relation to reading. *Journal of Educational Psychology,* 1959, 55, 8-14.

Gillung, T.B. and Rucker, C.N. Labels and teacher expectations. *Exceptional Children,* 1977, 43, 464-465.

Glanzer, M.S. and Clark, H.H. Accuracy of perceptual recall; An analysis of organization. *Journal of Verbal Learning and Verbal Behavior,* 1962, 1, 289-299.

Glanzer, M., Glaser, R. and Richlin, M. *Development of a Test Battery for the Study of Age-related Changes in Intellectual and Perceptual Abilities.* Randolph, Texas: USAF School of Aviation Medicine, 1958.

Glaser, R. Instructional technology and the measurement of learning outcomes: some questions. *American Psychologist,* 1963, 18, 519-521.

Glaser, R. and Bond, L. Testing: Concepts, policy, practice and research. *American Psychologist,* 1981, 36(10), whole October issue.

Glaser, R., Pellegrino, J.W. and Lesgold, A.M. Some directions for a cognitive psychology. In Lesgold, A.M., Pellegrino, J.W., Fokkema, S.D. and Glaser, R. (Eds), *Cognitive Psychology and Instruction.* New York: Plenum Press, 1977.

Glass, A.L., Holyoak, K.J. and Santa, J.L. *Cognition.* Reading, Mass.: Addison-Wesley Publishing Co., 1979.

Glasser, A.J. and Zimmerman, I.L. *Clinical Interpretations of the Wechlser Intelligence Scale for Children.* New York: Grune and Stratton, 1967.

Gleitman, H. *Psychology.* New York: W.W. Norton and Co., 1981.

Goddard, H.H. *The Kallikak Family.* New York: Macmillan, 1912.

Goldberg, R.A., Schwartz, S. and Stewart, M. Individual differences in cognitive processes. *Journal of Educational Psychology,* 1977, 69, 9-14.

Golden, C.J. *Diagnosis and Rehabilitation in Clinical Neuropsychology.* Springfield, Ill.: Charles C. Thomas, 1978.

Golden, C.J., Hammeke, T.A. and Purisch, A.D. Diagnostic validity of standardised neuropsychological battery derived from Luria's neuropsychological tests. *Clinical Neuropsychology,* 1979, **1** (1), 1–7.

Golden, C.J., Osmon, D.C., Moses, J.A.Jr. and Berg, R.A. *Interpretation of the Halstead–Reitan Neuropsychological Test Battery.* New York: Grune and Stratton, 1981.

Golden, N.E. and Steiner, S.R. Auditory and visual functions in good and poor readers. *Journal of Learning Disabilities,* 1969, **2**, 476–481.

Goldfarb, W. *An Investigation of Reaction Time in older Adults.* New York: Teachers College, Columbia University, 1941.

Goldstein, G. and Neuringer, C. Schizophrenic and organic damage in alcoholics. *Perceptual and Motor Skills,* 1966, **22**, 345–350.

Goldstein, K. Die Lokalisation in der Grosshirnrinde. In *Handbuch der Normalen Pathologischer Psysiologie.* Berlin: J. Springer, 1927.

Goldstein, K. The modifications of behavior consequent to cerebral lesions. *Psychiatric Quarterly,* 1936, **10**, 586–610.

Goldstein, K. *The Organism.* New York: American Book, 1939.

Goldstein, K. *Language and Language Disturbances.* New York: Grune and Stratton, 1948.

Goldstein, K.M. and Blackman, S. Assessment of cognitive style. In McReynolds, P. (Ed.), *Advances in Psychological Assessment.* Vol.4 San Francisco: Jossey Bass, 1978(a).

Goldstein, K.M. and Blackman, S. *Cognitive Style: Five Approaches and Relevant Research.* New York: Wiley, 1978(b).

Goldstein, K. and Scheerer, M. Abstract and concrete behavior: an experimental study with special tests. *Psychological Monographs,* 1941, **53**, (No.2).

Goodenough, D.R. The role of individual differences in field dependence as a factor in learning and memory. *Psychological Bulletin,* 1976, **83**, 675–694.

Goodman, K. Reading: A psycholinguistic guessing game. *Journal of the Reading Specialist,* 1967, **6**, 126–135.

Gorsuch, R.L. *Factor Analysis.* Philadelphia: W.B. Saunders, 1974.

Gottschaldt, K. uber den Einfluss der E fahning auf die Wahrnehmung von Figuren. *Psychologische Forschung,* 1926, **8**, 261–317.

Green, B.F. Current trends in problem solving. In Kleinmuntz, B. (Ed.), *Problem Solving: Research, Method and Theory.* New York: Wiley, 1966.

Green, R.F., Guilford, J.P., Christensen, P.R. and Comrey, A.L. A factor analytic study of reasoning abilities. *Psychometrika,* 1953, **18**, 135–160.

Greeno, J.G. Natures of problem-solving abilities. In Estes, W.K. (Ed.), *Handbook of Learning and Cognitive Processes: Human Information Processing,* Vol.5. Hillsdale, N.J.: Lawrence Erlbaum Associates, 1978.

Gregg, L.W. Internal representation of sequential concepts. In Klinmuntz, B. (Ed.), *Concepts and the Structure of Memory.* New York: Wiley, 1967.

Gregor, A.J. and McPherson, A. Personnel selection tests and nonliterate peoples. *Mankind Quarterly,* 1963, **3**, 151–58.

Guilford, J.P. When not to factor analyse. *Psychological Bulletin,* 1952, **49**, 26–27.

Guilford, J.P. Creative abilities in the arts. *Psychological Review,* 1957, **64**, 110–118.

Guilford, J.P. Zero correlations among tests of intellectual abilities. *Psychological Bulletin,* 1964, **61**, 401–404.

Guilford, J.P. Intelligence: 1965 model. *American Psychologist,* 1966, **21** (1), 20–26.

Guilford, J.P. *The Nature of Intelligence.* New York: McGraw Hill, 1967.

Guilford, J.P. *The Nature of Human Intelligence.* New York: McGraw Hill, 1969.

Guilford, J.P. Cognitive styles: what are they? *Educational and Psychological Measurement,* 1980(a), **40**, 715-735.

Guilford, J.P. Fluid and crystallised intelligences: Two fanciful concepts. *Psychological Bulletin,* 1980(b), **88**, 406-412.

Guilford, J.P. Cognitive psychology's ambiguities: some suggested remedies. *Psychological Review,* 1982, 29, 48-59.

Guilford, J.P. Transformation abilities of functions. *Journal of Creative Behaviour,* 1983 (Oct), **17** (2), 75-83.

Guilford, J.P. and Hoepfner, R. *The Analysis of Intelligence.* New York: McGraw Hill, 1971.

Guthrie, J.T. Models of reading and reading disability. *Journal of Educational Psychology,* 1973, 65, 9-18.

Guthrie, J.T. Principles of instruction: a critique of Johnson's remedial approaches to dyslexia. In Benton, A.L. and Pearl, D. (Eds), *Dyslexia: An Appraisal of Current Knowledge.* New York: Oxford University Press, 1978.

Haggerty, M.A. Intelligence and its measurements: A symposium. *Journal of Educational Psychology,* 1921, 12, 212-216.

Hakstian, A.R. and Cattell, R.B. *Comprehensive Ability Battery.* Champaign, Ill.: Institute for Personality and Ability Testing, 1976.

Hakstian, A.R. and Cattell, R.B. Higher stratum ability structures on a basis of 20 primary abilities. *Journal of Educational Psychology, 1978,* **70**, 657-69.

Halford, G.S. *The Development of Thought.* Hillsdale, N.J.: Lawrence Erlbaum Associates, 1982.

Hall, J.F. Learning as a function of word frequency. *American Journal of Psychology,* 1954, **67**, 138-140.

Hallahan, D.P. Distractibility in the learning disabled child. In Cruickshank, W.M. and Hallahan, D.P. (Eds), *Perceptual and Learning Disabilities in Children (Vol.2 Research and Theory).* Syracuse: Syracuse University Press, 1975.

Hallahan, D.P. and Cruickshank, W.M. *Psychoeducational Foundations of Learning Disabilities.* Englewood Cliffs, N.J.: Prentice Hall, 1973.

Hallahan, D. and Kauffman, J. *Introduction to Learning Disabilities: A Psychobehavioral Approach.* Englewood Cliffs, N.J.: Prentice Hall, 1976.

Hallahan, D.P. and Reeve, R.E. Selective attention and distractibility. In Keogh, B.K. (Ed.), *Advances in Special Education (Vol.1, Basic Constructs and Theoretical Orientations).* Greenwich, CT: JAI Press, 1980.

Hambleton, R.K., Swaminathan, H., Algina, J. and Coulson, D.B. Criterion-referenced testing and measurement: a review of technical issues and developments. *Review of Educational Research,* 1978, 48, 1-47.

Hamley, H.R. (Ed.), *The Testing of Intelligence.* London: Evans Bros., 1935.

Hammill, D.D. and Larsen, S.C. The effectiveness of psycholinguistic training. *Exceptional Children,* 1974, **11**, 5-14.

Harman, H.H. *Modern Factor Analysis.* Chicago: University of Chicago Press, 1976.

Harman, H.H., Ekstrom, R.B. and French, J.W. *Kit of Factor Reference Cognitive Tests.* Princeton: N.J. Educational Testing Service, 1976.

Harris, L.J. Sex differences in spatial ability, possible environmental, genetic and neurological factors. In Kimsbourne, M. (Ed.), *Asymmetrical Function of the Brain,* New York: Cambridge University Press, 1978.

Hartlage, L.C. and Reynolds, C.R. Neuropsychological assessment and the individualization of instruction. In Hynd, G.W. and Obrzut, J.E. (Eds), *Neuropsychological Assessment and the School Child.* New York: Grune and Stratton, 1981.

Hawkins, H.L. Parallel processing in complex visual discrimination. *Perception and Psychophysics,* 1969, 5, 56-64.

Healy, W. 1914 cited by Smith, I.M. *Spatial Ability*, 1964.
Healy, W. and Fenald, G.M. Tests for practical mental classification. *Psychological Monographs*, 1911, 13, No.54.
Hebb, D.O. *The Organization of Behavior*. New York: Wiley, 1949.
Hebb, D.O. *Textbook of Psychology*. Philadelphia: W.B. Saunders & Co., 1972.
Hebb, D.O. and Ford, E.N. Errors of visual recognition and the nature of the trace. *Journal of Experimental Psychology*. 1945, 35, 335–348.
Helton, G.B., Workman, E.A. and Matuszek, P.A. (Eds), *Psychoeducational Assessment: Interpreting Concepts and Techniques*. New York: Grune and Stratton, 1982.
Heron, A. and Chown, S. *Age and Function*. London: J. & A. Churchill Ltd, 1967.
Hertzka, A.F., Guilford, J.P., Christensen, P.R. and Berger, R.M. A factor analytic study of evaluation abilities. *Educational and Psychological Measurement*, 1954, 14, 581–597.
Heston, J.C. and Cannell, C.F. A note on the relation between age and performance of adult subjects on four familiar psychometric tests. *Journal of Applied Psychology*, 1941, 25, 415–419.
Hettema, J. Cognitive abilities as process variables. *Journal of Personality and Social Psychology*, 1968, 10, 461–471.
Hicks, M.M., Donlon, T.F. and Wallmark, M.M. Sex differences in item responses on the Graduate Record examination. Paper presented at the annual meeting of the National Council on Measurement in Education, 1976.
Hirst, W., Spelke, E.S., Reaves, C.C., Caharack, C. and Neisser, U. Dividing attention without alternation or automaticity. *Journal of Experimental Psychology: General*, 1980, 109, 98–117.
Hobbs, N. *Issues in the Classification of Children*, Vol.2. San Francisco: Jossey-Bass, 1975(a).
Hobbs, N. *The Futures of Children*. San Francisco: Jossey-Bass, 1975(b).
Hobbs, N. An ecologically orientated service based system for the classification of handicapped children. In Salzinger, S., Antrobus, J. and Glick, J. (Eds), *The Eco-system of the 'Sick' Child*. New York: Academic Press, 1980.
Hochberg, J. Attention in perception and reading. In Young, F.A. and Lindsley, D.B. (Eds), *Early Experience and Visual Information Processing in Perceptual and Reading Disorders*. Washington, D.C.: National Academy of Sciences, 1970.
Hock, H.S. The effects of stimulus structure and familiarity on same–different comparison. *Perception and Psychophysics*, 1973, 14, 413–420.
Hock, H.S., Gordon, G.P. and Marcus, N. Individual differences in the detection of embedded figures. *Perception and Psychophysics*, 1974, 15, 47–52.
Hoepfner, R. and Guilford, J.P. Figural symbolic, and semantic factors of creative potential in ninth-grade students. Paper as from the Psychological Laboratory, University of Southern California, No.35, June, 1965.
Hoffman, K., Guilford, J.P., Hoepfner, R. and Doherty, W. *A Factor Analysis of the Figural–cognition and Figural–evaluation Abilities*. Reports from the Psychological Laboratory, University of Southern California, No.40, December, 1968.
Holt, R.R. (Ed.) *Diagnostic Psychological Testing*. London: University of London Press, 1970.
Holzinger, K.J. and Harman, H.H. Comparison of two factorial analyses. *Psychometrika*, 1938, 3, 45–60.
Holzman, T.G., Pellegrino, J.W. and Glaser, R. Cognitive dimensions in numerical rule induction. *Journal of Educational Psychology*, 1982, 74, 360–373.
Holzman, T.G., Pellegrino, J.W. and Glaser, R. Cognitive variables in series completion. *Journal of Educational Psychology*, 1983, 75, 603–618.
Honzik, M.P. The development of intelligence. In Wolman, B.B. (Ed.), *Handbook of General Psychology*. Englewood Cliffs, N.J.: Prentice Hall, 1974.
Honzik, M.P. Life-span development. *Annual Review of Psychology*, 1984, 35, 309–331.
Horn, J.L. Intelligence: Why it grows, why it declines. *Transactions*, 1967, 4, 23–31.

Horn, J.L. Organization of abilities and the development of intelligence. *Psychological Review*, 1968, **75**, 242–259.

Horn, J.L. Organization of life-span development in human abilities. In Goulet, L.R. and Baltes, P.B. (Eds), *Life-span Developmental Psychology*. New York: Academic Press, 1970.

Horn, J.L. The structure of intellect: Primary abilities. In Dreger, R.H. (Ed.), *Multivariate Personality Research*, Baton Rouge, La: Claitor, 1972.

Horn, J.L. Psychometric studies of aging and intelligence. In Gershon, S. and Raskin, A. (Eds), *Aging (Vol.2): Genesis and Treatment of Psychological Disorders in the Elderly*. New York: Raven Press, 1975.

Horn, J.L. Human abilities: a review of research and theory in the early 1970s. *Annual Review of Psychology*, 1976, **27**, 437–485.

Horn, J.L. Human ability systems. In Baltes, P.B. (Ed.), *Life-span Development and Behavior* Vol.1. New York: Academic Press, 1978.

Horn, J.L. The rise and fall of human abilities. *Journal of Research and Development in Education*, 1979, **12**, 59–78.

Horn, J.L. Concept of intellect in relation to learning and adult development. *Intelligence*, 1980, **4**, 4, 285–319.

Horn, J.L. and Cattell, R.B. Refinement and test of the theory of fluid and crystallized intelligence. *Journal of Educational Psychology*, 1966, **57**, 253–270.

Horn, J.L. and Cattell, R.B. Whimsy and misunderstanding of gf–gc theory: A comment on Guilford. *Psychological Bulletin*, 1982, **91** (3), 623–633.

Horn, J.L. and Donaldson, G. On the myth of intellectual decline in adulthood. *American Psychologist*, 1976, **31**, 701–709.

Horn, J.L. and Donaldson, G. Faith is not enough: A response to the Baltes–Schaie claim that intelligence does not wane. *American Psychologist*, 1977, **32**, 369–373.

Horn, J.L. and Donaldson, G. Cognitive development in adulthood. In Brim, O.G. and Kagan, J. (Eds), *Constancy and Change in Human Development*. Cambridge, Mass.: Harvard University Press, 1980.

Horn, J.L. and Engstrom, R. Cattell's scree test in relation to Bartlett's chi-square test and other observations on the number of factors problem. *Multivariate Behavioral Research*, 1979, **14**, 283–300.

Horn, J.L. and Stankov, L. Auditory and visual factors of intelligence. *Intelligence*, 1982, **6**, 165–185.

Huey, E.B. *The psychology and pedagogy of reading*. Cambridge, Mass.: MIT Press, 1968. (originally published, New York: Macmillan, 1908).

Humphreys, L.C. The organization of human abilities. *American Psychologist*, 1962, **17**, 475–483.

Hunt, D. and Randhawa, B.S. Cognitive processes and achievement. *Alberta Journal of Educational Research*, 1983, **29**, 206–215.

Hunt, E. Mechanics of verbal ability. *Psychological Review*, 1978, **85**, 109–130.

Hunt, E. Intelligence as an information-processing concept. *British Journal of Psychology*, 1980, **71**, 449–474.

Hunt, E.B., Frost, N. and Lunneborg, C. Individual differences in cognition. In Bower, G. (Ed.), *The Psychology of Learning and Motivation: Advances in Research and Theory*, Vol.7. New York: Academic Press, 1973.

Hunt, E., Lansman, M. and Wright, J. *Some remarks on doing two things at once*. Technical Report Department of Psychology, University of Washington, Seattle, April , 1979.

Hunt, E.B., Lunneborg, C. and Lewis, J. What does it mean to be high verbal? *Cognitive Psychology*, 1975, **7**, 194–227.

Hunt, E. and McLeod, C.M. The sentence-verification paradigm: A case study for individual differences. In Sternberg, R.J. and D.K. Detterman, D.K. (Eds), *Human Intelligence: Perspectives on its Theory and Measurement*. Norwood, N.J.: Ablex, 1979.

Hunt, J. McV. *Intelligence and Experience.* New York: Ronald Press, 1961.

Ibarrola, R. Aportacion al estudio del ruvel mental de los indigenas de Guinea. *Archives del Instituto de Estudios Africanos,* 1951, 5, 7–29.

Inhelder, B. and Piaget, J. *The Early Growth of Logic in the Child.* London: Routledge and Kegan Paul, 1964.

Ippel, M.J. and Bouma, J.M. Closure factors: evidence for different modes of processing. In Friedman, M.P., Das, J.P. and O'Connor, N. (Eds), *Intelligence and Learning.* New York: Plenum Press, 1981.

Jackson, G. Another psychological view from the Association of Black Psychologists. *American Psychologist,* 1975, 30 89–93.

Jackson, M.D. *Memory access and reading ability.* Unpublished doctoral dissertation, University of California, San Diego, 1978.

Jackson, M. and McClelland, J. Sensory and cognitive determinants of reading speed. *Journal of Verbal Learning and Verbal Behavior,* 1975, 14 565–574.

Jackson, M.D. and McClelland, J.L. Processing determinants of reading speed. *Journal of Experimental Psychology: General,* 1979, 108, 151–181.

Jacobs, J. Experiments on prehension. *Mind,* 1887, 12, 75–79.

Jager, A.O. *Dimensioner der Intelligenz.* Gottinger: Verlag fun Psychologie, Hogrefe, 1967.

Jahoda, G. Cross-cultural use of the perceptual maze test. *British Journal of Psychology,* 1969, 39, 82–86.

James, W. *The Principles of Psychology* Vol.1. New York: Henry Holt & Co., 1890. (Republished by Dover, 1950).

James, W. *The Principles of Psychology* Vol.2. New York: Henry Holt & Co., 1890.

Jencks, C., Smith, M., Acland, H., Bane, M.J., Cohen, D., Gentis, H., Heyns, B. and Michelson, S. *Inequality: A Reassessment of the Effect of Family and Schooling in America.* New York: Harper, 1972.

Jensen, A.R. How much can we boost IQ and scholastic achievement? In *Environment, Heredity and Intelligence. Harvard Educational Review,* 1969, 39, 1–123.

Jensen, A.R. Individual differences in visual and auditory memory. *Journal of Educational Psychology,* 1971, 62, 123–131.

Jensen, A.R. g: outmoded theory or unconquered frontier? *Creative Science and Technology,* 1979, 2, 16–29.

Jensen, A.R. *Bias in Mental Testing.* New York: Free Press, 1980(a).

Jensen, A.R. Chronometric analysis of mental ability. *Journal of Social Biol. Structure,* 1980(b), 3, 181–224.

Jensen, A.R. and Munro, E. Reaction time, movement time and intelligence. *Intelligence,* 1979, 3, 121–126.

Johnston, W.A. and Heinz, S.P. Flexibility and capacity demands of attention. *Journal of Experimental Psychology: General,* 1978, 107, 420–435.

Juola, J.F. Pattern recognition. In Lachman, R., Lachman, J.L. and Butterfield, E.C. (Eds), *Cognitive Psychology and Information Processing z2: An introduction.* Hillsdale, N.J.: Lawrence Erlbaum Associates, 1979.

Kagan, J. Reflection—impulsivity and reading ability in primary grade children. *Child Development,* 1965, 36, 609–628.

Kahneman, D. *Attention and Effort.* Englewood Cliffs, N.J.: Prentice Hall, 1973.

Kail, R., Carter, P. and Pellegrino, J. The locus of sex differences in spatial ability. *Perception and Psychophysics,* 1979, 26, 182–186.

Kaiser, H.F. Varimax solution for primary mental abilities. *Psychometrika,* 1960, 25, 153–58.

Kaiser, H.F. Psychometric approaches to factor analysis. Paper presented at the Invitational Conference on Testing Problems, Princeton, N.J.: ETS, 31 October 1964.

Kaiser, H.F., and Caffrey, J. Alpha factor analysis. *Psychometrika,* 1965, 30, 1–14.

Kamin, L.J. *The Science and Politics of I.Q.*. Hillsdale, N.J.: Lawrence Erlbaum Associates, 1974.
Kanner, L. Autistic disturbances of affective contact. *Nerv. Child*, 1943, **2**, 217–250.
Kaplan, O.J. The place of psychology in gerontology. *Geriatrics*, 1951, **6**, 298–303.
Karrier, C. Ideology and evaluation. In Apple, M. et al. (Eds), *Educational Evaluation: Analysis and Responsibility*. Berkeley: McCutchan, 1973.
Kass, C.E. Psycholinguistic disabilities of children with reading problems. *Exceptional Children*, 1966, **32**, 533–539.
Katzell, R.A. and Dyer, F.J. Differential validity reviewed. *Journal of Applied Psychology*, 1977, **62**, 137–145.
Kaufman, A.S. Factor analysis of the WISC-R at eleven age levels between 6½ and 16½ years. *Journal of Consulting and Clinical Psychology*, 1975, **43**, 135–147.
Kaufman, A.S. *Intelligent Testing with the WISC-R*. New York: John Wiley and Sons, 1979.
Kaufman, A.S. The impact of WISC-R research for school psychologists. In Reynolds, C.R. and Gutkin, T.B. (Eds), *Handbook of School Psychology* New York: John Wiley and Sons, 1982.
Kaufman, A.S. and Kaufman, N.L. *Clinical Evaluation of Young Children with the McCarthy Scales*. New York: Grune and Stratton, 1977.
Kaufman, D. and Kaufman, P. Strategy training and remedial techniques. *Journal of Learning Disabilities*, 1979, **12** (6), 416–419.
Kearney, G.E. and McElwain, D.W. *Aboriginal Cognition*. New Jersey: Humanities Press, 1976.
Keating, D.P. and Bobbitt, B.L. Individual and developmental differences in cognitive-processing components of mental ability. *Child Development*, 1978, **49**, 155–167.
Keating, D.P., Keniston, A.H., Manis, F.R. and Bobbitt, B.L. Development of the search parameter. *Child Development*, 1980, **51**, 39–44.
Kelley, T.L. *Crossroads in the Mind of Man: A Study of Differentiable Mental Abilities*. Stanford, California: Stanford University Press, 1928.
Kellogg, R.T. Feature frequency in concept learning: What is counted? *Memory and Cognition*, 1981, **9**, 157–163.
Kendler, H.H. and Kendler, T.S. Vertical and horizontal processes in problem solving. *Psychological Review*, 1962, **69**, 1–16.
Kephart, N.C. *The Brain Injured Child in the Class-room*. Chicago: National Society for Crippled Children and Adults, 1963.
King, W.H. An experimental investigation into the relative merits of listening and reading comprehension to boys and girls of primary school age. *British Journal of Psychology*, 1959, **29**, 42–49.
Kinsbourne, M. and George, J. The mechanics of the word frequency effect on recognition memory. *Journal of Verbal Learning and Verbal Behavior*, 1974, **13**, 63–69.
Kinsbourne, M. and Wood, F. Short-term memory processes and the amnesic syndrome. In Deutsch, D. and Deutsch, J.A. (Eds), *Short-term Memory*. New York: Academic Press, 1975.
Kintsch, W. Recognition and free recall of organized lists. *Journal of Experimental Psychology*, 1968, **78**, 481–487.
Kintsch, W. *Learning, Memory and Conceptual Processes*. New York: Wiley, 1970.
Kirby, J.R. and Das J.P. Reading achievement, I.Q. and simultaneous-successive processing. *Journal of Educational Psychology*, 1977, **69**, 564–576.
Kirk, S. and Kirk, W. *Psycholinguistic Learning Disabilities Diagnosis and Remediation*. Urbana: University of Illinois Press, 1971.
Kirk, S.A., McCarthy, J.J. and Kirk, W.D. *Illinois Test of Psycholinguistic Abilities*. Urbana: University of Illinois Press, 1971.
Klahr, D. and Wallace, J.G. The development of serial completion strategies: an information processing analysis. *British Journal of Psychology*, 1970, **61**, 243–257.
Kleinsmith, L.J. and Kaplan, S. Paired-associate learning as a function of arousal and interpolated interval. *Journal of Experimental Psychology*, 1963, **65**, 153–161.

Knox, H.A. A scale based on the work at Ellis Island for estimating mental defect. *Journal of the American Medical Association*, 1914, **62**, 741–747.

Koehler, W. *Gestalt Psychology*. New York: Liveright, 1947.

Kogan, N. Creativity and cognitive style: A life-span perspective. In Baltes, P.B. & Schaie, K.W. (Eds), *Life-span Developmental Psychology: Personality and Socialization*. New York: Academic Press, 1973.

Kohs, S.C. The block-design tests. *Journal of Experimental Psychology*, 1920, **3**, 357–380.

Kossan, N.E. Developmental differences in concept acquisition strategies. *Child Development*, 1981, **52**, 290–298.

Kosslyn, S.M. *Image and Mind*. Cambridge, Mass.: Harvard University Press, 1980.

Kroll, N.E.A. Visual short-term memory. In Deutsch, D. and Deutsch, J.A. (Eds), *Short-term Memory*. New York: Lawrence Erlbaum Associates, 1975.

Krueger, L.E. Effect on bracketing lines on speed of 'same,' 'different' judgement of two adjacent letters. *Journal of Experimental Psychology*, 1970, **84**, 324–330.

Krueger, L.E. Effect of stimulus frequency on speed of 'same,' 'different' judgements. In Kornblum, S. (Ed.), *Attention and Performance IV*. New York: Academic Press, 1973.

Krutetskii, V.A. *The Psychology of Mathematical Abilities in School Children*. Chicago: Chicago U.P. (Translated from Russian by J.Teller, edited by J. Kilpatrick and I. Wirszup), 1976.

Kubota, M. Memory span and intelligence. *Japanese Journal of Psychology*, 1965, **36** (2), 47–55.

Kulpe, O. *Versuche uber Abstraktion*. Berlin: Internal Congress of Experimental Psychology Proceedings, 1904, pp. 56–58.

Lancy, D.F. and Goldstein, G.I. The use of non-verbal Piagetian tasks to assess the cognitive development of autistic children. *Child Development*, 1982, **53**, 1233–1241.

Lansman, M. *An attentional approach to individual differences in immediate memory*. Technical Report, University of Washington, Seattle, June, 1978.

Lawrence, D.H. Required distinctiveness of cues: II selective associations in a constant stimulus situation. *Journal of Experimental Psychology*, 1950, **40**, 175–185.

Lawrence, D.H. The tranfer of a discrimination along a continuum. *Journal of Comparative and Physiological Psychology*, 1952, **45**, 511–516.

Lawrence, D.H. The nature of a stimulus: some relationships between learning and perception. In Koch, S. (Ed.), *Psychology: A Study of a Science*, Study II, Vol.5. New York: McGraw Hill, 1963.

Layton, B. Perceptual noise and aging. *Psychological Bulletin*, 1975, (**82**), 875–883.

Lee, L.L., Koenigsknecht, R.A. and Mulhern, S.T. *Interactive Language Development Teaching: The Clinical Presentation of Grammatical Structure*. Evanston, Ill.: Northwestern University Press, 1975.

Leeuwenberg, E.L. Quantitative specification of information in sequential patterns. *Psychological Review*, 1969, **76**, 216–220.

Lennon, R.T. *Testing and the Culturally Disadvantaged Child*. New York: Harcourt, Brace and World, 1964.

Leontiev, A.N. *Problems in Mental Development*. Moscow: Izd Ahad Pedagog NAUK RSFSR [Press], 1959.

Lewis, M. (Ed.). *The Origins of Intelligence*. New York: Plenum Press, 1976.

Lewis, M. and Baldine, N. Attentional processes and individual differences. In Hale, G.A. and Lewis, M. (Eds), *Attention and Cognitive Development*. New York: Plenum Press, 1979.

Lewis, M. and Brooks-Gunn, J. Attention and intelligence. *Intelligence*, 1981, **5**, 231–238.

Lin, C.Y. Imagery in mathematical thinking and learning. *International Journal of Mathematics Education in Science and Technology*, 1979, **10**, 107–111.

Lindsley, D.B. Psychophysiology and motivation. In Jones, M.R. (Ed.), *Nebraska Symposium*. Lincoln: University of Nebraska Press, 1957.

Line, W. The growth of visual perception in children. *British Journal of Psychology. Monograph Supplement*, No.15, 1931.

Linn, R.L. A Monte Carlo approach to the number of factors problem. *Psychometrika*, 1968, **33**, 37–72.

Loftus, E.F. *Eyewitness Testimony*. Cambridge, Mass.: Harvard University Press, 1979.

Loftus, E.F. and Palmer, J.C. Reconstruction of automobile destruction: An example of the interaction between language and memory. *Journal of Verbal Learning and Verbal Behavior*, 1974, **13**, 585–589.

Lohman, D.F. *Spatial Ability: A Review and Reanalysis of the Correlational Literature*. Technical Report. Stanford, California: Aptitude Research Project, School of Education, Stanford University, October 1979(a).

Lohman, D.F. *Spatial Ability: Individual Differences in Speed and Level*. Technical Report No.9. Stanford, California: Aptitude Research Project, Stanford University, School of Education, 1979(b).

Lohman, D.F. and Kyllonen, P.C. Individual differences in solution strategy on spatial tasks. In Dillon, R.F. and Silmeck, R.R. (Eds), *Individual Differences in Cognition*, Vol.1. New York: Academic Press, 1983.

Lord, F.M. and Novick, M.R. *Statistical Theories of Mental Test Scores*. Reading, Mass.: Addison-Wesley Publishing Co., 1968.

Lovie, A.D. Attention and behaviourism—fact and fiction. *British Journal of Psychology*, 1983, **74**, 301–310.

Lundberg, F. *The Rich and the Super-rich*. New York: Lyle Stuart, 1968.

Lunneborg, C. Choice reaction time. What role in ability measurement? *Applied Psychological Measurement*, 1977, **1**, 309–330.

Lunneborg, C. Some information processing correlates of measures of intelligence. *Multivariate Behavioral Research*, 1978, **13**, 153–161.

Luria, A.R. *Human Brain and Psychological Processes*. New York: Harper and Row, 1966(a).

Luria, A.R. *Higher Cortical Functions in Man*. New York: Basic Books Inc., 1966(b).

Luria, A.R. The functional organization of the brain. *Scientific American*, 1970, **222** (3), 66–78.

Luria, A.R. *The Working Brain: An Introduction to Neuropsychology*, translated by Basil Haigh. New York: Basic Books Inc., 1973.

Luria, A.R. and Simernitskaya, E.G. Interhemispheric relations and the function of the minor hemisphere. *Neuropsychologia*, 1977, **15**, 175–178.

Lutey, C. *Individual Intelligence Testing: A Manual and Source Book*. Greeley, Colorado: C.L. Lutey, 1977.

McCarthy, J.J. and Kirk, S.A. *The Illinois Test of Psycholinguistic Abilities, Experimental Edition*. Urbana Champaign: University of Illinois, 1963.

McClelland, J. and Jackson, M. Studying individual differences in reading. In Lesgold, A; Pellegrino, J; Fokkema, S; and Glaser R. (Eds), *Cognitive Psychology and Instruction*. New York: Plenum Press, 1978.

McCormack, P.D. and Swenson, A.L. Recognition and memory and rare words. *Journal of Experimental Psychology*, 1972, **95**, 72–77.

McDermott, P.A. Congruence and typology of diagnoses in school psychology: An empirical study. *Psychology in the Schools*, 1980, **17**, 12–24.

McFarland, R.A. *Human Factors in Air Transportation and Occupational Health and Safety*. New York: McGraw-Hill, 1953.

McFarland, R.A. The sensory and perceptual processes in aging. In Schaie, K.W. (Ed.), *Theory and Methods of Research on Aging. Current Topics in Psychology of Aging: Perception, Learning, Cognition and Personality*. Morgantown, W. Virginia: 1968.

McFarland, R.A. The need for functional age measurements in industrial gerontology. *Industrial Gerontology*, 1973, **19**, 1–19.

McGee, M.G. Human spatial abilities: Psychometric studies and environmental, genetic, hormonal, and neurological influences. *Psychological Bulletin*, 1979, **86**, 889–918.

McGee, M.G. Spatial abilities: The influence of genetic factors. In Potegal, M. (Ed.), *Spatial Abilities Development and Psychological Foundation*. New York: Academic Press, 1982.

McHugh, R.B. and Owens, W.A. Age changes in mental organization—a longitudinal study. *Journal of Gerontology*, 1954, **9**, 296–302.

McNemar, Q. Lost: Our I.Q.? Why? *American Psychologist*, 1964, **19**, 871–882.

McReynolds, P. (Ed.), *Advances in Psychological Assessment*. Vol.5, San Francisco: Jossey-Bass Publishers, 1981.

MacArthur, R.S. Sex difference in field dependence for the Eskimo: replication of Berry's findings. *International Journal of Psychology*, 1967, **2**, 139–140.

Maccoby, E.E. and Jacklin, C.N. *The Psychology of Sex Differences*. Stanford, California: Stanford University Press, 1974.

MacCrone, I.D. Preliminary results from the Porteus maze tests applied to native school children. *South African Journal of Science*, 1928, **25**, 481–84.

Macione, J.R. Psychological correlates of reading disability as defined by the Illinois test of psycholinguistic abilities. Unpublished doctoral dissertation, University of South Dakota, 1969.

Mackworth, Jane F. *Vigilance and Habitation: A Neuro-psychological Approach*. Baltimore, Md: Penguin Books, 1970.

Mackworth, N.H. and Bruner, J.S. How adults and children search and recognise pictures. *Human Developments*, 1970, **13** (3), 149–177.

Mandler, G. From association to structure. *Psychological Review*, 1962, **69**, 415–417.

Mandler, G. Organization and repetition: Organizational principles with special reference to role learning. In Nilsson, L.G. (Ed.), *Perspectives on Memory Research: Essays in Honour of Uppsala University 500th Anniversary*. Hillsdale, New York: Lawrence Erlbaum Associates, 1979.

Mandler, J.M. and Johnson, N.S. Some of the thousand words a picture is worth. *Journal of Experimental Psychology: Human Learning and Memory*, 1976, **2**, 529–540.

Martin, R.C. and Caramazza, A. Classification in well defined and ill defined categories: Evidence for common processing strategies. *Journal of Experimental Psychology: General*, 1980, **109**, 320–353.

Matarazzo, J.D. *Wechsler's Measurement and Appraisal of Adult Intelligence*. Baltimore: Williams and Wilkins, 1972.

Maxwell, A.E. *Multivariate Analysis in Behavioural Research*. London: Chapman and Hall, 1977.

Mayeske, G.W., Okada, T., Beaton, A.E., Cohen, W.M. and Wissler, C.E. *A Study of Achievement of Our Nations Students*. Washington, D.C.: U.S. Government Printing Office, 1973.

Medin, D.L. and Smith, E.E. Concepts and concept formation. *Annual Review of Psychology*, 1984, **35**, 113–138.

Mehrens, W.A. and Ebel, R.L. (Eds). *Principles of Educational and Psychological Measurement: A Book of Selected Readings*. Chicago, Ill.: Rand McNally, 1967.

Meili, R. Die faktorenanlytische Interpretation der Intelligenz. *Schweizerische Zeitsehrift fur Psychologie*, 1964, **23**, 135–155.

Meredith, W. Notes on factorial invariance. *Psychometrika*, 1964, **29**, 177–185.

Messick, S. Multivariate models of cognition and personality: The need for both process and structure in psychological theory and measurement. In Royce, J. (Ed.), *Multivariate Analysis and Psychological Theory*. New York: Academic Press, 1973.

Messick, S. The standard problem: The meaning and values in measurement and evaluation. *American Psychologist*, 1975, **30**, 955–966.

Messick, S. Personality consistencies in cognition and creativity. In Messick, S. (Ed.), *Individuality in Learning*. San Fransisco: Jossey-Bass, 1976.

Messick, S. *The Values of Ability Testing: Implications of Multiple Perspectives about Criteria and Standards*. RR 82-19. Princeton, N.J.: Educational Testing Service, 1982.

REFERENCES

Messick, S. *Developing Abilities and Knowledge: Style and Interplay of Structure and Knowledge.* RR 83–2. Princeton, N.J.: Educational Testing Service, 1983.

Messick, S. and French, J.W. Dimensions of closure in cognition and personality. *Multivariate Behavioral Research*, 1975, **10**, 3–16.

Meumann, E. Vortrag.Z.Einf.iner experimentalischer Padagogik. 1907, **1**, 499–20. Cited in Smith, I.M. *Spatial Ability*, 1964.

Miles, T.R. On defining intelligence. *British Journal of Psychology.* 1957, **27**, 153–165.

Miller, G.A. The magical number seven, plus or minus two. Same limits on our capacity for processing information. *Psychological Review*, 1956, **63**, 81–97.

Milner, B. Some effects of frontal lobotomy in man. In Warren, J.W. and Akert, K. (Eds), *The Frontal Granular Cortex and Behaviour.* New York: McGraw Hill, 1964.

Money, J. Cytogenic and psychosexual incongruities with a note on space-form blindness. *American Journal of Psychiatry*, 1964, **119**, 820–827.

Money, J. On learning and not learning to read. In Money, J. (Ed.), *The Disabled Reader*, Baltimore: Johns Hopkins Press, 1966.

Moray, N. *Attention: Selective Processes in Vision and Hearing.* London, England: Hutchinson Educational Ltd, 1969.

Moray, N. *Attention: Selective Processes in Vision and Hearing.* New York: Academic Press, 1970.

Moses, B.E. The Nature of Spatial Ability and Its Relationship to Mathematical Problem Solving. Unpublished doctoral dissertation, Indiana University, 1977.

Moses, B.E. *The Relationship between Visual Thinking Tasks and Problem-solving Performance.* Unpublished paper presented at the annual meeting of the American Education Research Association, Boston. 1980.

Mosteller, F. and Moynihan, D.P. (Eds). *On Equality of Educational Opportunity.* New York: Vintage Books, 1972.

Moyer, R.S. and Bayer, R.H. Mental comparison and symbolic distance effect. *Cognitive Psychology*, 1976, **8**, 228–246.

Mueller, G.E. *Zur Theorie der Sinnlichen Aufmerksamkeit.* Leipzig: Edelmann, 1873.

Mueller, G.E. Zur Analyse der Gedachtnistatigkeit und des Vorstellungsret Laufes. III. Teil. *Zeitschrift fur Psychologie*, Erganzungsband 8, 1913.

Muhs, P.J., Hooper, F.H. and Papalia-Finlay, D. Cross-sectional analysis of cognitive functioning across the life span. *International Journal of Aging and Human Development*, 1979, **10**, 311–333.

Murdoch, B.B. and Walker, K.D. Modality effects in free recall. *Journal of Verbal Learning and Verbal Behavior*, 1969, **8**, 665–676.

Murphy, Roger J.L. Sex differences in examination performance: Do these reflect differences in ability or sex-role stereotypes? Paper presented at the International Conference on Sex Role Stereotyping, Cardiff, Wales, July, 1977.

Mutter, P. Very rapid forgetting. *Memory and Cognition*, 1980, **8**, 174–179.

Myklebust, H.R. Learning disabilities in psychoneurologically disturbed children: behavioral correlates of brain disfunction. In Zubin, J. and Gervis, G. (Eds), *Psychopathology of Mental Development.* New York: Grune and Stratton, 1967.

National Education Association. *Task Force and Other Reports*, presented to the fifty-second representative assembly of the National Education Association, July 1973. Washington, D.C.: National Educational Association, 1973.

Neale, M. *Neale Analysis of Reading Ability*, (2nd ed.). London: Macmillan, 1966.

Neisser, U. *Cognitive Psychology.* New York: Appleton-Century-Crofts, 1967.

Neisser, U. Changing conceptions in imagery. In Sheehan, P.W. (Ed.) *The Function and Nature of Imagery.* New York: Academic Press, 1972.

Neisser, U. *Cognition and Reality.* San Francisco: Freeman, 1976.

Neisser, U. *Memory Observed: Remembering in Natural Contexts.* San Francisco: W.H. Freeman and Co., 1982.

Newcombe, N. Sex-related differences in spatial ability: Problems and gaps in current approaches. In Potegal, M. (Ed.), *Spatial Abilities: Development and Physiological Foundations.* New York: Academic Press, 1982.

Newcomer, P.L. and Hammill, D.D. ITPA and academic achievement: A survey. *The Reading Teacher,* 1975, **28**, 731–741.

Newell, A. Learning, generality and problem solving. *Proceedings of the AFIP Congress,* 1963, **62**, 407–412.

Newell, A. Production systems: Models of control structures. In Chase, G.W. (Ed.), *Visual Information Processing.* New York: Academic Press, 1973.

Newell, A. and Simon, H.A. *Human Problem Solving.* Englewood Cliffs, N.J.: Prentice Hall, 1972.

Nickel, H. Der normale Entwicklungsverlauf von Wahrnehmungsprozessen im Kindesalter. In Berger, E. (Ed.), *Teilleistungsschwachen bei Kindern.* Bern: Hans Huber, 1975.

Nickerson, E.T. Some correlates of M. *Journal of Projective Techniques and Personality Assessment,* 1969, **33** (3), 203–212.

Nissen, H.W., Machover, S. and Kinder, E.F. A study of performance tests given to a group of native African Negro children. *British Journal of Psychology,* 1935, **25**, 308–55.

Norman, D.A. *Memory and Attention.* New York: John Wiley & Sons Inc., 1976.

Norman, D.A. *Memory and Attention: An Introduction to Human Information Processing,* (2nd ed.). New York: John Wiley & Sons Inc., 1979.

Norman, D.A. and Bobrow, D. On data-limited and resource-limited processes. *Cognitive Psychology,* 1975, **7**, 44–64.

Norman, D.A., Gentner, D.R. and Stevens, A.L. Comments on learning schemata and memory. In Klahr, D. (Ed.), *Cognition and Instruction.* Hillsdale, N.J.: Lawrence Erlbaum Associates, 1976.

Nunnally, J.C. *Psychometric Theory.* New York: McGraw Hill, 1978.

Nuttall, R.L. The strategy of functional age research. *Aging and Human Development,* 1972, **3**, 149–152.

Ogbu, J. *Minority Education and Caste.* New York: Academic Press, 1978.

Otis, A.S. An absolute point scale for the group measure of intelligence. *Journal of Educational Psychology,* 1918, **9**, 238–261.

Paivio, A. Images, propositions and knowledge. In Nicholas, J.M. (Ed.), *Images, Perception and Knowledge.* Dordrecht, Ontario: Reidel, 1977.

Paivio, A. and Csapo, K. Concrete-image and verbal memory codes. *Journal of Experimental Psychology,* 1969, **80**, 279–285.

Paivio, A. and Csapo, K. Picture superiority in free recall: Imagery or dual coding? *Cognitive Psychology,* 1973, **5**, 176–206.

Panek, P.E., Barrett, G.V., Sterns, H.L. and Alexander, R.A. Age differences in perceptual style, selective attention, and perceptual-motor reaction time. *Experimental Aging Research,* 1978, **4** (5), 377–387.

Pawlik, K. Concepts and calculations in human cognitive abilities. In Cattell, R.B. (Ed.), *Handbook of Multivariate Experimental Psychology.* Chicago: Rand McNally, 1966.

Payne, R.W. The effects of drugs on measures of thought disorder in schizophrenic patients. *Psychopharmacologia,* 1972, **24** (1), 147–158.

Payne, R.W. and Jones, H.F. Statistics for the investigation of individual cases. *Journal of Clinical Psychology,* 1957, **13**, 115–121.

Pelham, W.E. Selective attention deficits in poor readers: Dichotic listening speeded-classification, and auditory and visual central and incidental learning tasks. *Child Development,* 1979, **50**, 1050–1061.

REFERENCES

Pellegrino, J.W. and Glaser, R. Cognitive correlates and components in the analysis of individual differences. *Intelligence*, 1979, 3, 187–214.

Pellegrino, J.W. and Glaser, R. Components of inductive reasoning. In Snow, R.E; Frederico, P.H. and Montague W.E. (Eds), *Aptitude, Learning and Instruction*, Vol.1. Hillsdale, N.J.: Lawrence Erlbaum Associates, 1980.

Pellegrino, J.W. and Glaser, R. Analyzing aptitudes for learning: Inductive reasoning. In Glaser, R. (Ed.), *Advances in Instructional Psychology*, Vol.2. Hillsdale, N.J.: Lawrence Erlbaum Associates, 1982.

Pemberton, C.L. The closure factors related to temperament. *Journal of Personality*, 1952, 21, 159–175.

Peterson, J. Intelligence and learning. *Psychological Review*, 1922, 29, 366–389.

Piaget, J. *The Psychology in Intelligence*. London: Routledge and Kegan Paul, 1950.

Pichot, P. The Porteus maze test. *Revista De Psicologia General of Aplicada*, 1967, 22, 161–166.

Pieron, H. The problem of intelligence. *Pedagogical Seminary*, 1926, 33, 50–60.

Pintner, R. and Patterson, D.G. *A Scale of Performance Testing*. New York: Appleton, 1917.

Popham, W.J. *Educational Evaluation*. Englewood Cliffs, N.J.: Prentice Hall, 1975.

Popham, W.J. Domain specification strategies. In Berk, R.A. (Ed.), *Criterion-Referenced Measurement: The State of the Art*. Baltimore, Maryland: Johns Hopkins University Press, 1980, pp.15-31.

Porteus, S.D. *Primitive Intelligence and Environment*. New York: Macmillan, 1937.

Porteus, S.D. 1914, cited in Smith, I.M., 'Spatial ability,' 1964.

Porteus, Stanley D. *Porteus Maze Test 50 Year's Application*. Palo Alto, California: Pacific Books, 1965.

Porteus, S.D. and Gregor, J. Studies in intercultural testing. *Perception and Motor Skills*, 1963, 16, 705–24.

Posner, M.I. Short-term memory systems in human information processing. *Actor Psychologica*, 1967, 27, 267–284.

Posner, M.I. *Chronometric Explorations of Mind*. Hillsdale, N.J.: Lawrence Erlbaum Associates, 1978.

Posner, M.I. and Keele, S.W. Decay of visual information from a single letter. *Science*, 1967, 158, 137–139.

Posner, M.I. and Rossman, E. Effect size and location of informational transforms on short-term retention. *Journal of Experimental Psychology*, 1965, 70, 496–505.

Pylyshyn, Z.W. What the mind's eye tells the mind's brain: A critique of visual imagery. *Psychological Bulletin*, 1973, 80, 1–24.

Quereshi, M.Y. Patterns of psycholinguistic development during early and middle childhood. *Educational and Psychological Measurement*, 1967, 27, 353–365.

Raaheim, K., Kaufmann, G. and Bengtsson, G. Attempts to predict intelligent behavior. II A study of problem solving. *Scandinavian Journal of Psychology*, 1980, 21, 119–21.

Rabbitt, P.M.A. Age and discrimination between complex stimuli. In Welford, A.T. and Birren, J.E. (Eds), *Behavior, Aging and the Nervous System*. Springfield, Ill.: Charles C. Thomas, 1965.

Rabinowitz, J.C., Mandler, G. and Barsalou, L.W. Generation recognition as an auxiliary retrieval strategy. *Journal of Verbal Learning and Verbal Behavior*, 1979, 18, 57–72.

Rapaport, D., Gill, M.M. and Schafer, R. *Diagnostic Psychological Testing*. New York: International Universities Press, 1968.

Rapaport, D., Gill, M.M. and Schafer, R. *Diagnostic Psychological Testing*, revised edition by Holt, R.R. London: University of London Press, 1970.

Rasch, G. *Probabilistic Models for Some Intelligence and Attainment Tasks*. Copenhagen: Danish Institute for Educational Research, 1960.

Rasch, G. *Probabilistic Models for Some Intelligence and Attainment Tests*. (Revised edition) Chicago: University of Chicago Press, 1980.

Raven, J.C. *Mill Hill Vocabulary Scale*, Form 2 (Senior). Hawthorn: ACER, 1947.

Raven, J.C., Raven, J. and Court, J.H. *Mill Hill Vocabulary Scale*, Form 2 (Senior), Revised. London: H.K. Lewis and Co., 1982.

Reichard, S. and Schafer, R. The clinical significance of the scatter on the Bellevue scale. *Bulletin of the Menninger Clinic*, 1943, **7**, 93–98.

Reitan, R.M. Diagnostic inferences of brain lesions based on psychological test results. *Canadian Psychologist*, 1966(a), **7** (4), 368–383.

Reitan, R.M. Problems and prospects in studying the psychological correlates of brain lesions. *Cortex*, 1966(b), **2** (1), 127–154.

Reitan, R.M. A research program on the psychological effects of brain lesions in human beings. *International Review of Research in Mental Retardation*, 1966(c), **1**, 153–218.

Requin, Jean (Ed.). *Attention and Performance*. VII papers from the International Symposium on attention and performance held at Senanque, France, August 1–6, 1976. Hillsdale, N.J.: Lawrence Erlbaum Associates, 1978.

Resnick, L.B. (Ed.) *The Nature of Intelligence*. Hillsdale, N.J.: Lawrence Erlbaum Associates, 1976.

Resnick, L.B. Instructional psychology. *Annual Review of Psychology*, 1981, **32**, 659–705.

Restle, F. Theory of serial pattern learning: Structural trees. *Psychological Review*, 1970, **77**, 481–495.

Reynolds, C.R. and Gutkin, T.B. *The Handbook of School Psychology*. New York: John Wiley, 1982.

Reynolds, M.C. and Balow, B. Categories and variables in special education. *Exceptional Children*, 1972, **38**, 356–366.

Reville, W., Humphreys, M.S., Simon, L. and Gilliland, K. The interactive effect of personality, time of day and caffeine: A test of the arousal model. *Journal of Experimental Psychology: General*, 1980, **109**, 1–31.

Riegel, K.F. and Riegel, R.M. Development, drop, and death. *Developmental Psychology*, 1972, **6**, 306–319.

Riley, D.A. Memory for form. In Postman, L. (Ed.), *Psychology in the Making*. New York: Knopf, 1962.

Rimoldi, H.J.A. The central intellective factor. *Psychometrika*, 1951, **16**, 75–101.

Robinson, J.E. and Gray, J.L. Cognitive styles as a variable in school learning. *Journal of Educational Psychology*, 1974, **66**, 793–799.

Roid, Gale H. and Haladyna, T.M. *A Technology for Test-item Writing*. New York: Academic Press, 1982.

Rourke, B.P. Brain behavior relationships in children with learning disabilities. *American Psychologist*, 1975 (Sept), **30** (9), 911–920.

Rowe, H.A.H. *Problem Solving and Intelligence*. Hillsdale, N.J.: Lawrence Erlbaum Associates, 1985(a).

Rowe, H.A.H. *Non-verbal Ability Tests*. Hawthorn, Vic.: ACER, 1985(b).

Rowe, H.A.H. *Manual for the Non-Verbal Ability Tests*. Hawthorn, Vic.: ACER, 1985(c).

Royce, J.R. The conceptual framework for a multi-factor theory of individuality. In Royce, J.R. (Ed.), *Multivariate Analysis and Psychological Theory*. London: Academic Press, 1973.

Rubin, D. Very long-term memory for prose and verse. *Journal of Verbal Learning and Verbal Behavior*, 1977, **16**, 611–621.

Rubinstein, S.L. *Grundlagen der Allgemeinen Psychologie*. Berlin: Volk and Wissen, 1973.

Rugel, R.P. WISC subtest scores of disabled readers: A review with respect to Bannatyne's recategorization. *Journal of Learning Disabilites*, 1974, **7**, 48–55.

Rumelhart, D.E. *Introduction to Human Information Processing*. New York: Wiley, 1977(a).

Rumelhart, D.E. Towards an interactive model of reading. In Dornic, S. (Ed.), *Attention and Performance*, VI. Hillsdale, N.J.: Lawrence Erlbaum Associates, 1977(b).

Rutter, M. Diagnosis and definition of childhood autism. *Journal of Autism and Childhood Schizophrenia*, 1978, **8**, 139–161.

Rystrom, R. Toward defining comprehension: A second report. *Journal of Reading Behavior*, 1970, **2**, 144–158.

REFERENCES

Salthouse, T.A. *Adult Cognition: An Experimental Psychology of Human Aging.* New York: Springer, 1982.

Salthouse, T.A. and Somberg, B.L. Time accuracy relationships in young and old adults. *Journal of Gerontology*, 1982, 37, 349–353.

Samuda, R.J. *Psychological Testing of American Minorities: Issues and Consequences.* New York: Dodd, Mead and Co., 1975.

Santostefano, S. Cognitive controls versus styles: diagnosing and treating cognitive disabilities in children. *Seminars in Psychiatry*, 1969, 1, 291–317.

Santostefano, S. and Paley, E. Development of cognitive controls in children. *Child Development*, 1964, 35, 939–949.

Sattler, J.M. *Assessment of Children's Intelligence and Special Abilities.* (2nd edition). Boston, Mass.: Allyn and Bacon, Inc., 1982.

Saunders, D.R. A factor analysis of the picture completion items of the WAIS. *Journal of Clinical Psychology*, 1960, 16, 146–149.

Savage, R.D. *Psychometric Assessment of the Individual Child.* Middlesex: Penguin Books, 1968.

Schaie, K.W. The Seattle longitudinal study: A twenty-one year exploration of psychometric intelligence in adulthood. In Schaie, K.W. (Ed.), *Longitudinal Studies of Adult Psychological Development.* New York: Guilford, 1982.

Schaie, K.W. and Strother, C.R. A cross-sequential study of age changes in cognitive behavior. *Psychological Bulletin*, 1968, 70, 671–680.

Schneider, W. and Shiffrin, R.M. Controlled and automatic human information processing: I Detection, search and attention. *Psychological Review*, 1977, 84, 1–66.

Schonell, F.S. and Schonell, E. *Schonell Attainment and Diagnostic Tests of Reading and English.* Edinburgh: Oliver & Boyd, 1960.

Schwartz, D.W. and Karp, S.A. Field dependence in a geriatric population. *Perceptual and Motor Skills*, 1967, 24, 495–504.

Scott, D.H. *Bristol Social Adjustment Guides*, 5th edition. London: University of London Press, 1974.

Sharp, S.E. Individual psychology: A study of psychological method. *American Journal of Psychology*, 1898–1899, 10, 329–390.

Sherman, J. *Women and Mathematics: Summary of Research from 1977–1979.* NIE grant, final report. University of Wisconsin at Madison, 1979.

Siegel, L.S. The role of spatial arrangement and heterogeneity in the development of aspects of numerical equivalence. *Canadian Journal of Psychology*, 1973, 27, 351–55.

Silverstein, A.B. WISC subtest pattern of retardates. *Psychological Reports* 1968, 23, 1061–1062.

Silverstein, A.B. Variance components in the subtests of the WISC-R. *Psychological Reports* 1976, 39, 1109–1110.

Simon, H.A. Complexity and the representation of patterned sequences of symbols. *Psychological Review*, 1972, 79, 368–382.

Simon, H.A. The functional equivalence of problem solving skills. *Cognitive Psychology*, 1975, 7, 268–288.

Simon, H.A. Identifying basic abilities underlying intelligent performance on complex tasks In Resnick, L.B. (Ed.), *The Nature of Intelligence.* Hillsdale, N.J.: Lawrence Erlbaum Associates, 1976.

Simon, H.A. and Kotovsky, K. Human acquisition of concepts for sequential patterns. *Psychological Review*, 1963, 70, 534–546.

Simon, H.A. and Lea, G. Problem solving and rule induction: A unified rule. In Gregg, W.L. (Ed.), *Knowledge and Cognition.* Potomac, Md: Lawrence Erlbaum Associates, 1974.

Sims, M.T., Graves, R.J. and Simpson, G.C. Mineworkers scores on the group embedded figures test. *Journal of Occupational Psychology*, 1983, 56, 335–337.

Singer, H. Validity of the Durrell–Sullivan reading capacity test. *Educational and Psychological Measurement*, 1965, 25, 479–491.

Singer, H. and Ruddell, R.B. *Theoretical Models and Processes of Reading.* Newark, Del.: International Reading Association, 1970.

Smith, I.M. *Spatial Ability*. London: University of London Press, 1964.

Smith, I.M. Spatial ability and mental imagery. In Smith, I.M. (Ed.), *The Psychology of Mathematics Education*. London: Chelsea College (University of London). 1972.

Snow, R.E. Research on aptitudes: A progress report. In Shulman, L.S. (Ed.), *Review of Research in Education* (Vol.4). Itasca, Ill.: Peacock, 1977(a).

Snow, R.E. Individual differences and instructional theory. *Educational Researcher*, 1977(b), 6, 11–15.

Snow, R.E. Theory and method for research on aptitude processes. *Intelligence*, 1978(a), 2, 225–278.

Snow, R.E. Towards a theory of aptitude for learning: fluid and crystallised intelligence and their correlates. In Das, J.P. & O'Connor, N. (Eds), *Intelligence and Learning*. New York: Plenum Press, 1978(b).

Snow, R.E. Aptitude processes. In Snow, R.E., Frederico, P.A. and Montague, W.E. (Eds), *Aptitude, Learning and Instruction*, (Vol.1). Hillsdale, N.J.: Lawrence Erlbaum Associates, 1980.

Snow, R.E. Towards a theory of aptitude for learning: fluid and crystallised intelligence and their correlates. In Freidman, M., Das, J.P. & O'Connor, N. (Eds), *Intelligence and Learning*. New York: Plenum Press, 1981.

Snow, R.E. and Lohman, D.F. *Cognition and Learning in Young Adults*. Technical Report No.13, Aptitude Research Project. Stanford University, Department of Education, 1981.

Spearman, C. 'General intelligence' objectively determined and measured. *American Journal of Psychology*, 1904, 15, 201–293.

Spearman, C. *The Nature of 'Intelligence' and the Principles of Cognition*. London: Macmillan, 1923.

Spearman, C. *The Abilities of Man*. New York: The Macmillan Co., 1927.

Spearman, C. *The Spearman Visual Perception Test*. London: Macmillan, 1933.

Spencer, Herbert. (1820–1903) *Principles of Biology*. (Ref. Encyclopedia Britannica, 1864).

Stankov, L. Fluid and crystallized intelligence and broad perceptual factors among the 11 and 12 year olds. *Journal of Educational Psychology*, 1978, 70, 3, 324–334.

Stankov, L. Ear differences and implied cerebral lateralization on some intellective auditory factors. *Applied Psychological Measurement*, 1980, 4, 1, 21–38.

Stankov, L. Attention and intelligence. *Journal of Educational Psychology*, 1983, 75, (4), 471–490.

Stanley, G. Visual information processing in dyslexia. In Deutsch, D. and Deutsch, J.A. (Eds), *Short-term Memory*, New York: Academic Press, 1975.

Stephenson, W. Tetrad differences for non-verbal subtests. *Journal of Educational Psychology*, 1931 22.

Stern, W. The psychological method of testing intelligence. *Educational Psychology Monographs*, 1914, No.13.

Sternberg, R.J. *Intelligence, Information Processing and Analogical Reasoning: The Componential Analysis of Human Abilities*. Hillsdale, N.J.: Lawrence Erlbaum Associates, 1977.

Sternberg, R.J. The nature of mental abilities. *American Psychologist*, 1979, 34, 214–230.

Sternberg, R.J. Factor theories of intelligence are alright almost. *Educational Researcher*, 1980(a), 9(8), 6–13, 18.

Sternberg, R.J. Sketch of a componential subtheory of human intelligence. *Behavioral and Brain Sciences*, 1980(b), 3, 573–614.

Sternberg, R.J. Towards a unified componential theory of human intelligence: I. Fluid ability. In Friedman, M., Das, J.P. and O'Connor, N. (Eds), *Intelligence and Learning*. New York: Plenum Press, 1981(a).

Sternberg, R.J. The evolution of theories of intelligence. *Intelligence*, 1981(b), 5, 209–230.

Sternberg, R.J. Nothing fails like success: the search for an intelligent paradigm for studying intelligence. *Journal of Educational Psychology*, 1981(c), 73, 142–155.

REFERENCES

Sternberg, R.J. The nature of intelligence. *New York University Education Quarterly*, 1981(d), 12, 10–17.

Sternberg, R.J. (Ed.). *Advances in the Psychology of Human Intelligence* (Vol.1). Hillsdale, N.J.: Lawrence Erlbaum Associates, 1982.

Sternberg, R.J. *Beyond IQ: A Triarchic Theory of Human Intelligence*. New York: Cambridge University Press, 1984.

Stoddard, G.D. On the meaning of intelligence. *Psychological Review*, 1941, 48, 250–260.

Strang, R. *Diagnostic Teaching of Reading*. New York: McGraw-Hill, 1969.

Strauss, A.A. and Werner, H. Disorders of conceptual thinking in the brain injured child. *Journal of Nervous and Mental Diseases*, 1942, 96, 153–172.

Strowig, R.W. and Alexakos, C.E. Overlap between achievement and aptitude scores. *Measurement and Evaluation in Guidance*, 1969, 2, 157–167.

Swineford, F. Growth in the general and verbal Bi-factors from grade 7 to grade 9. *Journal of Educational Psychology*, 1947, 38, 257–272.

Swineford, F. A study in factor analysis: the nature of general, verbal and spatial Bi-factors. *Supplementary Educational Monograph*, 1948, No.67.

Talland, G.A. and Waugh, N.C. (Eds). *The Psychopathology of Memory*. New York: Academic Press, 1969.

Taylor, C.W.A. A factorial study of fluency in writing. *Psychometrika*, 1947, 12, 239–262.

Taylor, E.M. *Psychological Appraisal of Children with Cerebral Defects*. Cambridge, Mass.: Harvard University Press, 1959.

Terman, L.M. *The Measurement of Intelligence*. Boston: Houghton Mifflin, 1916.

Terman, L.M. Contribution to 'Intelligence and its easurement': A symposium. *Journal of Educational Psychology*, 1921, 12, 127–133.

Terman, L.M. and Merrill, M.A. *Stanford–Binet Intelligence Scale: Manual for the Third Revision Form L-M*. Boston: Houghton Mifflin, 1973.

Thomson, G.H. General versus group factors in mental activities. *Psychological Review*, 1920, 27, 173–190.

Thomson, G.H. *The Factorial Analysis of Human Ability*. London: University of London Press, 1939.

Thorndike, E.L. *Educational Psychology*. New York: Columbia University Press, 1913.

Thorndike, E.L. Tests of intelligence: reliability, significance susceptibility to special training and adaptation to the general nature of the task. *School and Society*, 1919, 9, 189–95.

Thorndike, E.L. Measurement of intelligence: I. The present status. *Psychological Review*, 1924, 31, 219–252.

Thorndike, E.L., Bregman, E.O., Cobb, C.V. and Woodyard, E. *The Measure of Intelligence*. New York: Teachers College Bureau of Publications, Columbia University, 1926.

Thorndike, E.L., Terman, L.M., Freeman, F.N., Coloin, S.S., Pintner, R., Ruml, B., Pressey, S.L., Hennon, A.C., Peterson, J., Thurstone, L.L., Woodrow, H., Dearborn, W.F. and Haggerty, M.E. Intelligence and its measurement: A symposium. *Journal of Educational Psychology*, 1921, 12, 123–147 and 195–216.

Thorndike, P.L. *Applied Psychometrics*. Boston: Houghton Mifflin Co., 1982.

Thorndike, R.L. (Ed.) *Educational Measurement*, (2nd ed.). Washington, D.C.: American Council on Education, 1971.

Thorndike, R.L. and Hagen, E. *10 000 Careers*. New York: Wiley, 1959.

Thurstone, L.L. The nature of intelligence. *Psychological Bulletin*, 1923, 20, 78–79.

Thurstone, L.L. *The Nature of Intelligence*. London: Harcourt Brace, 1924.

Thurstone, L.L. The factorial isolation of primary abilities. *Psychometrika*, 1936, 1, 175–182.

Thurstone, L.L. Primary mental abilities. *Psychometric Monographs*, 1938, 1, also published by University of Chicago Press, 1938(a).

Thurstone, L.L. The perceptual factor. *Psychometrika*, 1938(b), 3, 1–12.

Thurstone, L.L. Experimental study of simple structure. *Psychomtrika*, 1940, 5, 153–168.

Thurstone, L.L. A factorial study of perception. *Psychometric Monographs*, 1944, No.4.
Thurstone, L.L. *Multiple-factor Analysis: A Development and Expansion of 'The Vectors of the Mind.'* Chicago: University of Chicago Press, 1947.
Thurstone, L.L. Mechanical aptitude III. Analysis of group tests. *Psychometric Lab. Report*, No.55, Chicago: University of Chicago Press, 1949.
Thurstone, L.L. and Thurstone, T.G. *Factorial Studies of Intelligence*. Chicago: University of Chicago Press, 1941(a).
Thurstone, L.L. and Thurstone, T.G. Factorial studies of intelligence. *Psychometric Monographs*, 1941(b), No.2.
Titchener, E.B. *Lectures of the Elementary Psychology of Feeling and Attention*. New York: Knapp, 1908.
Trabasso, T. and Bower, G.H. *Attention in Learning Theory and Research*. New York: Wiley, 1968.
Traver, S.G. and Hallahan, D.P. Additional deficits in children with learning disabilities. A review. *Journal of Learning Disabilities*, 1974, 7, 560–569.
Traver, S.G. Underselective attention in learning-disabled children: Some reconceptualizations of the old hypotheses. *Exceptional Education Quarterly*, 1981, 2, 25–35.
Treisman, A.M. Selective attention in man. *British Medical Bulletin*, 1964, 20, No.1, 12–16.
Tuddenham, R.D. The nature and measurement of intelligence. In Postman, L. (Ed.), *Psychology in the Making*. New York: Knopf, 1963, pp.469–525.
Tulving, E. Theoretical issues in free recall. In Dixon, T.R. and Horton, D.L. Eds), *Verbal Behavior and General Behavior Theory*, Englewood Cliffs, N.J.: Prentice Hall, 1968.
Tulving, E. Episodic and semantic memory. In Tulving, E. and Donaldson, W. (Eds), *Organization of Memory*. New York: Academic Press, 1972.
Tulving, E. Ecphoric processes in recall and recognition. In Brown, J. (Ed.), *Recall and Recognition*. New York: Wiley, 1976.
Underwood, B.J. Are we overloading memory? In Melton, A. and Martin, E. (Eds), *Coding Processes in Human Memory*. New York: Wiley, 1972.
Underwood, B.J. The role of association in recognition memory. *Journal of Experimental Psychology*, 1974, 102, 917–939.
Vaidya, S. and Chansky, N. Cognitive development and cognitive style in mathematics achievement. *Journal of Educational Psychology*, 1980, **72**, 326–330.
Vallett, R.E. *The Remediation of Learning Disabilities: A Handbook of Psychoeducational Resource Programs.* Palo Alto, Calif.: Fearon Publishers, 1967.
Vernon, M.D. *Backwardness in Reading*. Cambridge: Cambridge University Press, 1960.
Vernon, P.E. *The Structure of Human Abilities*. London: Methuen, 1950.
Vernon, P.E. *Intelligence and Cultural Environment*. London: Methuen, 1969.
Vernon, P.E. The nature of field independence. *Journal of Personality*, 1972, 40, 366–391.
Vernon, P.E. *Intelligence: Heredity and Environment*. San Francisco: Freeman, 1979.
Vernon, P.E. *The Abilities and Achievement of Orientals in North America*. New York: Academic Press, 1982.
Vitz, P.C. and Todd, R.C.A. A coded element model of the perceptual processing of sequential stimuli. *Psychological Review*, 1969, 76, 433–449.
Vygotsky, L.S. Problemaemotsii (Problem Solving). Vop Psikhol. 1957, 4, 125–134.
Vygotsky, L.S. *Razvitie Vysshikh Psikhicheskikh Funktsii*. (The development of higher psychic functions). Moscow, USSR: RSFSR Academy of Pedagogical Sciences, 1960.
Vygotsky, L.S. *Thought and Language*. Cambridge, Mass.: MIT Press, 1962.
Vygotsky, L.S. *Mind and Society*. Cambridge, Mass.: Harvard University Press, 1978.
Wachtel, P.L. Field differentiation and psychological differentiation: Reexamination. *Perceptual and Motor Skills*, 1972, 35, 179–189.
Wagner, R.F. *Dyslexia and Your Child*. New York: Harper and Row, 1971.

REFERENCES

Walker, E.L. Action decrement and its relation to learning. *Psychological Review*, 1958, 78, 103–106.

Warren, J.L. Syndrome differences in the cognitive processing of mildly retarded children and adolescents. Unpublished doctoral dissertation. University of Washington, Seattle, 1978.

Warren, N. (Ed.). *Studies in Cross-cultural Psychology.* London: Academic Press, 1980.

Warrington, E.K. and Weiskrantz, L. Amnesic syndrome: consolidation or retrieval? *Nature*, 1970, 228, 628–630.

Wason, P.C. and Johnson-Laird, P.N. *Psychology of Reasoning: Structure and Content.* London: Batsford, 1972.

Watkins, M.J. and Watkins, O.C. The postcategorical status of the modality effect in serial recall. *Journal of Experimental Psychology*, 1973, 99, 226–230.

Wechsler, D. *The Measurement of Adult Intelligence.* Baltimore: Williams and Wilkins, 1939.

Wechsler, D. *Wechsler Intelligence Scale for Children. WISC.* New York: The Psychological Corporation, 1949.

Wechsler, D. *Manual for the Wechsler Adult Intelligence Scale.* New York: The Psychological Corporation, 1955.

Wechsler, D. *The Measurement and Appraisal of Adult Intelligence.* Baltimore: Williams and Wilkins Co., 1958.

Wechsler, D. The IQ is an intelligent test. *New York Times Magazine*, June 26, 1966.

Wechsler, D. *Wechsler Intelligence Scale for Children—Revised*, WISC-R. New York: The Psychological Corporation, 1974.

Wechsler, D. *Wechsler Adult Intelligence Scale—Revised, (WAIS-R).* New York: The Psychological Corporation, 1981.

Wechsler, D. *Wechsler Adult Intelligence Scale—Revised, WAIS-R.* New York: The Psychological Corporation, 1982.

Weikard, D.P., Rogers, L., Adcock, C. and McClelland, D. *The Cognitively Oriented Curriculum: A Frame Work for Preschool Teachers.* Urbana, Ill.: University of Illinois Press, 1971.

Weiner, I.B. Behavior therapy in obsessive-compulsive neurosis: Treatment of an adolescent boy. *Psychotherapy: Theory, Research and Practice.* 1967, 4 (1), 27–29.

Weiner, I.B. (Ed.). *Clinical Methods in Psychology.* New York: Wiley Interscience, 1976.

Weiner, M. Organization of mental abilities from ages 14 to 54. *Educational and Psychological Measurement*, 1964, 24, 573–587.

Weisenburg, T., Roe, A., and McBride, K.E. *Adult Intelligence. A Psychological Study of Test Performance.* New York: Commonwealth Fund, 1935.

Weisman, A.G. Intelligent testing. *American Psychologist*, 1968, 23, 267–274.

Weissenberg, P. and Gruenfeld, L. Relationships among leadership dimensions and cognitive style. *Journal of Applied Psychology*, 1966, 50, 392–395.

Welford, A.T. *Skill and Age: An Experimental Approach.* London: Oxford University Press, 1951.

Welford, A.T. *Skilled Performance: Perceptual and Motor Skills.* Glenview, Ill.: Scott, Foresman & Co., 1976.

Welford, A.T. Motor performance. In Birren, J.E. & Schaie, K.W. (Eds), *Handbook of the Psychology of Aging.* New York: Van Nostrand, 1977.

Werdelin, I. *Geometrical Ability and the Space Factor in Boys and Girls.* Lund, Sweden: Gleerups, 1961.

Werner, H. *Comparative Psychology of Mental Development.* New York: Follet, 1940.

Werner, H. and Strauss, A.A. Pathology of figure background relation in the child. *Journal of Abnormal and Social Psychology*, 1941, 36, 58–67.

Wertheimer, M. *Principles of Perceptual Organization.* Leipzig: Breitkopf and Haertel, 1923.

Wessells, M.G. *Cognitive Psychology.* New York: Harper and Row, 1982.

Whipple, G.M. *Manual of Mental and Physical Tests.* Baltimore: Warwick and York, 1910.

Whitely, S.E. Solving verbal analogies: Some cognitive components of intelligence test items. *Journal of Educational Psychology.* 1976, 68, 234–242.

Whitely, S.E. Information processing on intelligence test items: Some response components. *Applied Psychological Measurement*, 1977, **1**, 465–467.

Whitely, S.E. Latent trait models in the study of intelligence. *Intelligence*, 1980(a), **4**, 97–132.

Whitely, S.E. Multicomponent latent trait models for ability tests. *Psychometrika*, 1980(b), **45**, 479–494.

Whitely, S.E. Measuring aptitude processes with multi-component latent trait models. *Journal of Educational Measurement*, 1981, **18**, 67–84.

Whiteman, M. and Jastak, J. Absolute scaling of tests for a state-wide sample. *Educational and Psychological Measurement*, 1957, **17**, 338–346.

Wiggins, J.S. *Personality and Prediction: Principles of Personality Assessment*. Reading, Mass.: Addison-Wesley, 1973.

Willoughby, R.R. Family similarities in mental test abilities (with a note on the growth and decline of the abilities). *Genetic Psychology Monographs*, 1927, **2**, 235–277.

Wilson, R.C., Guilford, J.P., Christensen, P.R. and Lewis, D.J. A factor-analytic study of creative thinking abilities. *Psychometrika*, 1954, **19**, 297–311.

Wissler, C. The correlation of mental and physical traits. *Psychological Monographs*, 1901, **3**, 1–62.

Witkin, H.A. A cognitive style approach to cross-cultural research. *International Journal of Psychology*, 1967, **2**, 233–250.

Witkin, H.A. and Berry, J.W. Psychological differentiation in cross-cultural perspective. *Cross-cultural Psychology*, 1975, **6**, 4–87.

Witkin, H.A., Dyk, R.B., Faterson, H.F., Goodenough, D.R. and Karp, S.A. *Psychological Differentiation: Studies in Development*. New York: Wiley, 1962, (reissued 1974).

Witkin, H.A., Goodenough, D.R. and Karp, S.A. Stability of cognitive style from childhood to young adulthood. *Journal of Personality and Social Psychology*, 1967, **7**, 291–300.

Witkin, H.A., Goodenough, D.R. Field dependence and interpersonal behavior. *Psychological Bulletin*, 1977, **84**, 661–689.

Witkin, H.A., Goodenough, D.R. *Cognitive Styles: Essence and Origins*. New York: International Universities Press, 1981.

Witkin, H.A., Moore, C.A., Goodenough, D.R., Cox, P.W. Field dependent and field independent cognitive styles and their educational implication. *Review of Educational Research*, 1977, **47**, 1–64.

Witkin, H.A. and Oltman, P.K. Cognitive style: patterning in congenitally totally blind children. *Child Development*, 1968, **39**, 768–786.

Witkin, H.A. and Oltman, P.K., Raskin, E. and Karp, S.A. *A Manual for the Embedded Figures Test*. Palo Alto, Calif.: Consulting Psychologist Press, 1971.

Wittenborn, T.R. Factorial equations for tests of attention. *Psychometrika*, 1943, **8**, 19–35.

Wittig, M.A. and Petersen, A.C. (Eds). *Sex Related Differences in Cognitive Functioning*. New York: Academic Press, 1979.

Wohlwill, J.F. Methodology and research strategy in the study of developmental change. In Goulet, L.R. and Baltes, P.B. (Eds), *Life-span Development Psychology*. New York: Academic Press, 1970.

Wolf, V.C. Age and sex performance differences as measured by a new non-verbal visual perceptual test. *Psychonomic Science*, 1971, **25**,, 85–87.

Woodward, A.E., Bjork, R.A. and Jongeward, R.H. Recall and recognition as a function of primary rehearsal. *Journal of Verbal Learning and Verbal Behavior*, 1973, **12**, 608–614.

Woodworth, R.S. *Experimental Psychology*. New York: Holt, 1938.

Woodworth, R.S. and Schlosberg, H. *Experimental Psychology* (Revised edition). London: Methuen, 1954.

Woo-Sam, J., Zimmerman, I.L. and Rogal, R. Location of injury and Wechsler indices of mental deterioration. *Perceptual and Motor Skills*, 1971 (April), **32** (2), 407–411.

Worden, P.E. Memory strategy instruction with the learning disabled. In Pressley, M. and Levin, J.R. (Eds), *Cognitive Strategy Research: Psychological Foundations*. New York: Springer, 1983.

Wright, B. and Stone, M.H. *Best Test Design: Rasch Measurement*. Chicago: Mesa Press, 1979.

Wrigley, C., Saunders, D.R. and Neuhaus, J.O. Applications of the quartimax method of rotation to Thurstone's primary mental abilities study. *Psychometrika*, 1958, **23**, 151–170.

Wundt, W. *Grundzuge der Physiologischen Psychologie*. Leipzig: Breitkopf und Hartel, 1873.

Yarmey, A.D. *The Psychology of Eye-witness Testimony*. New York: Free Press, 1979.

Yerkes, R.M. and Anderson, H.M. The importance of social status as indicated by the results of the point scale method of measuring mental capacity. *Journal of Educational Psychology*, 1915, **6**, 137–150.

Yoakum, C.A. and Yerkes, R.M. *Army Mental Tests*. New York: Holt, 1920.

Young, F.A. and Lindsley, D.B. (Eds). *Early Experience and Visual Information Processing in Perceptual and Reading Disorders*. Washington, D.C.: National Academy of Sciences, 1970.

Ysseldyke, J. Diagnostic prescriptive reading: The search for aptitude treatment interactions. In Mann, L. and Sabatino, D. (Eds), *First Review of Special Education*. New York: Grune and Stratton, 1973.

Ysseldyke, J. and Mirkin, P.K. The use of assessment information to plan instructional intervention: A review of research. In Reynolds, C.R. and Gutkin, T.B. (Eds), *The Handbook of School Psychology*. New York: Wiley, 1982.

Zeaman, D. and House, B.J. The role of attention in retardate discrimination learning. In Ellis, N.R. (Ed.), *Handbook of Mental Deficiency*. New York: McGraw Hill, 1963.

Zimmerman, I.L. and Woo-Sam, J. The utility of the Wechsler preschool and primary scale of intelligence in the public school. *Journal of Clinical Psychology*, 1970, **26**, 472.

Zimmerman, I.L. and Woo-Sam, J. Research with the Wechsler intelligence scale for children: 1960–1970. *Psychology in the Schools*, 1972, **9**, 232–271.

Zimmerman, I.L. and Woo-Sam, J. and Glasser, A.J. *Clinical Interpretation of the Wechsler Adult Intelligence Scale*. New York: Grune and Stratton, 1973.

Zimmerman, W.S. A revised orthogonol rotation solution for Thurstone's original primary mental abilities test battery. *Psychometrika*, 1953, **18**, 77–93.

INDEX OF AUTHORS

Numbers in *italics* indicate pages with complete bibliographic information.

Ackerman, P.T., 113, *245*
Acland, H., 8, *252*
Adcock, C., 84, *265*
Alexakos, C.E., 178, *263*
Alexander, R.A., 73, 93, 113, *240, 258*
Algina, J., 31, *249*
Allen, M.J., 235, *239*
Anastasi, A., 14, 49, 61, 93, 136, 139, 160, *239*
Anderson, H.M., 14, *267*
Anderson, J.R., 30, 32, 125, 127, *239*
Arenberg, D., 74, *239*
Aristotle, 8, 138
Arthur, G., 86, 96, *239*
Atkinson, R.C., 24, 66, 80, 116, 118, *239, 242*
Austin, G.A., 24, *241*
Australian Council for Educational Research, 223, *239*
Ayres, A.J., 235, *239*

Baldine, N., 113, *254*
Balow, B., 222, *260*
Baltes, P.B., 69, 76, *239*
Bamber, D., 78, *239*
Bane, M.J., 8, *252*
Bannatyne, A., 235, *239*
Bardon, J., 222, *239*
Baron, J., 107, *239*
Barrett, G.V., 73, 93, 113, *240, 258*
Barron, F., 6, *240*
Barsalou, L.W., 126, *259*
Barsch, R., 66
Bartlett, C.J., 49, *240*
Bartlett, F.C., 126-127, *240*
Batchelder, B.L., 132, *240*
Bateman, B., 208, *240*
Bauer, R.H., 109, *240*
Bauman, G., 92, *240*
Beaton, A.E., 8, *256*
Becker, D., 78, *245*
Bender, 43, 65
Bengtsson, G., 83, *259*
Bennett, V., 222, *239*
Berg, C., 74, *240*
Berg, R.A., 35, 94, 99, *248*
Berger, R.M., 16, *250*

Berlyne, D.E., 112, *240*
Berry, J.W., 91, *240, 266*
Bessel, F.W., 10
Bien, E.C., 91, 94, *240*
Bilash, I., 75, *240*
Bindra, D., 78, *240*
Binet, A., 5-6, 10-14, 62, 86, 96, 132, 181-182, 223-224, 226, 232, *240*
Birren, J.E., 73, *240*
Bishop, A.J., 71, *240*
Bjork, R.A., 125, *266*
Blackman, S., 93, *248*
Blankenship, A.B., 129, *240*
Blankstein, K.R., 130, *243*
Blum, J.E., 76, *240*
Bobbitt, B.L., 24, 66, 80, *253*
Bobko, P., 49, *240*
Bobrow, D., 79, 122, *258*
Boehm, V.R., 49, *241*
Boersma, F.J., 93, *241*
Bolton, T.L., 129, *241*
Bond, L., 14, *247*
Boring, E.G., 6, *241*
Botwinick, J., 73, *241*
Botzum, W.A., 93, *241*
Bouchard, T.J., 8, 24, *241*
Bouma, J.M., 93, *252*
Bourne, L.E., 106, *241*
Bower, G.H., 69, 109, 125, 127, *239, 264*
Boyle, M., 72, *247*
Brainerd, C.J., 84, *241*
Broadbent, D.E., 68, 73, 79, 109, 116, *241*
Brooks-Gunn, J., 7, *254*
Broverman, D.M., 67, *241*
Brown, A.L., 26, 38, 129, *241*
Brown J., 125-126, *241*
Bruininks, R.H., 72, *241*
Bruner, H.J., 24, *241*
Bruner, J.S., 68, 130, *241, 256*
Buffart, H.F., 81, *247*
Buriel, R., 91, 94, *241*
Buros, O.K., 65, 219, *241*
Burt, C., 110, 146, 160, *241*
Butcher, H.J., 24, *241*

INDEX OF AUTHORS

Caffrey, J., 143, *252*
Caharack, C., 123, *250*
Campione, J.C., 26, 38, 129-130, *241*
Cannell, C.F., 74, *250*
Caramazza, A., 78, *256*
Carey, S.T., 126, *241*
Carmichael, L.C., 127, *242*
Carpenter, P.A., 66, *242*
Carroll, J.B., 1, 5, 11, 12, 13, 16, 17, 21, 22, 24, 26, 58, 69, 81, 158, *242*
Carter, P., 97, *252*
Cattell, J.McK., 10, 11, *242*
Cattell, R.B., 8, 15, 16, 18, 19, 58, 59, 74, 83, 89, 90, 93, 98, 101, 110, 138, 143, 158, 160, 177, 233, *242, 251*
Ceci, S.J., 128, *242*
Chansky, N., 91, 93, *264*
Chaplin, J.P., 62, *242*
Chein, I., 8, *242*
Cherry, E.C., 79, 107, *242*
Chi, M.T.H., 127, *242*
Chiang, A., 24, 66, 80, *242*
Child, D., 138, 141, 143, *242*
Chown, S., 63, 75, 103, 113, *250*
Christensen, P.R., 16, *248, 250, 266*
Clark, H.H., 101, *247*
Clark, L.W., 73, *243*
Cleary, T.A., 49, *243*
Clements, S.D., 113, *245*
Coates, S.W., 92, *243*
Cohen, A.S., 72, 94, *243*
Cohen, D., 8, *252*
Cohen, J., 86, 98, 147, 165, 194-195, *243*
Cohen, W.M., 8, *256*
Comalli, P.E. Jr, 73, *243*
Comalli, P.F., 91, *243*
Comfort, A., 63, *243*
Comrey, A.L., 16, *248*
Cooley, W.W., 17, *243*
Coombs, C.H., 16, *243*
Cooper, L.A., 71, 78, 81, 97, *243*
Cornell, E.L., 96, *243*
Coulson, D.B., 31, *249*
Court, J.H., 225, *259*
Cox, P.W., 89, 94, *266*
Coxe, W.C., 96, *243*
Craik, F.I.M., 73, 113, 121, 123, 130, *243, 244*
Cronbach, L.J., 24, 57, 59, 135, 234, *244*
Crowder, R.G., 127, *244*
Cruickshank, W.M., 66, *249*
Csapo, K., 127, *258*
Curran, L., 72, *247*

Daniels, J.C., 229, *244*
Darwin, C., 9
Das, J.P., 111, *253*
Davey, C.M., 58, *244*
David, K.H., 98, *244*
Da Vinci, L., 38
Davis, F.B., 189-190, *244*
Dawson, J.L., 98, *244*
Day, R.S., 70, *244*
Deffenbacher, K.A., 130, *244*

Dempster, F.N., 129, *244*
Denny, D.R., 91, 94, *244*
Denny, M.R., 132, *240*
Descartes, 9
Detterman, D.K., 26, 38, 79, *244*
Deutsch, A., 218, *244*
Deutsch, D., 79, *244*
Deutsch, J.A., 79, *244*
Diak, H., 229, *244*
Dirken, J.M., 63, *244*
Dirks, J., 129, *244*
Doherty, W., 177, *250*
Doll, E.A., 226, *244*
Dominowski, R.L., 106, *241*
Donaldson, G., 74, *251*
Donderi, D.C., 78, *240*
Donlon, T.F., 50, 51, *245, 250*
Doppelt, J.C., 160, 161, *245*
Douglas, V.I., 91, 109, *245*
Drenth, P.J.D., 220, *245*
Droege, R.C., 178, *245*
Duffy, J., 222, *245*
Duncan, D.B., 202, 205, *245*
Dunn, L.M., 224, *245*
Dwyer, C.A., 50, *245*
Dyer, F.J., 49, *253*
Dyk, R.B., 91, 93, *266*
Dykman, R.A., 113, *245*

Eakin, S., 91, *245*
Ebbinghaus, H.E., 124, 127, *245*
Ebel, R.L., 84, 220, *245, 256*
Echternacht, G., 49, *245*
Edgerton, H.A., 17, *246*
Edwards, A.S., 8, *245*
Egan, D.E., 24, *245*
Egeth, H., 78, 109, *245*
Einstein, A., 38
Ekstrom, R.B., 16, 69, 89, 90, 101, 110, 139, 177, *245, 249*
Elithorn, A.A., 98, *245*
Elliott, C.D., 190, *245*
Ellison, M.L., 17, *246*
English, A.C., 135, 139, *246*
English, H.B., 135, 139, *246*
Engstrom, R., 159, *251*
Estes, W.K., 7, 72, 116-118, *246*
Evans, J., 70, *246*
Eysenck, H.J., 113, 130, *246*
Eysenck, M.W., 128, *246*

Fairweather, H., 51, *246*
Faterson, H.F., 91, 93, *246, 266*
Fenald, G.M., 95, *249*
Fennema, E., 50, 71, *246*
Ferguson, G.M., 21, *246*
Ferrara, R.A., 26, 38, 129, *241*
Fiebert, M., 90, *246*
Field, J.G., 235, *246*
Fischer, C.T., 7, 17, *246*
Fishman, J.A., 220, *244, 246*
Flaugher, R.L., 49, *246*
Ford, E.N., 127, *249*

Foulds, G.A., 76, *246*
Fozard, J.L., 63, *246*
Frank, G., 102, 162, *246*
Frederiksen, J.R., 72, 89, *246*
Freeman, B.J., 43, *246*
Freeman, F.N., 6, *246, 263*
French, F.N., 16, 111, 112, 139, *246*
French, J.W., 16, 69, 70, 89, 90, 93, 108, 139, *245, 246, 249, 257*
Frost, N., 24, 66, *251*
Frostig, M., 66
Fruchter, B., 138, *247*
Furth, H., 42, *247*

Gallistel, E., 72, *247*
Galton, F., 10, 11, 12, 129, *247*
Gardner, H., 32, *247*
Garrett, H.E., 7, 8, 21, 160, *247*
Gates, A.I., 209, *247*
Gathercole, C.E., 7, 219, *247*
Geen, R.J., 130, *247*
Geissler, H.G., 81, *247*
Gelman, R., 42, *247*
Gentis, H., 8, *252*
Gentner, D.R., 102, *258*
George, J., 125, *253*
Ghiselli, E.E., 46, *247*
Gibson, J.J., 79, *247*
Gilbert, L., 80, *247*
Gill, M.M., 7, 83, 85, *259*
Gilliland, K., 130, *260*
Gillung, T.B., 222, *247*
Glanzer, M.S., 63, 101, *247*
Glaser, R., 14, 24, 29, 31, 63, 101, 102, *247, 250, 259*
Glass, A.L., 131, *247*
Glasser, A.J., 86, 87, 97, 231, *247, 267*
Gleitman, H., 115, *247*
Goddard, H.H., 11, *247*
Goldberg, R.A., 24, *247*
Golden, C.J., 35, 94, 99, *248*
Golden, N.E., 72, 209, *248*
Goldfarb, W., 75, *248*
Goldstein, G.I., 42-43, 99, *248, 254*
Goldstein, K.M., 66, 84, 93, 96, 129, *248*
Goodenough, D.R., 89, 91, 92, 94, *248, 266*
Goodman, K., 209, *248*
Goodnow, J.J., 24, *241*
Gordon, G.P., 79, *250*
Gorsuch, R.L., 138, 142, *248*
Gottschaldt, K., 89, *248*
Graves, R.J., 93, *261*
Gray, J.L., 91, 94, *260*
Green, B.F., 17, *248*
Green, R.F., 16, *248*
Greeno, J.G., 102, *248*
Gregg, L.W., 101, *248*
Gregor, A.J., 98, *248, 259*
Gropper, R.L., 72, *241*
Gruenfeld, L., 91, *265*
Guay, R.B., 71

Guilford, J.P., 15, 16, 17, 67-68, 70, 91, 95, 101, 110, 113, 132, 139, 140, 147, 158, 177-178, 206, 226, 233, *248, 249, 250, 266*
Guthrie, J.T., 209, *249*
Gutkin, T.B., 235, *260*
Guttman, L., 143

Hagen, E., 46, *263*
Haggerty, M.A., 7, *249*
Hakstian, A.R., 18, 110, *249*
Haladyna, T.M., 31, *260*
Halford, G.S., 129, *249*
Hall, J.F., 125, *249*
Hallahan, D.P., 66, 108, 109, 222, *249, 264*
Hambleton, R.K., 31, *249*
Hamley, H.R., 71, *249*
Hammeke, T.A., 35, *248*
Hammill, D.D., 72, 235, *249, 258*
Harman, H.H., 16, 69, 89, 90, 110, 138, 139, *245, 249, 250*
Harrington, D.M., 6, *240*
Harris, L.J., 51, *249*
Hartlage, L.C., 233-234, 238, *249*
Hawk, J.A., 178, *245*
Hawkins, H.L., 78, *249*
Hawthorn, M., 72, *247*
Healy, W., 86, 95, *249*
Hebb, D.O., 58, 70, 127, *249*
Heinz, S.P., 123, *252*
Helton, G.B., 221, 227, *250*
Heron, A., 63, 73, 75, 103, 113, *241, 250*
Hertzka, A.F., 16, *250*
Hertzog, C.K., 74, *240*
Heston, J.C., 74, *250*
Hettema, J., 89, *250*
Heyns, B., 8, *252*
Hicks, M.M., 50, *250*
Hirst, W., 123, *250*
Hobbes, 9
Hobbs, N., 222, *250*
Hochberg, J., 79, *250*
Hock, H.S., 78-79, *250*
Hoepfner, R., 16, 17, 177, *249, 250*
Hoffman, K., 177, *250*
Hogan, H.P., 127, *242*
Holt, R.R., 227, *250*
Holyoak, K.J., 131, *247*
Holzinger, K.J., 16, *250*
Holzman, T.G., 102, *250*
Honzik, M.P., 73, 103, *250*
Hooper, F.H., 74, *257*
Horn, J.L., 8, 15, 16-17, 18-19, 23, 58, 59, 74, 113, 158, 159, 160, 178, *250, 251*
House, B.J., 108, 109, *267*
Huey, E.B., 80, *251*
Hume, 9
Humphreys, L.C., 17, 21, 49, *243, 251*
Humphreys, M.S., 130, *260*
Hunt, D., 112, *251*
Hunt, E.B., 24, 66, 70, 74, 80, 97, 107, 108, 109, 129, *240, 251*
Hunt, J. McV., 21, *252*

INDEX OF AUTHORS

Ibarrola, R., 98, *252*
Inhelder, B., 84, *252*
Ippel, M.J., 93, *252*

Jacklin, C.N., 50, 92, *256*
Jackson, G., 14, *252*
Jackson, M.D., 72, 80, 111, *252, 255*
Jacobs, J., 129, *252*
Jacoby, L.L., 121, *243*
Jaeger, A.O., 16, *252*
Jahoda, G., 98, *252*
Jakobovics, E., 91, *243*
James, W., 106-107, 109, 125, *252*
Jarvik, L.F., 76, *240*
Jastak, J., 75, *266*
Jencks, C., 8, *252*
Jenkins, 202, 206, 211, 212
Jensen, A.R., 6, 24, 49, 110, 209, 233, *252*
Johnson, N.S., 129, *256*
Johnson-Laird, P.N., 24, *265*
Johnston, W.A., 123, *252*
Jones, H.F., 235, *258*
Jongeward, R.H., 125, *266*
Juola, J.F., 68, *252*
Just, M.A., 66, *242*

Kagan, J., 91, *252*
Kahneman, D., 79, 110, 112, 122-123, 127, *252*
Kail, R., 97, *252*
Kaiser, H.F., 16, 144, *252*
Kamin, L.J., 14, *253*
Kanner, L., 43, *253*
Kaplan, O.J., 63, *253*
Kaplan, S., 130, *253*
Karp, S.A., 67, 73, 91, 92, 93, *261, 266*
Karrier, C., 14, *253*
Kass, C.E., 72, *253*
Katzell, R.A., 49, *253*
Kauffman, J., 222, *249*
Kaufman, A.S., 59, 132, 165, 181-182, 186, 188, 190, 195, 231, 235, *253*
Kaufman, D., 231, *253*
Kaufman, N.L., 181-182, 231, 235, *253*
Kaufman, P., 231, *253*
Kaufmann, G., 83, *259*
Kearney, G.E., 14, *253*
Keating, D.P., 24, 66, 80, *253*
Keele, S.W., 127, *259*
Kelley, T.L., 146, *253*
Kellogg, R.T., 78, *253*
Kendler, H.H., 109, *253*
Kendler, T.S., 109, *253*
Kendricks, S.A., 49, *243*
Keniston, A.H., 24, *253*
Kephart, N.C., 66, 235, *253*
Kinder, E.F., 98, *258*
King, W.H., 51, *253*
Kinsbourne, M., 125, 129, *253*
Kintsch, W., 125, *253*
Kirby, J.R., 111, *253*
Kirk, S.A., 66, 72, 128, 160, 224, 235, *255*
Kirk, W.D., 72, 126, 224, 235, *253*

Klahr, D., 101, *253*
Kleinsmith, L.J., 130, *253*
Knowles, J.B., 73, *243*
Knox, H.A., 86, 96, *254*
Koehler, W., 9, 66, 121, *254*
Koenigsknecht, R.A., 38, *254*
Koffka, K., 66
Kogan, N., 73, 218, 242, *254*
Kohs, S.C., 90, 96, *254*
Kossan, N.E., 78, *254*
Kosslyn, S.M., 70, *254*
Kotovsky, K., 101, *261*
Kroll, N.E.A., 128, *254*
Krueger, L.E., 78, *254*
Krutetskii, V.A., 71, *254*
Kubota, M., 132, *254*
Kulpe, O., 106, *254*
Kyllonen, P.C., 97, *255*

Labouvie, E.W., 76, *239*
Lancy, D.F., 42, *254*
Lansman, M., 108, *251, 254*
Larsen, S.C., 235, *249*
Lawrence, D.H., 109, *254*
Layton, B., 73, *254*
Lea, G., 102, *261*
Lea, S.E.G., 128, *242*
Lee, L.L., 38, *254*
Leeuwenberg, E.L.J., 81, 101, *247, 254*
Lennon, R.T., 220, *254*
Leontev, A.N., 68, *254*
Lesgold, A.M., 25, 29, *247*
Lewis, D.J., 16, *266*
Lewis, J., 24, 66, 129, *251*
Lewis, M., 5, 7, 113, *254*
Lin, C.Y., 71, *254*
Lindsley, D.B., 109, 129, *254, 267*
Line, W., 58, *254*
Linn, R.L., 17, *255*
Lipsitt, L.P., 69, *239*
Locke, 9
Lockhart, R.S., 119, 126, *241, 243*
Loftus, E.F., 106, 126, *241, 254*
Lohman, D.F., 19, 69, 92, 97, *255, 262*
Lohnes, P.R., 17, *243*
Lord, F.M., 17, *255*
Lord, M., 91, *243*
Lovie, A.D., 106, 109, *255*
Lucker, W.G., 72, *241*
Lundberg, F., 8, *255*
Lunneborg, C., 24, 66, 70, 129, *251, 255*
Luria, A.R., 1, 34-36, 46, 59, 68-69, 94, 113, 129, 233-234, *255*
Lutey, C., 132, *255*

McBride, K.E., 74, *265*
McCarthy, J.J., 72, 128, 160, 224, *255*
McClelland, D., 84, *265*
McClelland, J.L., 72, 81, 111, *252, 255*
McCormack, P.D., 125, *255*
McDaniel, E.D., 71
McDermott, P.A., 184, *255*
McElwain, D.W., 14, *253*

McFarland, R.A., 63, 73, 255
McGee, M.G., 51, 71, 255, 256
McHugh, R.B., 160, 256
McLeod, C.M., 97, 251
McNemar, Q., 6, 146, 255
McPherson, A., 98, 248
McReynolds, P., 219, 255
MacArthur, R.S., 96, 256
Maccoby, E.E., 50, 92, 256
MacCrone, I.D., 98, 256
Machover, R.S., 98, 258
Macione, J.R., 72, 256
Mackworth, J.F., 112, 113, 128, 256
Mackworth, N.H., 130, 256
Mandler, G., 109, 125-126, 256, 259
Mandler, J.M., 129, 256
Manis, F.R., 24, 253
Marcus, N., 79, 250
Martin, R.C., 78, 256
Matarazzo, J.D., 46, 132, 256
Matuszek, P.A., 221, 227, 250
Maxwell, A.E., 138, 256
Maxwell, S.E., 24, 242
Mayeske, G.W., 8, 256
Medin, D.L., 77, 256
Mehrens, W.A., 218, 256
Meili, R., 16, 256
Meredith, W., 158, 256
Merrill, M.A., 182, 263
Messick, S., 31, 67, 70, 89, 93, 111, 220, 256, 257
Meumann, E., 80, 256
Michelson, S., 8, 252
Mihal, W.L., 113, 240
Miles, T.R., 8, 257
Mill, J., 9
Miller, G.A., 117, 257
Milner, B., 129, 257
Mirkin, P.K., 235, 267
Money, J., 108, 129, 257
Moore, C.A., 89, 94, 266
Moray, N., 111, 112, 257
Morton, J., 127, 244
Moses, B.E., 71, 257
Moses, J.A.Jnr, 35, 94, 99, 248
Mosteller, F., 8, 257
Moynihan, D.P., 8, 257
Mueller, G.E., 109, 125, 257
Muhs, P.J., 74, 257
Muir, W., 93, 241
Mulhern, S.T., 38, 254
Munro, E., 24, 252
Murdoch, B.B., 127, 257
Murphy, R.J.L., 51, 257
Murray, D.J., 190, 245
Mutter, P., 127, 257
Myklebust, H.R., 208, 257

National Education Association, 218, 257
Neale, M., 229, 257
Neisser, U., 79, 123, 127, 129, 177, 244, 250, 257-258
Nesselroade, J.R., 76, 239

Neuhaus, J.O., 16, 267
Neuringer, C., 99, 248
Newcombe, N., 51, 258
Newcomer, P.L., 72, 258
Newell, A., 25, 101, 207, 258
Nickel, H., 37, 258
Nickerson, E.T., 78, 258
Nishisato, S., 78, 240
Nissen, H.W., 98, 258
Norman, D.A., 79, 102, 108, 122-123, 258
Novick, M.R., 17, 255
Nunnally, J.C., 136, 258
Nuttall, R.L., 63, 258

Ogbu J., 14, 258
Okada, T., 8, 256
Oltman, P.K., 67, 90, 266
Osmon, D.C., 35, 94, 99, 248
Otis, A.S., 12, 112, 225, 258
Owens, W.A., 160, 256

Paivio, A., 127, 258
Paley, E., 91, 261
Palmer, J.C., 126, 254
Panek, P.E., 73, 93, 113, 240, 258
Papalia-Findlay, D., 74, 257
Patterson, D.G., 86, 96, 259
Pawlik, K., 177, 258
Payne, R.W., 222, 235, 258
Peabody, 224
Pearson, L.S., 10, 190, 245
Pelham, W.E., 109, 258
Pellegrino, J.W., 24-25, 29, 97, 101, 102, 247, 252, 259
Pemberton, C.L., 91, 93, 259
Peters, J.E., 113, 245
Peters, K.G., 109, 245
Petersen, A.C., 51, 266
Peterson, J., 6, 259, 263
Piaget, J., 7, 84, 252, 259
Pichot, P., 98, 259
Pieron, H., 6, 8, 259
Pine, S.M., 49, 240
Pintner, R., 86, 96, 259, 263
Plato, 9, 138
Platt, G.J., 130, 244
Popham, W.J., 31, 136, 259
Porteus, S.D., 98, 259
Posner, M.I., 110, 117, 127, 259
Price, L.A., 16, 89, 247
Purisch, A.D., 35, 248
Pylyshyn, Z.W., 70, 259

Quereshi, M.Y., 160, 259

Raaheim, K., 83, 259
Rabbitt, P.M.A., 73, 259
Rabinowitz, J.C., 86, 126, 259
Randhawa, B.S., 112, 251
Rapaport, D., 7, 83, 85, 86, 100, 102, 103, 132, 259
Rarnahm, R., 93, 241
Rasch, G., 17, 259
Raskin, E., 67, 266

INDEX OF AUTHORS

Raven, J., 225, *259*
Raven, J.C., 76, 225, *246, 259*
Reaves, C.C., 123, *250*
Reese, H.W., 69, *239*
Reeve, R.E., 108, *249*
Regan, D.T., 71, 80, *243*
Reichard, S., 86, *260*
Reitan, R.M., 35, *260*
Requin, J., 81, *260*
Resnick, L.B., 24, 25, *260*
Restle, F., 101, *260*
Reville, W., 130, *260*
Reynolds, C.R., 233-235, 238, *249, 260*
Reynolds, M.C., 222, *260*
Richlin, M., 63, *247*
Riegel, K.F., 76, *260*
Riegel, R.M., 76, *260*
Riley, D.A., 127, *260*
Rimoldi, H.J.A., 16, *260*
Ringstrom, M.D., 128, *242*
Ritvo, E.R., 43, *246*
Robinson, J.E., 91, 94, *260*
Roe, A., 74, *265*
Rogal, R., 87, *266*
Rogers, L., 84, *265*
Roid, G.H., 31, *260*
Rorschach, 65
Rossman, E., 117, *259*
Rourke, B.P., 38, *260*
Rowe, H.A.H., 2, 24, 41, 60, 97, 134, 231, *260*
Royce, J.R., 89, 177, *260*
Rubin, D., 86, 126, *260*
Rubinstein, S.L., 37, *260*
Rucker, C.N., 222, *245*
Ruddell, R.B., 207, *261*
Rugel, R.P., 89, 132, *260*
Rumelhart, D.E., 72, 79, *260*
Rutter, M., 43, *260*
Rystrom, R., 209, *260*

Salthouse, T.A., 5, 63, 73, 74, 103, *261*
Salvia, J., 222, *245*
Samuda, R.J., 220, *260*
Santa, J.L., 131, *247*
Santostefano, S., 67, 91, *260*
Sarris, V., 81, *247*
Sattler, J.M., 98, 132, 190, 231, 235, *261*
Saunders, D.R., 16, 86, *261, 267*
Savage, R.D., 7, 227, *261*
Schafer, R., 7, 83, 85, 86, *259, 260*
Schaie, K.W., 75, 76, 103, *239, 261*
Scheerer, M., 84, 96, *248*
Schlosberg, H., 109, *266*
Schneider, W., 110, *261*
Schonell, E., 228-229, *261*
Schonell, F.S., 228-229, *261*
Schwartz, D.W., 73, 91, *261*
Schwartz, S., 24, *247*
Scott, D.H., 224, *261*
Scott, M.S., 129, *241*
Sharp, S.E., 10, *261*
Sherman, J., 71, *261*
Shiffrin, R.M., 110, 116, 118, *239, 261*

Siegel, L.S., 42, *261*
Silverstein, A.B., 132, 195, *261*
Simernitskaya, E.G., 59, 205, *255*
Simon, H.A., 24, 25, 101-102, *258, 261*
Simon, L., 130, *260*
Simon, T., 6, 10, 11, *240*
Simpson, G.C., 93, *261*
Sims, M.T., 93, *261*
Singer, H., 178, 207, *261*
Smith, E.E., 77, *256*
Smith, I.M., 16, 19, 47, 71, 77, 80, 90, 94, 95, *262*
Smith, M., 8, *252*
Snow, R.E., 19, 20, 23, 24, 57, 92, 97, *262*
Somberg, B.L., 73, *261*
Spearman, C., 10, 15, 22, 58, 73, 81, 101, 110, 146, 175, 206, *262*
Spelke, E.S., 123, *250*
Spencer, H., 9, *262*
Stanford, 181-182, 223, 224, 232
Stankov, L., 110, 111, 112, 113, 178, *251, 262*
Stanley, G., 129, *262*
Steiner, S.R., 72, 209, *248*
Stephenson, W., 58, *262*
Stern, W.L., 7, *262*
Sternberg, R.J., 2, 18, 24, 25, 26, 38, 51, 79, 97, 101, 107, 233, *244, 262, 263*
Sterns, H.L., 73, 93, 113, *240, 258*
Stevens, A.L., 102, *258*
Stewart, M., 24, *247*
Stoddard, C.D., 7, *263*
Stone, M.H., 17, *267*
Strang, R., 208, *263*
Strauss, A.A., 66, 94, *263, 265*
Strother, C.R., 75, *261*
Strowig, R.W., 178, *263*
Swaminathan, H., 31, *249*
Swenson, A.L., 125, *255*
Swineford, F., 160, 161, *263*

Talland, G.A., 127, *263*
Tarver, S.G., 109, *264*
Taylor, C.W.A., 16, *263*
Taylor, E.M., 231, *263*
Terman, L.M., 7, 10, 182, *263*
Thomson, G.H., 15, 146, *263*
Thorndike, E.L., 7, 8, 15, 22, *263*
Thorndike, P.L., 139, 142, *263*
Thorndike, R.L., 46, 234, *263*
Thurstone, L.L., 6, 7, 15, 17, 22, 58, 70, 81, 89, 90, 91, 101, 139-140, 146-147, 176, 206, *263, 264*
Thurstone, T.G., 101, 139, 147, *264*
Titchener, E.B., 106, 109, *264*
Todd, R.C.A., 101, *264*
Trabasso, T., 69, 109, *264*
Treisman, A.M., 79, 109, *264*
Tucker, J., 222, *245*
Tuddenham, R.D., 8, *264*
Tulving, E., 118, 121, 126, *243, 264*

Underwood, B.J., 6, 126, *264*

Vaidya, S., 91, 93, *264*

Vallett, R.E., 235, *264*
Vernon, M.D., 129, *264*
Vernon, P.E., 14, 90, 92, 95, 98, 110, 146, *264*
Vitz, P.C., 101, *264*
Vygotsky, L.S., 68, *264*

Wachtel, P.L., 67, *264*
Wagner, R.F., 128, *264*
Walker, E.L., 130, *265*
Walker, K.D., 127, *257*
Wallace, J.G., 101, *253*
Wallmark, M.M., 50, *250*
Walters, A.A., 127, *242*
Warren, J.L., 108, *265*
Warren, N., 8, 14, *265*
Warrington, E.K., 129, *265*
Wason, P.C., 24, *265*
Watkins, M.J., 121, 127, *244*, *265*
Watkins, O.C., 127, *265*
Waugh, N.C., 127, *263*
Wechsler, D., 7, 11, 18, 43, 45, 55, 59, 73-74, 75, 81, 85, 86-87, 96, 98, 100, 102, 110, 132, 182, 187, 190, 220, 223-224, 231, 232, 233, 235, *265*
Weikard, D.P., 84, *265*
Weiner, I.B., 27, 161, 235, *265*
Weiner, M., 160, 178, *265*
Weisenburg, T., 74, *265*
Weiskranktz, L., 129, *265*
Weisman, A.G., 7, 14, *265*
Weissenberg, P., 91, *265*
Welford, A.T., 73, 103, 113, *265*
Werdelin, I., 16, *265*
Werner, H., 66, 90, 94, *263*, *265*
Wertheimer, M., 66, *265*
Wesman, A., 49, *243*
Wessells, M.G., 122, *265*
Whipple, G.M., 12, *265*
Whitely, S.E., 2, 24, 29, 101, *265*, *266*

Whiteman, M., 75, *266*
Wiggins, J.S., 184, *266*
Williams, M.A., 130, *244*
Willoughby, R.R., 74, *266*
Wilson, R.C., 16, *266*
Wilton, K., 93, *241*
Wisler, C.E., 8
Wissler, C., 10, *256*, *266*
Witkin, H.A., 67, 89, 90-92, 93, 94, 95, *246*, *266*
Wittenborn, T.R., 111, 112, *266*
Wittig, M.A., 51, *266*
Wohlwill, J.F., 158, *266*
Wolf, V.C., 37, 92, 94, 95, *266*
Wood, F., 129, *253*
Woodward, A.E., 125, *266*
Woodworth, R.S., 109, 127, *266*
Woo-sam, J.W., 86-87, 181, *266*, *267*
Worden, P.E., 109, *267*
Workman, E.A., 221, 227, *250*
Wright, B., 17, *267*
Wright, J., 108, *251*
Wrigley, C., 16, *266*
Wundt, W., 106, *267*

Yarmey, A.D., 126, *267*
Yen, W.M., 235, *239*
Yerkes, R.M., 11, 14, 86, 96, *267*
Yoakum, C.A., 11, 86, 96, *267*
Young, F.A., 129, *267*
Ysseldyke, J., 222, 235, *245*, *267*

Zeaman, D., 108, 109, *267*
Zimmerman, I.L., 86-87, 97, 181, 231, *247*, *266*, *267*
Zimmerman, W.S., 16, *267*
Zubek, J.P., 75, *240*

INDEX OF SUBJECTS

aborigine, 98, 161-162, 169, 171, 173, 175, 176, 177, 179
abstract thinking, 7, 37, 89, 138, 174, 222
ACER Tests of Learning Ability (TOLA), 225
achievement, 8, 14, 19, 27, 28, 29, 31, 36, 47, 59, 67, 71, 73, 88, 91, 94, 96, 107, 111, 134, 137, 175, 185, 187, 197, 199, 201, 202, 207, 209, 220, 226
adaptability, 7, 25, 58, 96
adaptation, 7, 9, 25, 28, 59, 89, 94
adolescent, 37, 55, 69, 85, 91
adult, 9, 18, 19, 37, 51, 55, 62, 66, 69, 72, 73, 74, 85, 92, 103, 104, 126, 137, 157, 160, 163, 171, 174, 177, 198, 223
age, 7, 10, 11, 12, 13, 18, 28, 36, 43, 50, 53, 55, 61, 62-64, 73-76, 87, 91, 93, 96, 98, 103, 113, 129, 135, 144, 147, 157, 161, 164, 167, 168, 169, 171, 174, 175, 176, 179, 184, 186, 188, 193, 225
aim, 2, 3, 15, 30, 46, 57, 105, 123, 133, 167, 206
alcohol, 104
analogical reasoning, 25, 138, 146
animal, 9, 138
anxiety, 45, 69, 85, 88, 96, 99, 132
aphasia, 131
Aristotle, 9, 138
arithmetic, 18, 85, 223
Army Beta Test, 87, 96
arousal, 113, 130
art, 47
assembly model, 207, 209
assimilation, 7
association, 6
attention, 31, 42, 43, 45, 53, 69, 73, 79, 80, 81, 88, 98, 100, 105-114, 115, 122, 132, 134, 136, 162, 163, 167, 173, 174, 205
attention factor, 177
attitude, 14
autistic children, 43
automatization, 24, 25, 30, 37, 84, 110, 127, 177

behaviourism, 9, 107
Bender Visual Gestalt Test, 43, 65
bias, 14, 41, 48-50, 57, 61, 94, 144, 220, 225
Binet, 10, 12, 132
blindness, 90
Bloch Design Test, 18, 59, 95

Brain, 9, 34, 46, 59, 68, 193
brain damage, 45, 46, 47-48, 58, 66, 83, 85, 88, 94, 96, 99, 103, 114, 129, 187
Bristol Social Adjustment Guides, 226
British Ability Scale, 190

categorization, 8, 42, 77, 85, 117
centroid method, 146
chess, 103
childhood, 92, 160
classification, 56, 62, 85, 221
cocktail party phenomenon, 107
cognition, 7, 11, 16, 23-24, 25, 36, 58, 59, 63, 97, 115
cognitive style, 23, 38, 66, 68, 73, 89, 90, 93, 94, 110, 177
communality, 142, 178, 195, 217
communication, 43, 46
compensation, 64, 208
complexity, 7, 9, 10, 17, 26, 27, 40, 43, 53, 55, 69, 70, 77, 87, 90, 94, 113, 129, 178, 194, 209
components, 25, 29, 32, 33, 34, 36, 37, 38, 44, 59, 60, 61, 72, 74, 86, 87, 95, 100, 102, 106, 115, 129, 133, 137, 140, 141, 165, 169, 181, 185, 187, 193, 194, 201, 202, 209
comprehension, 6, 15, 18, 59, 72, 74, 100, 102, 123, 223
concentration, 45, 87
concept formation, 63, 85, 86, 94, 102, 133, 156, 166, 177
conceptual factor, 31, 53, 164, 167, 174, 176
consciousness, 85, 106
context, 14, 64, 93, 126
control processes, 118
creativity, 23, 73, 96
criterion referenced, 31, 38, 218
criticism, 13, 14, 125
cross-cultural differences, 48, 92, 98, 218
crystallized intelligence, 18, 19, 30, 58-59, 60, 74, 110, 111
cue, 128, 130
culture, 1, 7, 14, 33, 42, 50, 59, 64, 144, 186, 219, 220, 225, 227

Darwin, 9
deafness, 43, 90
deficit, 38, 99, 128, 194, 210
depression, 85
deprivation, 14, 45

development, 55, 62, 63, 64, 65, 72, 74, 91, 92, 102, 129, 133, 158, 160, 167, 168, 174, 208, 218
diagnosis, 2, 36, 38, 41, 43, 44, 45, 47, 53, 57, 64, 66, 78, 79, 86, 116, 128, 132, 179, 182, 184, 187, 193, 206, 218, 219, 220, 221, 230
difficulty, 7, 11, 12, 39, 43, 45, 60, 69, 70, 86, 114, 127, 171, 203, 225
digit span, 129, 132, 223
digit symbol, 74
disadvantage, 1, 28, 36, 43, 44, 45, 128, 177
diversity, 15, 17, 61, 91
dreams, 138

education, 8, 17, 22, 27-28, 44, 46, 59
efficiency, 25, 29, 30, 37, 38, 56, 68, 71, 79, 108, 113, 117, 144, 198, 218
elite, 25
emotion, 7, 14, 45, 85, 93, 96, 99, 108, 114, 130
engineering, 47, 71
environment, 7, 9, 14, 21, 30, 33, 45, 58, 59, 67, 68, 79, 88, 91, 96, 102, 104, 105, 107, 108, 111, 116, 122, 123, 127, 130, 132
episodic information, 118
error, 187, 189, 194
ethnicity, 14, 49, 50, 161, 164, 173, 218
evaluation, 59, 177, 184, 206, 219
evolution, 9
expectation, 45, 198
experience, 37, 59, 60, 64, 69, 92, 94, 96, 107, 115, 122, 182
extraversion, 130

factor, 14-21, 22, 37, 53, 87, 88, 101, 102,133, 137-138, 139, 142, 143, 144, 147, 160, 163, 164, 167-179, 187, 188
fatigue, 108
feedback, 33, 210
field-dependence, 89-90
flexibility, 9, 18, 59, 80, 85, 91, 95, 97, 123, 164, 174
fluency, 15
fluid intelligence, 18-19, 30, 53, 58-59, 60, 74, 91, 110, 111
functional system, 31, 32, 35, 36, 74, 109, 115, 165, 174, 194, 201, 202, 205, 206, 207, 208

'g', 10, 15, 17, 32, 53, 58, 70, 76, 85, 88, 96, 98, 101, 102, 110, 111, 139, 142, 146, 147, 156, 160, 161, 163, 167, 169-176, 178, 179, 195, 206
geometry, 47
Gestalt psychology, 9, 66, 68, 107, 109
giftedness, 37, 47, 181, 182
go, 103
Grace Arthur Test, 87, 94
grade, 13, 94
group tests, 12-13, 185

handicapped person, 86, 115
health, 108
heredity, 58
heterogeneity, 146, 147, 158, 201

Hobbes, 9
homogeneity, 12, 29, 39, 58, 61, 160, 202, 225
Hume, 9

identification, 66, 129
Illinois Test of Psycholinguistic Abilities (ITPA), 72, 128, 160, 224
immigrant, 43
incidental learning, 59
income, 8
individual differences, 1, 2, 5, 8, 9-10, 11, 22, 24, 36, 57, 58, 63, 69, 70, 81, 89, 91, 103, 107, 108, 129 158, 203
individualization, 23, 57, 94, 198, 220
infancy, 9
information, 14, 18, 21, 23, 24, 29, 32, 33, 36, 38, 46, 57, 65, 66, 67-68, 69, 71, 72, 78, 79, 86, 94, 101, 105, 108, 109, 112, 113, 115, 116, 120, 124, 129, 146, 174, 207, 208, 217, 218, 223
innovation, 11
input, 33, 68, 72, 127, 131
insight, 9, 97
intellectually handicapped, 174, 179, 198
intellectual strengths, 2, 5-8, 23, 28, 29, 30, 37, 39, 43, 44, 57, 61, 68, 133, 137, 184, 185, 186, 194, 197, 198, 203, 219
interest, 108
interpretation, 70, 95, 133, 135, 164, 179, 182, 219
intervention, 1, 2, 23, 29, 30, 32, 43, 44, 45, 47, 48, 53, 57, 61, 66, 78, 79, 86, 103, 173, 178, 184, 187, 198, 199, 218, 220, 233, 234
introversion, 130
IQ, 19, 29, 30, 31, 68, 140, 147, 181, 182, 184, 185, 186, 201, 206, 207, 211
isomorphism, 68
item, 13, 57, 58, 61, 68, 111, 125

Jenkins Non-Verbal Test, 202, 206, 211
judgment, 6, 59, 68, 73, 87, 100, 102

Kaiser's criterion, 143, 144
knowledge, 13-14, 18, 24, 30, 37, 44, 46, 55, 59, 65, 72, 73, 83, 87, 111, 118, 136, 138, 219
Kohs Blocks, 90
KR20 formula, 141

labelling, 36, 47, 56, 128, 183, 184, 201, 220, 222
language, 8, 11, 14, 15, 18, 23, 32, 42-43, 46-47, 58-59, 60, 61, 70, 72, 85, 96, 102, 116, 125, 132, 147, 175, 198, 220, 221, 224
latent trait, 24, 50
learning, 6, 19, 21, 26, 27, 30, 37, 38, 59, 64, 78, 88, 91, 94, 96, 105, 108, 115, 124, 125, 130, 184, 187, 198
learning disabilities, 23, 37-38, 44, 45, 47, 48, 66, 103, 108, 128, 129, 132, 187, 198, 207
left-handed testees, 98
level of performance, 45, 67, 124, 132
limitation, 14-15, 117, 119, 220
Locke, 9
Luria's Model, 34-35

INDEX OF SUBJECTS

maladjustment, 86
malleability, 25, 28, 32, 38, 193
manipulation, 26, 35, 46
mathematics, 15, 18, 36, 47, 71, 84, 91, 102, 118, 123, 131, 133, 134, 138, 178, 205
maturation, 21, 38, 160
maze, 18
mechanics, 47
memory, 14, 15, 19, 23, 31, 32, 36, 45, 48, 53, 60, 68, 69, 70, 76, 80, 87-88, 91, 100, 105, 115, 117, 130, 136, 174, 193, 224
Mental Measurement Yearbook, 217
metacognitive skills, 23
metalwork, 47
methodology, 11, 12, 16, 17, 21, 24, 39, 41, 42, 45, 84, 100, 218, 220
Mill Hill Vocabulary Scale, 224
Mill, James, 9
Mill, John Stuart, 9
mind, 9, 10, 138, 140, 146
minority-groups, 1, 28, 164
misuse, 5
modality, 127, 128
money, 8
motivation, 7, 14, 29, 43, 46, 55, 61, 85, 96, 100, 112, 113, 180, 186, 229
motor skills, 32, 43, 60, 63, 91, 110
multiple choice, 13

NAT model, 35-38
Nature-Nurture, 21
Neale Analysis of Reading Ability, 229
need, 30
nervous system, 66, 109
non-cognitive factors, 16, 46, 88, 92, 95, 229
norm, 6, 13, 28, 38, 44, 62, 159, 185, 187, 225
'nous', 9, 138

Object Assembly, 18, 74
omnibus tests, 58, 201
Otis Test of Intelligence, 112

pattern, 38, 39, 41, 44, 45-46, 66, 68, 88, 97, 99, 117, 137, 162, 172, 184, 193, 212
Peabody Picture Vocabulary Test, 224
peer, 7, 13
percentile rank, 183
perception, 10, 15, 30, 31, 37, 45, 53, 58, 59, 66, 68, 72, 80, 81, 89, 90, 98, 108, 121, 134, 136, 156, 167, 174, 175, 177
perseveration, 114
personality, 11, 16, 46, 93, 184, 186, 229
philosophy, 9, 14, 138
physical development, 63
physical measurements, 11-12
physical properties, 116
physiology, 112
Picture Arrangement, 18, 74, 99, 102
Picture Completion, 18
planning, 100, 102, 103, 177, 178
Plato, 9, 138
pluripotentiality, 35
point scale, 12
politics, 14

pragmatism, 6, 11
prediction, 8, 10, 25, 28, 29, 39, 44, 46, 47, 49, 64, 71, 126, 129, 137, 144, 199, 201, 202
prejudice, 50
'prescientific', 22
prestige, 8, 14, 46
'primary mental abilities', 15, 23, 139, 147, 206
principal components analysis, 135, 141, 142, 143, 144, 147, 157, 161, 168, 193
problem solving, 6, 7, 13, 18, 23, 30, 32, 38, 41, 59, 60, 70, 84, 90, 94, 102, 123, 187, 207
profile, 1, 32, 38, 39, 41, 42, 44, 46, 48, 64, 67, 131, 133-134, 164, 167, 178, 179, 181, 183, 185, 186, 187, 189, 193, 194, 197, 198, 202, 211, 218, 221
Project Talent, 17
psychiatric patient, 99, 114
psychoanalysis, 11, 107
psychological processes, 8, 22, 23, 33
psychology: cognitive, 28, 57, 66, 146
psychology: developmental, 9, 28, 29, 37, 57, 146
psychology: differential, 1, 146
psychology: educational, 1, 29, 37, 57
psychology: experimental, 1, 9, 10, 11, 24, 28, 29
psychometrics, 1, 2, 5, 11, 15-22, 24, 28, 29, 37, 57, 66, 67, 74, 103, 110, 134, 146, 206, 233
psychopathology, 103
psychophysics, 107
psychotic, 85
purpose of the assessment, 219, 221
puzzles, 55, 59, 96

rationale, 1-2, 28, 30, 32, 53, 65, 83, 100, 135, 207
reaction time, 9, 11, 73
reading, 13, 46, 67, 68, 71, 72, 80, 85, 88, 94, 102, 115, 118, 123, 129, 132, 136, 186, 207, 208, 209
reasoning, 6, 9, 11, 15, 17, 18, 23, 45, 48, 60, 85, 95, 97, 100, 103, 107, 140, 147, 174, 176, 177, 220, 223, 224
recall, 60, 124, 127, 131, 132
recognition, 60, 105, 115, 124, 127, 132
reference group, 28, 185, 225
reflex, 9, 30
reliability, 2, 12, 141, 184, 190, 194, 220
requirement, 13, 23, 25, 30, 36, 38, 43, 56, 60, 61, 63, 80, 88, 90, 94, 100, 101, 112, 147, 156, 178, 184, 197, 205, 233, 234
resource allocation, 123
retardation, 45, 62, 66, 108, 129, 131, 144, 157, 163, 169, 171, 174, 177, 182, 187
Rorschach Test, 65
rote learning, 36
rule induction, 102

's', 10, 15, 32
sample, 13, 28, 31, 60, 69, 92, 96, 144, 171, 176, 219
scaling, 2, 11, 63, 182, 196
schizophrenia, 85

scholastic achievement, 19, 129, 227
Schonell Attainment and Diagnostic Tests, 228-229
school, 10, 14, 17, 48, 56, 59, 62, 64, 71, 94, 129, 132, 137, 144, 184, 195, 198, 199, 202, 205, 206, 209, 219, 220, 225
science, 18
score, 12, 14, 15, 24, 26, 27, 28, 29, 30, 31, 32, 42, 44, 45, 47, 49, 61, 64, 68, 74, 75, 76, 99, 133, 137, 139, 144, 167, 173, 179, 181, 182, 184, 185, 188, 190, 194, 197, 220
scree test, 143, 144
selection, 28, 30, 46, 47, 56, 60, 63, 69
senility, 130
sensation, 10, 63, 68, 106, 109, 116, 127
sequencing, 36, 48, 60, 83, 85, 97, 100, 132
sex differences, 49, 50, 61, 92
similarities, 18, 59, 223
society, 8, 14, 18, 25, 33, 42, 64, 92, 186, 209, 224, 225
socioeconomic level, 14
soul, 9, 138
spatial ability, 15, 19-21, 47, 51, 60, 69, 71, 74
speech, 68
speed, 15, 23, 67, 69, 70, 75, 76, 79, 80, 89, 97, 99, 111, 112, 140, 156, 164, 175
spelling, 36, 85
Spencer, 9
Standard Reading Tests, 229
stanine, 183
statistics, 10, 15, 18, 22, 23, 45, 55, 76, 94, 133, 134, 138, 156, 184, 195, 218
stereotyping, 50, 84
strategy, 23, 29, 30, 37, 61, 64, 68, 70, 78, 87, 93, 94, 98, 127, 156, 168, 174
stress, 108
'Structure-of-the-Intellect', 15, 16, 17, 67, 110, 132
subskills, 165, 194-198, 209, 212
supplementary measures, 199
symbol, 7, 18
syndrome analysis, 1
system, 23, 33, 35, 37, 68, 70, 91, 113, 125, 201, 207, 208, 209, 210

taxonomy, 21
teacher assessment, 212
technical aspects, 2, 41
technology, 11, 13, 22, 26, 44, 110

test development, 13, 14, 31, 41-44, 57, 133, 137, 140
testing time, 221
test theory, 22
test producer, 56
Tests in Print, 217
test taker, 56, 57
test user, 56-57, 134, 167, 188, 194, 219-220, 233
Thematic Apperception Test, 65
theology, 9
theory, 3, 5, 9, 10, 11, 16, 22, 31, 32, 37, 44, 57, 59, 72, 79, 101, 116, 117, 124, 125, 137, 138, 139, 140, 146, 199
thinking aloud, 79
time, 12, 37, 61, 89, 108, 109, 110, 112, 113, 124, 130, 174
training, 19, 25, 26, 28, 35, 36, 38, 43, 46, 56-57, 59, 79, 86, 92, 95, 185, 198, 219, 220
transfer of learning, 21
trial and error behaviour, 7, 9, 98
typology, 11

underachiever, 206, 207
understanding, 6, 11, 24, 59, 71, 72, 73, 105, 133, 137, 164, 167, 219
uniqueness, 35
user requirements, 1, 5

validity, 1, 2, 14, 29, 31, 32, 41, 44, 47, 48, 49, 55, 56, 58, 60, 63, 64, 76, 89, 110, 116, 133, 135-137, 140, 141, 146, 147, 173, 179, 182, 184, 186, 188, 194, 198, 199, 201, 202, 218-221, 233, 234
variability, 44, 63, 111, 144, 171
variety, 36, 71, 101
vigilance, 113
Vineland Social Maturity Scale, 226
vision, 60, 88, 96, 128
visualization, 19, 43, 48, 58, 59, 69, 70, 71, 92, 164, 176
Vocabulary, 18, 74, 223
vocational guidance, 184

Wechsler tests, 18, 132, 147, 163, 190
wood work, 47
Word Knowledge, 138, 220, 223

z-score, 183